BATHROOMS
How to Plan, Install & Remodel

Rick Harrison

HPBooks®

Published by HPBooks, Inc.
P.O. Box 5367
Tucson, AZ 85703
602/888-2150
ISBN: 0-89586-218-2
Library of Congress Catalog
Card Number: 84-81515
©1984 HPBooks, Inc.
Printed in U.S.A.
First Printing September 1984

Publisher:
Rick Bailey

Editorial Director:
Randy Summerlin

Editor:
Jim Barrett

Art Director:
Don Burton

Book Design:
Paul Fitzgerald

Typography:
Cindy Coatsworth, Michelle Claridge

Photography
All photography by Rick and Betty
Harrison, except as noted in
captions.

Illustrations
Rick Harrison

ACKNOWLEDGMENTS

A book such as this is never the product of one person, or even a few people. Many have contributed time, effort, ideas, information and contacts with others who might help. Included are the many homeowners who allowed us to photograph their bathrooms.

Our thanks to these people extends to any we might have inadvertently omitted in the following list. Special thanks to those manufacturers listed here who have contributed photographic material for use in this book.

American Olean Tile Co., Lansdale, PA
Armstrong World Industries Inc., Lancaster, PA
Roger Beckmann, Lightbending Designs Inc., Fall City, WA
Chuck and Barbara Blodgett, Kitchens & Baths by Blodgett, Seattle, WA
Jeff Case, CKD, Scan Design, Bellevue, WA
Country Floors Inc., New York, NY
Ed and Shirley Day, D & S Construction, Issaquah, WA
Ditz-Crane Associates, Tucson, AZ
Skip Driscill, Quality Mark, Tucson, AZ
DuPont Co., Wilmington, DE
Chuck and Barbara Hertzler, Fine Wood Cabinets, Oak Harbor, WA
Jacuzzi Whirlpool Bath, Walnut Creek, CA
Kohler Co., Kohler, WI
Jim Monyhan, Decor Tile, Tucson, AZ
Marian and George Noble, Redmond, WA
David Soleim, New Country Homes, Issaquah, WA
United States Ceramic Tile Co., Canton, OH

Special thanks to Russell W. Platek, CKD, for reviewing this book for technical accuracy. Mr. Platek is Director of Training for the National Kitchen & Bath Association. The NKBA promotes the kitchen and bath industries by setting quality standards and a code of ethics for NKBA members. It also awards the title, Certified Kitchen Designer (CKD), to qualifying members.

Cover Photograph:

Color scheme of this beautifully decorated bathroom is based on large stained-glass window. Skylight in ceiling provides additional natural light. Carpeted steps make transition from floor to mosaic-tile tub platform, mirror behind tub visually expands space. This bathroom is featured on pages 14 and 15. *Photo by Rick and Betty Harrison.*

CONTENTS

Your Bathroom

Plants add pleasant contrast to light color scheme of this bathroom. Clear glass shelves on adjustable brackets form attractive storage and display area. Radiused corners on shelves help prevent accidents.

Like it or not, most of us start each day by spending some time in the bathroom. That start can be pleasant, efficient and safe—a good beginning to a pleasant day for everyone in the family. Or the start can be hurried, unpleasant, difficult and even dangerous. In this way, the bathroom can affect your whole day, day after day.

Your bathroom or bathrooms may be functional, spacious and well designed, but are worn out or shabby looking. So you may want to remove and replace fixtures and finish materials without changing the layout.

However, most bathrooms could use some design improvements, and many need all the design help they can get. A modern, efficient bathroom is worth the effort it takes to create. *Create* is the operative word.

GOOD DESIGN

Like any design work, good bathroom design requires foresight. As you sketch designs for your proposed bathroom, visualize the lines on paper as a real room.

Relate that room to real people, with real knees and elbows. Because bathrooms are usually the smallest rooms in the house, it's critical to design them for free and unobstructed movement.

Consider the needs of both large and small users, in all potential postures. For instance, a shower may look fine on paper, but can you shampoo your hair in it without banging your elbows? Can you bend over to pick up a dropped cake of soap without stepping outside the shower? Can you step in and out of the bathtub or shower without barking your shins on the toilet?

If you can't visualize the bathroom on paper, make rough cardboard models—one of the old bathroom and surrounding rooms, and one of the proposed alterations. Also, don't be afraid to chalk in changes on bathroom walls and floor, or build fixture mockups out of cardboard boxes as work progresses. These techniques may enable you to spot problems early and correct them.

Many homes are afflicted with one or both of two design problems—the *leftover bathroom* and the *minimum bathroom.* The leftover bathroom, as the name implies, is an afterthought. After space was allotted to all other rooms in the house, the leftover space became the bathroom.

Leftover bathrooms are also a result of filling an odd-shaped space created by remodeling. The bathroom shape is the tipoff—the walls jog in and out at random and do not accommodate the bathroom fixtures. The bathroom door may bump into the bathtub, or the toilet may be wedged into what used to be a closet.

The minimum bathroom is also easy to spot. It usually measures 5x7', with all plumbing in one wall. The tub is at one 5-foot end. The toilet is next to the tub, in your way as you reach for the tub faucets. The lavatory is next—same wall—using up the space between the toilet and the other 5-foot wall, where the door is usually located. Opening the door while someone is using the sink usually results in a collision.

Both the leftover bathroom and the minimum bathroom call for artful reworking of surrounding space to provide room for a functional bathroom. Sometimes there's enough space, but the problem is a poor original design. Other times it's necessary to enlarge the bathroom. This can be done by stealing floor space from an adjoining room or adding floor space by means of a room addition. The chapter, *Planning & Design,* starting on page 48, covers the techniques for analyzing and reworking space, and for reviewing other important design considerations.

Glass panels at side of shower have been fitted to tub platform. White tile also covers end of tub platform that's inside shower. Contrasting grout in tile emphasizes lines of tub and shower enclosure. Foil wallpaper is water resistant.

Privacy—An essential part of bathroom design is providing privacy. Privacy goes far beyond putting a door on the bathroom. In addition to the actual bathroom layout, review the main traffic pattern to and from existing bathrooms and dressing areas.

Poor placement of a bathroom door is a frequent design fault. The inside of the bathroom and people's comings and goings are visible from the more formal parts of the house. When designing your bathroom, consider door placement and views into the bathroom from outside.

Noise—There are two kinds of noise involved in bathrooms. One is noise that bothers the user. The other is noise that bothers everybody else in the house. Noise within the bathroom is difficult to control because of the smooth, hard surfaces that reflect sound instead of absorbing it. Any sound-absorbent materials you can introduce will help—curtains, acoustical ceiling, resilient flooring or textured wall coverings. Also some plumbing fixtures are inherently quieter than others.

Noise leakage from a bathroom can

Mirrors can be used to visually expand space. Marbling in mirrors reflects marbling in tub and platform. Single row of tiles protects reflective backing on mirrors from water damage. Adjustable glass shelves in alcove form display area for figurines. Light from top of alcove passes through shelves.

often be traced to the plumbing. Noise from pipes and fixtures is amplified by the intervening walls. Many bathroom noises can be damped by installing insulation around pipes and fixtures such as bathtubs. A detailed review of potential noisemakers and their cures can be found on pages 122-123.

Lighting—Most bathrooms have insufficient lighting. In many older bathrooms, the only available light comes from a wall-mounted light fixture over the medicine cabinet. It has one standard light bulb inside a frosted-glass globe, and an electrical outlet mounted on the side of the chrome-plated base with rust speckles popping through the plating.

This sort of lighting is next to useless. Good lighting relates directly to activities that take place in the bathroom. There must be enough light, of the right kind. Also, placement of fixtures is just as important as the amount of light provided.

Consider both general illumination and special-purpose lighting. For instance, light required for applying makeup must not only be the correct intensity, but it must be the right color and come from the right direction.

There are many specialized light fixtures made for bathrooms. But you can use any lighting equipment you want, from kitchen-style luminous ceilings to antique floor lamps. One light fixture rarely used in a bathroom but works quite well is the swag lamp, like the one shown on page 5.

The only hard-and-fast rule is that any movable lamps or other electrical equipment should be positioned so they can't accidentally come into contact with water, creating a shock hazard. This might only require shortening a lamp cord so it can't accidentally fall in the shower, tub, sink or toilet and remain plugged in at the same time. For more on lighting, see pages 56-57.

Storage—Most bathrooms, especially in mass-produced housing, are short on storage space. A central linen closet is useful, but separate linen storage should be provided in each bathroom, even if the storage is only a small area. Point-of-use storage is also needed for toilet paper, cleaning supplies and extra soap. At least a small storage space should be planned for each family member who uses the bathroom. Also, don't forget storage for blow-dryers, electric hair curlers and a dozen other gadgets that

haven't even been invented yet.

Flexibility—This is the characteristic of good bathroom design most often overlooked. A good design adapts to changing family needs over the years. A good bathroom is also flexible enough to adapt to the needs of varied individuals and uses throughout the day.

Many times, other functions can be combined in a bathroom. Laundry equipment can often be included, as can exercise gear or a photographic darkroom.

GETTING IT DONE

Remodeling a bathroom or installing a new one can be challenging. But nothing dates a house more quickly than an obsolete bathroom. Poor bathroom facilities, or not enough of them, can make a home almost unlivable. Sooner or later, most of us realize we must remodel the bathroom, or add one, like it or not.

An expensive but perfectly good solution is to hire a designer and a remodeling contractor to do the entire job. After explaining your wishes to them, you can pack up and go on vacation while the work is being done. Another expensive solution is to buy another home, preferably a new or modern one, and leave the problem of the old bathroom to the next owner of the old home.

There is a better solution. If you're reasonably competent with basic tools and able to follow instructions, you can do anything required to repair, remodel or build a bathroom. After all, builders are normal people too. When they started, they probably knew no more about remodeling than you do. Don't be afraid to tackle the work yourself, or at least as much as you care to. Area by area, chapter by chapter, this book covers every technique you need to know—from initial planning to final cleanup.

You can contract as much of the work as you want, from all of it to none of it. Even if a contractor or subcontractors do all the work, this book will help you understand what they're doing and why.

The greatest source of friction between tradespeople and their clients isn't shoddy work or poor materials. It's the mistrust and suspicion that can arise because the client doesn't know if the work or materials are poor, and suspects the worst.

Other problems between clients and builders are misinterpretation and a failure to communicate. This book can help you understand what's possible and what isn't, what a contractor's bids and contracts mean and how the builder is likely to interpret what you say to him. Construction people seldom have the time or ability to stop and explain complicated procedures. The more you can learn about these procedures and techniques, the less chance of misunderstanding between you and the builder.

A contractor's personnel may not do everything exactly as described in this book. Specialized tools, a trained eye and long experience count for a lot in the kind of handcrafted work found in residential construction. Also, the procedures described here have been selected to be as foolproof as possible for the do-it-yourselfer. They require a minimum of specialized tools, and apply to as many situations as possible. As you repeat jobs you've learned here, you'll find yourself adapting procedures to your own taste and finding personal shortcuts.

DEFINITIONS

Over the years, people have used many euphemistic terms for the bathroom and its fixtures. Luckily, this ancient trend is starting to die out. All such terms will be ignored in this book. After all, the Elizabethan "necessary house" was only an outhouse. And a "porcelain convenience" was, and is, a toilet. Standard but relatively informal terms will be used here, not cutesy pseudonyms or any of the more-confusing industry terms.

The fixture designed for deposit and disposal of body wastes is referred to as a *toilet*. The fixture made much like a toilet, but not designed to flush, is called a *bidet* (pronounced bih-DAY). It is designed for wet cleansing of the perineal area. A flushing fixture designed only for deposit of liquid wastes is a *urinal*.

A basin with water-supply and drain fittings, roughly at waist level, made for hand and face washing, is a *lavatory*. The cabinet enclosing the space below the lavatory is called a *vanity*. A *shower* is designed to spray water on you from above and collect and drain away that water. A device made to contain water for whole-body immersion is called a *tub*, whether or

Especially in a small bathroom, space over toilet tank is a likely place to add an extra storage cabinet to keep frequently used items close at hand. In this bathroom, cabinets, accessories and trim are solid oak.

not it's also equipped to serve as a shower receptor.

As to the rooms themselves, if any provision is made for whole-body cleansing—tub or shower—the room will be called a *bathroom*. If there is no such provision, just a toilet and a

lavatory, the space will be called a *powder room*. The term *outhouse*, of course, is self-evident: An old home so equipped was once described in a real-estate ad as having "three rooms and path."

2

Case Studies

Tile covering tub platform extends across bathroom floor and up walls behind shower. Molded-fiberglass shower receptor matches tub color.

When the bathroom first came indoors, little thought or effort was applied to making it more than a service area. Early bathrooms often had all the charm of a boiler room in a basement, and were about as comfortable. Slowly, people came to realize that a bathroom can be pleasant and comfortable. In fact, a bathroom deserves as much design and decorating attention as any room in the house.

There's a major problem facing anyone who sets out to design and build a really good bathroom. We've all seen dozens, perhaps hundreds, of examples of other rooms—living rooms, dining rooms, kitchens, foyers. These examples ranged from excellent to poor, from inspired to disastrous. From all of them we've learned what works and what doesn't, what we like and what we don't. More importantly, we've learned what's possible and roughly how to achieve it.

Very few people have had this much experience with bathrooms. You've probably seen relatively few bathrooms, and many of those have ranged from ordinary to poor.

This chapter is a collection of outstanding bathrooms. They're different from each other, in size as well as in style. All function well, but the design approaches are as varied as the personalities of their owners and designers. The photographs, floor plans and accompanying text should enable you to develop some sense of what works, and to decide what you like and dislike. The chapter, *Planning & Design,* starting on page 48, will show you how to design your own unique new bathroom or successfully redesign an existing one.

Treetop View

The ground outside this bathroom slopes away sharply, so the bathroom opens out onto its own raised deck. Treetops shield the bathroom from a more distant view. Greenery inside echoes the colors of the trees outside.

The soft pastel green, gray and rose pattern in the wall covering contrasts with the dark-stained cherry trim and gold accents. The quiet color scheme leans heavily on the dark wood trim to give it definition, especially the crown molding where walls meet ceiling.

The basic floor plan is simple. The door to the right of the bidet opens on a large linen and storage closet. To the left of the toilet, beyond the planter, is the door from the dressing area. The dressing area has a long vanity on one side and a walk-in closet on the other.

This bathroom has a spacious and open floor plan. The large areas of open wall space around the perimeter contribute to the feeling. In most bathrooms, space along the walls is occupied by fixtures and cabinets. The light color scheme also creates a feeling of spaciousness.

Design: Rick Harrison for D & S Construction.

Bathroom opens onto private deck and treetops beyond. Tub is equipped with hydro-massage jets. Telephone keeps owners, both active business people, in touch without having to leave tub.

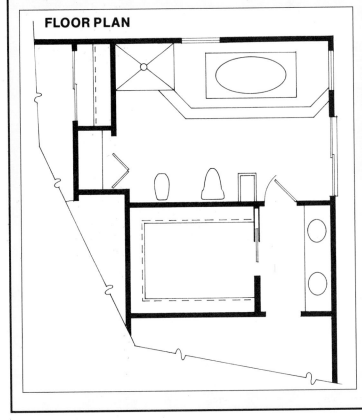

FLOOR PLAN

Major fixture manufacturers offer matching toilet and bidet sets like the one shown here. Vertical pipes behind bidet are vacuum breakers to isolate fixture from water-supply lines. Required in many jurisdictions, vacuum breakers are installed for sanitary reasons. They're available from fixture manufacturer.

Southwest Heritage

This magnificent Southwest-style bathroom is designed around its tile. The intricate red, blue-black and gray pattern comes from an American Indian blanket that hangs in the master bedroom. The tiles were handmade to match the blanket design—in the large version over the tub, and in small, single tiles on the vanity top.

All other bathroom elements harmonize with the pattern, against a background of rough white plaster and natural beams. Attention to detail counts. The white stripe in the red towels echoes the small white squares in the red field of the tile pattern.

The north-facing greenhouse windows in the tub area provide plenty of natural light, and a view of the mountainside above. The light and humidity make for happy plants all year long. Additional natural light comes through the glass door between the end of the vanity and the wall of the toilet compartment.

There's also a skylight over the space between the vanity and the shower enclosure. Two infrared heat lamps are mounted inside the skylight opening. Natural light comes into the toilet compartment through a tall, narrow stained-glass window; it also echoes the main pattern of the tile.

Design: Jose Pujada for D.F. Fraker Design & Building Corp.

Long vanity is equipped with two lavatories, topped with long mirror that includes a mirrored medicine cabinet at each end. Design motif in tile over tub is repeated on vanity top.

Sunken planter and greenhouse window occupy one end of bathing area. Frosted glass provides privacy. Clear glass above affords view of mountains. Faucet handles of tub fitting are located for easy operation from both outside and inside of tub.

FLOOR PLAN

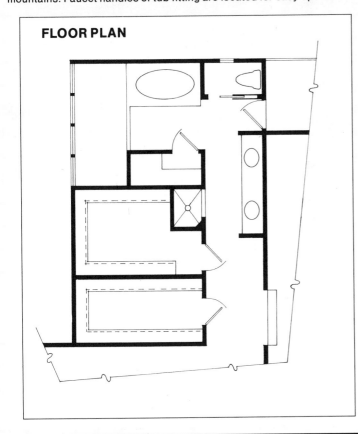

Skylight with heat lamps provides natural light to both vanity and shower enclosure. Stained-glass window provides natural light in toilet compartment.

Island Vanities

Arranged in an L-shape around an atrium garden, this combined bath and dressing room makes imaginative use of mirrors. The mirror-faced bypass doors on the two closets visually expand the space, as does the full-wall mirror over the tub. But the mirrors over the back-to-back vanities are more than they appear to be at first glance.

Actually, what seems at first to be a rectangular mirror over one vanity is a rectangular sheet of clear plate glass mounted between two vanities. Two circular mirrors are mounted back-to-back, one on each side of the clear glass, to serve each side of the island. Because the other bathroom elements are mostly at right angles to each other, and all the wall and ceiling surfaces carry the same strongly figured wall covering, you can rarely tell whether you're looking in a mirror or through clear glass. When you walk up to the lavatory to use it, the round mirror becomes just a mirror. Viewed at an angle, it all but disappears.

What appears to be two skylights over the tub is actually one skylight and its reflection in the mirror beyond. The skylight might seem to be unnecessary with all the glass into the atrium. But it serves the important purpose of balancing the light from the atrium, effectively reducing glare in the bathing area. The all-glass shower enclosure lets both natural-light sources reach the shower area.

In a zoned bath-dressing room like this, the toilet would customarily be located in the bathing area. In this bathroom, a small area that's usually wasted—the corner between two closets at right angles—has been used. A standard closet depth of 2 feet would ordinarily create a 2x2' space in the corner. In this case, closets were held back about 3-1/2 feet each way to make room for the toilet. A translucent-glass door closes off the toilet area, across the diagonal, but still lets in light from the rest of the room.

Tub is mounted *under* the synthetic-marble platform material, as are undercounter lavatories. Atrium at right provides light and a place for private sunbathing. Cat on tub platform is realistic porcelain figure.

Back-to-back vanities carry unusual round mirrors attached to sheet of clear plate glass. Fluorescent-light enclosure over vanities provides direct lighting.

The dressing area opens to the adjoining master bedroom with double doors. Normally, this would cause the dressing area to feel somewhat like part of the bedroom. The placement of the double vanity shifts the sense of the dressing room over to more a part of the bathroom. Part of the effect is a result of the boxed-in light centered over the vanity. At the same time, the vanity serves the dressing needs of two people without crowding.

Design: Herder Construction Co.

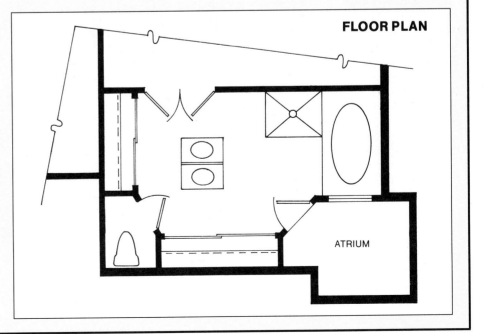

FLOOR PLAN

ATRIUM

Stained Glass

A skylight in the sloping wood ceiling provides the natural light in this bathroom. This makes it possible for the bathroom window to serve as a focal point, done in stained glass that picks up the colors in the bathroom.

Full-wall mirrors above tub and opposite vanity multiply the impact of the stained-glass window by generating multiple images of it in both directions. The resulting optical illusion is a statement of the owner's feelings about the relationship of man's works and the infinite.

One entire wall of the bathroom is an integrated cabinet system. It incorporates two lavatories, a makeup area and storage for linens and personal items. The makeup area includes knee space under a dropped section of vanity for convenient sitdown use. Drawers flanking the makeup area, and in the bottoms of storage cabinets, make it possible to store large quantities of clutter.

The tile backsplash below the mirror is tall enough to keep stray water drops off the mirror. It also raises the bottom edge of the mirror so that the hinged outer panels clear the lavatory fittings. There's additional storage behind the mirror panels. Note that the seams in the mirror line up with the steps in the vanity top.

The top of the tub platform is tiled to match the vanity top. The tile surround helps protect the carpeted steps from splashed water. The tub's fitting design is extremely practical, because the threaded nuts below the fitting body permit it to be completely removed for servicing and repair.

The toilet and a large shower are in a separate compartment to the left of the tub platform, separated by a pocket door. The shower and compartment floor are finished in the same blue mosaic tile as the tub platform and the vanity top.

Makeup counter between vanities is dropped to comfortable seating height. Drawer stacks beside makeup area hold more items than would shelves in same location. Drawers also keep things better organized.

Drawers in bottom of linen-storage cabinet hold personal items. Upper portion holds linens and towels on adjustable shelves.

Carpeted steps make transition to tiled tub platform. Mirrored wall behind tub faces vanity mirror, causing "tunnel-to-infinity" effect.

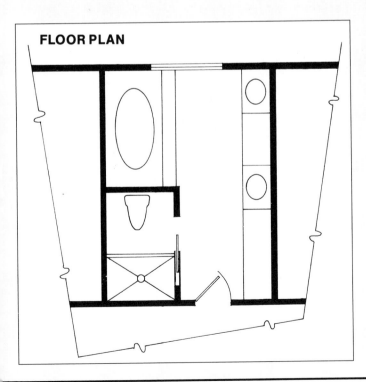

FLOOR PLAN

Stained-glass window is focal point of this bathroom. Skylight in ceiling above window lets in additional natural light. Mosaic tiles at undercounter lavatories have been laid individually to make finished edge.

Sculpture in Tile

This bathroom shares a fireplace with the adjoining bedroom. A fireplace screen on the bathroom side keeps stray sparks under control; solid-iron fireplace doors on the bedroom side preserve privacy. A fire is a pleasant addition to a soak in the deep, Japanese-style soaking tub. The soaking tub is tall and narrow, with a small interior ledge for a seat.

The shower needs no door or curtain. While the control is on the back wall, the showerhead is in the curve of the free-standing wall. So any splashed water is contained by the shape of the shower.

Custom-shaped tubs and showers like these need to be planned carefully so that access is adequate and safe. In this bathroom, there are two steps up to the soaking tub for easy access. The shower floor is at the same level as the main bathroom floor. The first step up to the tub serves as a curb for the shower. The seat inside the soaking tub serves as a step while getting in and out. This arrangement should be easy for most people to negotiate.

It's important to design steps at least 4 inches tall. Low steps, ledges or curbs can be tripped over because they're less visible. Even full steps can be tripped over if the floor material camouflages them.

Taking a cue from the wood ceiling, the rest of the bathroom is trimmed in oak. This includes vanity cabinets, medicine cabinet, towel bars, toilet seat and paper holder. Edge and backsplash on the vanity top are also in matching oak.

Design: Roger Beckman of Light-bending Designs.

Fireplace is elevated to same height as rim of Japanese-style soaking tub, opens on other side to bedroom.

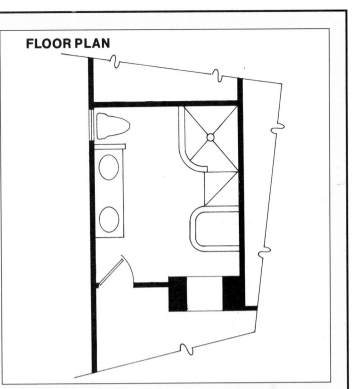

Drawer stack between lavatories provides plenty of storage. Stub wall at right separates vanity from toilet.

Curved wall of shower presents construction challenge, but small size of mosaic tile makes it easy to finish. First step up to tub at right acts as curb for shower. Shower fitting on back wall controls showerhead located in curve.

Something Old, Something New

Just because you're building a new bathroom, or even a new home, the bathroom doesn't have to look like a new one. In this case, the house was new, but the style of this bathroom revolved around an old-fashioned tub the owners had stored away years before. The enamel was chipped and the outside was spotted with rust, but it *had* to be good for something more than a horse trough or planter.

A local refinisher was able to make the old tub look like new again. The feet were removed, bead blasted—a process similar to sand blasting—and brass plated. The owners then spent several months tracking down all the other fixtures and pieces to match the refurbished tub and make an old-style bathroom. As it ended up, not one other piece in the bathroom is old. Each is a modern reproduction. The owners even found out that they didn't need to start with the old tub. Reproductions of old clawfoot tubs are also available.

Refinished tub looks as good as new, maybe better. Two different wall coverings in related colors were selected to fit the period style.

FLOOR PLAN

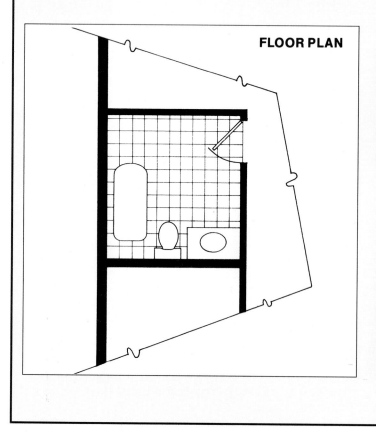

Tub fitting, drain and soap dish are all newly manufactured reproductions.

Period bath features refurbished antique tub, new toilet, medicine cabinet and vanity in same style. Note notching of chair rail to fit supply tube up to wall-mounted toilet tank.

Use an Extra Room

This old Victorian-era home originally had three upstairs bedrooms and a tiny upstairs bathroom. When the present owners restored it, they enlarged one of the bedrooms for a master bedroom, and turned another small bedroom into a master bath. Much of the original detailing and trim was either preserved or duplicated.

The window locations in the old bedroom dictated the new bathroom's layout to a great extent. The vanities couldn't be identical, because the door placement was dictated by the layout of the toilet-shower area, which in turn was dictated by the window location. Further problems developed in fitting in the new heating system, making it necessary to conceal the registers in the toe-board space under the vanity cabinets. The register shown in the ceiling above the window in the photo at right is the cold-air return.

Because they're in constant use, the doors between the dressing area and the toilet-shower area had to be solidly mounted. So the owners used restaurant-style commercial double-swing hinges. The doors swing freely in both directions, and will stay fully open in either position.

Louver doors lead to smaller compartment that contains toilet, bidet, shower and walk-in linen closet.

In contrast to cream tones of rest of room, shower is lined with intricately shaped bright blue tile.

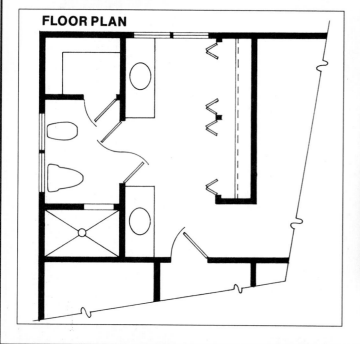

FLOOR PLAN

Dressing area includes two well-lighted vanities with plenty of drawer space. Bare-bulb incandescent lights give yellowish cast to cream-colored room. Louver doors allow plenty of air circulation between rooms.

Blue and Rose

This bathroom makes use of an unusual color combination. The blue in the tile and the rose color of the carpet are repeated in lighter tones in the wall covering and picked up again in the towels and accessories. But there's more to this sort of color use than picking the basic colors.

The two colors are used in solid form only in the carpet and the vanity cabinets. Everywhere else the two colors—and the cream of the trim—are used in opposition, or in *tension*. Otherwise, the relatively quiet basic colors would have produced a flat effect. For example, the blue tile is set off with cream-colored grout, to change the effect of large areas of solid blue. The background of the wall covering isn't plain, lighter rose. It's masked with a blue cross-hatching that echoes the shape of the tile-grout lines, but on the diagonal.

From the standpoint of space planning, it's obvious that planning is easier when you have this much room to work with. But good integration makes the space work in ways that

FLOOR PLAN

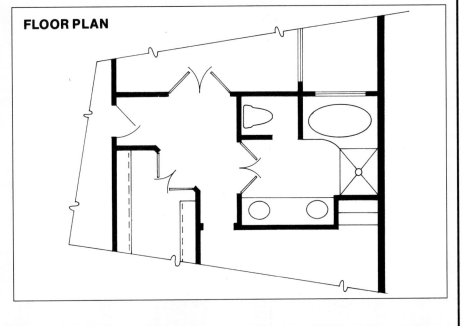

apply just as well to smaller bathrooms. The toilet compartment lines up with the tub platform. The tub platform makes use of the space in the corner, while smoothly turning to integrate with the shower enclosure. The blocked-out corner avoids conflict between

shower and vanity, while providing storage for the master bedroom on the other side of the wall.

The large window opening to an enclosed atrium is a good example of extending lines of sight to create the illusion of space.

Design: Herder Construction Co.

Only other view into atrium is from study off master bedroom. Privacy can be gained by closing shutters, if necessary.

Carefully plan platforms, tile installation and shower enclosures so they work together. This enclosure was fitted after tile installation was complete.

Redefined Space

The remodeling of an upstairs bathroom involved reorganizing the floor space of the bedroom next to the bathroom. Originally there was a walk-in closet beyond the wall behind the tub. This squeezed the bathroom into too small a space.

The wall was torn out when the bathroom was gutted, along with the wall between the bedroom and bathroom. Stealing some space from the bathroom and some from the bedroom created a new standard-depth closet running the length of the wall, except for a small section used for bathroom-linen storage.

This made room for a hydromassage tub set in a Corian-surfaced platform alongside a shower, where the walk-in closet used to be.

The front of the shower is enclosed with a glass door, but the side toward the tub is completely open. This makes it possible to take a shower while the tub is filling, then step across for a soak or a hydromassage. The entire area is lined with water-resistant materials—Corian panels and ceramic tile.

The remodeled bathroom is on the third floor of an older home with winding stairs. The bathtub weighed 1,100 pounds. Even if the tub could fit up the stairwell, there was the question of whether the stairs could support the tub's weight. It was necessary to remove the window, enlarge the window opening and hoist the tub up the side of the building and in. The hole was later filled with a larger window.

The pedestal lavatory wasn't high enough for the owner, so it was raised several inches on a base of Corian shaped to fit the bottom of the pedestal. To augment the surface area of the lavatory, the wall behind it has been stepped out to form a ledge at the bottom of the mirror.

Design: Jeff Case, CKD.

Pedestal lavatory has been raised by Corian spacer under pedestal to suit height of owner.

Jog in corner between toilet and lavatory conceals old chimney. Wall behind lavatory has been stepped out to provide extra surface area. Top is finished with ceramic tile.

There's no panel separating shower from tub. White plastic grab bar bridges gap.

FLOOR PLAN

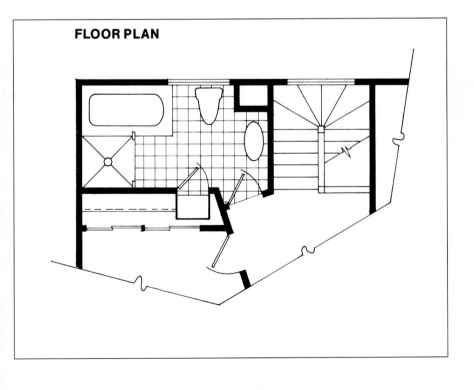

Terra Cotta Tile

Two distinctly different ceramic tile selections were used in this pretty but durable family bath. The red floor tile has been carried in from the hall serving both the bathroom and the nearby bedrooms. The tan tile is used on both the tub surround and the vanity top. Because very few trim shapes were available for the tan tile, it was necessary for the tile setter to miter the tiles at the ends of the vanity backsplash.

Matching lavatories and tub are high-durability enameled cast iron. The fittings were also selected for heavy use.

Considerable storage space is available in the vanity drawers and cabinets. Linen storage is in a tall closet that also serves to partially screen the toilet from the rest of the room.

Design: Rued Construction.

Custom ceramic soap dish adds a luxury touch to tub.

Tub is set a few inches back into alcove to ease fitting of tile. Tile runs to ceiling of alcove.

FLOOR PLAN

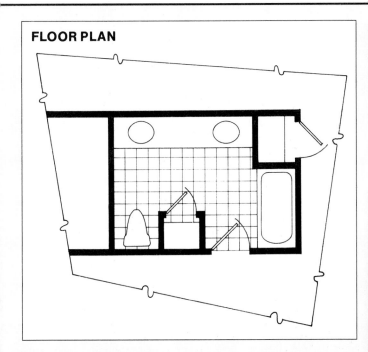

Long vanity provides plenty of storage. Ceramic-tile floor withstands heavy traffic.

Lavatory is centered in tile pattern, which takes careful advance planning.

Divide and Conquer

Compartmented bathrooms don't necessarily have jogs and odd shapes. This example is rectangular except for one offset. The first area has two vanities on opposite walls, the second area a tub and linen storage, the third a toilet and a shower enclosure. Each area has unusual custom touches.

The lavatories, set in solid-color plastic laminate, are hand-thrown pottery, made up and glazed to the owner's design. If you do this, make sure the potter understands how an overflow channel works, and has the actual drain fitting to fit the bowl to.

The backsplashes on the vanity tops are wood, matching the cabinets. In this case, the backsplash has been extended upward to form a frame for the mirrors.

Due to the probability of water exposure, the tub platform is trimmed with oiled red cedar rather than oak. The cedar strips are attached with screws and plugs, in case removal is ever required for recaulking or refinishing.

When the backsplash was installed, a height conflict developed between the upper edge of the tub spout and the upper edge of the backsplash around the tub. It was neatly resolved by shaping the backsplash to follow the contour of the spout. See photo at right.

Cedar tub-surround sets off yellow tub. Note how trim was cut to fit around tub spout.

To provide linen storage, a simple system of open bins was hung on the wall opposite the tub. This was originally intended to have doors, but the owners moved in before the doors were ready. They liked the open shelves so well they decided not to add the doors.

The three compartments are separated by pocket doors. The narrow, half-round case trim for doors and windows has been used throughout the house. For pocket doors, the radiused case trim was applied separately. For swing doors, the case trim was milled as a part of the door jambs, made in inner and outer halves.

This bathroom layout works well as a master bath, but would present access problems if used as the home's one-and-only bath. If an access door were provided at the other end, more than one person could use the bathroom at once without invading privacy.

Design: Chris Saxman, The Design Co. Built by: Connole-Crawford Construction.

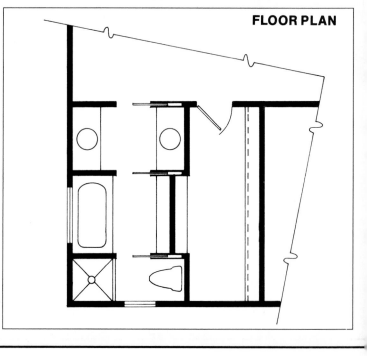

FLOOR PLAN

First compartment has two vanities, second has tub and linen storage, third contains toilet and shower.

Wood trim forms backsplash, surround for mirror. Ceramic lavatory is handmade to owner's specifications.

High towel bar over foot of tub keeps towels close at hand. Window looks out over woods, has narrow blinds for privacy.

Art Deco

The style of this bathroom originated in the 1920s and has since become a classic decorating approach. The basic color elements in this case are black, white, silver and gray. Major areas range from pure silver—the foil wall covering in the toilet enclosure—to pure black countertops. Even the exercise cycle fits the color scheme.

It's stretching the term somewhat to refer to this as a "bathroom," made up as it is of six rooms or compartments. This is really a well-integrated system of activity and storage areas. So it can be examined room by room, looking at the function and detailing of each.

The bathing area incorporates both an oversize hydromassage tub and a large shower compartment. The door opens on a walkway to the pool outside. All the flooring and much of the wall finish in this area is ceramic tile, either black with white grout or white with white grout. The planter at the foot of the tub is lined with metal, painted black.

Continued on page 30

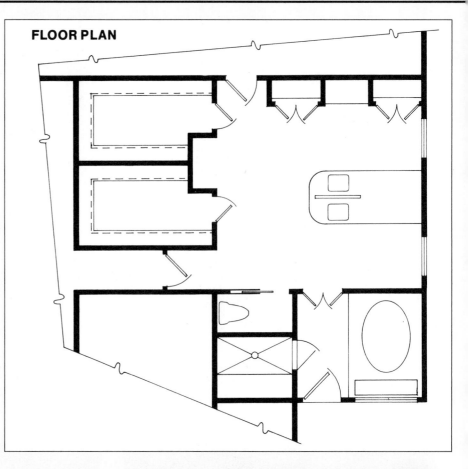

FLOOR PLAN

Peninsula vanity has two lavatories, on opposite sides. Soaking tub is in separate room beyond. Shower compartment is off tub room.

Hydromassage tub, tile platform, wall coverings and window treatment all carry out the black/white/silver color scheme.

Art Deco

Continued from page 28

The shower compartment has a full-length seat and is equipped with a steam generator, so it also serves as a steam room. Two different shower valves, and two shower heads at different heights, are fitted to suit the differing needs of the owners. Even the ceiling is tiled to protect it from water and steam. The seat is sloped to drain. Because the shower compartment also serves as a steam room, the glass door must seal tightly. So the shower compartment has its own ventilating fan.

There are two well-organized walk-in closets behind the mirror doors on either side of the alcove housing the exercise cycle. The his-

and-hers closets are a good idea if you have the space available. But the same principles can apply to two smaller conventional closets, or to opposite sides of one walk-in closet. Life is easier if each person has his or her own storage area.

The alcove that holds the exercise cycle may seem too small for the use of the cycle. In this case, the user can operate the cycle quite well in the space provided, because the only movement is a rather limited leg motion. The more-complicated models that incorporate handlebar motion linked at the pedals would need some more space in both directions.

The peninsular vanity neatly provides two lavatories, at non-conflicting locations. The peninsula

could have been built as an island, but extending one end to the wall left more floor space on the side toward the closets.

The activity of applying makeup has been separated from the lavatories and given a place of its own. The makeup counter has knee space underneath and is flanked by two shallow storage closets. Makeup storage is in two tall, narrow drawers on either side of the knee space, and in a wide shallow drawer above it.

Ceramic tile has been used on the floor at the makeup vanity and the peninsula. This not only protects from spills and splashes, but prevents the development of worn spots in the carpet in these high-traffic locations.

Makeup table is opposite vanity, flanked by shallow storage closets.

Roomy shower compartment also serves as steam room. Ceiling is tiled to protect it from moisture.

Foil-walled toilet compartment has skylight, pocket door.

Behind mirrored doors are his-and-hers walk-in closets. Alcove between provides room to use exercise cycle.

3

Surfaces & Equipment

A number of surface materials can be used in a bathroom. In this one, wood, ceramic tile and wallpaper provide the background. Vanity is plastic laminate. Corner tub is drop-in type. *Photo courtesy of American Olean Tile Co.*

A new bathroom starts as a concept. The wide range of ideas and products available means you have many choices to make. To assure a workable bathroom, the choices must remain true to the concept.

Suppliers will tell you what features and advantages their products have, but not what's available from other suppliers. They may not even know alternative features or products exist. It is up to you to research what is available, compare products and fea-tures and make the best choices for your bathroom.

This chapter does not cover all available products and their var-iations. Its purpose is to give you an overall idea of what products and fea-tures are available, what to look for and where to start looking. When you know which features you want and which are available, you can begin shopping and comparing products.

Basic bathroom fixtures change little over time. Other products, such as decorating materials, wall coverings and floor coverings, change rapidly. Colors and patterns are changed, added or discontinued yearly. Some products and features described in this chapter may soon be outdated. But you can get up-to-date informa-tion from the manufacturers. A list of manufacturer names and addresses can be found on page 190.

This chapter is divided into two major categories, *surfaces* and *equipment*. While some items, such as vanity tops, belong to both categories, the two categories cover about everything you'll be working with in finishing your bathroom. The section on surfaces covers wall and floor coverings. The section on equipment covers vanities, plumbing fixtures and fittings.

SURFACES

Walls, floors and ceilings form most of the visible area in a bathroom. Materials available for finishing these surfaces are covered in this section.

Bathrooms need durable surfaces if they're to continue looking good for any length of time. Surfaces must survive steam, splashed water, spilled cosmetics and strong cleaning products. Don't select materials on the basis of looks alone.

CHOICES IN FLOOR COVERINGS

One important factor must be considered at all times when deciding on a bathroom flooring material. Users will often be barefoot, and their feet will often be wet. The floor must be safe, which means relatively skidproof under wet feet. Second, a floor must feel good—no rough or sharp edges and not overly cold to the touch.

The relative coldness of a floor depends partly on the actual temperature and partly on how quickly the flooring material conducts heat, called its *heat conductivity*. A ceramic-tile floor installed directly over an uninsulated concrete slab is going to feel colder than a vinyl floor installed over a wood subfloor. Masonry materials like brick and ceramic tile have fairly high conductivity—they take heat out of your feet readily and in large amounts. So even when relatively warm, high-conductivity materials are going to feel cooler than low-conductivity ones. A wood floor or a resilient floor would be a better choice than brick or tile for a bathroom in a cold climate.

Check Existing Floors—In selecting a flooring material, consider the floors of adjoining areas. All sorts of trim strips are available to bridge seams where two kinds of flooring meet. But some floor combinations can be unsightly and even dangerous. Avoid significant changes in level be-

Finish materials can be used in unorthodox ways to good result. Here, carpet has been extended up the tub apron and short strips of oak used on the walls. Both are normally flooring materials.

tween adjacent floor coverings. Sometimes adjoining floor areas can be built up to the same level as the new bathroom floor.

Before selecting materials such as thick ceramic tile or brick, examine the existing floor structure. These heavy, brittle materials require a strong, rigid subfloor. If your present floor is not strong or rigid enough, it may sag under the added load, or flex and cause the finish floor to break up. You will have to reinforce the subfloor. Check local codes for subfloor requirements.

On the other hand, if the subfloor is rough, lumpy concrete, it may require too much work to make it smooth and level enough for a flexible, resilient floor covering. Quarry tile in a thick mortar bed might be a better solution.

Certain bathrooms need floor coverings with resistance to abrasion. If mud and grit are regularly tracked into the bathroom, the finish on a

high-gloss wood floor will quickly be destroyed. A cushioned-vinyl floor with a strong pattern to hide dirt would be more suitable. It would also be more skid resistant under wet feet.

CARPET

Bath carpet is different from ordinary carpet, and from indoor-outdoor carpet. Bath carpet is all-synthetic, will withstand frequent cleaning and has a waterproof backing. Most ordinary carpets contain natural materials that can absorb water and harbor bacteria. The backing is usually porous. Indoor-outdoor carpet is usually all synthetic, but the backing is designed to let water drain through and away, which is not suitable in a bathroom.

The comfort and resiliency of bathroom carpet are hard to match with any other material, but spills and routine cleaning are major drawbacks. Constant water exposure can result in

Today's resilient-flooring materials often masquerade as other materials, but are easier to install and maintain, and are more durable. This resilient sheet flooring simulates ceramic tile, but is softer and warmer underfoot. *Photo courtesy of Armstrong World Industries Inc.*

short carpet life. A good compromise might be loose-laid carpet or an area rug. If the carpet or rug is washable, it can be picked up and thrown into the washing machine when it gets soiled or soggy.

RESILIENT FLOOR COVERINGS

Thanks to modern polymers, there are many choices in resilient materials for bathroom floors. The wide variety of resilient flooring materials has led to some confusion about installation techniques. With the early linoleum and asphalt tile, you first put down a layer of evil-smelling brown-black mastic and laid the floor covering over it. Now each type of resilient-flooring material requires its own special adhesive and installation technique, depending on use.

Resilient tiles usually require adhesive over the whole floor surface. Some resilient tiles are self-adhesive. You peel release paper from the backs and drop them into position. Some sheet floorings only require adhesive around the perimeter. A few sheet floorings can be stapled around the perimeter and not glued at all.

Asphalt Tile—The first resilient tile was made from asphalt and fillers. It isn't readily available today. Colors are limited and it is made only in a marbleized pattern. Asphalt tile is brittle and subject to staining from grease and other substances. If you want the look of asphalt tile, perhaps for a 1930s or 1940s period bathroom, there's a solid-vinyl look-alike available.

Vinyl-Asbestos Tile—This product is made up of a patterned layer of vinyl over a fibrous backing, with or without a clear vinyl or urethane top layer. Vinyl-asbestos tile is economical. It is inexpensive to produce and long-lasting. As a result, it's widely used in new construction. A wide variety of colors, patterns and grades are available. Tile size is 12x12''.

Solid-Vinyl Tile—These are more expensive than vinyl-asbestos, but more luxurious. Some types are manufactured by printing a pattern on a layer of vinyl. Others, called *inlaid vinyl,* have small vinyl particles of several colors fused into the tile, arranged to form a pattern. Both types are made with or without a clear surface coating, called a *wear layer.* Solid-color

vinyl tiles are also available. Tile size is 12x12''.

One type of solid-vinyl tile is made by rolling out and fusing the factory's scraps and trimmings from other vinyl tile production. This produces a mottled, marbleized pattern that looks similar to the old asphalt tile. These tiles are usually inexpensive, and make an excellent substitute for asphalt tile in a period bathroom. They're as durable as the other solid vinyls. Tile size is 12x12''.

Vinyl Sheet Flooring—Vinyl sheet flooring is made in long rolls 6, 9, 12 and 15 feet wide. Sheet vinyl may or may not have a clear vinyl or urethane wear layer. Many patterns and colors are available.

Printed vinyl is generally the least expensive. The vinyl top layer is printed with a pattern and laminated to a felt backing. Better grades are embossed, and have a clear wear layer.

Cushioned vinyl has a layer of resilient foam between the patterned vinyl layer and the backing. This produces a cushioned feeling underfoot. A textured, cushioned vinyl is ideal for floors subjected to grit and mud. The cushioning helps prevent grit particles from cutting into the floor surface.

A top-line variation of the cushioned vinyl floor consists of a clear wear layer, pattern layer, cushioning and backing—all of them vinyl. The resilience of cushioned vinyl has its drawbacks. The top surface is subject to dents and punctures from sharp or heavy objects.

Inlaid-vinyl sheet flooring is made by creating the color pattern with small granules of vinyl, then fusing the granules together into a solid sheet. This process makes for brilliant coloring and high durability.

Resilient Floor Quality—The signs of quality are similar for all resilient flooring materials. Generally, the thicker the flooring, the higher the quality. Also, the thicknesses of the clear wear layer and the pattern layer are good indicators. If possible, ask the salesman for a sample and check it for damage resistance. Check the clear wear layer for its reaction to burns, such as from a dropped cigarette. Also check the material for abrasion resistance. Damage caused by such mishaps can be repaired, but a clear wear layer that's resistant to damage is preferable.

WOOD

Wood is one of the oldest and most widely used flooring materials. Some wood-floor materials come prefinished, some presanded but unfinished, and others must be sanded and finished after installation. Some thin wood floorings can be glued down. Others are nailed over resin paper.

Parquet—Wood-block flooring is available in a wide variety of types, sizes, thicknesses and wood species. *Parquet* flooring consists of a number of small wood pieces preassembled into blocks. Originally, parquet floors were painstakingly assembled in place from many small pieces of wood, using inlay techniques. Many of today's parquet blocks duplicate the old patterns. Parquet flooring is sold prefinished or unfinished. Parquet comes in many block sizes—12x12" is the most common.

A common parquet flooring looks like several short lengths of strip flooring splined together into a block, with tongues and grooves milled on the edges. It is usually thick enough to be *blind-nailed* like strip flooring, page 114, or it can be applied with adhesive.

Some parquet flooring is laminated flat, like plywood. Plies are offset to form tongues and grooves. The wear surface might be one piece of wood, or several pieces joined in a pattern.

Parquet is sometimes made by joining strips of wood together with a paper facing. The paper preserves the relationship of the strips in the pattern. This type usually has square edges. It can be difficult for the do-it-yourselfer to work with.

Installation is much the same as for resilient tile, but any curving of the wood segments during installation tends to scoop adhesive off the floor, extruding it under the paper facing. The resulting blotch can be difficult to remove because it's often discovered only after removing the facing paper.

Strip Flooring—Wood strips come in a number of sizes, species, grades and finishes. Strips are usually 3/4-inch thick and vary in width from 1-1/2 to 3-1/4 inches. They are sold in bundles of random lengths, from 2 to 8 feet. Strips of other widths and thicknesses are available, as are random-width planks with plugs to simulate the old pegged-plank floors.

Wood-strip flooring is available in many species, but oak is the most popular. If protected from water

Blue floor tiles provide the basis for color scheme of this bathroom. Tiled tub platform was extended to make room for large houseplants. *Photo courtesy of American Olean Tile Co.*

damage, oak flooring is almost as durable as ceramic tile. With proper maintenance, an oak floor will outlast most other materials in the house.

The basic problem with wood flooring in a bathroom is water penetration into cracks between the strips. In water-prone areas, plan on installing unfinished wood flooring. Sanding and finishing will seal the joints. Two coats of polyurethane will usually protect a wood floor from water damage.

Another solution is to use a wood-veneer/vinyl composite tile. Installed like vinyl tile, it's made of a clear wear layer, a layer of real-wood veneer, and a vinyl-backing layer, all fused together. The veneer can be cut from wood species that are too expensive or fragile to use as strip flooring.

CERAMIC TILE

Since the advent of indoor bathrooms, ceramic tile has been used for bathroom surfaces in all parts of the world. Thus, it is easy to find tile to fit any style bathroom. Tile's durability, water resistance and ease of cleaning are hard to equal. Tile is one of man's oldest manufactured construction materials. There are examples several thousand years old that are all but indistinguishable from tiles still made today.

Unglazed Tile—These tiles are the color of the clay used in their manufacture, modified by the heat of firing. Colors range from brick-red to pale green or tan.

Unglazed tile must be sealed after laying because it's absorbent. See page 157. Shapes include square, hexagonal, octagonal and serpentine. Sizes are usually larger than glazed tiles, averaging from 6x6" to 16x16". Larger tiles usually go under the names, *quarry tile, patio tile* or *Mexican tile.* Because they haven't been fired as long, unglazed tiles are usually softer than glazed tiles.

Glazed Tile—To make glazed tile, the tile body is first hard fired with an undercoating glaze, producing a gritty but skidproof coating, called bisque. The bisque glaze mostly serves as a bonding coat for a final, colored glaze. Temperature of the final firing controls the degree of melting of the final glaze and therefore the finish on the tile. Finishes for glazed tile range from glossy to semi-matte to matte.

The finish is a major indicator of the skid-resistance of a tile. Glossy tile will be slick under wet feet, unless there's a molded pattern under the high gloss to help provide traction.

Sizes of glazed tiles range from barely 1/2 inch across to 14 or 15 inches on a side. All sorts of shapes are commercially available. Tiles can also be custom-made.

Using Tile—Ceramic tile makes an excellent floor. It's long lasting, stays good looking and needs a minimum of care. The wide range of colors, patterns and shapes makes it possible to use ceramic tile in almost any bathroom. But the hard surface of ceramic tile reflects sound, and it feels harder underfoot. Ceramic tile can also feel cold to the touch.

If you drop a fragile object on a ceramic-tile floor, it's more likely to break than if dropped on a more resilient floor. If you drop something heavy, it can crack a tile or two. A repair job can be difficult unless you've kept spare tiles and some matching grout. A rigid subfloor is required to hold the weight of the tile and prevent cracking. Check local codes for subfloor requirements.

MASONRY

Usually considered outdoor-paving materials, brick and stone are often used for floors. Like ceramic tile, these masonry materials are heavy and require a strong, rigid subfloor.

Brick—You can use brick for a bathroom floor, although it's hard, heavy work to install. Use brick pavers specifically made for flooring. Paving

Because brick is almost always a lo-

cally made product, sizes and thicknesses vary slightly with each manufacturer. Colors available are usually similar to unglazed-tile colors, which are derived from local clay colors. Brick floors are even more porous than unglazed tiles and should be sealed or finished.

Stone—If it's available in your area, stone makes an interesting and attractive bathroom floor. Because of the extreme weight and the expense of shipping, stone is rarely transported more than a few hundred miles. If there's a local source of a good flooring stone, a stone floor is entirely feasible. But the installation is so specialized and difficult that it should be left to an experienced stonemason, with one exception.

In some parts of the United States and Canada, it's possible to buy *gaged stone.* Slate is most often found in this form. Marble is sometimes available as gaged stone. Gaged slate, for instance, has been ground on the back to an approximately uniform thickness—1/4 to 1/2 inch.

It is then sawed into regular squares and rectangles. The face is just as it was originally split.

Gaged stone products come in a box, just like tile, and are installed and finished much the same as unglazed tile. Also available are slate and marble squares ground to a highly polished finish. However, these may be too slick to use on a bathroom floor.

WALLS AND CEILINGS

Most walls and ceilings in a house consist of drywall covered with a coat of paint. If you decide to use paint in a bathroom, it must be carefully applied. Use a primer-sealer and a finish coat of high-quality semigloss or gloss enamel. Flat paints are less resistant to water and cannot be washed when the wall gets dirty. For maximum resistance to washing and scrubbing, you can use an exterior acrylic-enamel house paint.

Gloss and semigloss enamels are made in water-base (acrylic-latex) and solvent-base (alkyd) forms. Each has its benefits, but the differences have become minor. The water-base products have the advantages of faster drying, easier cleanup, less smell and a more manageable consistency.

Solvent-base paints tend to *self-level* a bit better, reducing brush marks.

Hiding power and durability might also be better. Paint thinner or other solvent is required to clean paint off tools and surfaces. Whichever type you decide to use, don't skimp on quality. A high-quality product of one type will outperform an average-quality product of the other type.

Colored paints are easy to work with. But white, strangely enough, can be tricky. Plain white is generally too stark to use, and is hard to find anyway—most paint labeled white is actually blue-white. Paint marked *off-white* is often a depressing gray-white. It rarely complements home decor.

Usually, some variation of a cream-white, usually marked *cottage white* or *antique white,* is the best choice. This is especially true when colors in the room are earth or wood tones. These whites have warmer tones and provide a good background for most decorating schemes.

The shade of white you use should provide the correct background for the color scheme you've chosen. If the paint dealer can't provide the right shade, you can start with plain white, or an off-white that's "off" in the right color direction. Then add a small quantity of paint, or tinting color from the paint store, matched to another major color in the room. You'll find you can add quite a bit of color, and the white will still look white once it's dry.

Put the entire amount of paint to be used into one container. Then slowly add small amounts of color until the desired tone is achieved. Test color frequently by applying it to a small section of wall and letting it dry.

Textures—You can use textures to add interest to walls and ceilings. Commercial textures are available for use on drywall, or you can make your own, using drywall-joint compound and one of several readily-available additives. See page 101.

Texturing is best done before all fixtures, except the tub, and cabinetry go in. However, a too-heavy texture can present problems with fixture and vanity installation. Avoid placing lumps and bumps where anything will meet the wall. If you don't, you'll have to scrape and sand the wall later to get cabinets and fixtures to fit.

Like heavy textures, all types of masonry walls present some fitting problems. About the only realistic solution is to plan on scribing moldings to fit the contour of the wall. See page 177.

Wall Coverings—These can be used in a bathroom, but must be selected carefully. Ordinary wallpaper is subject to water and humidity damage. It should not be used without a protective coating. Vinyl-impregnated wallpapers, vinyl-coated wallpapers and all-vinyl wall coverings are more resistant to moisture damage, but are more difficult to apply. Foil wall coverings also work well, as long as they are not directly exposed to water.

Wall coverings require an adhesive to hold them in place. Some come *prepasted,* with adhesive already applied. You dip the strips in water to moisten the adhesive before hanging. Although convenient, prepasted paper doesn't allow the use of high-strength adhesives or adhesive additives. Such adhesives and additives are better at withstanding exposure to steam and water, common to a bathroom environment.

Strippable wall coverings have a lower-strength bond to the wall than nonstrippable kinds. They tend to come loose when exposed to moisture. *Peelable wall coverings* are designed to split between the face and backing layers when you remove the covering. When removed, they leave adhesive and paper backing on the wall. Complete removal is a tedious chore, should you want to paint the wall in the future.

Hundreds of variations of wall coverings are available. The best source of information is a knowledgable wall-covering dealer. Explain the project you're doing, and he or she will help you select the right wall covering and adhesive for the job.

Wood Paneling—You can panel bathroom walls and ceilings with 4x8' wood panels or tongue-and-groove wood paneling strips. Bare wood isn't very tolerant of moisture, and isn't washable at all. The finish has to take most of the punishment. Some types of prefinished paneling and varnished tongue-and-groove paneling won't survive steam, water and repeated scrubbing. Several coats of a clear polyurethane make a fairly durable surface for these conditions. Polyurethane comes in satin, semigloss and gloss surfaces. A penetrating polyurethane will protect wood from moisture while maintaining the wood's original surface texture.

Wall coverings don't have to be dull and retiring—they can be the boldest element in a bathroom, as is this animal print. Note how wall covering was extended into light well of skylight.

Many kinds of prefinished paneling can be found on the market. Some have a surface of wood veneer laminated to a backing of thin plywood or tempered hardboard. Others have a vinyl surface with printed or photographically reproduced wood grain. Simulated-wood paneling is often the only way to get the appearance of rare or expensive wood, or wood that doesn't cut well into veneer. Usually, the more expensive the paneling, the more realistic it looks.

Many colors and patterns of paneling are available besides simulated woods. Finishes range from a thin paint coating to plastic laminate. Durability and resistance to scratches, stains and water vary widely. Check the manufacturer's literature to see if a particular paneling is recommended for bathroom use.

Ceramic Tile—The tile you use on walls need not meet the same requirements as that used for floors. It need not be skid resistant—in fact, tile with a smooth, glossy glaze is often used because it's easier to clean than a rough-surface tile. Wall tiles can be thinner and more brittle than floor tiles. The same tiles used for vanity tops and tub surrounds can be used on the wall. There is a much wider selection of these tiles than floor tiles.

On bathroom walls, tile is most often used as a *wainscot* that extends from the floor to a height of 3 to 5 feet up the wall. A tile wainscot is especially suitable around plumbing fixtures to protect the wall against splashed

Ceramic tile is probably the most widely used material for all kinds of bathroom surfaces. It is also one of the best materials for expressing personal creativity. *Photo courtesy of American Olean Tile Co.*

water. Because ceramic tile is easy to clean and lends a sanitary appearance to a bathroom, you often see this type of treatment in commercial restrooms.

However, you don't have to design your bathroom to look like a public facility. There are many imaginatve ways to use tile on walls. For instance, you can use it to tie other tiled areas together, such as a vanity backsplash to a shower enclosure or tub surround.

Ceilings—Any material or treatment that's used on walls can be used on a ceiling. Ceilings also have three finish materials of their own—*acoustical tile, acoustical coatings* and *luminous-ceiling panels*.

Acoustical tile is a natural solution for a bathroom that tends to be noisy, or has too high a ceiling. Many colors and patterns are available. The tile can

be applied directly to the present ceiling or suspended below it on a metal framework designed for that purpose.

An acoustical-tile ceiling won't solve the problem of an old, loose, broken plaster or drywall ceiling. Acoustical tile may disguise the mess for a year or two, but there is a danger of it all coming down. Avoid this by removing the old ceiling material and installing new drywall, plaster or an acoustical-tile ceiling that will stay in place.

Acoustical tiles should not be used in areas subject to steam or moisture condensation, such as over a shower enclosure. Water can stain or warp the tiles.

Acoustical coatings are applied with a paint roller or by spraying. They have a light, fluffy texture and are

more sound-absorbent than ordinary drywall texture. They do not absorb sound nearly as well as acoustical tile. Acoustical coatings are not resistant to steam and high humidity unless specially treated with a water sealer. Such coatings aren't really suitable for small, enclosed bathrooms with high humidity levels.

The early acoustical-ceiling coatings often contained large amounts of asbestos. Such coatings are dangerous because of their tendency to shed carcinogenic asbestos particles. They're especially dangerous to remove. If you're working with an older acoustical ceiling, contact the local air-quality or public-health agency for information on how to make such ceilings safe, either by sealing in the asbestos, or by removing the coating.

A luminous ceiling can provide large amounts of nondirectional light in a bathroom, without the clutter of light fixtures. Most luminous ceilings consist of a recessed light fixture covered with a translucent diffuser panel. Panels are usually set flush with the ceiling surface. The diffuser panels used for luminous ceilings can also serve to diffuse light from skylights.

Any translucent material can be used for diffuser panels. Sheets of rigid plastic are made for this purpose. They come in many patterns, colors and degrees of translucency. Stained-glass panels can also be used.

Diffuser panels can be suspended on the same metal framework made for acoustical ceilings, or suspended on wood frames. Wood frames can be finished to match cabinets or trim work. Be sure to allow adequate clearance from hot light bulbs. For more on installing acoustical and luminous ceilings, see pages 175-176.

EQUIPMENT

As you're selecting surfaces for the bathroom, consider what type of equipment you'll install. In most cases, surfaces and equipment are chosen simultaneously to fit the overall bathroom design. Or your choices in both may revolve around a single major design element, such as a hardwood floor, stained glass window or large hydromassage tub.

Major plumbing fixtures such as lavatories, toilets, bidets and tubs are available in matching styles and colors. Fixture designs range from ultra-modern, like the ones shown on page 46, to antique reproductions, as shown on page 19. Prefabricated vanities and tops are available in numerous traditional and contemporary styles, or you can custom design a vanity to fit your bathroom decor. Prefabricated showers are available, but more often these are custom designed and built on site. Accessories, such as towel bars, paper holders and soap dishes are made to fit virtually any style bathroom.

VANITY CABINETS AND TOPS

Cabinetwork is playing an increasing role in bathrooms, providing storage and visual interest. Bathroom cabinets don't have to match the rest of the cabinets in the house. You can harmonize the bathroom cabinets with the rest of the bathroom. The cabinets must be resistant to water and other damaging materials.

Custom cabinets can be built either on the job or in a local shop. Or you can install prefabricated cabinets. These are factory-produced to standard sizes and types. The type of cabinets you choose depends on time, money and demands of the bathroom you're creating.

You can solve just about any design problem with custom cabinets, including odd sizes and shapes, and poor storage. If your new bathroom is unusual, a custom cabinetmaker can deal with it.

Cabinet Construction—Two basic construction methods are common to all vanity cabinets made today. *Face-frame* cabinets have a frame attached to the front of the basic box, visible between the doors. Other cabinets have no face frames, or narrow, concealed ones. The exposed face is all doors and drawer fronts.

The finish surfaces of most cabinets are made of wood or plastic laminate. Wood cabinets have wide appeal. Well cared for, they develop a pleasing patina with the passing of time. Plastic-laminate cabinets look sleek and modern, are easy to keep clean, wear well and tolerate some moisture. Plastic-laminate doors and drawer fronts are available with many kinds of wood, plastic or metal trim.

Whatever the exterior finish of a prefabricated vanity cabinet, the structure will be built of plywood, or particle board or wafer board in cabinet-grade density. On wood cabinets, face

This novel vanity design would have been relatively easy to do in plastic laminate or wood veneer. Solid oak is used here.

frames, doors and drawer fronts are often made of solid wood.

Look for solid cabinet construction with rabbeted, glued and fastened joints. Edges should be as well finished as the rest of the cabinet, especially where they will show. Hardware, especially for drawers, should be sturdy and of high quality. Drawers should be built of solid wood or plywood, not lightweight particle board. High-quality molded-plastic drawer assemblies have recently appeared on the market. Quality plastic drawers have the potential to outlast wood drawers.

When assessing the quality of wood cabinets, check the way the entire cabinet is finished. Wood constantly absorbs and releases moisture as humidity rises and falls. This causes the wood to swell and shrink. If two sides of a wood door or drawer front have been finished differently, they will swell and shrink differently. This

can cause doors to warp, or drawers to stick.

Look for panels that are treated the same on both sides, so they will swell and shrink in unison. If the face of a door is finished with plastic laminate, see if the back of the door has a similar finish. The back laminate may be a different color than the face laminate, but that will have no effect if they're both the same material. If the back is covered with only a coat of paint, the cabinet may warp.

Also, high-quality plastic-laminate cabinets will have laminate on door and drawer edges, as well as on both faces. On cheaper cabinets, the edges will be painted plywood or particle board. In the high humidity of a bathroom, these types of cabinets may be subject to warping, swelling or delamination.

Customizing—You don't necessarily have to use the hardware that comes with prefabricated cabinets. Most hardware stores and home-improvement centers have a good selection of decorator handles, latches, pulls and hinges. Or, you can order hardware through a custom cabinet shop. Cabinetmakers often have sources for the more exotic hardware not available at most local retail outlets.

In addition to adding custom hardware, many kinds of custom moldings can be attached to flat doors and finished to match or contrast with the door faces. Doors that have inset panels can be altered by removing panels and substituting metal mesh, etched glass, stained glass or fabric.

VANITY TOPS

The basic requirements for vanity tops is that they be waterproof and resistant to stains from makeup, medicines and other toiletry items. All materials discussed here are suitable, if installed correctly.

Plastic Laminate—This surface material is more widely used than you might think, often masquerading as other materials. Consider substituting plastic laminate if you want the appearance of a fragile or hard-to-work-with material such as slate or leather. Often, laminate is easier to find and apply than the material it simulates. Wear characteristics and moisture resistance may be better than the real item. Plastic laminates also come in many unique designs and patterns of their own.

Plastic laminates come in standard widths of 24, 30, 36 and 48 inches. Standard lengths are from 4 to 12 feet in 2-foot increments. Thicknesses are normally 1/16 inch for tops and 1/32 inch for wall areas and cabinets.

Post-Form Tops—These are the fastest and easiest vanity tops to install. They consist of plastic laminate pre-formed over a particle-board core. Post-form tops have a curved, molded backsplash and front edge. They come ready to install and are widely available. They're sold in stock lengths, usually in 2-foot increments, priced by the running foot. Clean lines, quick installation and moderate price are their main advantages.

Post-form tops have drawbacks for more elaborate vanity installations. Corners and finished ends can be troublesome, and width is not adjustable for narrow areas or irregular shapes. Colors and patterns are often limited.

Ceramic Tile—Along with wood, ceramic tile is among the oldest and most versatile building materials. It is much more appropriate than wood for a vanity top. Most glazed tile is impervious to water, heat, cold, acids and cleaning products, although its grout joints are not. Grout sealers should always be used for tiled vanity tops. Unglazed tiles should be sealed with a waterproof sealer, available from the tile dealer.

You can use any kind of tile for a vanity top. Smooth, glossy tiles are the easiest to keep clean. The tile can either match or complement tile used in other parts of the bathroom—floor, wall, shower or tub surround.

Tiles 4x4" or larger are best used for large, flat surfaces. Small mosaic tiles are better for contoured or irregular surfaces. See page 154 for information on installing ceramic-tile tops.

Marble, Real and Synthetic—Real marble is sometimes used for vanity tops, but it is easily stained and scratched. For this reason, synthetic substitutes are often used. Synthetic-marble materials come in two kinds. One is an acrylic resin, often having marble chips or marble dust as a filler. The other is a DuPont product called *Corian*.

The acrylic type is suitable for light-duty areas, but the glossy finish is thin and subject to wear. Corian is the same all the way through, so marred areas can be sanded and polished fairly easily. Both can be worked with hand and power tools, and are easy to install. Corian can also be milled into complex shapes with sandpaper, files or a router. Carbide-tip blades and bits are recommended for working both types; regular blades and bits are quickly dulled.

Many producers of synthetic marble make vanity tops with an integral lavatory bowl and backsplash. These tops are made in standard sizes to fit prefabricated vanity cabinets. Holes are predrilled in the top to accept standard faucet and drain fittings. Check with local suppliers for the available sizes, shapes and bowl configurations.

PLUMBING FIXTURES AND FITTINGS

Plumbing fixtures and fittings form the functional part of a bathroom. A plumbing *fixture* is a water receptacle. Tubs, showers, toilets, bidets and lavatories are fixtures. A plumbing *fitting* attaches to the fixture to deliver water to it or drain water from it. Faucets, showerheads, toilet-flushing mechanisms and drain assemblies are fittings.

The day of strictly functional fixtures is over. Today, fixtures are an integral part of bathroom decoration.

Many synthetic marble and Corian tops have integral lavatory bowls. Custom sizes and shapes are available, such as this double-bowl Corian top. *Photo courtesy of DuPont Company.*

Modern fixtures are available in both pastels and saturated colors. Sizes and shapes vary. Patterns are becoming available for some fixtures.

The first distinction among fixtures is the basic materials they're made of. Depending on the fixture, these materials include enameled steel, cast iron, vitreous china or fiberglass.

Enameled Steel—Some lavatories, tubs and prefabricated shower enclosures are made of enamel-coated steel. Enameled steel comes in several colors, but the selection of shapes is limited. The enamel coating is subject to chipping and shows marks. Scouring powder will remove some marks. Touch-up kits are available to cover chipped areas.

Cast Iron—Used for tubs and lavatories, cast iron is much more durable than enameled steel. Available in a variety of colors and shapes, cast-iron tubs are solid and quiet. Sheer mass reduces noise.

The coating on cast-iron fixtures is powdered glass, fused to the iron at high temperature. You must take certain precautions with this type of finish. The thin, fused surface of the coating can be quickly worn away by abrasive cleaners such as scouring powder. Once the glass-smooth finish is abraded, stains and dirt penetrate the coating. Then, the harder you scrub it, the worse it will look. If you don't use abrasive cleaners on a cast-iron fixture, it will look new for years.

Defects in cast-iron fixtures are primarily lack of bonding between the iron and the coating, and an excess of carbon specks in the coating. Unfortunately, both of these problems can develop months after the fixture is installed. Loss of coating bond is cause for replacing the fixture under warranty. But some carbon specks are unavoidable in the manufacturing process, and are allowable under warranty.

Because the coating on enameled cast iron is glass, previously invisible carbon specks can bloom on the surface of a fixture months after firing. If some appear that you consider objectionable, contact the manufacturer for the detailed industry standards that apply. Or ask for a service representative to stop by and have a look.

Vitreous China—A few lavatories and most toilets and bidets are made of vitreous china. Essentially the

PLUMBING-FIXTURE MATERIALS

Fixture	Enameled Cast Iron	Enameled Steel	Vitreous China	Fiberglass	Other Plastics	Synthetic Marble	Ceramic Tile
Conventional Tub							
Tub with Surrounds							
Hydromassage Tub							
Shower							
Toilet							
Bidet							
Wall-Hung Lavatory							
Pedestal Lavatory							
Drop-in Lavatory							
Undercounter Lavatory							

This chart includes the more-common bathroom fixtures and materials. Plumbing fixtures and their parts have also been made from many other kinds of materials—wood, metal and masonry. Metals range from sheet copper to hammered silver. Other materials include ordinary concrete, exposed-aggregate concrete, real marble, stones set in mortar and even gem minerals, such as jade or onyx.

In the materials listed above, *fiberglass* refers to fiberglass-reinforced polyester (FRP), with an acrylic or gelcoat finish. *Other plastics* refers to all molded-plastic fixtures that are *not* fiberglass-reinforced. All fixtures listed, except those made of ceramic tile, are prefabricated units, either custom-made or factory-made. Ceramic-tile fixtures are built in place. Ceramic drop-in lavatory bowls are made by the same process as ceramic tile or pottery.

same material used for china dishes, vitreous-china fixtures are molded from white clay. The clay is ground fine, mixed to a slurry like consistency called *slip*, and poured into plaster molds. Left to stand several hours, the plaster mold absorbs water from the slip, gradually depositing a layer of clay particles on the inside of the mold. Each mold shapes only a part of a plumbing fixture.

After an adequate thickness is built up, the excess slip is poured off and the part removed for air drying. When the parts are dry enough to hold their shape, they're assembled into a plumbing fixture, using slip to stick the pieces together. A light first firing further hardens the fixture. After cooling, the fixture is dusted with powdered glaze and fired again. This produces *bisque ware*. You can see what this finish looks like by checking the inside of a toilet tank or the underside of the tank lid. A final glaze is applied as a powder, the fixture is fired again, inspected, the mechanical parts installed, and the fixture is boxed and shipped.

Because vitreous-china fixtures involve an essentially handcrafted production process, some irregularities are to be expected. Defects to watch for are missing areas of final glazing

and cracks, especially at the assembly seams.

Cracks in vitreous-china fixtures can develop after the fixture is shipped from the factory. Because a new fixture shows a hairline crack, it doesn't necessarily mean the inspector at the factory missed it. If there was stress generated in the china during the firing, a crack may develop days, weeks or even months later. The only remedy is to replace the fixture under the manufacturer's warranty.

Plastic—Once sneered at as inferior, plastic plumbing products are becoming accepted and widespread. Plastic has some major advantages, which led to its initial use for pipes and internal parts for fittings. Plastics are noncorroding. Water impurities don't affect them. Scale and other deposits don't stick to plastic. Many plastics are self lubricating.

Molded-plastic, drop-in lavatories have been available for several years, and seem to wear well. Recently, one major manufacturer has introduced a molded-plastic one-piece toilet, with considerable success. Installation is easier because it weighs considerably less than a vitreous-china toilet.

Fiberglass—The term, *fiberglass,* is an abbreviation of the actual material used for bathroom plumbing fixtures.

Most manufacturers offer matching fixtures. The ones shown here are Kohler's *Raspberry Puree Set. Photo courtesy of Kohler Co.*

The full name of the material is *fiberglass-reinforced plastic*. Some manufacturers use the terms, *fiberglass-reinforced polyester*, or *FRP*.

The fixtures consist of a fiberglass-plastic shell covered with a smooth *gelcoat* finish or *acrylic* skin. Gelcoat is applied as a liquid to the fiberglass shell; the color of the fixture is added to the gelcoat layer. Acrylic comes in thin sheets, which are formed in a mold, then sprayed with a fiberglass-impregnated resin to add rigidity to the fixture. Gelcoat usually comes in solid colors. Acrylic comes in both solid colors and marbleized patterns.

Look for thick, solid fiberglass, a uniform gelcoat or acrylic finish, and support ribs built into the structure to carry the weight of water and user. Many lines of fiberglass tubs and showers are coated on the back and bottom with insulating foam. The foam provides support for the floor of the fixture, deadens sound and keeps the water in tubs from cooling too quickly.

Common defects in plastic and fiberglass fixtures are poor molding and trimming, delaminations and surface irregularities. Before you take delivery of a large fiberglass fixture, check it for stress-cracking caused by flexing in shipment and for dents and dings.

FITTINGS

Almost all new faucets and fittings avoid the old problems of washer-and-seat construction. The operating parts are most often contained in a cartridge. The cartridge is relatively trouble free and easily replaced if it malfunctions.

The familiar two-handle faucets are still available, but single-handle faucets are more widely used.

The finish on a fitting can be matched with the rest of the metal trim and accessories in the bathroom. Brass and chrome in polished and brushed finishes are most common. Unusual handle designs and materials are available from some specialty manufacturers. Fitting handles are made of metal, vitreous china, and clear or tinted crystal, along with plastic look-alikes.

If you want the look of polished-brass, you can't strip the plating from a brass fitting to get it. Due to casting and machining requirements, different parts are made from different types of brass alloy. The color of the brass underneath the plating is likely to be different than the brass used for plating.

To get a brass finish, you have to remove any other plating, polish the surfaces, then brass-plate the fixture to get a uniform color. If a local plating shop can't brass-plate, or even if they can, consider gold-plating instead.

Despite the cost, gold-plated fittings are really quite practical. The plated finish is long wearing and resistant to corrosion and tarnishing. The look is similar to polished or brush-finish brass, but gold requires no protective coatings.

BATHTUBS

Bathtubs are made in all shapes and sizes. The basic types are the *conventional tub*, in recessed and corner models, the *receptor tub*, the *drop-in*, the *conventional tub with integral wall surrounds*, and the *hydromassage unit*. Tubs are made of enameled steel, enameled cast iron and fiberglass.

Conventional Tubs—The familiar conventional tub with front apron is made in 4-1/2, 5 and 5-1/2-foot lengths. Typical widths, front to back, are 28 to 32 inches. Overall height is usually 14 or 16 inches.

The *apron* of a tub is the finished front or end panel that extends from the tub rim to the floor. Conventional tubs are made with an apron only on one side for installation in a recess; or with an apron on one side and one end for installation in a corner. Most conventional tubs have full-height aprons, but some are made with a short apron for partially sunken installation.

Integral-Surround Tubs—These are usually molded fiberglass. They have wall-surround panels molded integrally with the tub. This eliminates the seam where tub meets wall and takes the place of waterproofing materials required for the wall surround. Once the unit is in place and connected, it's ready for use.

These tubs are particularly suitable if you're redoing your one-and-only bathroom and require a quick installation, or if the walls are in bad shape and would require extensive patching to install another type of material.

Such integral-surround tubs are bulky—you may have difficulty getting one up stairs and through doorways. They're also somewhat delicate to handle before they're installed. This is because the unit is flexible and prone to stress-cracking where the end panels of the surround meet the apron of the tub. If handling or access to the bathroom is a problem, there are fiberglass tubs with separate surround panels that are attached after the tub is in place. They are much easier to transport.

Receptor Tubs—These are roughly square. They're built like a conventional tub, only shallower. Recess models are 3 to 4 feet on a side. Corner models often have the projecting corner cut off on a diagonal. Receptor tubs are designed to function better than a conventional tub when used as a shower, but to still work as a tub when needed. Most are made in enameled cast iron.

Drop-In Tubs—The drop-in tub is a recent development. It has no apron, but the edges are turned down on all four sides so it can be recessed in a horizontal surface, in the same way as a countertop lavatory. Usually, the tub fitting is also deck-mounted, either by drillings in the tub rim, or in the horizontal surface alongside. See photo at right. Sizes are usually large, up to 5x6'.

Drop-in tubs can be installed in the floor so the rim is at floor level, installed in a raised platform or surround that provides seating, or simply skirted in to conceal the tub body. The finished rim height can be anywhere from floor level—or even slightly below—to 24 inches high or so. Raised tubs should be installed at a height that allows easy access and comfortable seating around the perimeter.

Except for the integral-surround types and the drop-ins, all the above tubs have a flange or lip where the tub edges meet walls. The lip is installed against the wall framing, and the waterproof surround material installed over the lip. This directs water back into the tub and helps prevent leaks where the tub meets the surround.

All tubs except the drop-ins are either *left-hand* or *right-hand*. The hand is determined by which end the drain hole is on as you stand facing the front of the tub. Be sure you know the correct hand before ordering a tub.

Freestanding Tubs—The old freestanding tubs—the ones with the claw feet—are still around, a few of new manufacture but mostly old ones. On old tubs, if the enamel on the interior is still in good condition, the outside can be easily refinished.

Drop-in tub can be installed at floor level or on a raised platform.

If your bathroom has one of these tubs and you plan to keep it, save all of the old exposed pipes and fittings. They can be nearly impossible to replace. For the same reason, don't buy one of these tubs without the pipes and fittings.

The exposed pipes were often solid brass, nickel-plated brass, or, in a few cases, solid nickel. Like many other metal antique items, they can be either cleaned and polished or replated.

Hydromassage Tubs—All the tubs discussed so far are made only for taking baths and showers. There are other tubs made for additional functions, whether therapeutic or recreational. Hydromassage tubs are made in both forms.

It's possible to replace a standard 5-foot recess tub with a similar model that has hydromassage capabilities. Other hydromassage tubs are more like small spas. Generally longer and wider than a conventional tub, there is often room for more than one occupant. The working equipment—pump, heater, hydrotherapy jets and related plumbing—is usually nestled around the body of the tub. Extra space may be needed to accommodate the equipment and its connections.

When installing a hydromassage tub, provide access for servicing and repair of working components. Check the manufacturer's literature during the planning stage to make sure you can meet all the requirements for space, plumbing and electrical hookups, and equipment access.

The hydromassage tub was first developed for physical-therapy use in the treatment of sprains and other muscle and joint injuries. The equipment was soon adapted for home use, simply because it felt good.

High-pressure streams of water are directed into the water in the tub through one or more swivel nozzles, called *hydrothearapy jets,* so the flow can be directed. The jets have an air-induction passage that pulls air into the water stream to produce a bubbling effect. Water-flow intensity, air volume and jet direction are all adjustable.

If you have the space and the inclination, you can install an actual spa or hot tub in the bathroom. If this idea appeals to you, see HPBooks' *Spas & Hot Tubs, How to Plan, Install & Enjoy,* by A. Cort Sinnes.

An interesting variation of the hot tub comes from Japan. For centuries, the Japanese have used small but deep tubs, called *ofuros,* not for bath-

ing but for soaking and relaxing. Before central heating, these tubs were one of the few places one could thaw out in the winter. The original ofuro was wood, but many current ones are fiberglass. Several American manufacturers make versions, usually about 3-1/2 feet square, for drop-in installation.

SHOWERS

The prefabricated-metal shower is still available, but has largely been replaced by the fiberglass-reinforced plastic version. These are made in one-piece and component-type models. They are similar to the integral-surround tubs mentioned on page 42. Sizes range from 32x32" to 3x5'.

Most showers are built on site. A combination of building materials are used to build the shower enclosure. For the most part, shower enclosures are surfaced either with ceramic tile or a waterproof plastic laminate made for that purpose.

There are several prefabricated products used to build showers. Premolded shower-floor pans come in many shapes, sizes and colors. There are recess, corner, and diagonal-corner pans ranging from 32x32" to 36x60". Premolded shower-floor pans can be combined with almost any wall finish, simplifying a shower installation. Premolded shower pans

Working parts of hydromassage tub are preplumbed around tub body. On most models, you must build your own tub surround to hide the equipment. Surround shown here was tiled to complement ceramic-tile floor. *Photo courtesy of American Olean Tile Co.*

Surround for this hydromassage tub was done in bathroom carpet and oak trim to match vanity cabinets.

Tubs and showers with integral sidewalls are a quick solution to the problem of deteriorated walls due to water exposure. The one shown here is a combination shower/whirlpool bath. *Photo courtesy of Jacuzzi Whirlpool Bath.*

are made of fiberglass-reinforced plastic, mineral-filled plastic, and cast-masonry materials.

If you build the entire shower in place, including the floor, special waterproofing measures are often needed. There are heavy folding waterproofing membranes to do the job.

Of course, the old installation techniques are workable, but more cumbersome. These include forming a pan of sheet copper or sheet lead and soldering the corner seams. Another method involves applying a waterproofing layer of hot-mopped roofing asphalt. Most of these techniques require specialized skills and equipment. The job is best left to a subcontractor.

TOILETS

The basic toilet is available in a wide variety of choices. First, there are four basic operating systems, discussed below, and four basic construction types, discussed at right. Next, you have a choice of either wall-hung or floor-mount models. Another choice is the bowl shape, either round-front or elongated.

After these major choices have been made, there are several secondary considerations. These are water use—ranging from normal to no water at all—and seat height. Of course, there's also a wide array of colors.

This diversity wouldn't be as confusing if every choice in each category were available with every choice in the other categories. Some choices are integral with others. The discussion that follows includes as much information as possible on what choices tend to come in groups.

Operating Systems—The basic operating systems for toilets are the *washdown, reverse-trap, siphon-jet* and *siphon-vortex* designs. The type you choose will determine how efficiently and quietly the toilet operates.

The washdown type is largely obsolete. It is the noisiest, least efficient and least expensive. It doesn't clear bowl contents well, tends to get dirty fast and is somewhat difficult to clean. Not many are sold anymore. In some jurisdictions they're no longer permitted because of their marginal function.

The reverse-trap toilet is somewhat better, but still noisy. A low residual

Most showers are built on site. In this bathroom, shower wall and floor are Corian. Custom doors are brass plated to match shower and lavatory fittings. *Photo courtesy of DuPont Co.*

water level in the bowl still contributes to soiling problems, but function is better than a washdown. Because the trap opening is toward the front of the bowl, instead of the rear, cleaning can be difficult.

The siphon-jet toilet is what most people think of as the basic modern toilet. The bowl is more concave than the washdown and reverse-trap types. A higher water level in the bowl makes cleaning easier. Bowl-clearing is more positive, due to the action of a water-jet positioned so it accelerates the bowl contents down the trapway during flushing. Cost is somewhat more than the first two, but still moderate. Noise level is fairly low.

Of all categories, the siphon-vortex is the top of the line. During flushing, water flow into the bowl sets up a strong swirling action. This swirling action produces a self-cleaning effect and positive bowl clearing with little noise. The siphon-vortex design is expensive to produce, and is usually

used on the most expensive models.

Construction Types—All toilet bowls are roughly similar, but the method of supplying water for flushing varies. For many years, the tank was mounted on the wall, and a metal pipe connected it to the bowl. The first toilets had tanks mounted near the ceiling, as shown on pages 19 and 116. But the pipe and its connections were subject to corrosion and leaks.

Later designs used a tank mounted directly on the back of the bowl, free of the wall. This is called a *close-coupled* toilet. The water connection between the two parts is by a cone-shaped gasket.

The *one-piece* toilet is made with tank and bowl in one unit. Because the process is more complex, one-piece toilets are expensive. The operating system is usually either siphon-jet or siphon-vortex. Many wall-hung toilets are of one-piece design.

The *flush-valve* design is used pri-

The one-piece, low-tank toilet is today's top-of-the-line fixture. Matching bidets are almost always available.
Photo courtesy of Armstrong World Industries Inc.

marily for commercial installations, but can be installed in the home. These toilets have no tank, but use direct water pressure for their flushing action. They're made in floor-mount and wall-hung versions, usually with an elongated bowl. Operation is almost always siphon-jet type. To function correctly, a flush-valve toilet requires a higher water pressure and a larger-diameter water-supply pipe than the other toilets.

Note: Bowls for flush-valve and wall-hung toilets look superficially the same, but they're not interchangeable. The internal design is entirely different. Carefully check the bowl's model number against the manufacturer's catalog to make sure you have the right kind.

Wall-Hung or Floor-Mount?—Most toilets are mounted on the floor, but models are available that can be hung on the wall, using a sturdy device called a *carrier.*

A wall-hung toilet eases floor cleaning. Because the bowl must be massive and strong to support its own weight and that of users, and because of the need for the carrier, wall-hung toilets are usually more expensive than floor-mount models. Operating systems for wall-hung toilets are siphon-jet and siphon-vortex.

When you buy a wall-hung toilet, the carrier will not come with it. The carrier is ordered separately to fit the requirements of your specific installation. Each wall-hung toilet model has several carriers that will fit it. The supplier who sells you the toilet should be able to supply the correct carrier for your circumstances. Be prepared to give the supplier specific details of your installation.

Round-Front or Elongated?—All of the less-expensive toilets are made with round-front bowls. The more expensive ones are available in both round-front and elongated versions. The elongated bowl is a few inches longer front to back. Most commercial installations use elongated-bowl toilets, and many people prefer these toilets in their home. The decision is usually based on comfort to the user.

Water Use—In some areas, water conservation is vitally important. The average toilet uses 5 to 7 gallons per flush. If you need to conserve water, pick a toilet that uses less.

Many such water-saver toilets are made. A typical model has a water consumption of 3-1/2 gallons per flush. The supplier should be able to give you details for any particular toilet model he sells. Water authorities estimate that a water-saver toilet can cut average water use by as much as 7,500 gallons a year. For more water-efficient fixtures, see page 63.

Seat Height—The standard seat height of a toilet is approximately 15 inches. Some manufacturers make special toilets for children with seat heights of 10 or 13 inches. Many manufacturers make toilets with an 18-inch seat height for the special needs of the infirm and the handicapped. These special needs are discussed on pages 64-65. Of course, it's also possible to mount a wall-hung toilet at a non-standard height if you want to. A special adjustable carrier will be needed.

Toilet Seats—The key to the comfort and utility of a toilet is the seat, and it's too often an afterthought. There is a great range of toilet seats available, both in design and in material.

The least expensive and most common toilet seat is made of molded wood covered with a coat of paint. The paint coating tends to wear, chip and stain quickly.

Better-quality toilet seats are made of molded plastic. Not only is a plastic seat more durable, but models are available that are shaped to better fit the user.

Plastic seats tend to be less prone to damage and breakage than molded-wood ones. If you want the ultimate in seat durability, investigate high-pressure plastic seats used for commercial installations. Some are surprisingly good looking and are ideal for high-traffic home use. They're also more expensive.

Specialty toilet seats are available, both for special purposes and to fit various decorating schemes. Seats in pastel colors are readily available. The old-fashioned solid-oak seat is back, and it looks good with oak cabinets or in a period bathroom. Also available are decorator seats with embossed or hand-painted designs. There are even padded seats on the market.

BIDETS

Long popular in Europe, bidets first became available in the U.S. after World War II. Most major plumbing-fixture manufacturers now make bidets. They are available in styles and colors to match other fixtures in their lines. They're used for washing the perineal area of the body, and are little more than a specialized lavatory. The bidet has found some following, but it seems that most Americans are accustomed to using a shower or tub for bathing the whole body.

LAVATORIES

Wall-hung and pedestal lavatories form one broad class, countertop lavatories another. Wall-hung and pedestal lavatories are made either of vitreous china or enameled cast iron,

Undercounter lavatory allows custom top treatment around bowl. Here, small mosaic tiles easily conform to oval bowl.

Pedestal lavatories are making a comeback, but with modern, sleek designing. Most modern pedestal lavatories are wall-hung—the pedestal is for appearance only.

with the exception of one very expensive line of lavatories carved from solid blocks of marble, onyx and other minerals. Round, rectangular and oval lavatories are made in all types, in a wide range of sizes.

Countertop lavatories are made in all the basic fixture materials, including molded plastic, in a wide array of colors, some with patterns.

Mounting is by a metal rim, by a self-rim molded onto the lavatory, or by mounting clips from underneath the counter. Makers of synthetic marble and DuPont Corian offer lavatory bowls molded directly into a vanity top. See photo on page 40.

If you want a custom-made lavatory, consider a glazed-ceramic lavatory like the one shown on page 27. Some pottery shops specialize in custom-made lavatories.

4

Planning & Design

Dividing bathroom into separate compartments can lend privacy if more than one person will use it.

As with most other home-improvement projects, adding a bathroom or reworking an existing one starts with pencil and paper. To end up with the bathroom you want, spend sufficient time planning it.

Early in the planning process, look over all your present bathroom facilities. Bathroom planning can't stop at the boundary of the existing bathroom. If you restrict planning to the bathroom space as it now exists, you're limiting your options. At the least, consider the immediate area around the bathroom. Then you can make sure everything works together in meeting your needs.

Review your family's lifestyle and living habits, even the size and shape of each family member. Their privacy needs are also an important consideration. The planning process involves a jigsaw-puzzle fitting of the new bathroom or bathrooms to the available space, and to the people who'll be using the facilities. This chapter reviews the processes for gathering the necessary information and how to plan effectively.

UNDERSTANDING SPACE

One of the first steps in designing your bathroom is to distinguish *real* space from *apparent* space. Real space is the actual square footage of floor, wall and ceiling space in the bathroom. Apparent space is the amount of space you perceive, or see.

The spaces you see are affected by

several optical illusions. One illusion is caused by color. You can alter the *apparent* size and shape of a bathroom by the way you handle color.

For instance, in a long, narrow bathroom, light colors on the long walls and dark colors on the short walls make the room seem much more square. This is because dark colors always seem closer, light colors farther away. A light ceiling seems higher, a dark one lower.

Patterns are also used to create optical illusions. Patterns with strong horizontal lines make a room seem lower and wider. Patterns with strong vertical lines make the room seem higher and narrower. Consider this effect when selecting your wall and floor coverings.

Mirrors—The illusions created by mirrors can work for or against you, depending on how the mirrors are used. Mirrors visually expand space in a bathroom, in proportion to mirror size. A small mirror has a small effect. Mirrors covering an entire wall double the apparent size of the room.

Installing mirrors on a whole wall can introduce unpredictable problems if you're not careful. For instance, a full-wall mirror not only doubles space, it visually doubles the fixtures and any clutter. You see two tubs, two toilets, two vanities, and so forth. Wall coverings or graphics on adjoining walls are also doubled, possibly causing what started out as an accent to become overpowering.

Another illusion created by mirrors is the "tunnel-to-infinity" effect. Commonly seen in barbershops and beauty salons, this effect occurs when you install two mirrors facing each other. The reflections go on forever in both directions.

Unless you want this effect, it can be visually irritating. The effect can also occur, and is even more disconcerting, when large mirrors are installed on both sides of a corner.

Lines of Sight—Another way to manipulate apparent size and shape of a space is by altering *available lines of sight*. This means shortening or extending a view from a particular spot in the room.

To increase the apparent size of the bathroom, avoid partitioning it into a series of small closetlike compartments. How far you can see determines how big the space feels. Keep

Multiple mirrors can cause surprising and unexpected effects—pleasant or unpleasant. Consider such effects before installing more than one large mirror in a bath.

compartment dimensions as generous as you can.

Subject to the demands of privacy, open up a bathroom whenever you can—to an enclosed garden or courtyard, treetops or to the sky. The bathroom itself will feel much larger. A large opening or window to these areas is more effective than a small one in achieving a spacious feeling. The floor plans on page 50 show how a boxed-in bathroom can be opened up to give the illusion of more space.

A good bathroom design carefully combines several illusions to create the desired effect. When designing the floor plan and selecting bathroom elements, consider the space illusion you want to create.

STYLE SELECTION

In most cases, you'll want the bathroom style to match the rest of the house. If your house has low, beamed ceilings, pine paneling and antique furniture, you'll probably be more comfortable with a country or colonial look in the bathroom. If the house has soaring angular spaces and is full of chrome and glass, contemporary or Scandinavian bathroom styles will fit best.

Spatial illusions can sometimes be used to minimize effect of odd-shaped rooms, such as in this modest-sized powder room with an excessively high ceiling. Lattice shelf was added at normal ceiling height and portion above was painted plain white. With no light fixtures or other eye-catching features above lattice, ceiling height is visually minimized.

But style is a matter of personal choice and preference. A few well-chosen accessories can tie a bathroom of one style into a house of another style, or can integrate several styles into one bathroom.

Style selection should not be dictated only by fashion. A well-built bathroom lasts a long time. You don't want the bathroom or its permanent elements—especially cabinets and plumbing fixtures—to become dated because of a short-lived fad. A well-planned bathroom can provide a neutral background for periodic updating with style accents such as wall and floor coverings and surface-mounted accessories.

YOUR LIFESTYLE

Your family's needs will affect your bathroom design more than any other factor, except the amount of space available. By now you've probably begun to assess these needs and ask yourself many questions. Beyond the obvious questions are others you might not think to ask. Some of these questions are listed here, along with answers that may be helpful.

Does it seem there's always someone waiting for someone else to leave the bathroom? Would some family members share the bathroom for some uses, but can't?

Having to take a number for the bathroom is most often a symptom of a shortage of facilities—simply not enough bathrooms. But if you don't have space or budget to add one or more additional bathrooms, consider how you can rework the existing one so more than one person can use it at a time.

If the bathroom is well organized, two or three children can often brush their teeth or attend to other things at the same time. In a master bath, one person might soak in the tub while another takes a shower or shaves. This can be accomplished by careful selection of fixtures and judicious use of partitions. There's more information on compartmented baths on page 26.

Do you often run out of things such as towels, toilet paper or shampoo while using the bathroom?

Bathrooms must have adequate storage—not down the hall but at point of use. Running out of ordinary supplies is a sign that more storage is needed in the bathroom. Often, you can alter closets that adjoin a bathroom so some storage is available from the bathroom side for larger items. For storage ideas, see pages 183-185.

Is the bathroom always cluttered with supplies and toiletries in plain sight?

Same problem—a shortage of adequate storage. In this case, the first place to look for more storage is a better medicine cabinet—not only larger, but with better organization of shelves.

Especially in a bathroom used by several people, plan space under the vanity for a stack of drawers for smaller personal items. Then each person can be allotted a drawer of their own. Drawers hold large amounts of ordinary medicine-cabinet contents, are easier to organize and are spillproof. Also, if the problem is simply that people leave their toiletries out, they'll soon learn that such items are easily picked out of an open drawer and dropped right back in again.

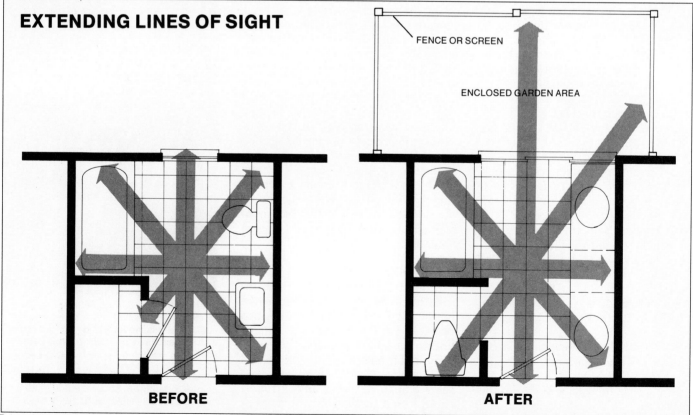

EXTENDING LINES OF SIGHT

FENCE OR SCREEN

ENCLOSED GARDEN AREA

BEFORE

AFTER

Privacy considerations often prevent opening up too many lines of sight in a bathroom, but anything helps, even a patch of sky. Often, a small area of garden can be enclosed outside the bathroom, and a large window or sliding-glass door installed, as shown here. Also note how bathroom was remodeled to make more efficient use of space.

Another option for small items is to build shelves between the wall studs. Open shelves can be used for some of the less-ugly toiletry items, such as perfumes and decorator-type bottles. Or, you can install a mirrored door to hide the contents—in effect, add another medicine cabinet. This option makes use of otherwise unused space.

Walls with plumbing in them are usually deeper than standard walls, sometimes even double-wall construction. If there's space, you can install deeper recessed cabinets for larger items. If the medicine cabinet is in this wall, consider replacing it with one that has deeper shelves. Check locations of plumbing and wiring in the wall before installing cabinets.

Does water frequently get splashed or spilled in the bathroom, such as when someone showers?

Poor water control and inadequate protection of surfaces is a chronic bathroom problem. Give special attention to control measures when planning. Surfaces prone to water exposure should be ceramic tile or other water-resistant material. A leak-proof tub or shower enclosure helps reduce the amount of water on the floor after bathing.

Water control also extends to plumbing. When the toilet clogs and overflows, it's nice to have the shutoff valve in plain sight, within easy reach. Also, some lavatories and fittings seem to splash more water on the vanity top than others. The cause may be bowl shape and depth, fitting design and location, or whether or not the bowl is topset or recessed below the vanity-top surface.

If your present bathroom has any of these problems, track down the source and correct it. Also, check for any damage the water may have caused over the years. See page 103 for details.

Is the bathroom plagued with bad odors, perhaps including damp, musty ones?

Obviously, persistent odors indicate a need for adequate room ventilation, but look at other things also. If there's a hamper or other storage for soiled clothes and used towels, it also needs to be well ventilated. Otherwise, wet towels and dirty sweatsocks will ferment.

Anywhere water collects and can't dissipate or evaporate, odors will develop. The problem may be as

Stack of drawers in vanity or inside linen closet can hold as many items as a half-dozen medicine cabinets.

simple as inadequate caulking or sealing around a bathtub or other fixture. Or leaky plumbing may be causing persistent dampness inside walls or floor.

Persistent musty or soapy-sewerlike odors can indicate long-term plumbing leaks, with attendant water damage. Or the problem might be one or more ineffective traps that siphon out and don't seal because of inadequate or plugged vents, or a broken wax seal on the toilet. This allows sewer odors to seep into the bathroom.

If possible, find the cause of any persistent odors in your present bathroom. Plan to correct the problem when you remodel. If there is water damage, use the information on page 103 to find the source and repair it. Pages 102-104 provide information on repairing floors damaged by water. Ventilation is discussed on pages 142-145 and plumbing repairs on pages 188-189.

Is the bathroom noisy when you're

in it, or when you're outside and someone else uses it?

Bathroom equipment and the supply and drain pipes are capable of generating a variety of noises. Also, some plumbing fixtures are inherently noisier than others. Analysis of the noises can give you a lot of help in minimizing them. See the feature on pages 122-123 for causes and cures of noisy bathrooms.

Is the bathroom too hot, or more commonly, too cold?

Few bathrooms are too hot. When one is, the cause is usually a balance problem in the heating or cooling system. Some bathrooms will remain uncomfortably warm and muggy after the shower has been used. Adequate ventilation will solve this problem.

Bathrooms are often cold, not because of an actual temperature difference from the rest of the house, but because higher temperatures are needed. The temperature needed for comfort of an unclothed person is about 86F, far higher than normal home temperatures. In warmer climates, reducing the cooling in the bathroom can solve the problem, at least in the summer. The solution in other circumstances is supplemental heating. This is particularly important in dry climates, where rapid water evaporation from wet skin compounds the problem.

Some surfaces tend to feel colder than others, even if all surfaces in the bathroom are the same temperature. This has to do with the *heat conductivity* of the surface. See page 33.

Is the bathroom poorly lighted?

In older bathrooms—and some newer ones—light levels are low and lighting is poorly organized. Often there's nothing more than one wall-mounted fixture directly over the lavatory, or a small fluorescent fixture located in the center of the ceiling. Careful planning of fixtures will help put light where it's needed, and provide enough of it. See pages 56-57.

When you apply makeup in the bathroom, does the makeup look different once you're outside?

This is a subtle but important problem that has to do with the color of light. Our eyes automatically adjust to off-colors in light, so most light looks like white light. But direct daylight has a blue cast, incandescent light an amber cast, and most fluorescent light a blue, green or pinkish-green cast. Also, reflecting surfaces can change light color. For instance, incandescent light reflecting off green walls becomes amber-green.

Light color affects color perception, and moving into a different light produces a different perception. The correct light for makeup application strikes an average balance between the various types of light, so the colors are never very far off, no matter what light is encountered later.

Are there always traffic jams among people going to and from the bathroom?

Traffic jams are another reason to examine the area around the bathroom during the planning stage. You may be able to correct the problem by relocating an awkwardly placed door or fixing a tight spot in a hall.

Do people keep having accidents in the bathroom?

Bathrooms, especially tubs, are one of the most accident-prone locations in the home. It's sometimes helpful to have family members review all accidents and near-accidents they've had over the past year or so. A list of these can help you spot trouble areas for correction. The main problems are slippery surfaces, poor lighting and layouts that cause people to move awkwardly or in an unbalanced way.

Do family members have difficulty finding a place to plug in equipment like hair dryers and electric shavers?

Good electrical service in a bathroom is essential. Often, you can locate outlets so the equipment can be left plugged in and ready to use, but still stored neatly out of the way. Make sure you locate outlets where they won't tempt people to use electrical equipment while in the tub or shower. Also locate outlets so a plugged-in device can't accidentally fall in the lavatory, tub or toilet.

How many steps does the usual daytime trip to the bathroom take?

When a home has only one bathroom, it's usually located convenient to the bedrooms. But it's often *inconvenient* to the rest of the house. If this is the case, you may opt to install a convenient powder room, postponing the remodeling of the main bathroom until later. A powder room has a toilet and lavatory only, with no provision for bathing. Another option is to install a lavatory and toilet as part of a laundry room. Besides, it's much easier on all concerned if you don't start remodeling the home's only bathroom before providing other facilities.

Can the bathroom be planned to accommodate any other functions, needs or activities?

When planning a bathroom, review all the other things that the bathroom can accomplish for you. A vanity of adequate size makes a great place for baby care—dressing, diaper changing and baths. You may want to install a lavatory that can be used for baby bathing. You can also plan space for a changing-storage table.

A bathroom can double as a photographic darkroom. You'll need storage for photo supplies and surfaces that are resistant to photo chemicals. You'll also need well-placed electrical outlets to run equipment.

A shower might convert to a steam bath. Also consider enlarging the bathroom to include a spa, hot tub or adjoining sauna.

Look for convertible functions wherever you can find them. For instance, a small bathroom next to a small utility room offers an opportunity to improve both. Take out the wall between, build a closet to enclose washer and dryer, and absorb the rest of the floor space into the bathroom.

COMPROMISES

Design is compromise. Most creative work lies in identifying and resolving conflicts. The largest is the conflict of square footage in the house for bathroom activities versus square footage for all other home activities. Close behind comes the conflict of space for fixtures in the bathroom versus storage space and moving-around space.

The first approach to resolving these problems is setting priorities. List the conflicting items in order of their importance to you. Then include as many as you can of the top items on the list and pass up those farther down. For example, not every bathroom has space for a large sunken shower in addition to a 6-foot soaking tub. Sometimes it's necessary to provide enough space for the most important elements so they function properly, and do without other desirable elements.

Consider borrowing space wherever it can be found. A powder-room door looks like any other door, so a powder room can be anywhere it's convenient. A hall closet could be converted, for instance.

If the conflict is mostly financial, your perfect bathroom can be staged over a period of months, or even years. Make changes a step at a time, starting with the most important ones. Planning this process is tricky, but it's possible. Make sure each modification follows your overall plan, so all elements in the finished bathroom fit together when the project is complete.

You may need to make some design compromises if you want a spacious corner tub like this one, though such a tub can be space-efficient. Both natural and artificial lighting are provided over the tub area.

COLOR

When planning your bathroom, choose a color scheme early. This will help you select fixtures, cabinets, floor and wall coverings, and other materials.

The characteristic we call *color* is produced by the frequency, or wavelength, of light reflected from an object. The correct name for a particular frequency band, for a color's exact position in the spectrum, is *hue*. For instance, *sky blue* is a specific hue of the color blue.

At the same frequency, a color can have many *values*, depending on how much light is absorbed and how much reflected. Values range from high (light) to low (dark). For example, *navy blue* has a low value, *sky blue* a high value.

Intensity describes the purity of the reflected light frequency. In other words, reflected light of other frequencies can muddy up the main color. The lower the intensity, the more neutral the color.

Whether a surface is *glossy* or *matte* also has to do with the reflection of light. A glossy surface reflects light directly, without scattering the light rays. The more matte a surface is, the more it scatters light rays as it reflects them.

The Color Wheel—Shown below, the color wheel is the basic tool of color selection. Applying various patterns to the wheel generates color combinations we perceive as harmonious. Each segment represents a light-frequency range that we recognize as a separate color.

About half of the wheel is sensed as *warm* and the other half as *cool*. Color segments marked "P" are *primary colors,* from which all others can be blended. Ones marked "S" are *secondary colors,* formed by blending equal parts of the primary colors on either side of them on the wheel. Segments marked "T" are *tertiary* colors, formed by a 1/4-3/4 blend of the primaries on either side.

Color Schemes—You can apply any of the patterns below to the color wheel to come up with harmonious color combinations. Start with a color that is a fixed part of the overall bathroom design, such as the fixture color, and work from there. Before you start selecting colors, get an idea of values and intensities you want for various areas.

A *monochromatic* color scheme (pattern A) uses several colors from one segment of the color wheel, in a range of values and intensities. A *related* color scheme (pattern B) uses colors from two or more segments that are side by side on the color wheel. Start by picking the central segment, and working out from there. A *complementary* color scheme (pattern C) uses colors from two segments directly opposite each other. A *related-complementary* color scheme (pattern D) uses colors from two pairs of segments, directly opposite each other. A *split-complementary* color scheme (pattern E) uses colors from one segment and the two segments on either

side of the one opposite it. A *triad* color scheme (pattern F) uses colors from three segments equally spaced around the color wheel. A *tetrad* color scheme (pattern G) uses colors from four segments equally spaced around the color wheel. All of these patterns can be rotated to any position on the color wheel.

Color Accents—Towels, curtains and plants afford opportunities for strong color accenting. Keep accent-color options open so you can vary accents from time to time. Different towels, rugs, flowering plants and other accessories or decorator items can be used to generate a fresh look every few months. High-intenstiy, low-value colors work well for accents. You can pick accent colors from the color schemes shown below.

Accent colors can also be picked from wall coverings or other patterns in the bathroom. Just match a minor color in the pattern, and use it at full intensity for an accent.

Color Tips—Color and light are interrelated. While color shading in artificial "white" light is faint, it's still there. Incandescent light is slightly yellow or amber. Fluorescent light can have a faint green, blue or pink cast. The light source you use can slightly alter the color of room surfaces and objects. Try to view color samples under the actual mix of lighting you'll be using, day and night.

Basically, the closer a color is to the color of the light, the more it's intensified. The farther away a color is

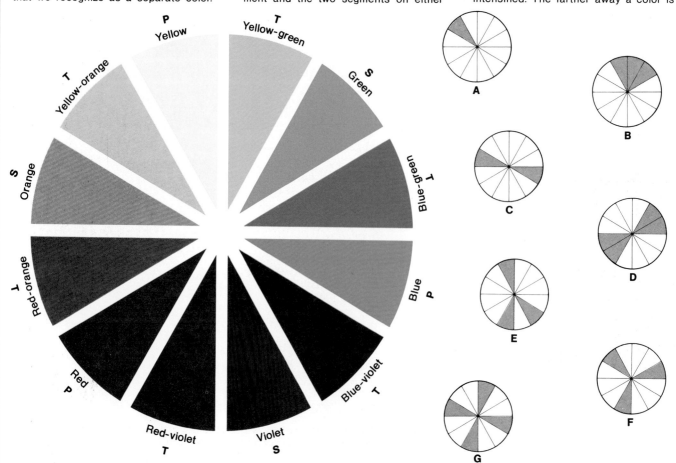

from the color of the light, the more it fades. For instance, the color of natural-oak cabinets is accentuated by incandescent lighting, and suppressed by fluorescent lighting that has a blue or green cast.

Color at Makeup Areas—The application of makeup can be strongly affected by the colors around the makeup area. As discussed on pages 56-57, color of light is critical, and the color of a surface changes the color of the light reflected off it. So the color of walls, ceilings and vanity tops in a makeup area may have to be adapted to prevent problems.

One color complication often overlooked is the mirror. First, if you're sitting in front of a mirror, you'll see the entire area behind you. This visible area must also be considered, or makeup-color distortions can result. Second, the mirror can have a color cast, commonly blue or green. Make sure the mirror you install is as neutral as possible in color rendition. This not only prevents makeup problems, but avoids changing the look of the room. If mirrors with a green cast are applied to a whole wall of a room with pink walls, you'll see three pink walls—and one pinkish-green wall.

Color plays an important part in creating the desired bathroom atmosphere. Here, pastel greens suggest a cool, calm environment. Floral wallpaper and towel provide complementary accent color. Wallpaper color and pattern mimic plants in atrium.

LIGHTING

Natural Light—Because a bathroom is used a lot in the daytime, admitting natural sunlight can help conserve electricity. If the bathroom has an outside-facing wall, it will probably already have a small window. You can provide additional light by adding a skylight or high clerestory windows, or by enlarging the present window. A skylight can be added to a bathroom with no outside-facing walls. See pages 174-176.

Direct sunlight is generally bluish-white unless it's tinted by window glass or diffuser panels. But once direct sunlight strikes a surface, it picks up some of its color. Reflected, indirect sunlight can be more useful than direct sunlight in creating the desired lighting in a bathroom.

Glare from direct sunlight on glossy surfaces can be a problem. Textured surfaces can also create glare. Another difficulty is high contrast between sunlit areas and shaded ones. This contrast can be hard on your eyes.

You can reduce glare by several means. Fixed or movable diffuser panels on windows and skylights will reduce and scatter direct sunlight. Outside sunshades or awnings can cut off direct sun altogether, allowing only scattered skylight to enter the room. Landscaping outside a window can make a big difference. Trees, vines and tall shrubs can directly shade a window. Lawns, ground covers and low plantings reduce the amount of reflected sunlight through the window. Curtains or blinds help change the character and the color of the light that enters the window.

It's important to plan orientation of windows, skylights and clerestories. North-facing windows and clerestories rarely admit direct sun. East-facing ones admit morning sun. West-facing windows let in afternoon sun, and possibly excessive heat and glare. South-facing windows and clerestories admit direct sun most of the day, with attendant problems.

Skylights, especially clear ones, are less predictable. Depending on the slope and orientation of the roof, the amount of sunlight admitted can differ. For instance, a skylight in a flat roof will light the center of the west wall of the room on a summer morning, then the floor, then the east wall in the afternoon. In the winter the same skylight will admit light that moves from the north end of the west wall, across the north wall to the east wall. A skylight in the north slope of a pitched roof may admit direct sun only in the summer, being shaded by the roof the rest of the year.

Before installing a skylight, think about how the sun moves throughout the year. To reduce glare, use translucent skylights or diffuser panels.

Artificial Light—The job of artificial lighting is to substitute for sun when it isn't there, and to supplement sun when it is.

Letting in as much natural light in as possible can cut electric bills. Here, natural light is admitted through skylight and large window to enclosed atrium. Swag lamp illuminates tub area at night.

There are two basic sources of artificial light.

Incandescent lights are small, bright light sources that generate heat as well as light. Power consumption is higher for the amount of light generated than with fluorescents. Incandescent light has a gold or amber cast, though your eyes will automatically adjust for the color shift from natural sunlight.

Basic incandescent fixture types are recessed, surface-mounted and suspended. Recessed fixtures are installed in a ceiling or wall. Luminous ceilings, page 175, fall into this category. Surface-mounted fixtures are made in both fixed types and directional spots and floods. In these groups are track assemblies that let you move lights anywhere you want along a track. Strip lighting for vanities also fall into this category. Suspended fixtures hang down from the ceiling, and are useful for lighting a bathroom when the ceiling is high or sloping. These include swag lamps like the one shown above.

Incandescent bulbs vary widely in price and lifespan. Bulb cartons usually list the wattage and the amount of light produced, measured in *lumens*. Bulbs that produce the highest number of lumens per watt generally have the shortest life, especially in a fixture that doesn't vent accumulated heat very well. So if a bulb shape is expensive, or a fixture is hard to get to, pick a bulb with the lowest lumens-per-watt you can find.

Fluorescent lights produce two or three times as much light per watt as incandescents. They emit relatively little heat. The light is produced over a fairly large surface. Light from early fluorescent tubes had an unpleasant greenish cast. Tubes are now available that emit a "warm" light and others that emit a "cool" light.

Fluorescent light fixtures are limited in size and shape by the fluorescent tubes themselves. Also, the box that forms the body of the fixture includes room for the ballast, or transformer, required to make the tube function. Most fluorescent fixtures tend to look utilitarian. Unless the utilitarian look fits with your design, plan on disguising fluorescents behind diffuser panels, or in an enclosed fixture.

General Lighting—General lighting ideally provides relatively uniform and shadowless light over the entire bathroom. Fluorescent fixtures work well for this, as do regular patterns of incandescent lights. For fluorescent lights, comfortable light levels run around 1-1/4 watts per square foot of surface to be lit—about 3-1/2 watts per square foot with incandescent lights. Considerable variation from these levels may be necessary to adapt to a light-colored or reflective bathroom, or to a dark-colored or light-absorbent one. For instance, a dark wood wall can absorb large quantities of general light, leaving the bathroom dim.

Special-Purpose Lighting—Lighting for makeup, shaving, hair care and other special purposes should be planned separately from general lighting. The first principle of makeup lighting is to eliminate shadows. This usually means that light should be coming from both high and low positions, and from both sides.

The traditional theatrical-makeup lighting arrangement consists of a series of small bulbs on top and sides of a mirror. This arrangement is commonly used for vanities and makeup areas because it produces even, shadowless light.

Glare is the biggest problem with this kind of lighting. The mirror must be large enough that the bulbs are out of the user's direct line of sight. If the mirror can't be that large, consider some sort of translucent cover or shade over the bulbs to reduce glare. Or use special bulbs with metallic covers. Also, the surfaces around a makeup area should be carefully chosen so they don't pick up light and become a source of glare.

The required intensity of special-purpose lighting is difficult to judge. Generally, the light level should be just enough to let the user see clearly. Too high a light intensity washes out all detail. The age of the user or users has a direct effect. Usually, the older you are, the more light you need to see clearly, by a fairly wide margin. Makeup work is more sensitive to too high a light intensity than is shaving or hair care. If more than one person uses an area for more than one purpose, a dimmer switch can be installed to adjust light level.

Light color relates more to makeup work than to other tasks. Makeup light color is critical. Not only must you consider the color of the light source, but also the color of light reflected from surrounding surfaces. This is explored more fully in the section on color, pages 54-55.

The best makeup lighting is a mixture of diffuse daylight and incandescent light. This balances the bluishness of the sunlight against the amber cast of

Fluorescent fixture over vanity provides even, shadowless light. Fluorescents use less electricity than incandescent lights for the same amount of light produced. Fluorescent lights often have a greenish cast, which is usually not suitable for makeup application.

Lighting for makeup application is important. At this vanity, a multiple-bulb fixture blends with natural light from overhead skylight to provide the right light color and intensity. Special bulbs are available for makeup lighting.

the incandescent to give neutral, full-spectrum light. Makeup applied under this light will look the closest to natural under any other light.

Fluorescent light fixtures equipped with full-spectrum bulbs can also be used, but standard fluorescent bulbs emit the wrong-color light for makeup application. Most ordinary fluorescent bulbs produce light with some parts of the spectrum missing—some colors of light aren't there—and usually with an overdose of blue, green or pink. Makeup applied under light with a blue or green cast will tend to look excessively ruddy under whiter light.

One good way to judge if a lighting setup is going to be suitable for makeup use is to assemble a group of color samples. These should be in the color range to be used, perhaps just dabs of makeup on white paper. Study the samples under white light, then under the makeup lighting. Or take two Polaroid photos of each sample, one under each kind of lighting. You'll be surprised at the color changes that can take place. A good source of white light is direct skylight on a mildly overcast day, away from any colored reflective surfaces.

Special-Effect Lighting—Lighting can be installed for effect rather than purely functional reasons. Just as a spotlight might be used to highlight a painting on a wall, objects in a bathroom can be highlighted by spotlights or showcase lights. A row of miniature lights might be installed, not for its contribution to

general lighting, but to illuminate a dark area. Many such treatments are possible.

Controls—Lights can be controlled either by standard switches or by dimmer switches. Make sure dimmer switches have adequate capacity for the lights they're controlling. If the bathroom has two entrances, a switch for general lighting should be installed at each one. This may require three-way switching. See page 136. Special-purpose lighting, on the other hand, is best controlled where it's used.

LIGHTING TIPS

● Avoid glare from exposed bulbs, especially those at eye level.
● Soft, even lighting and a light color scheme make the bathroom seem larger.
● A low ceiling requires a light color and flat or recessed light fixtures—or a large, flush luminous area.
● A high ceiling allows use of larger suspended fixtures, to dramatize the room volume.
● Small light sources produce sharp shadows, large light sources produce more diffuse shadows.
● Lighting color should harmonize with decorating colors, not clash with them.
● Bright light stimulates, soft light calms.
● Warm light colors are cheerful, cool light colors are restful.
● Low light levels, especially in the amber color ranges, can make a bathroom look depressing.

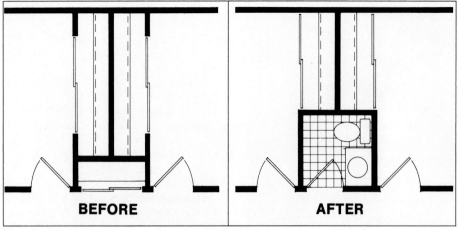

Many homes have a closet configuration similar to the one shown at left. Space can be rearranged to accommodate a small powder room while retaining enough closet space for adjoining bedrooms.

MEASURING

Accurate measurements are important to successful design. Measure the bathroom area and all the rooms or spaces surrounding it. Once you get these measurements down on a floor plan, many improvements will suggest themselves. The relationships of various spaces may not be apparent until they're on paper.

After living in a house for several years, you may be so used to it you no longer notice its problems. A floor plan gives you a fresh two-dimensional view.

If you measure and draw only the present bathroom, you'll probably end up with a design much like it, flaws and all. Also include adjoining spaces. Relocating a wall can often be a small price to pay for a substantial improvement.

If you want to clarify the space even more, don't measure existing fixtures and cabinets. Measure the space as if

nothing had yet been installed. But note fixture locations—the farther away you move the new fixture from the old one, the more complex the plumbing change will be.

Accurate measurements are essential for sizing cabinets and fixtures to existing spaces. You'll also need them when you make modifications to walls, floors and other structural elements in the bathroom.

ROUGH SKETCH FIRST

Draw a rough sketch of the area you're going to measure. It doesn't need to be fancy or to scale. But the rough sketch must show that walls have thickness, and it must give you enough space to note dimensions. Show all windows and doorways on the sketch, but ignore doors themselves. If you draw in a door as it is, right- or left-hand, you might keep yourself from seeing that the door should be hinged the other way. Or that there should be a pocket door there. Or no door at all. A sample rough sketch is shown below.

DIMENSIONS

Mark two sets of *dimension lines* on the sketch. One is an overall dimension line for each wall of each space. The other is a dimension line that

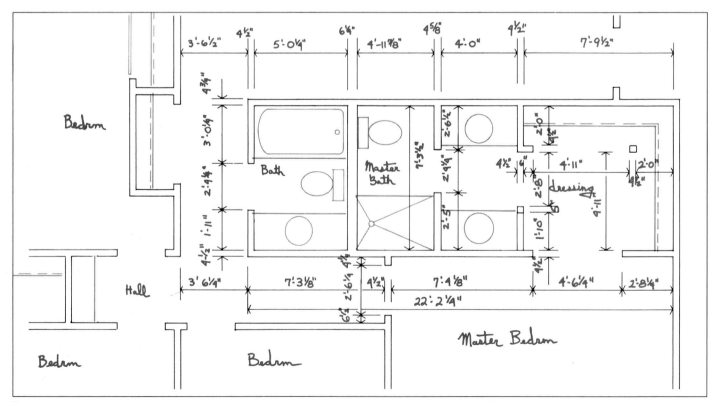

Draw a rough sketch of the bathroom and surrounding area. Measure and note all dimensions. Crosscheck your measurements by adding step-by-step measurements and comparing to overall measurements. If they don't match, one of them is incorrect.

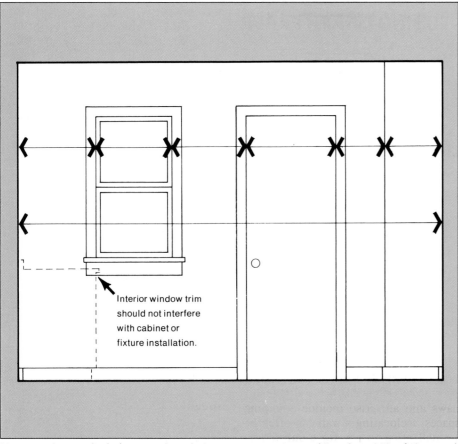

Measure door and window openings between arrows shown. Allow for width of door and window trim when planning locations for fixtures and cabinets.

breaks at each interruption—door or window edge, jog or offset—in the wall. On this second line, note wall thicknesses.

Measure the overall dimensions of the walls first, noting them on the sketch. Don't assume that walls at opposite ends of a room are exactly the same length. Often they're not.

Ignoring baseboards and door and window casings, measure from each interruption to the next for each wall.

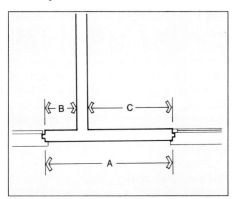

To determine the thickness of a wall with no openings, first measure between openings in adjacent rooms (A). Then measure from wall to opening in each room (B and C). Subtract total of B and C from measurement A to get wall thickness.

Measure to the face of any door or window jamb. Also measure the thickness of each wall. Don't assume that all walls are the same thickness. If there isn't a door, window or other opening that indicates wall thickness, find a way to measure from fixed points, as shown in the drawing below. Then subtract to get wall thickness. Indicate wall thicknesses on the sketch.

When you have all the measurements, add all the shorter dimensions. Compare them to the overall dimensions to detect any errors in measurement.

SQUARENESS, LEVEL AND SAG

Walls and floors are rarely straight, level and square. You should note any of these peculiarities of the space you're working with.

To find these wall problems, you need a 4-foot level and a perfectly straight length of 1x2. Move the 1x2 on edge from place to place on all surfaces where you might want to install fixtures, mirrors or cabinets. Note any humps or hollows greater than 1/8 inch, or so. Look for curving or

bowing of walls. Where you measure on the curve can affect the accuracy of your measurements. Always work with the shortest dimension between two walls.

Use the level and a 1x2 on edge to detect any bowing or sagging in floor and ceiling, and to find high spots. Any ceiling-height measurements should be based on the vertical distance between highest point on the floor and the lowest point on the ceiling.

Also use the level to find any leaning walls. If any walls lean, your dimensions should take this into account. Otherwise, square objects like cabinets won't fit in where you think they will. They'll be slightly too large for the space.

CORNERS

When you're sizing up your existing space, check corners last. Corners are rarely square. When drywall or plaster corners are finished, plaster or joint compound builds up, so the last 4 or 5 inches at the corner may have a curve. If it's a minor deviation, it can be ignored. If the curve is severe—over 1/8 inch or so—correct it before installing fixtures or cabinets. This can be done by shaving down the corner or building up one or both walls to the level of the corner. Decide now which you're going to do so you can adjust your dimensions accordingly.

The second cause of out-of-square corners is more serious: Sometimes walls don't meet at a 90° angle. This corner problem is more difficult to detect. Sometimes you'll be tipped off when walls at opposite ends of the room are not the same length.

You can find out-of-square problem corners with a framing square. Check corners near floor and at vanity-top height.

You can use a framing square to check for out-of-square corners, as shown in the photo on page 59.

Out-of-square corners can cause problems with vanities if they turn the corner. Pre-mitered tops are ruled out, unless you're willing to recut the corner miters, which is not an easy job. Large ceramic tiles are also out, unless you don't mind tapered grout joints near the corner. Most other materials can be adapted fairly well.

DRAWING PLANS

After you've gathered the data on your new bathroom space, make an accurate scale drawing. The drawing not only serves as a reference while remodeling, but it will assist you in getting a building permit if major changes are to be made. See page 67. If you're having a contractor or sub-contractors do the work, the drawing will help you better communicate your remodeling plans.

Making a quality scale drawing isn't as difficult as you might think. The secret is in the kind of paper you use. Don't use common school-type graph paper with the 1/4-inch grid. Find a store that sells drafting supplies and buy some tracing paper with an accurately printed 8x8 *fadeout grid*. The grid is a network of faint blue or blue-green lines that do not reproduce on a blueprint machine. An 8x8 grid has heavy lines at 1-inch spacing and light lines at 1/8-inch spacing. Tracing papers with fadeout grids come in rolls or precut sheets.

If you work on 8x8 fadeout grid paper in 1/2"=1'-0" scale, 1/2 inch on the paper equals 1 foot in reality. Each big block equals 2x2', and each small block equals 3x3".

TOOLS

Once you have the right paper, you need only a few basic tools to do good drawings. The simplest tool kit includes a *straightedge,* a roll of *masking tape,* a fairly hard *lead pencil* and a piece of *fine sandpaper.* The sandpaper is used to keep a sharp, even point on the pencil lead. Any smooth, hard surface will do for a work area—a table with a plastic-laminate top works well.

Many other tools are available at a drafting-supply store. These can make the process quicker and easier, though it's possible to get by without them.

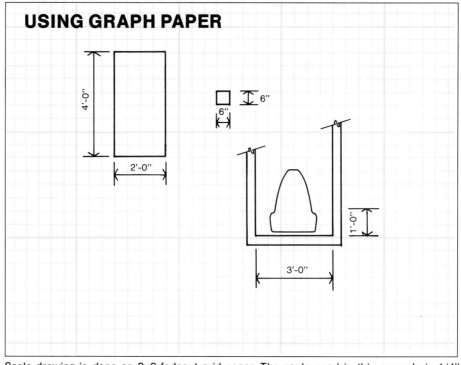

USING GRAPH PAPER

Scale drawing is done on 8x8 fadeout grid paper. The scale used in this example is 1/4" equals 1'-0". Each small square equals 6x6" and each large square equals 4x4'. This example is slightly larger than actual size.

The first extra tool to consider is a *scale rule.* Shown below, a scale rule has several different scales on it, and makes it possible to read scaled measurements directly instead of having to count squares on the graph paper. A scale rule reads differently than a ruler. There's a zero point near one end of each scale. Whole feet are marked from the zero point, going *away* from that near end. You'll find a finely divided section extending from the zero point *toward* the near end. These small divisions subdivide a

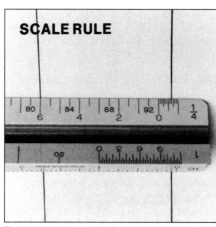

SCALE RULE

Read inches to right from the zero mark, feet to left from the zero mark. Lines above are 6'-8" apart in 1/4"=1'-0" scale.

single foot, usually into 2-inch increments on smallest scales, up to 1/8-inch increments on largest scales.

If you have a table with at least one straight side and a hard, smooth edge such as plastic laminate, you could make use of a small *T-square* and one or two convenient-size *triangles.* The head of the T-square hooks over the table edge and slides along to let you draw parallel horizontal lines. The triangles butt against the T-square so you can make parallel, perpendicular or diagonal lines.

For another few dollars, you can add a *mechanical drafting pencil* of the type pioneered by Pentel. It accepts leads that are a uniform 0.3, 0.5, or 0.9 mm in diameter. This makes it easy to get consistent line widths in your drawings. Leads for these pencils come in varying degrees of hardness. These range from 6B (softest) to 6H (hardest). Experiment with different leads to find the grade you like.

Templates are especially handy for bathroom planning. They're pieces of flexible plastic with die-cut fixture outlines cut in them. A template in the proper scale makes it easy to visualize and draw the sizes and shapes of various fixtures as you plan. Check the template to make sure it has most or all of the fixtures you might want to work with.

GETTING STARTED

Use masking tape to attach a sheet of tracing paper to your tabletop or drafting board. Be sure to position your drawing so it's oriented the *same direction* as the spaces you're drawing, even if you're working in an another room. If the drawing is rotated from the real thing, you're more likely to confuse yourself as you translate your notes onto paper.

Look at your rough sketch and find an outside wall. Add up the dimensions from the outside wall to the innermost area you want to draw. Roughly center that measurement on the sheet. That gives you a starting location for the outside wall.

Lightly draw in a pair of *guidelines* for the outside wall. The lines should show actual wall thickness. These guidelines form the framework for the actual drawing. Make them just dark enough to see, and as thin and as accurately placed as possible. Find the next wall parallel to the outside wall, mark your measurements and draw in another pair of guidelines. When parallel walls are marked by guidelines, do the same for all cross walls. If a wall isn't parallel to the others, adjust guidelines to match the actual wall location.

When all guidelines are in place and checked, refer to your sketch and draw in openings, one wall at a time. When openings in a wall are marked with heavy end lines, fill in wall locations with heavy lines, right over the guidelines.

TRIAL SOLUTIONS

When you've drawn in lines indicating walls and openings, don't do anything more to the drawing. It will be your *base drawing* on which to sketch your various ideas on tracing-paper *overlays*.

Tape a second piece of tracing paper over the base drawing, aligning grids on top and bottom sheets. Label this sheet with a number 1 in the corner so you can identify it. You'll be able to see the heavy lines of the first drawing right through the overlay sheet. Work out the new bathroom design you've got in mind on the top sheet.

When you're done with sheet 1, take an important step. Pull sheet 1 off the base drawing and put on anoth-

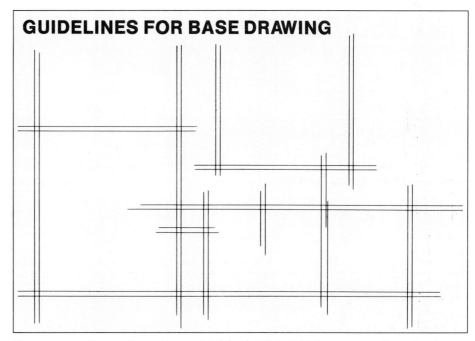

Measure overall room dimensions and lightly sketch in guidelines on your base drawing, as shown here. Guidelines should indicate wall thicknesses.

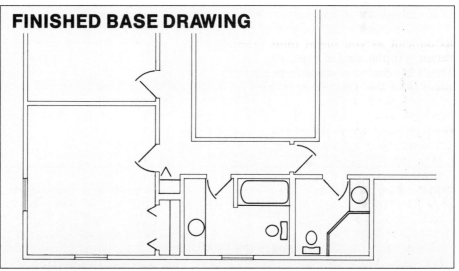

Finished base drawing is a floor plan of bathroom as it now exists. It should include accurate sizes and locations of doors, windows, fixtures and cabinets. Changes are indicated on tracing-paper overlays.

er sheet of tracing paper. Label this sheet 2. Now ask yourself: "If I never had the first idea I just took off the board, how would I handle this bathroom space?"

After you've done a second trial solution, do a third. Keep this up until you start repeating yourself. Trial solutions don't have to be carefully

drawn. Freehand work with a felt-tip pen is good enough. But the scale of fixtures and vanities must be close to correct. The purpose of this exercise is to free up your thinking. Ideas and details may occur to you that you hadn't thought of. Jot down these ideas or sketch them out so you can compare them with each other.

TRIAL SOLUTIONS

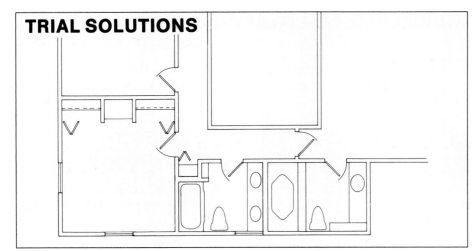

Shown here are two possible remodeling solutions for the floor plan shown on the previous page. In each case, the closet in the adjoining bedroom was relocated so there would be enough space to add a bathtub to the right-hand bathroom.

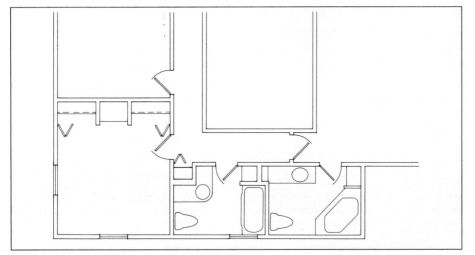

Special features like this laundry chute to utility room below require careful planning, including detailed measurements on both floors.

Your first thoughts may have been the right ones. Or your first thoughts may have been blocking you from thinking further. Getting those first thoughts out on sheet 1 lets you have a look at what occurs to you next.

Analyzing Trial Solutions—Don't try to weigh the relative merits of solutions as you draw them. Critical analysis comes after all trial solutions are on paper.

Movement space is the first point to check in analyzing trial solutions. Make sure floor space is arranged so people can move freely in all parts of the bathroom. Look for elbow-bangers and shin-bumpers. Visualize a person bending over to pick something up off the floor, not only in the

PLANNING HOT-WATER SUPPLY

While you're planning your new bathroom, take a look at the way you're currently providing hot water. Having to wait for hot water to reach the tap is not only a nuisance, but wastes water. When you shut off the hot water, the pipe from the water heater is full of hot water that you paid to heat. Some changes in the hot-water system can save money and aggravation.

If you do nothing else, insulate any hot-water pipes you can get to, preferably all of them. Closed-cell foam insulation is available at most plumbing and building suppliers. There are two basic types—insulating tape and insulating jackets to fit standard pipe sizes. Hot water in an insulated pipe stays warm a long time, so a second user gets hot water faster, and it's water that would otherwise be wasted.

If you're designing a complete plumbing system for a new home, you can make a loop of the hot-water supply line, and install a small circulating pump. Hot water for the fixtures is then tapped out of the loop near the point of use rather than being drawn all the way from the water heater. Such a loop should be insulated, and can add significantly to your hot-water storage capacity.

One of the best ideas is to relocate the water heater, or add a second one, near the bathroom. This reduces the traveling distance to only a few feet. Several manufacturers make undercounter water heaters that can be installed inside a vanity, right in the bathroom, or in a nearby closet. At least one manufacturer makes demand heaters that generate hot water only while you're drawing it from the tap. Because it doesn't store any hot water, a demand heater is only about the size of a briefcase and is easy to find room for.

main floor space but in the tub or shower. Bear in mind that someone who is over 6 feet tall may be using that bathroom someday.

Check the direction of door swings. This means *all* doors—the entry door, all cabinet doors and doors on tub and shower enclosures. It's possible to design a bathroom so there's enough space when the entry door is open or closed, but no place to stand while opening or closing the door—unless you're willing to climb up on the toilet.

A major consideration is the overall feasibility of the new design. Compare the work needed with your own abilities, and with the time, energy and money you have available.

Start by looking at how much struc-tural work is needed. Check the fit of the new design to existing fixed features like walls, doors, windows. For instance, narrowing a window opening 6 inches is easy, even if the sill height of the window must be changed. Widening a window opening by 6 inches is much more difficult. But widening a window opening 3 feet isn't any more difficult than widening it 6 inches.

Consider the feasibility of the required plumbing and electrical changes. Modifying the electrical layout usually isn't a problem, especially if most or all of the old wall-finish material is going to be removed. But reworking the plumbing to the new design can be difficult if new fixtures will be any distance from existing drain lines and water-supply pipes.

Concrete-slab floors can introduce large amounts of extra work when drain lines must be relocated. If you have a slab floor, check to see if plumbing lines are overhead (easy to modify) or under the slab. Water pipes under the slab are no problem if you can rework them inside a wall. If you're planning to remove a wall with pipes coming up inside it, you'll have to chop concrete to relocate the pipes.

As you look over all of the trial solutions, some will rise to the top of the pile, often because they'd be so much more pleasant and livable. When it comes to the final decision, the design you and your family are going to be happiest with is the one to pick.

WATER CONSERVATION

About 75% of all water used in the home is used in the bathroom. Water conservation should be part of planning for new bathrooms and remodeling existing ones. Even if you're reusing the existing fixtures, much can be done to conserve water.

Toilets—The average older toilet uses about 6 gallons of water per flush. New water-saver models flush properly with only about 3-1/2 gallons of water. There's even a toilet that uses compressed air to assist flushing. It uses as little as 1/2 gallon of water per flush. The compressed-air toilet may not be readily available in your area, but water-saver toilets from many manufacturers are available at most plumbing suppliers. In certain code jurisdictions, water-saver toilets are required.

There are easy ways cut water use of an existing toilet. Bending the float arm down, to lower the water level in the tank, is *not* one of the ways. Any water-saving method has to keep the original water level in the tank so there's adequate pressure for correct flushing action.

A 1-gallon plastic jug weighted with a few handfuls of gravel, filled with water and inserted in the tank, will save a gallon a flush. Plastic dams that wedge into the tank and hold back part of the water are another inexpensive way to cut water use. Some water departments give their customers water-conservation kits that include a heavy plastic bag that can be filled with water and hung in the tank. Also, the old brick-in-the-tank trick works, though the brick may eventually disintegrate.

Whatever method you use, make sure the item you're using to displace the water doesn't interfere with the operating mechanisim in the tank. Be especially careful that the tube to the top of the overflow pipe still functions. When the toilet flushes, the little stream of water from the tube isn't being wasted. It's refilling the bowl to maintain the water seal in the toilet trap, to keep sewer gases out of the bathroom.

Perhaps the best water-saving technique for toilets is user education. Ash trays are ash trays and waste baskets are waste baskets—toilets are neither. Using a toilet solely for its intended purpose also cuts down on blockages in the drain system.

Tubs and Showers—Not much can be done with a tub from the conservation standpoint. About all you can do is fill it a little less when you use it. Showers, however, respond well to conservation methods. Some of the older shower-heads have a flow rate of as much as 15 gallons per minute, so a 20-minute shower can use up as much as 300 gallons. If you're installing a new shower or replacing the showerhead on an old one, check with the dealer and make sure you're getting a showerhead with a flow rate of 3 to 4 gallons per minute.

If you'd rather keep you present showerhead, you can insert a *flow restrictor* in the pipe behind the showerhead. A flow restrictor looks like a washer with a small hole in it, and can be obtained from many water companies or plumbing suppliers. If they don't have any, try washers with various-size holes until you find one that minimizes water use but still provides an acceptable shower.

Lavatories—A lavatory fitting turned to maximum flow can use as much as 5 gallons per minute. An aerator in working order can cut usage drastically, by mixing air with the water. Aerators cut down on splashing too. Even if a lavatory fitting seems to have an aerator, it might only be a trim ring. Or someone may have removed the inside parts instead of cleaning and replacing them. If the stream of water isn't soft and full of air bubbles, get a new aerator and install it. Check any new fittings before you buy them to make sure they have aerators and not just a *stream diverter,* a fancy term for the trim ring.

Sensible use is a good way to conserve water at the lavatory. It isn't necessary to let the water run continuously while you shave or brush your teeth.

Leaks—A dripping fitting seems harmless enough, but can waste hundreds of gallons a week. Fix it—the directions are on pages 188-189. More insidious is the leaking toilet. If a toilet makes whistling or gurgling noises when it's not in use, the float valve is probably leaking. If no noise is evident, add some ink or food coloring to the tank. Check the bowl after a few minutes. If the coloring is starting to show up in the bowl, the flush valve is leaking. Directions for fixing leaky toilets are on page 188.

Note: The above information was adapted from a handbook entitled Water Conservation for Domestic Users, *prepared by the University of Arizona for the City of Tucson Water Department.*

BATHROOMS FOR THE HANDICAPPED

Aside from custom features, there are general considerations that apply to all bathrooms for the handicapped. They involve *access, ease of use* and *safety.*

ACCESS

The most critical access concerns apply to wheelchair users. The bathroom door should be at least 32 inches wide. The door swing must not interfere with passage—pocket doors are well suited to this application. The hall or room adjoining the bathroom must allow room for the chair to swing and maneuver, coming and going. Clearance inside the bathroom is needed for easy turnaround.

Toilets and tubs or showers require additional maneuvering room, correctly organized for transfer from and to the wheelchair. The grab bars and other aids that assist transfer can also serve an important safety purpose, as discussed on the facing page. In general, a shower is preferable to a tub for wheelchair users. Lavatories must have clearance underneath for the chair.

Access for the ambulatory is much easier to arrange in the conventional home than is access for the wheelchair user. However, basic approaches to designing bathrooms for the ambulatory handicapped may vary considerably, depending on the disability. Many ambulatory handicapped people prefer to have support near at hand at all times, so the bathroom can be quite small, often long and narrow.

SAFETY

Bathrooms can be unsafe even for those who are not disabled. Safety features for the handicapped must be planned even more carefully. A basic starting point is to select skid-resistant flooring materials. Materials include carpet or any of the softer, textured resilient-flooring materials. Grab bars are usually required, both for safety and to aid in maneuvering.

To avoid confusion, don't install regular towel bars in a bathroom that also has grab bars—use a properly mounted grab bar instead. This is especially important if there's any visual impairment. Then there's no risk of the user grabbing the towel bar by mistake, and having it come loose from the wall.

Don't plan on the regularly used grab bars for towel storage—provide extras. Towels can interfere with gripping. One good method is to install a towel-storage grab bar a few inches below another grab bar, so the top bar is always clear.

Grab bars and safety rails are made in all sorts of shapes and sizes, to suit all sorts of circumstances and disabilities. A knowledgeable supplier and the user's physical therapist can recommend setups that will best suit the user's needs and capabilities. More-common grab-bar arrangements for each fixture

are described with the fixture, below.

Scalding from overly hot water, and burns from hot water pipes, such as those under lavatories, are recurring problems. If the user's pain nerves are impaired, scalding and burns can occur without any warning. All exposed hot-water pipes should be insulated. Foam pipe insulation works well. Hospital-type thermostatic mixing valves can solve the problem of scalding, but they're fairly expensive.

A good alternative is to install an adjustable blending valve in an inconspicuous place, such as a nearby closet. Then install a hospital-type water-line dial thermostat where it's visible in the bathroom. In this way, the blending valve can be adjusted to give the normal warm-water temperature when the hot faucets are full on. The user can monitor the temperature to determine if the blending valve needs readjusting, and can tell when the water is warm. It's especially useful when the user has difficulty making fine adjustments of water flow.

FIXTURES

There are some special fixtures made for the handicapped, but in most circumstances it's advisable to work with standard fixtures or readily available variations of them. For each fixture, the problems of access, support, maneuvering and ease of use must be approached separately.

Toilet—For the wheelchair user, space for the wheelchair alongside the toilet is usually necessary to make possible the transfer from wheelchair to toilet. Some wheelchair users may prefer to pull the wheelchair up nose-to-nose with the toilet. Transfer is then made by a 180-degree turn from the one to the other. Whichever transfer method is preferred, safety bars will be needed for support.

A toilet in a corner is best equipped with safety bars on both walls, positioned so at least one is reachable at all times.

A toilet placed along a straight wall can be equipped with projecting bars on each side of the toilet.

For an existing toilet, or for temporary use, there are safety bars made up in a free-standing frame. This assembly can be placed over the existing toilet, and removed when no longer needed.

One arrangement for transfer from wheelchair to toilet that's too seldom used is a horizontal overhead bar. The bar should extend across both the toilet and the wheelchair parking position, so the user can move back and forth, using his arms for lifting. Check with the wheelchair user for the preferred position, usually between shoulder and forehead height, centered directly above the front edge of the toilet bowl. If the toilet is installed in a compartment, bar ends can be fastened to side walls. If not, bar ends can be supported from the floor by an upright, with a brace to the back wall for structural stability.

The ambulatory disabled can also benefit from adequate safety bars at the toilet, most commonly on a side wall. Often, a raised toilet is useful for the disabled, especially those with limited lower-limb joint mobility.

Several manufacturers make versions of their standard toilets with 18-inch seat height instead of the standard 15 inches. It's also possible to install a wall-hung toilet higher than normal, provided the toilet's wall carrier will adapt to the desired height. A wall-hung toilet may also be more convenient for the wheelchair user, because of the clearance under the bowl for footrests and other projections.

An existing toilet—or a new standard-height one—can be installed on a wood platform to raise seat height. Such wood platforms should be carefully finished at the edges to allow easy cleaning.

For temporary use, or a quick fix to the problem of toilet height, you can buy an extended or extra-thick toilet seat, up to

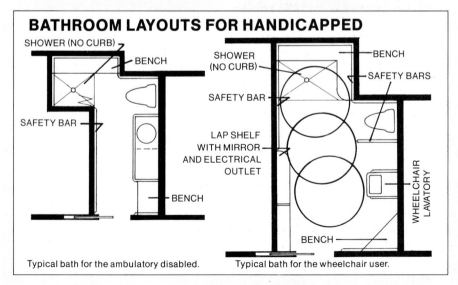

BATHROOM LAYOUTS FOR HANDICAPPED

SHOWER (NO CURB)
BENCH
SAFETY BAR
BENCH

Typical bath for the ambulatory disabled.

SHOWER (NO CURB)
BENCH
SAFETY BARS
SAFETY BAR
LAP SHELF WITH MIRROR AND ELECTRICAL OUTLET
WHEELCHAIR LAVATORY
BENCH

Typical bath for the wheelchair user.

about 4 inches thick. Some bolt on in place of a regular seat. Others snap onto the regular seat, and can be removed and replaced.

Lavatory—Any normal lavatory will usually serve the needs of the ambulatory disabled, provided the fitting handles can be easily operated by the user. The wheelchair user needs some special arrangements to provide clearance under the lavatory. For this reason, a wheelchair lavatory must be relatively shallow. Most major manufacturers make special wall-hung lavatories for this application. Any fairly shallow drop-in lavatory will also work if it's mounted in a countertop on wall brackets or adjacent cabinets, with no cabinet or vanity directly underneath the lavatory.

Lavatory pipes require special attention. The trap and supply pipes should be located as high as possible, and should easily clear all parts of the wheelchair and the user. All sharp edges must be covered or rounded off. The hot-water supply pipe and valve must be insulated, as mentioned previously. Wrap all the under-lavatory pipes with foam insulation. A metal trap full of hot water can cause a burn just as easily as a hot-water supply pipe can. The insulation can also protect against accidental bumps and scrapes.

Tub—It's difficult for many handicapped people to negotiate the rim of a tub. If a tub is a must or you're stuck with one, many aids are available. These range from simple seats anchored by suction cups to hydraulically operated lifters. Hydraulic lifters are bulky and expensive, and often require the assistance of a nurse or other attendant.

One particularly useful aid for a tub is a bench at rim height, extending from outside the tub to inside. A portable bench across the foot of the tub and projecting out a couple of feet can be added to an existing tub. It will ease entry and exit for many users. In a new or remodeled bathroom, such a bench can be built in.

Safety bars are vital at a tub, so the user can move from standing to sitting and back, and to prevent falls. Both low- and high-level bars are usually required. To provide a grip for wet hands, safety bars at a tub should be knurled, or should be wrapped in nonskid tape. Both the bottom of the tub and the front rim should also be nonskid.

Shower—Far better than a tub for handicapped bathers, the shower still needs some special adaption for wheelchair access. The curb that keeps the water in should be eliminated, or ramped on both sides. The floor in the splash zone must slope to the shower drain, and the rest of the bathroom floor should be completely waterproof. To avoid getting the wheelchair wet, a folding, permanently mounted or built-in shower seat, or a castered shower chair can be used. A shower seat or waterproof chair can be useful for the ambulatory disabled as well as for the wheelchair user.

Splash control can be achieved by a shower curtain or a conventional enclosure, with or without a curb. If there is no curb, the floor slope should extend beyond the curtain or enclosure. If the bathroom is properly arranged, a curtain or enclosure may not be necessary.

Safety-bar arrangements for a shower should include a continuous bar at about

waist level for all users. The waist-level bar should extend several feet out of the shower. For the wheelchair user, the waist-level bar should extend to the wheelchair parking area. The ambulatory disabled may benefit from additional safety bars at about shoulder height. As with the tub, all safety bars serving a shower should either be knurled or wrapped with nonskid tape.

Fittings—Many disabled or handicapped people can cope with normal lavatory, tub or shower fittings. But many have some degree of impairment of hand or arm function. Lever-style, single-handle fittings are the easiest to manage, require very little effort, and don't need fine control if the blending-valve system mentioned is installed. Existing two-handle fittings can often be equipped with large lever handles to make them easier to operate. One kind, often used in hospitals, is paddle-shaped and is called a *wrist-control* handle. It's meant to be moved by the wrist so the hands don't touch it. These handles can usually be added to an existing fitting.

Normally, a showerhead is at a stationary height and the user moves around to accomodate to the location of the stream. This is often impractical for the handicapped.

Also, a showerhead for handicapped use is often located for a *sitting* person, and may not be usable by other people in the household. A hand-held showerhead on flexible tubing is often the best solution. There are several brands on the market, and at least one brand is available at most plumbing suppliers. You can accomodate standing and sitting showering by mounting hooks on the wall to hold the showerhead, or by mounting a vertical bar with a sliding hook.

Shower/toilet area includes wall-mounted toilet and shower bench. Shower curb has been eliminated for wheelchair access. Entire floor is waterproof, has four drains. Movable showerhead directs water stream where needed while user is in sitting or standing position.

Vanity is designed for wheelchair user. Towel bar and lower shelves of medicine cabinet are accessible from sitting position.

5

Preparing to Build

Preparation is essential to any bathroom remodel, especially in an older home such as this one. At least minor repairs and patching will be required to apply new wall and floor coverings. *Photo courtesy of American Olean Tile Co.*

Preparation is essential to a successful bathroom installation. Before you start actual remodeling work, you should have detailed plans for your project, as described in the previous chapter. Then you'll need to have your plans approved by the local building department and get necessary permits.

When your plans are approved, the next step is to purchase required materials so they'll be on the job when you're ready to use them. This chapter tells you how to organize purchasing, so you'll know what to buy, where to buy it and how much it should cost.

Before you order materials, you should plan the job sequence, as described on page 69. The job sequence and supplier lead times will determine when you place your orders.

Planning the job sequence is also important if you're hiring subcontractors. Most important, it will indicate how long the job will take. This chapter will help you think through the entire project to avoid time delays and unforseen costs after you start the work.

CODES, PERMITS AND INSPECTIONS

To issue building permits, your building department will probably require you to submit a detailed scale floor plan. They may also ask for other detailed drawings and information. Include such structural information as lumber sizes and material descriptions, both for new work and for the existing structure. Also include detailed information on plumbing and electrical changes. If your plans call for changes to outside walls, you may also need to submit exterior-elevation drawings. These drawings should show sizes and locations of new and existing framing members.

Get the building department's application form and fill it out at home, rather than at the building department. Print in ink, or type. Prepare a list of any technical questions and get them answered when you go to the building department to file the application. Get the name of the person answering your questions in case you have to cite answers to the inspector during building inspections.

BUILDING CODES

Most local building codes are based on master codes published by regional groups. In the Eastern U.S., master codes are issued by Building Officials and Code Administrators (BOCA) or by the Southern Conference of Building Officials (SCBO). In the Western U.S., the master codes are the Uniform Building Code, the Uniform Mechanical Code, and the Uniform Plumbing Code. These are issued every 3 years by the International Conference of Building Officials (ICBO) in Whittier, California. For electrical work, the master code is the National Electrical Code, issued by the National Fire Protection Association (NFPA), Boston, Massachusetts.

In Canada, each province issues its own set of master codes for building, plumbing and electrical work. Even if a master code has been adopted in your area, local variations often apply. You can get details on any local variations—and often a copy of the code—from your local building department.

If you're not sure whether some part of your work will comply with the codes, don't guess. Call the building department and ask about it. Or check the codes at your local library.

BUILDING PERMITS

Work beyond minor redecorating or nonstructural changes usually requires a building permit. Separate permits are usually required for plumbing and electrical changes. If you're remodeling, call your local building department before you go beyond the planning stage. Building-department requirements and procedures vary widely from place to place, so check local requirements for your area.

Permit Costs—Costs also vary from place to place. Permit costs usually include inspection fees, although some jurisdictions may charge extra for reinspections. In addition to permit fees, a plan-check fee may be charged. As a general rule, permit fees range from 0.5% to 3% of the cost of the work.

BUILDING OFFICIALS

Building officials include administrators, plan checkers, inspectors and others. When applying for a permit in all but the smallest jurisdictions, you'll deal with someone other than the inspector who will actually inspect your work.

Dealing with building officials can be frustrating but it is necessary. Officials can make your remodeling job easy or difficult, depending on their assessment of your attitude. Take the rules as seriously as they do, and make sure they know you do. In short, cooperate. Some building officials may even help you with your plans and offer useful advice on design and construction techniques.

BUILDING INSPECTIONS

The number of inspections required depends on the extent of your remodeling project. Inspections are made as various stages of work are completed. Most departments require a structural inspection when the rough framing is complete, and plumbing and electrical inspections when rough wiring and plumbing are installed. In some jurisdictions, one inspection may cover all of these. Initial plumbing and electrical inspections are made while framing is still exposed so all rough wiring and plumbing work can be inspected.

The final inspection is usually made when the job is complete. It's your responsibility to notify the building department and arrange for inspections. Find out at what stages the department requires inspections. Don't proceed past each stage until the work is approved—the inspector may require you to rip out subsequent work to make the inspection.

The inspector may look at your work in great detail. This attention on his part is not malicious. The house you're working on will be standing for years to come. Every building official feels a strong obligation to the health and safety of all present and future owners and occupants.

Above all, don't take an inspection personally. If you feel you must debate a point, don't start an argument with the inspector. Discuss the matter calmly with the inspector or his superior. The superior will be much more likely to deal objectively with the matter, because he or she is not directly involved in the dispute.

PURCHASING

Before you buy fixtures and materials, make material lists from your drawings. If you're unsure of material needs, read the appropriate sections in this book on the installation of the materials in question. List materials by supplier on separate sheets of paper. On bulk materials such as lumber, wall coverings, pipe, electrical wiring and tile, add 10% to the estimated amount you'll need. In most cases, you can return any materials you don't use.

It's better to have leftover materials than to run short of them during installation.

GETTING THE BEST PRICES

After material lists are made, refer to the Yellow Pages to make a list of suppliers you want to get quotations from. Call or visit suppliers to get quotations for materials on your list. Quotations should indicate exactly what the dealer intends to supply, and should be priced item-by-item.

Find out delivery arrangements and costs, payment terms and whether you can return leftover materials. Don't accept *estimates* that do not commit the supplier to a firm price.

You'll also need to know the *lead times* on items that must be ordered by the dealer. Lead time is the time from placement of order to delivery of goods.

Get at least three prices on each item. Normally, prices should fall within a range of about 5%. If prices vary much more than 5%, get additional quotations until two or three prices for an item fall in the 5% range. Scattered prices often indicate you're asking suppliers to provide something they don't normally handle. They may be willing to get the item for you, but the cost may be high. Because this kind of service carries varying markups, the prices will vary. Once you find the correct suppliers for a material, the prices will fall into line.

Carefully check any sensationally low prices. They may be legitimate—the result of an oversupply or a closeout, or efficient operation by a supplier. But the supplier may have misunderstood what you wanted, or made a mistake in the figures. Double-check any extremely low prices so a later correction by the supplier doesn't upset your job budget. Also make sure the lower-priced goods are of comparable quality to those offered at standard prices.

You may find one or more suppliers in your area who can supply all materials for the job. If so, ask if there is an additional discount if you give them the order for the whole job. Be sure their total price is at or below the sum of your separate quotations.

As an owner-builder, you'll often be required to pay for materials on delivery. If payment will be c.o.d., inquire about prompt-payment discounts. Many suppliers give a 2% or 3% prompt-payment discount to their open-account customers. They may give you one if you ask.

A c.o.d. shipment is not a reflection on your credit rating. The red tape involved in opening an account may not be justified for one order, so the supplier may not offer payment terms.

Comparative shopping requires a lot of work, but it can cut material prices by 20% to 25%. One of the reasons you're doing your own bathroom is to save money. Buying right can maximize that saving.

After you've obtained quotations, take one more money-saving step. Check do-it-yourself stores in your

TYPICAL SUPPLIER LEAD TIMES

Product	High-volume, local stock	Low-volume, factory or regional stock	Factory-made to order or custom-made
Cabinets	2 to 10 days	1 to 6 weeks	3 to 13 weeks
Plumbing fixtures & fittings	2 to 7 days	1 to 8 weeks	3 to 13 weeks
Lights & vents	2 to 10 days	1 to 8 weeks	3 to 13 weeks
Plastic laminates	2 to 10 days	2 to 8 weeks	Not available
Ceramic tile	2 to 7 days	2 to 13 weeks	2 to 26 weeks
Floor covering	2 to 15 days	1 to 13 weeks	3 to 13 weeks
Brick & stone	2 to 14 days	2 to 8 weeks	1 to 26 weeks

Note: Lead times are approximate and can vary according to manufacturers and suppliers you're dealing with. Also, the state of the construction industry has a bearing on lead times. When building is brisk, both suppliers and manufacturers build up their inventories to meet demand. Many low-volume items can be obtained more quickly. But if building is booming, extreme demand can lead to spot shortages and backorders of even common materials. Conversely, during slow times, manufacturers and custom shops are usually more able and eager to get out a special or custom order without delay.

area. Their overall prices may be slightly higher than conventional suppliers, but these stores sometimes have loss-leaders or closeouts on materials you need. Make sure you're getting top-quality, comparable goods. Closeout items are sometimes damaged or shopworn.

Discontinued Items—The problem of discontinued items occurs most often with floor coverings, plastic laminates and colors of speciality fixtures. Many manufacturers change their lines every year. Some add products and discontinue others almost constantly.

If an item of a certain pattern or color is essential to your design, buy or order it early and store it. Or, if a dealer has the item in stock, you can place a firm order for it and make a deposit, if necessary. The dealer probably won't mind storing the item if he knows it's sold. One risk you take is the dealer might accidentally sell the item to someone else. In any case, always have several alternate choices for such items.

SCHEDULING

After you've planned the space and the budget, plan the time. If you're working in your spare time, the work will probably take longer than you think. Problems may come up in remodeling, the boss wants you to

work some overtime or emergencies happen. Figure the amount of time a particular phase will take, then double it. You'll come out about on schedule.

Job Sequencing—Use the table on page 69 to plan out the construction sequence for your bathroom. Start at the top of the table and write down the first operation that applies. Then write down successive operations. When you've finished, review the list, starting at the bottom and working back to the top. This will help you see if you've missed any operations that should precede the next. Adjust the sequence to suit your own needs.

Next, mark approximate start and finish dates for each operation on the list. Note where in the sequence you'll need materials on hand to keep the job going. Working from the lead times your suppliers gave you, fit ordering dates into the schedule. Don't be afraid to modify your schedule later, as actual work progresses.

Lead Times—With the best of intentions, suppliers will sometimes make promises they or the manufacturers can't keep. So treat all supplier lead-time projections as educated guesses at best.

Ordinary goods such as 2x4s, 1/2-inch plywood or a standard-size white bathtub should be readily available and rarely back-ordered. If one

BATHROOM REMODELING SEQUENCE OF OPERATIONS

Plan space.
Plan money.
Plan time.
Plan purchasing.
Obtain permit.
Arrange for temporary facilities.
Remove all bathroom contents and decorations.
Seal off area.
Remove toilet, plug floor flange and cap off water supply.
Remove lavatory and cap off water supply.
Remove electrical fixtures and cap all exposed wires.
Remove vanity top or tops.
Remove cabinets.
Remove baseboards, trim and built-ins.
Remove finish-floor materials.
Remove wall coverings.
Remove unwanted non-bearing walls.
Remove tub or shower.
Clean up and remove trash and debris.
Repair floors.
Shore up and remove unwanted bearing walls.
Revise and repair wall framing.
Revise and repair ceiling framing.
Install new tub or shower.
Install windows or exterior doors.
Revise and repair water supply.
Revise and repair drainage.
Revise and repair wiring.
Revise and repair insulation in floor, ceiling and exterior walls.

Clean up and remove trash and debris.
Get rough-in inspections.
Install drywall.
Tape and finish drywall.
Install other wall and ceiling finish materials.
Paint walls and ceiling.
Install wall coverings or surface materials.
Install interior doors.
Install floor coverings.
Install cabinets.
Install cabinet trim.
Build vanity tops.
Install vanity tops.
Install top finish materials.
Install baseboards and trim.
Install and hook up lavatory and fitting.
Install and hook up toilet; install seat.
Install and hook up finish electrical.
Install accessories.
Clean up and remove trash and debris.
Test all systems—repair and touch up as required.
Get final inspections.

Note: This sequence is a general one that will fit most bathroom remodeling jobs but by no means all. Add, subtract, or rearrange to suit your particular job conditions and preferences.

supplier doesn't have a standard item, another probably will. This is not always the case with low-volume materials, such as custom vanities or bath fixtures in decorator colors.

If you have to place a special order for a hard-to-get item, do it before you start the job. In some cases, it's best to wait for delivery of the item before starting the job. Waiting to start the job can be frustrating. Doing without the bathroom for three months while you wait for an essential fixture is worse.

A week to ten days after the order is placed, the supplier should be able to provide you with a projected manufacturer's shipping date. Even these dates aren't infallible, but any information is a help.

Some suppliers will require a deposit for special orders. Make sure it's noted on the receipt that the deposit is refundable if some reasonable and specific delivery date is not met.

STORAGE

You'll need storage space for new materials and for old fixtures and debris to be removed. If supplies will be delivered by truck, you'll need to provide access to the storage area.

Also, many new materials for your bathroom will be susceptible to weather and water damage. Store these materials in your garage if you have one. The driveway will provide good access and materials will be more secure from theft.

If you don't have space in the garage, look for other suitable storage places. Materials such as lumber can be stacked outside and covered until used. Block lumber stacks off the ground to prevent moisture damage. Have materials unloaded where you're going to store them, to avoid double handling.

Store more-valuable and easily damaged materials in a room or closet convenient to the work area. You'll need space about equal in size to the bathroom you're working on. Do not store anything in the bathroom because you'll need elbow room to work. Provide storage space for fixtures or other components you'll be reinstalling.

TO SUB OR NOT TO SUB

Time, effort and money are tied together. The way to remodel a bathroom in the least time and with the least effort is to hire a general contractor. You tell the contractor what you want and pay the bill. This is usually the most expensive way to go.

The least expensive way is to do *all* the work yourself. Unless you're familiar with all phases of remodeling work and can devote a major portion of your time to the job, this is also the most time-consuming way to remodel. If you're limited to evenings and weekends, a substantial remodeling job can take several weeks to a month or more. A general contractor could probably do the same job in 3 to 5 days.

There is a full range of options between these two extremes. If you act as your own contractor, you can do any amount of work you want and hire subcontractors to do the rest.

This book guides you through every phase necessary to remodel an existing bathroom or install a new one. After you've read this book, you may decide you don't have the ability or inclination to do certain phases of the work.

Jobs such as modifying plumbing lines or setting ceramic tile in a shower enclosure can be messy and time-consuming. An experienced plumber or tilesetter has both the experience and tools to do the work quickly and efficiently. This does not necessarily mean a subcontractor will do a better job than you could. There are good ones and bad ones.

Investigate and weigh all alternatives. Consider the amount of work you're able to do and how quickly you need the job done. Only you can decide what mix, if any, of your effort and subcontractor effort should be put into your bathroom.

HIRING QUALIFIED HELP

If you want to have some or all of the work on your bathroom project done by a contractor or subcontractor, the procedure for selecting either is much the same. Check out everything, every step of the way. Don't take shortcuts because the size of the contract is small. No matter what the amount of the contract, the potential liabilities are much the same.

To simplify the following discussion, both general contractors and subcontractors, such as plumbers and tilesetters, will be referred to by the general term, *contractors*.

Finding a Contractor—The best place to get the names of prospective contractors is from people you already know—friends, relatives, neighbors and co-workers. Look for completed arm's-length transactions, that is, contractors who did work for these people, did it well and on time. Disregard any obviously biased referrals.

Another good source of contractor names is the local building department. They will *not* make specific recommendations. However, they can usually give you a list of local contractors who are in good standing with the building department. You can draw your own conclusions if a particular name isn't on the list. In a big city, it doesn't mean much. In a small town, the absence can be significant.

In many areas, there are contractor's and trade associations, such as a local chapter of a national association, like the National Association of Home Builders (NAHB), the National Kitchen and Bath Association (NKBA) or a strictly local group. While not every good contractor is necessarily affiliated with any such group, the associations are still a good source of referrals. You might also ask if the association sponsors any competitions among the membership. If so, the names of the last few years' winners should be available. These will give you a good reading of whose work is considered outstanding by their peers.

A last source of contractor referrals is the Yellow Pages. You may be surprised how much information you can get from the ads.

Some contractors may list only a name and a phone number. Others may include the names of principals in a contracting company, number of years in business, memberships in or certifications by professional and trade associations, the exact kinds of work the contractor specializes in, what equipment he has, licensing and insurance information and more. Even if you already have a contractor's name and phone number, still check the Yellow Pages for any additional information that might be there.

Checking Contractors—Before calling any contractor, do some preliminary checking. Almost all states now license contractors. Most require a security bond and proof of insurance coverage.

Call the state contractor's board or licensing agency to find out if the contractors you've selected are licensed. Find out if their bonds and insurance coverage, if required, are up to date. Also ask if there are any past or pending complaints or claims against them. If so, get details. Of course, some complaints may be groundless. But a consistent pattern of complaints can mean the contractor either does substandard work or is just plain hard to get along with.

Some construction trades are exempt from licensing in some states. An alternate source of information is the local Better Business Bureau. They can give you any past or present complaints from their files, and the resolutions. Whether or not a contractor is a member of the local Better Business Bureau is essentially meaningless. Some join and some don't. What counts is the complaint history, if any, and the resolutions of the complaints.

If you want to be really thorough, you can check both sources, the BBB and the state licensing agency. On a big contract, you may also want to check with the county recorder's office for lawsuits, assignments for the benefit of creditors, defaults, delinquencies and judgements. Any of these can indicate a shaky financial position, and possibly a future inability to perform the job.

Quotations—When you have a list of four or five potentially good contractors, call and ask them to inspect the job and give you a quotation. At this point, find out when the contractor will be able to start the job.

Beware of any contractor that quotes complex work over the phone without first seeing the job. There are some operations that are so standardized or routine that they can be priced that way, but most work can't.

Also look out for the contractor who offers you a great bargain, but only if you sign the contract immediately. If he can't wait a day or two, he's in too much of a hurry to do the job correctly.

A contractor's quotation should be

Dealers of specialty items, such as this large whirlpool bath, often offer installation services. Some code jurisdictions may require a spa or whirlpool bath be installed by a licensed plumber or electrician. This is one job you may want to subcontract. *Photo courtesy of Jacuzzi Whirlpool Bath.*

in writing, and it should contain the essential elements. These include a complete breakdown of the materials and labor to be provided, a timetable for the work and a proposed payment schedule. Sometimes, you may have to go to the contractor's place of business to pick out materials or fixtures before he can give you a final price.

A quotation usually has a time limit—find out what it is. Material and labor prices keep shifting, so a contractor can't be bound by his quotes forever. But the time limit should give you a reasonable amount of time to get additional quotes and further check the contractor's credentials, if necessary.

When calling for a quote, ask the contractor for the names and numbers of satisfied customers. Also get information on the contractor's insurance coverage, both liability and workmen's compensation. The easiest way to check this is to ask for the name of the contractor's insurance agent, and call him. If the contractor doesn't have adequate insurance, *you could be held responsible* if there's an injury or property damage connected to your job.

After you've got the quotations, you must decide who you want to do the work. Don't hire a contractor you don't personally get along with. Without a certain amount of trust, respect and communication, even a small job can turn into a headache.

Check each bid carefully. Price, job starting time, time to job completion and amount of detail in cost breakdowns are often good indicators of a contractor's ability and desire to do the job. The contractor who submits a high bid and can't start the job for three months obviously has more work than he wants or needs. The consistent prize-winner may charge more due to the excellence of his work, and past customers should confirm that.

The low bidder may have low overhead, working out of his home and doing all the work himself. Or the low bidder may be desperate for work, or is simply not aware of what his competitors charge.

The above reasons don't necessarily reflect quality of work or the contractor's ability to complete the job. On the other hand, a low bidder may not know what he's bidding, or is intentionally submitting an incomplete bid to undercut the competition. Either

way, this often results in the contractor trying to tack on extra charges when it comes time to sign the contract, or after the job is in progress. The best way to avoid this trap is to study materials and labor breakdowns in the bid.

First, the bid should be complete. Make sure there are no missing items. Also, materials should be described in detail. The bid should indicate lumber and plywood grades, make and model numbers of fixtures and so forth. Materials and equipment should be of comparable quality to those indicated in higher bids. Man hours required to complete the work should also be comparable.

The Contract—Don't let a contractor do any work or deliver any materials until you have a written contract. A contract should contain exactly the same information as the quotation, and any subsequent verbal agreements. If a verbal agreement isn't in the contract when it's signed, that verbal agreement *no longer exists.*

The contract should specify when the job is to start, and when it's to be completed. It should spell out what is to happen if the job doesn't start and finish on time, or doesn't finish at all. Payment details should be spelled out, along with the specifics of any warranties.

Warranty information should not only include what's covered and for how long, but exactly *who* is warranting the product. Some manufacturers warrant only their product, not replacement labor cost or other damage that occurs due to failure of the product. In that case, if the contractor doesn't warrant the replacement labor costs in the contract, you're responsible for them.

Payment—It's normal for some amount of money to be payable on signing the contract. In some legal jurisdictions, the contract isn't valid without at least a token payment. Because the contractor has *lien rights* against the property where the work is done, he should not ask you for too much money before work starts. Lein rights are discussed at right. Find out what the payment arrangements are when you get bids. Reviewing bids from several contractors will show you what payment schedules are customary in your area.

Generally, the payment schedule in a contract should leave you enough

money at all times to have the work completed by someone else if the contractor fails to complete it. The last payment should not be made until all the work is done and all inspections completed.

Liens—It's possible to pay for the same work twice. If the contractor does the work and collects from you, but doesn't pay his suppliers, employees or subcontractors, they can file a lien against your home for the money due them. The fact that you paid the contractor will not keep you from having to pay all over again. This is another reason why you should check out a contractor carefully.

The basic defense against this kind of problem is a *lien waiver* or *release of lien.* When a contractor asks for a payment, he should be prepared to give you one of these documents from each supplier that provided material and each employee or subcontractor that worked on the job up to the date of payment. The contractor doesn't sign the waiver—the supplier, employee or subcontractor does. A good contract states the contractor's intent to provide these documents.

What the document means is that if the signer has to go after somebody for the money owed, he'll pursue the contractor, not you. It doesn't necessarily mean that the contractor has already paid—just that his credit and reputation are good enough for them to let you off the hook.

In some legal jurisdictions, a supplier may record a *Notice of Intent to File Lien* shortly after delivery. Don't get rattled—this is only a formality required by local lien laws to preserve the right to file a lien at some future date, should it become necessary. The later release of lien or lien waiver should be worded to take this into account.

Outside Review—As you can see, contracting for work on your home can be complex and confusing. Local laws and customs vary, and you're bound by all of them. If you're not completely confident of your ability to handle these details, especially the documents, have an attorney review everything before signing. The fee for such a review is usually reasonable, and can help you avoid future problems.

Also, if you're financing the work, the lender may have requirements regarding the bidding and the contract, especially payment provisions. Check with them before you sign.

GETTING READY

The first step in remodeling a bathroom is to clear out everything that isn't nailed or screwed fast. The second step is to remove everything that *is* nailed or screwed fast.

Load a cardboard box with everything you'll need to use while the bathroom is out of commission. Then box everything else and store it. Don't leave anything behind that will get in the way—hampers, shower curtains, throw rugs and so forth.

Tools—Basic tools for tearout work are a *hammer with ripping claws, brick set, 3-inch scraper, 3/32-inch pin punch, utility knife, screwdrivers, adjustable wrenches, and a small, flat pry bar.* Specialized tools for various tearout phases are listed where required.

If you don't already have a flat pry bar, get one that's fairly thin, sharp-edged, and spring tempered. They're available at hardware stores. A brick set looks like a broad-blade cold chisel except the blade is beveled on one side only. Hardware stores and masonry suppliers carry this tool.

Removal Tips—Brute force has its place in demolition work, such as removing masonry walls or old concrete. For most interior remodeling, the secret is not force but removal of all fasteners and the judicious use of wedging and leverage. Whenever something won't move, check for hidden fasteners and remove them. Then decide how you can apply some leverage or wedging action. Let your tools do the work.

Be alert to the possible presence of electrical or plumbing lines inside walls, floors, ceilings and cabinets. If you're careful, you can often leave plumbing or electical lines in place after removing walls or cabinets. Then you can remove or reroute the lines separately.

Dust Control—During the early phases of remodeling, take steps to keep dirt and dust from spreading through the house. Remove all heating and cooling registers in the room or rooms you'll be working in. Then block off the ducts with cardboard attached with duct tape. Also seal off any cold air returns. Protective measures should stay in place until all cleanup and sanding is done.

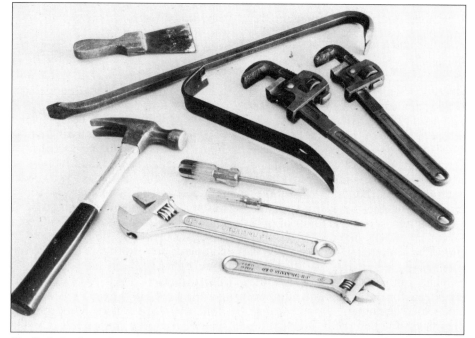

The first step toward a new bathroom is tearing out the old one. Only simple tools are needed, as shown here. Be prepared to cap off plumbing and electrical connections as you disconnect fixtures.

TOILET REMOVAL

There are three types of toilet-mounting systems. In the most common floor-mounted type, the toilet bowl is bolted to the floor and/or drain flange and the tank is bolted to the bowl. On some older toilets, the bowl is bolted to the floor and the tank bolted to the wall. On wall-mounted toilets, the tank and bowl, often one piece, are bolted to a heavy carrier in the wall. The early steps of removal are similar for all three types.

Turn off the water at the *stop valve* below the toilet, or at the main valve if there is no stop valve. A typical stop valve is shown on page 73. Remove the tank lid. Flush the toilet and hold the flush valve open to drain as much water from the tank as possible.

If water is still running into the tank, the stop valve isn't completely shut off. Stop valves often build up deposits on the seats that don't allow them to close all the way. To fix this, turn off the main valve, dismantle and clean the stop valve, replace worn washers, if any, and reinstall.

Dismantle and remove the *supply riser* between the stop valve and the tank. Use a towel or sponge to remove any water remaining in the tank. Bail out remaining water in the bowl with

a small cup or can. Mop out the last of the water in the bowl with a sponge or towel.

To remove a toilet with a bowl-mounted tank, first remove the ceramic or plastic bolt caps covering the floor bolts or screws. Then remove the nuts and washers or screws at the base of the bowl.

If a toilet has been in place for many years, the flange bolts may be corroded or frozen. In this case, the bolt heads will turn in the flange when you try to remove the nuts. There are several ways of dealing with this situation, depending on individual circumstances.

An expendable toilet bowl can be broken away from around the bolts. Use suitable safety precautions if you do this. If you have to save the toilet bowl, steady the bolt with a pair of vise-grip pliers, then cut off the bolt at the bottom of the nut. You can use a hacksaw if there's access. A metal-cutting blade inserted into a keyhole-saw frame works well. Or you can tape the broken end of a broken hacksaw blade and use the taped end as a handle.

If you have one, you can use a flex-shaft grinder or hand-held grinder to grind away the side of the nut to free it from the bolt. Or an automotive-type nut splitter will split and release the nut.

Some toilets have holes that are larger than the nut, but smaller than the washer under the nut. In these cases, you can sometimes pry up the edge of the washer and grip it with diagonal wire cutters. Repeated left-and-right twisting of the wire cutters will fatigue and split the washer. Once the washer is removed, you can lift the toilet bowl off bolts and nuts.

When the screws or nuts and washers are removed, lift straight up on the tank-and-bowl assembly. If the bowl is stuck to the floor, don't use tools to pry it loose unless you don't care if the bowl breaks. Gently rock the bowl from side to side until it comes loose.

If the tank is mounted on the wall, it will swivel on the elbow to the bowl. Loosen the large slip nut that holds the elbow to the bottom of the tank. Support the tank while you remove the screws holding the tank to the wall. Lift off the tank and put it aside. Then remove the bowl as described earlier.

Wall-mounted toilets should be supported by a helper while you're removing them. Unscrew the bottom bolts or nuts first, then the upper ones. Rock the toilet sideways slightly to break it loose from the wall, then pull the toilet straight out.

If you have an existing wall-mounted toilet in good shape, consider keeping it. If you're planning to get a new one that will fit the old wall carrier, you may have some difficulty finding a replacement. The bolt locations for wall-mounted toilets vary

The first step in toilet removal is shutting off and disconnecting water supply. In most cases, the *supply riser* (vertical pipe from stop valve to bottom of tank) can be removed to make more room to maneuver toilet.

greatly. Not all carriers have provisions for adjusting the bolt locations to fit more than one bolt layout. You may have to get a new carrier for the replacement toilet. If you want to convert to a floor-mounted toilet, you'll have to rework water-supply and drain pipes to fit it.

When the toilet is off, remove the flange bolts from the flange. Use a putty knife or chisel and a stiff wire brush to clean the drain opening and flange. Remove all loose rust and pieces of wax seal sticking to the flange and underside of toilet. Clean drain opening and surrounding area with a strong chlorine bleach solution. Stuff several wads of newspaper into the drain opening and tape a piece of cardboard over it with duct tape.

TOILET TYPES

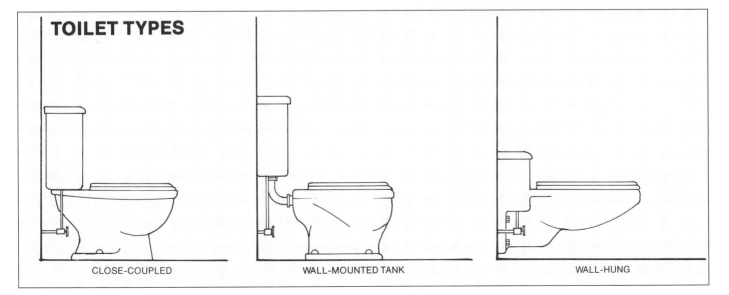

CLOSE-COUPLED   WALL-MOUNTED TANK   WALL-HUNG

LAVATORY REMOVAL

First, study the way the trap is put together. The trap parts are usually held together by a series of slip nuts. Then take apart the trap and remove it. If the trap won't come apart, you can avoid mangling the drain pipe by cutting the trap with a hacksaw. You can deal with the remaining trap piece later.

Turn off the water at the supply valves and disconnect or cut the risers. If the supply valves won't shut off all the way, turn off the main valve. Then remove the supply valves from the wall stubs. Either clean the supply valves and put them back, or cap the pipes so you can turn on the main valve.

If the lavatory is wall-hung, there may be one or more clamps holding it to the wall bracket. After the clamps are removed, you can lift the lavatory off the bracket. To avoid damaging the surrounding wall surface, use a utility knife to cut away any sealer or accumulated paint where the lavatory meets the wall.

You may need some help lifting the lavatory off the bracket. Many old wall-hung lavatories are heavy cast iron. Those that aren't cast iron are breakable vitreous china, the same material as a toilet.

Drop-in lavatories can be left in the vanity top and removed with it. Disconnect the trap and supply lines as you would for a wall-hung lavatory.

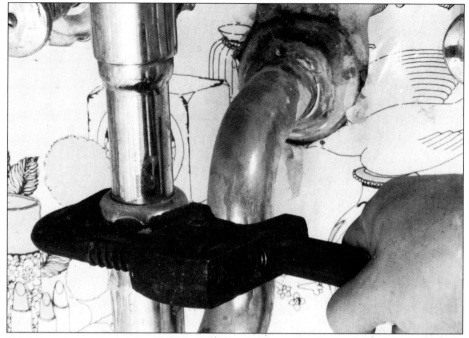

Most trap assemblies can be taken apart after all slip nuts are loosened with wrench. If slip nuts won't loosen, use hacksaw to cut through trap body, or a cold chisel to split the nut.

VANITY REMOVAL

If there are any moldings or fillers, pry them off. Remove any drawers and look inside the vanity for mounting screws or nails. Remove the mounting screws or nails holding the cabinet to the wall. If the vanity has been nailed in place, set a 3/32-inch pin punch in the center of each nailhead. Then drive the nail right through the cabinet. This technique also works on badly corroded or stripped screws.

Use a utility knife to cut any sealer or old paint at the seam between the vanity top and the wall. The vanity should then lift or slide out. If necessary, use the pry bar to lever the cabinet away from the wall.

Some old cabinets have been built in place rather than being built and then installed. The way to deal with these is to puzzle out the sequence the original builder followed. Then reverse the process, prying off one piece at a time.

TUB REMOVAL

The single biggest problem in tearing out an old bathroom is removing the tub. Bathtubs weigh anywhere from 200 to 600 pounds and up. Water supply and drain pipes are complex and often inaccessible. The tub itself is often locked into a recess. All these factors make tub removal difficult and disruptive.

Access to Plumbing Connections—If you have to tear out the old tub, start by looking for an access opening on the other side of the wall from the fitting end of the tub. If you don't find an access opening, you'll have to cut one. Follow the instructions for removing drywall or plaster on pages 79-80. Make the access opening generous in size so you have room to work, but don't exceed 4 feet in either dimension. That way you can make a cover panel from drywall or plywood without having to contend with a seam.

Some highly economical bathroom-plumbing installations are laid out with plumbing fixtures for adjacent bathrooms on both sides of a core wall containing all the plumbing. The two bathrooms are mirror images of each other. In such a situation, special measures must be taken to gain access to tub plumbing.

First, remove everything else from the bathroom you're working on, so there's nothing in there but you and the bathtub. Then cut an access opening in the wall alongside the tub at the fitting end. This access opening should be at least as tall as the tub, and at least as wide as one stud bay. This will give you access to the tub drain from the side. You'll have to work blind, but at least the other tub's connections will serve as a guide. A second access opening will be required

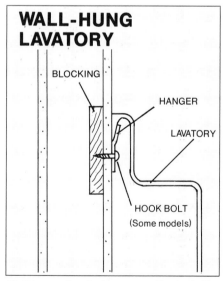

WALL-HUNG LAVATORY

BLOCKING

HANGER

LAVATORY

HOOK BOLT
(Some models)

Wall-hung lavatories are attached by clamps to a wall bracket. When clamps are removed, lavatory will lift off bracket. Do *not* remove bracket from wall to remove lavatory.

around the fitting over the tub.

A crawl space or basement can also give you access for dismantling drain connections, but you'll still have to cut an upper access hole around the fitting to disconnect the water-supply lines.

Disconnect Drain Plumbing—The drain assembly doesn't have to be removed from the tub, but you must disconnect the drain assembly from the drain line. At the outlet end of the tub drain, the drain assembly will have a tailpiece that looks like a lavatory drain. The tailpiece will be tied into the drain pipe with a slip nut. Unscrew the slip nut. Use a pair of channel-lock pliers to unscrew the tailpiece out of the drain assembly. If it won't unscrew, crush the tailpiece with the pliers until you can unhook the fine threads at the upper end from the drain assembly. Then work the tailpiece free of the drain line.

On old tubs, you may find a section of soft-lead pipe with wiped-lead joints tying the drain assembly to the drain line. Treat lead connections and unbudgeable tailpiece connections the same. Use a hacksaw to cut through the tailpiece or lead connection at an angle. Use pliers to wiggle the pieces free.

Disconnect Supply Pipes—Turn off the main water valve and disconnect

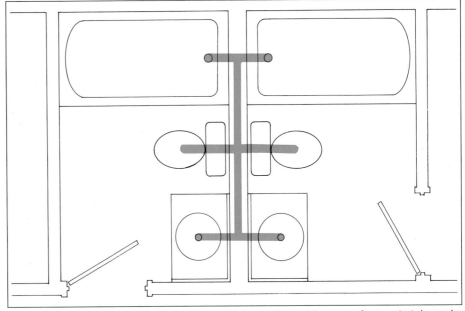

Mirror-image bathrooms make most economical use of plumbing runs. Access to tub can be difficult. Remove lavatory and toilet first, cut access opening next to tub.

If you're lucky, access to tub plumbing will be available from other side of wall at head of tub. All connections can be unhooked and capped from adjacent room. If there's no existing access opening, you can make one, if it will be in an unobtrusive place.

and remove the water-supply fitting. In most cases you'll find brass unions connecting the hot and cold water pipes to the bottom of the fitting. Unscrew the union nuts to remove the unions.

If the fitting does not have a *shower riser,* you can now remove any trim parts on the tub side and withdraw the body of the fitting from the wall. See drawing on page 76. If the fitting does have a shower riser, unscrew the showerhead and the pipe nipple extending from the wall over the tub.

Then from the access-opening side, use a pair of channel-lock pliers or a pipe wrench to unscrew the shower riser from the top of the fitting body. Usually the shower riser and the elbow at the top will rotate in its straps.

In rare cases you may have to enlarge the access opening to free the shower riser so it can rotate. If the new tub is not going to be installed in the same location, leave the riser in place, to be entombed in the wall. Then cap the pipes so you can turn on the water.

Remove the Tub—There are several ways to remove the tub. One way is to take the tub out the way it went in. Most recess tubs were installed before the drywall or plaster was applied to the bare studs. If your plans call for removing the drywall or plaster from the walls at either end of the tub, do so before removing the tub. The tub will then slip right out.

If you plan on preserving the walls in the bathroom, consider taking the old tub out endways, through the wall at the head or foot. Make sure the wall you're cutting into is not a bearing wall—see pages 84-85. Also make sure there is room on the other side of the wall to maneuver the tub—in other words, don't try to take the tub out into a narrow hallway.

Then remove a section of plaster or drywall on the other side of the wall opposite the tub. The opening should allow 6 to 8 inches clearance from top and sides of the tub.

Remove the plaster or drywall on the tub side also, allowing 6 to 8 inches clearance. The sides of the hole you made should be centered over studs so there will be backing when you nail in the drywall replacement patch. Remove any plumbing in the way of the tub and cap the lines.

Use a circular saw with a carbide-tip blade to cut out any studs within the opening. Knock the lower cut pieces sideways and pry them loose from the bottom plate. Make two cuts in the bottom plate and pry out the loose piece. There may be a stud at the corner that's tough to cut or to get out. This stud can be left in place, but you'll have to lever the tub away from the back wall about 2 inches to clear the stud before the tub will be free to move.

The toughest inch of the moving process is the first one. A tub that has been in place for more than a few

TUB/SHOWER PLUMBING

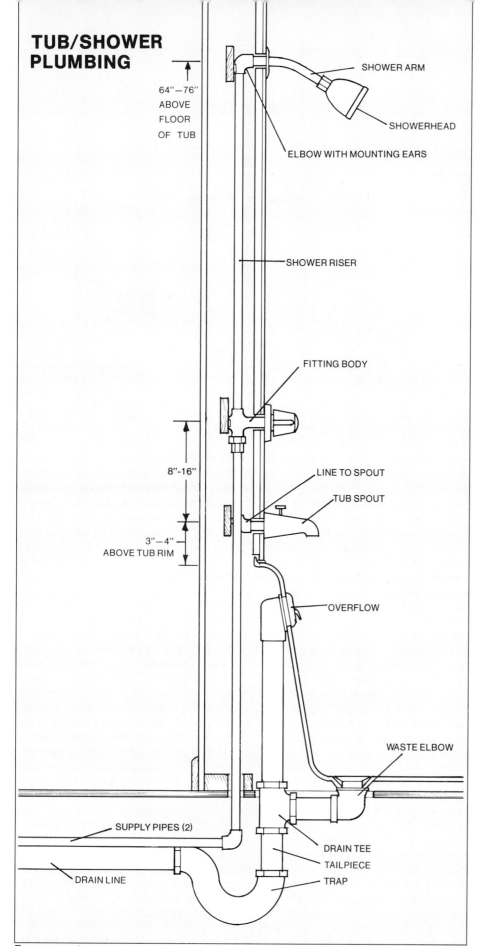

64"–76" ABOVE FLOOR OF TUB

SHOWER ARM

SHOWERHEAD

ELBOW WITH MOUNTING EARS

SHOWER RISER

FITTING BODY

8"-16"

LINE TO SPOUT

TUB SPOUT

3"–4" ABOVE TUB RIM

OVERFLOW

WASTE ELBOW

SUPPLY PIPES (2)

DRAIN TEE

TAILPIECE

DRAIN LINE

TRAP

To remove tub plumbing, first disconnect drain assembly from drain line by removing tailpiece between trap and drain tee. Assembly can be left on tub, if desired. Next, shut off main water valve and disconnect supply pipes.

years is probably stuck fast. Use a utility knife to cut loose any sealer, grout or putty at the joint between the tub and the remaining walls.

If the tub is anchored with nails or screws in the flanges along the remaining walls, remove some of the wall-finish material with a chisel and remove the fasteners.

The next step requires long sleeves, gloves and goggles to protect you from flying chips. Use a crowbar to wedge between the opposite end of the tub and the studs in that wall.

Once you've gained an inch or two, you can continue to work with the crowbar and some wood blocks to move the tub a foot or so. If the old tub is enameled steel, you and a helper or two should now be able to pick up the tub by the ends and move it through the hole in the wall. If the tub is one of the heavy cast iron ones, four or five helpers may be needed.

Ingenuity is often needed to move a heavy cast-iron tub. If there is a window or door opening in the opposite wall, you can rig a couple of long lengths of 2x4 across the opening. Make sure the 2x4s span enough wall on either side of the opening to reduce stresses. These can be used as the anchor point for a block and tackle, a come-along, a chain hoist, or other force-multiplying device. Or you can use an automobile bumper jack between the other end of the tub and the wall. Old broom handles or scrap lengths of pipe can be used as rollers under the tub.

A heavy cast-iron tub can easily damage floor covering in the room it's exiting into. Either remove floor coverings or protect them with plywood or scrap pieces of lumber.

After the tub is out in the open, whether in the bathroom or in an adjoining room, the hardest part is over. You can either tip the tub onto its front apron and onto a dolly, or you can upend the tub and use a hand truck. Don't try to upend a heavy cast-iron tub if you can possibly avoid it. If you must do so, use at least four strong helpers and proceed with caution.

REMOVING SHOWER STALLS AND TUB SURROUNDS

Tearing out old ceramic-tile shower stalls and tub surrounds is a dirty chore. Water damage to wall and floor structures is sometimes extensive but not visible on the surface. If possible, inspect from behind or underneath before planning to leave old tile in place.

If a ceramic-tile wall or shower pan must come out, be ready for some heavy, messy chopping. Older ceramic-tile shower pans were often set in mortar, as shown on page 147 for floors, but with a lead, copper or hot-mopped asphalt waterproofing layer beneath the mortar. Newer installations usually have fiberglass or molded-cement shower pans.

In older installations, the wall tile was set in mortar, referred to as *mudset* tile. The setting mortar was applied over plaster or over a scratch coat of mortar, reinforced with chicken wire or expanded-metal lath. The total thickness from tile surface to studs will often exceed 1-1/2 inches. In newer installations, you'll find the tiles adhered with a mastic adhesive directly to a backing of waterproof drywall.

Removing Mudset Wall Tile—Safety precautions are important when removing mudset wall tile. Wear steel-toe shoes if you have them. If not, keep your feet out of the way as much as possible, and use a cardboard box turned on its side to protect your toes when you need to. Large chunks of old masonry can let go unexpectedly and seriously injure your feet. Eye protection is a must, because of flying tile chips. Wear heavy gloves and heavy clothing to protect you from sharp edges and ragged metal reinforcing.

Protect the floor with an old tarpaulin or layers of cardboard so falling chunks don't make extra repair work. To protect an existing tub for reuse, start by covering it with a layer of cardboard, secured with duct tape. Then put a folded tarp in the bottom, or use a piece of scrap plywood big enough to cover the entire top of the tub. If you use a piece of plywood, be sure it's sturdy and stable enough to use as a working platform.

The wisest course is usually to remove the old tile-and-mortar layer in one thickness rather than trying to peel off layer after layer. Tools you'll need include a heavy mason's chisel, a 3- or 4-pound short-handle hammer, a heavy crowbar and sheet-metal shears.

Start at the bottom of a section of tile, preferably near an edge. If you

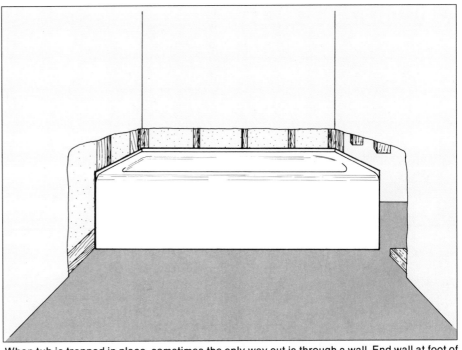

When tub is trapped in place, sometimes the only way out is through a wall. End wall at foot of tub is the easiest, provided there's space on other side of wall to maneuver tub. Remove only as much wall covering as necessary. Cut off studs at angle for easy removal.

start at the top you risk the whole section peeling off at once, with you underneath it as it falls. Chop off a few tiles with hammer and chisel, then chop away the mortar down to the reinforcing mesh. The layer of mortar on the back of the reinforcing mesh can be knocked off with a hammer from the front. As you do this, avoid hitting the studs with your hammer. Cut away the exposed mesh with sheet-metal shears.

Gradually work your way outward from the hole. The crowbar is helpful where reinforcing mesh is nailed to the studs. You can also insert the hooked end of the crowbar into the wall and use it to knock loose the tile-and-mortar layer from behind. Use the hammer and chisel when necessary to encourage the tile-and-mortar layer to break into manageable chunks as you pull it off. Use the shears when necessary to cut through reinforcing mesh and to separate loose pieces from the wall.

As you work, frequently remove tile and mortar debris from the work area and dispose of it. This may seem like extra work, but it is dangerous to let debris pile up and get in your way while working.

Finish by pulling all nails from studs and cleaning up any remaining mess.

Removing Mastic-Set Wall Tile—In

newer installations, the tiles will be glued with a waterproof mastic adhesive directly to the finish-wall surface, usually waterproof drywall. Mastic-set tiles are easily removed from the wall with a hammer and brick set. An old wood chisel also works well, but make sure it's one that you don't plan to reuse for woodworking after the job is done.

When removing tiles, wear gloves, safety glasses and heavy clothing to protect yourself from flying chips. Protect the tub or shower pan and the floor with canvas dropcloths or pieces of cardboard. The dropcloths also provide a cushion for falling tiles, should you wish to save whole ones for reuse.

Start at a top outside corner of the shower stall or tub surround and remove individual tiles until you've completed the job. If you're careful, you may be able to salvage most of the tiles. But you probably won't be able to reuse them for the shower or tub surround. Inevitably, a few tiles will break when you're removing them and it's extremely difficult to find new tiles that exactly match the old. Consider using the salvaged tiles for another project.

If the backing material is drywall and in relatively poor condition, you may be better off to cut the drywall and remove it, tile and all. This can be a timesaver when the drywall will

Use floor-repair compound and scraper to fill and level imperfections in old floor. Remove all loose material first.

have to be replaced anyway.

Removing Shower Pans—Old fiberglass and molded-cement shower pans will usually come out easily, once the drain is disconnected. First remove the drain cover plate from the drain fitting. The drain fitting is usually threaded into the drain body underneath the pan. If the drain fitting isn't corroded too badly, try inserting the handles of an old pair of pliers and unscrewing with a pipe wrench. If that doesn't work, or if everything is corroded together, try using a blunt chisel and a hammer to drive the drain fitting counterclockwise, unthreading it. Penetrating oil may help. If all else fails, chop out the shower pan around the drain with a hammer and cold chisel. Be careful to protect yourself from flying chips.

Removing a mudset ceramic-tile pan is much like removing a mudset tile wall. Use a heavy mason's chisel and a 3- or 4-pound short-handled hammer to remove tiles and mortar down to the waterproofing layer.

If the waterproofing layer is hotmopped asphalt, use a hammer and old wood chisel, or the ripping claws of the hammer, to tear off the material down to the subfloor framing.

If the waterproofing layer is copper or sheet lead, it is usually attached to the framing with roofing nails. Use a pry bar to remove nails and pry out the waterproofing layer.

On concrete subfloors, the tiles are usually set in mortar directly over a formed-concrete recess. Remove tiles and mortar as previously described. Use a mason's chisel or brickset to chip any remaining pieces of mortar from the concrete.

FLOOR COVERING REMOVAL

Not all old resilient floor covering has to be removed. If the adhesive is holding well and the surface is relatively smooth, repair the old floor covering and leave it in place. Find any loose spots and reglue. Put a layer of kitchen plastic wrap over any reglued spots and add weights to force the patch flat. Low spots and small broken-up areas can be filled in with floor-patching compound.

Do not repair floor imperfections with any materials other than water-resistant floor-patching compounds. You don't want the patch coming loose in a year or two.

Old floor coverings that are spot-glued or badly loosened can be eased up with a scraper or a flat pry bar. Some of the backing will usually stay on the subfloor. The last of the backing can be removed with a hammer and a brick set. Take care not to dig into the subfloor with the brick set.

Loose-laid sheet flooring can be rolled up and hauled off. If necessary, use a utility knife to cut the sheet flooring into manageable pieces.

Wood Floors—Old, sound wood flooring usually doesn't have to be taken up. Often it can be sanded and refinished. Or you can renail where necessary and put down a new floor directly over it. Some sanding may be needed to flatten out cupped or warped boards, though it's sometimes easier to split them with a chisel and nail down the halves separately.

Sometimes relocating walls or reducing finish-floor height makes it necessary to remove old wood-strip flooring. It's a good idea to salvage some of the flooring for future repairs to floors in the rest of the house. Most old flooring is nearly impossible to match.

Remove any baseboard or shoe molding that overlaps the flooring. Pick a strip near a wall and split it with a hammer and chisel all along its length. Start near the wall the tongues are pointing toward—you can get clues at openings in the floor. If you guessed wrong, move to the opposite wall and start over. Because wood-strip flooring is blind-nailed through the tongue, you need access to the tongue edge to remove strips with minimal damage.

Pry out the pieces of the split strip to give you access to the tongue of the next strip. Drive a flat pry bar under the strip near each nail and lift gently until the strip comes loose. Remove the nails from each strip by driving out from the underside. Keep going until all the wood flooring material is pulled up.

Ceramic Tile Floors—Once a ceramic tile floor is worn out, there's no effective way to refinish it, as you often can with a wood floor. You either have to rip it out or cover it up. If the ceramic tile was originally laid with a mastic adhesive, chip off the tiles with a hammer and brick set. Long sleeves, gloves and safety glasses or a face shield are required for this job.

If the ceramic tile was *mudset*—laid in a bed of wet mortar 1/2 to 2 inches thick—it's best to use the cover-up method described in the following text. If both the tile and mortar bed are in bad condition or breaking up, remove the entire floor down to the joists or concrete subfloor. Frame floors are usually constructed as shown on page 147. Joists under mudset tile often have tapered tops to minimize cracking. After removing tile and mortar bed, nail *scabs*, either

2x4s or 2x6s, alongside each joist to restore the bearing surface. Then lay a new subfloor as a base for the new flooring.

If the old ceramic tile floor is sound, and the extra floor height presents no problems, you can cover it with new flooring. Thoroughly sand the tile surface with coarse sandpaper. Then install a layer of plywood underlayment with construction adhesive. Construction adhesive comes in cartridges to fit a caulking gun. Follow instructions on the adhesive cartridge for flooring and underlayment work.

STRUCTURAL TEAROUT

Some older bathrooms are well designed and functional. But like all other parts of a house, bathroom fixtures and surfaces can wear out. A worn-out bathroom can be given new life by removing old fixtures and finishes, making some minor repairs, and installing new fixtures and decorations.

Many times, older bathrooms need major renovation because they are too small or poorly laid out. You may need to steal space from adjoining rooms, or rearrange partitions in the space you have. In any event, you'll need to gain access to plumbing and wiring to rework them to the new layout. This requires cutting into or removing walls. This sections shows you how.

Before doing anything, examine all floors and suspicious wall areas for signs of rot and deterioration. Probe with a screwdriver or an icepick around the old plumbing-fixture locations—especially around the toilet. See pages 102-104 for repair instructions on rotted floors.

DRYWALL AND PLASTER REMOVAL

To remove drywall, use a utility knife to cut along any adjoining walls and ceiling. This will prevent damage to adjoining surfaces from the joint reinforcing tape that wraps around the corner. To remove part of a wall, mark a pencil line on the wall at the cut. To get the line vertical, use a plumb bob or level. Leave some extra drywall if you're not sure of the exact location of the cut. Surplus drywall can easily be trimmed later.

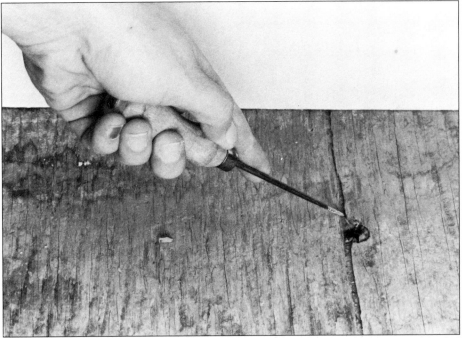

Thoroughly check all floor and wall framing for deterioration. Water leaks can go undetected for years, doing considerable damage.

In the drywall area to be removed, chop a small hole with the ripping claws of a hammer. Slide the end of a tape measure through the hole sideways and mark the locations of the adjoining studs. If the cut line is on a stud, make a rough cut first at the edge of the stud toward the tearout area. Then pry the drywall out slightly to pop the nails. Remove the nails and make the final cut.

To cut the drywall, repeatedly score with a utility knife until you've gone all the way through. Chop an opening at the cut line in the drywall to be removed. Starting at the bottom, pull off the drywall in pieces. As you remove pieces, be alert for places where the drywall you're removing is still attached. Cut these free with a utility knife as you go along.

Removing part of a plaster wall is much more difficult than removing the whole wall. Often, the easiest course is to remove all the plaster from the wall, down to bare studs. You can then rework the framing and later apply drywall to the part of the wall that's to remain.

To remove plaster from an entire wall, chop the plaster loose from any adjoining walls and ceiling with a hammer and brick set. Keep the brick set at an extreme angle and cut only the plaster, not the lath underneath. Then drive the short end of a pry bar into the plaster in the middle of the

wall, but not into the lath. Starting in the middle, pry the plaster off the lath in chunks. Most plaster walls will be edged with *plaster grounds*. These are wood strips that were used to level the initial coats of plaster. Remove the plaster grounds with a pry bar.

After the plaster is off, the lath is all that's left. The lath may be perforated gypsum board, in which case you can remove it like drywall. Or the lath may be thin wood strips. To remove wood lath, pry it off a strip at a time. Pull any lath nails that stay in the studs.

At adjoining walls, lath ends may overlap so the lath you're removing is trapped. If so, start at the bottom and ease out the free ends of a dozen or so strips. Slide a brick set in behind the strips and chop off the lath nails holding them. You can then withdraw them. Then work your way up, levering each successive lath strip downward to pull its nail out. Don't pull straight out from the adjoining wall, or you'll break loose some of the plaster you wanted to save.

If you must remove part of a plaster wall, the remaining plaster must not be dislodged from the lath behind it. One method is to use a circular saw with a carbide-tip blade. Do not use a regular blade; plaster is abrasive and there may be imbedded nails. Make a plunge cut near the bottom and push the saw up the wall. Wear long

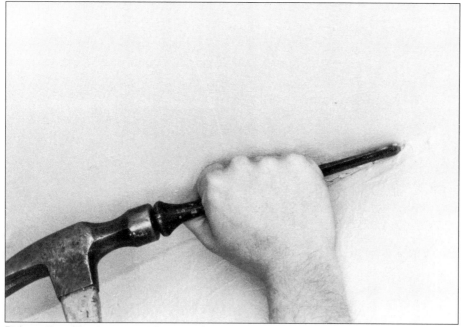
Before attempting to remove plaster, make clean separation at adjoining wall or ceiling without disturbing lath underneath.

CUTTING PLASTER

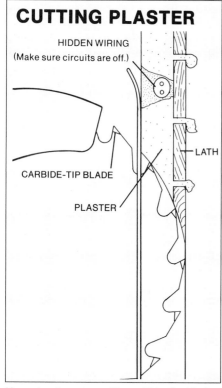

HIDDEN WIRING
(Make sure circuits are off.)

CARBIDE-TIP BLADE

PLASTER

LATH

Use circular saw with carbide-tip blade for cutting plaster. On rare occasions, wiring may have been buried directly in plaster during previous repair or remodeling. Check for signs of surface patching as evidence of this. To be safe, turn off nearby circuits when cutting plaster.

sleeves, goggles and a painter's respirator to protect yourself from plaster dust. If you have a shop vacuum, have someone move the nozzle along ahead of the saw as you cut. This will catch most of the dust. Set the blade only as deep as the bottom of the lath. Move the saw slowly so the blade speed stays up to prevent excessive vibration.

FRAMING REMOVAL

Walls are either bearing or non-bearing. See pages 84-85 to figure out which is which. Non-bearing walls can come out immediately. You can remove the surface materials from bearing walls. But bearing-wall framing should not be removed until you are ready to replace the support provided by the wall. Do not depend on temporary shoring any longer than absolutely necessary.

If you strip a bearing wall to the studs, temporarily brace the wall to prevent lateral movement. Nail on a diagonal 1x4 extending from the top plate to the bottom plate, and nail at the plates and at each stud. It's necessary to drive the nails completely into the brace to be effective. If you want, you can use *duplex nails* for the brace. A duplex nail has two heads, one about 1/4-inch below the other. You can drive a duplex nail in to the first head. The second head protrudes so you can pull out the nail easily.

Other than the shoring techniques for bearing walls shown on page 86, removal is the same for both bearing and non-bearing walls. Use a saw to cut through the middle of each stud to be removed. Cut on an angle so the saw doesn't bind. Then pull the cut pieces off the nails at the top and bottom plates. Cut the top and bottom plates flush at the ends and pry the plates loose.

When removing studs, cut on diagonal to avoid binding saw blade. Carbide blade is recommended because of nails in old lumber.

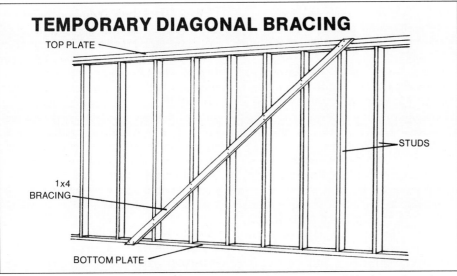

TEMPORARY DIAGONAL BRACING

TOP PLATE

STUDS

1x4
BRACING

BOTTOM PLATE

When drywall or plaster is removed from a bearing wall, the wall should be braced as shown here.

SALVAGING OLD MOLDINGS AND TRIM

When remodeling a relatively recent house, you may prefer to replace existing moldings and trim with new material. In most cases, you can find currently available materials that are similar or identical in shape, size and wood species.

When working on an older house, matching moldings is not as easy, especially when you want an authentic restoration. Three basic solutions are available. Specialty houses can supply new moldings to match some of the old patterns. Custom fabricators can make replacement moldings to order. Specialty houses and custom fabricators often run ads in some of the publications for old-house restoration enthusiasts. Both of the above solutions are expensive.

The third solution is to remove the existing moldings and trim, then refurbish and reuse them. To make up for shortages, small lengths of matching moldings can be salvaged from out-of-the-way places. Attics, basements, and the inside-front walls of closets are good places to rob. Replace robbed pieces with the best match you can manage.

It's difficult to remove moldings and trim intact after a century or two in place, if both the molding and the wall must be preserved. In such cases, leave the molding in place and work around it, if at all possible. If the piece has to come off, be prepared to damage the wall to preserve the molding.

First, use a utility knife to cut through any putty, filler, or paint and varnish at all joints. This helps prevent chipping. Check the molding surface for indications of putty or filler over nailheads. If you find any, use a thin pin punch to drive the nail through the molding—do not try to dig it out.

If your search for nails is fairly successful, the piece—or at least an end—will come loose. If only an end comes loose, spring the end out and insert the hooked end of a flat pry bar behind the molding. Ease out successive nails without letting the pry bar contact the edge of the molding. Apply the pressure to the back of the molding and let the wall take any damage that results. It's easily patched.

Trim will often be nailed into studs, so concentrate any pry-bar work directly above and below nails. You'll often be prying against the stud under the plaster, which results in much less damage to the wall. Twisting the bar rather than levering it can also confine most of the wall damage to the area behind the trim, where it will be concealed on replacement.

If a piece of trim is stuck tight and you can't get a start anywhere, resist the temptation to drive a tool behind it and pry. What you think is a molding might be molded plaster and a part of the wall itself. Scratch it in an easily patched place to find out. You'll encounter this kind of trim most often where walls meet the ceiling, and removing and replacing such molded-plaster trim is practically impossible.

If the molding or trim is wood, use a brick set or old screwdriver and dig into the material, usually plaster, behind the end of the piece. Excavate behind the piece of trim until you can insert a small wood block and the hooked end of a flat pry bar. Use the wood block to keep the pry bar from contacting the exposed edge of the piece. Then gradually coax the piece loose. You may have to repeat this process several times on a large piece of trim.

SURFACE PREPARATION

No matter what finish material you're applying or what kind of surface you're applying it to, there are some basic rules of surface preparation that apply. First, the old surface must be solid, no matter what it is. Any material that is loose, severely chewed up or water damaged should be removed. Then new drywall or plywood can be installed to provide a good foundation for the new finish. Peeling paint or wallpaper will continue to peel under the new finish materials. Strip or sand down to a solid base.

Paint or adhesives won't stick to glossy surfaces. Dull the entire surface with fine sandpaper—don't leave any glossy patches. A washing solution of trisodium phosphate (TSP) will degloss some paints with little or no sanding, as will commercially available deglossing solutions.

Wax, dirt, grease or oil will resist bonding by anything, as will soap scum. Trisodium phosphate washing solution will remove them. Stubborn deposits can often be removed with paint thinner or acetone. Some heavy soap-scum deposits will require scraping before scrubbing.

Some surface materials are too porous to accept paint or adhesive. This is especially true of new drywall or plaster. A seal coat of paint or primer, or a skim coat of adhesive, may be needed to reduce the porosity so the finish coats can bond correctly. For more specific information, check the label on the finish paint or adhesive you'll be applying.

Wall preparation is as important with wall coverings as it is with paint. The steps are much the same. Seal porous surfaces and remove grease, wax and dirt. Thoroughly degloss shiny surfaces. After the wall surface is ready, you may need to *size* it before you hang the wall covering. Sizing is a material applied to the wall surface to help ensure a better bond. Check with your wall-covering dealer to obtain the correct sizing for your particular project.

TRASH DISPOSAL

Trash disposal is a major part of a bathroom remodeling job. Keep trash cleaned up as you work so it doesn't get in the way. The garbage man will accept small amounts of debris with your regular garbage, but garbage cans full of plaster and broken concrete will be ignored.

Old cast-iron fixtures can often be sold to a scrap yard. If the fixtures are pre-1930 or so, they may have some antique value. If so, you may be able to sell them to an antique dealer or through the classified ads of the newspaper. Old claw-foot bathtubs and pedestal sinks are often sought by those restoring turn-of-the-century homes to their original state.

If you have a fireplace, wood debris can be cut up with a carbide-tip blade in a circular saw and stockpiled for kindling. If you call the local solid-waste agency, they'll tell you how and where you can dispose of what's left.

Don't dump your trash where it doesn't belong. The proper place for debris is the local landfill. If you don't have or can't borrow a pickup truck, check the newspaper classified section under *light hauling*. Such services are available almost anywhere and are usually reasonable.

If you'll be generating a large trash pile, contact a dumpster service if there is one where you live. Dumpsters are large wheeled trash containers that commercial businesses use. If you can't find a dumpster service listed in the phone book, look behind the local supermarket. If their dumpster doesn't have the company's name and phone number on it, ask the supermarket manager who to call.

Dumpster companies have temporary drop and pickup services that are fairly economical. General contractors use them frequently. If possible, get a dumpster or roll-off container that will handle the job in one load. Make sure you have enough space for the dumpster and access for the delivery truck. Look out for potential driveway damage from the large roll-off containers.

TEMPORARY FACILITIES

More than for any other room, temporary or substitute bathroom facilities are essential. The substitute facilities don't have to be elaborate, just enough to get by with com-

fortably. Of course, if you have two bathrooms your problem is solved, provided you only tear out and rebuild one at a time.

If you only have one bathroom, temporary facilities are more of a problem. If you own or can borrow a travel trailer, motor home or other self-contained RV, park it in the yard and use it as if you were on the road. Perhaps you can make arrangements with a neighbor or a nearby relative or friend.

In some areas, it's possible to rent a portable toilet—the kind used on construction sites and for outdoor public functions—for the time necessary to tear out a bathroom and replace it. Access and privacy should be considered before you take this course, though. Portable chemical toilets sold for camping use are a good alternative for indoor use. A kitchen or laundry room can be used for washing hands, taking sponge baths, and so on. When planning the job, take into consideration the length of time the bathroom can be out of service without too much disruption.

SAFETY

Accidents don't happen, they're caused. Take precautions to prevent not only the obvious hazards but the more subtle ones also. You can't finish remodeling a bathroom if you're in a cast or otherwise out of action.

Your personal limitations are an important safety consideration. You'll be doing a lot of heavy lifting in awkward positions. Everybody's knees and back have limits, and a little forethought can save much pain. If your weak points are knees, ankles or wrists, strap the joints with an Ace bandage before doing any heavy lifting. If a job requires kneeling for prolonged periods, knee pads are helpful. These are available at building and masonry suppliers.

To avoid straining your back, always lift objects correctly, even fairly light ones. Center yourself over the load so all back muscles take the strain, not just one side or the other. Then use the major muscles of upper arms and upper legs to provide the lifting power, not lower leg, lower arm, and especially not the back. Never lift *anything* unless your body is ready to take the load. Even bending over and snatching something off to the side

can be hazardous. You can overload the muscles on the opposite side of your back and cause a lingering injury.

Most importantly, don't work when you're tired—either physically or mentally. If you overwork yourself physically, you're more likely to strain or injure your body. If you tire yourself physically or mentally, you will make mistakes or perhaps have an accident. Either way, you stand to lose more time than you gain by working that extra half hour after your body tells you to quit.

HEALTH HAZARDS

Remodeling a bathroom inevitably involves exposure to sewage and drain pipes. The buildup of organic materials inside drain pipes and traps is an ideal growing medium for all sorts of microorganisms, some of them dangerous. It's helpful to flush the drain lines with a cup or so of chlorine laundry bleach a few hours before you start working. This treatment will reduce the microbe population.

Maintain basic sanitation when working on old fixtures, and drain and sewer lines. Don't eat, smoke, or touch your face, mouth or eyes while your hands might be contaminated. Don't contaminate any scratches or other damaged skin areas you may have. Scrub down thoroughly after you're done and wash any tools that may have been contaminated. After washing tools, rinse them in a weak chlorine-bleach solution. Severe and crippling infections can be contracted from a single casual exposure to sewage. Don't take any chances.

Any remodeling work carries with it the risk of *tetanus,* also known as *lockjaw.* Any of your tools or the old materials you're ripping out can carry tetanus. The organisms can live indefinitely under the right conditions. If you haven't had a tetanus inoculation in the last few years, get one before you start working. You can be infected through any minor scratch or puncture. Once contracted, tetanus is difficult to treat and sometimes fatal.

ELECTRIC SHOCK

Electricity can be a major hazard while you're working on a new bathroom. Do not work on any electrical circuit unless the circuit is definitely known to be turned off. Use a piece of tape on the breaker or fuse holder so someone else doesn't turn on the

If circuit must be turned back on while switch or outlet box is dismantled, first clip off exposed wire ends and cap them with wire nuts. Fold wires back into box. Leave all bare or green safety grounds attached to box instead of capping them.

circuit while you're working. Be sure any loose wires are capped off and safely covered before turning on the circuit.

Power tools are big current users. Check the fuses or circuit breakers to determine the maximum amperage capacity of the circuits you're using. If necessary, string heavy-duty extensions from other parts of the house to distribute the electrical load.

Look at the specification plate on power tools for amperage ratings. Bear in mind that some motors will draw a surge current when they're starting that exceeds their rated current draw. This is why a 10-amp tool will sometimes blow a 15-amp fuse. If you can't find a stated amperage on a tool, try to determine motor horsepower or wattage. One motor horsepower is roughly equivalent to 6 amps at 120 volts. If you can find a wattage figure, divide the watts by the volts to get the amps. For example, a 2HP motor at 120 volts draws about 1800 watts. Divide 1800 by 120 to get 15 amps. If you plug a 15-amp tool into a 15-amp circuit, you're likely to trip the breaker or blow the fuse if anything else is drawing current from that circuit at the time.

All power tools should be either the newer double-insulated type or should be grounded. Use 3-wire heavy duty extensions, not household lampcord extensions. Lightweight extensions cut down the voltage available at the power tool. Heat will quickly destroy the insulation on the extension, and the low voltage can burn out the power tool. Heavy duty

extensions are a better solution. Look for an amperage rating on the label of the extension, and buy one rated above the current draw of your biggest power tool.

The size of the electric shock risk depends on the grounding available. Look out for wet conditions when you're using electricity. Water provides a good ground for any leaking current, through you. If you must work in wet conditions with electrical equipment, install a *ground fault circuit interrupter* (GFCI) in the circuit you're using. Unlike a conventional circuit breaker, a GFCI detects the presence of potential current leakage and shuts off the current before you get shocked.

GFCIs can be sensitive and under certain circumstances can pop off repeatedly. But the annoyance is nothing compared to a possible lethal shock. If your house is wired with circuit breakers rather than fuses, it's possible you can unplug any 120-volt breaker in the panel box and plug in a GFCI. Or you can wire a junction box into your extension cord and install a GFCI there. GFCIs are fairly expensive, but the circuits in all new bathrooms are required to be protected with them. For more on wiring bathroom circuits, see pages 134-141.

TOXIC SUBSTANCES

Airborne dust from sanding or paint spraying is a nuisance and can be hazardous to your health. When necessary, use a molded-paper res-

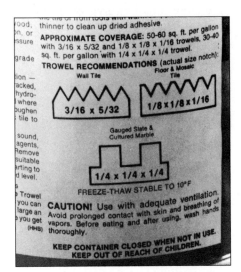

Read every word on fine-print labels like this. Some compounds and solvents are totally harmless. Others must be handled with extreme caution to avoid hazards.

pirator mask, available at any paint store. Don't sand old lead-base paint or asbestos-bearing floor tile, because the dust created is dangerous.

A mask won't protect you from volatile solvents present in some of the materials you'll be using. Many of the liquid materials involved in bathroom construction are solvent-based. These include adhesives, paints and varnishes, degreasers and cleaners. Ventilation is imperative when using these products. Open doors and windows. Set up an electric fan if there isn't enough air circulation. Move the work outdoors if you can. Some solvents will make you sick; others can do permanent damage.

Also, some volatile solvents are flammable or explosive. Check the labels carefully for specific information on this. Make sure all open flames are extinguished before working with flammable solvents. Some solvent vapors are so sensitive that even the tiny spark from a light switch or a power tool can set them off. Also, solvent fumes can travel great distances to an ignition source.

PERSONAL INJURIES

Power tools are the source of many injuries on home construction and remodeling jobs. Wear safety goggles and earplugs. When doing tearout work, a hard hat is also advisable. Keep loose clothing away from the machinery. Securely clamp the piece you're cutting or drilling. Make sure tools and materials are out of the way of the moving parts of power tools. Precautions are detailed in the manual that came with the tool. In addition to these precautions, don't let yourself be distracted. When operating a circular saw or any other power tool, don't let your mind wander. Force yourself to concentrate only on what you're doing. Don't let anyone or anything distract you until the power tool is shut off and secured.

Especially in small, enclosed areas such as a bathroom, noise is a big problem with power tools. Some tools can do permanent damage to your hearing. If you can't find suitable hearing protection where you buy your tools, there are many good hearing protection products made and sold for target shooters. Check with the nearest gunsmith, shooter's supply store, or sporting goods store with a firearms department.

Walls

You can build some excitement into your new bathroom if you think of the structure itself, especially the walls, as shapeable. Walls don't have to be flat or straight. Finishing may take a little extra time and care, but the effect can be worth it.

Once you've removed the old plumbing fixtures and finish materials from your bathroom, the walls will need some repairs or changes. At the very least, you'll have to patch nail and screw holes, and miscellaneous dents and dings. In older bathrooms, water-damaged walls will need repair or replacement. Sections of wall may have to be added or removed to fit the new plan. Access openings may have to be cut to work on plumbing or electrical lines.

With one exception, this chapter covers all the work you might have to do on walls, from simple repairs to framing to finish work. The exception is ceramic tile installation. Because ceramic tile is a common bathroom material with so many applications, a complete chapter has been devoted to its installation, starting on page 146.

WORKING WITH WALLS

Before cutting into any existing wall, find out if it's a *bearing wall*. Bearing walls support the roof or the second floor of a two-story house.

You must treat bearing walls more cautiously than non-bearing walls, but any wall can be modified. Bearing walls require shoring while you're working, as shown on page 86. Working on bearing walls can be hazardous if you don't provide adequate shoring. The entire structure can collapse if any major structural elements are removed.

IDENTIFYING BEARING WALLS

You can assume that all exterior walls are bearing, but interior bearing walls can be difficult to spot. In a one-story house or on the top floor of a two-story house, a look at framing in the attic will often reveal bearing-wall locations. If the roof is constructed with *trusses*, only walls below that support the ends of trusses are bearing. A roof truss is a preassembled unit made up of many small members held together by metal fastening plates or plywood gussets. See drawing at right.

If the roof is built of separate rafters and ceiling joists, all walls under splices or overlaps in ceiling joists are bearing walls. Even if the ceiling joists are continuous over a wall, treat it as a bearing wall if you can't find a definite bearing wall within 12 feet or so. Any wall perpendicular to ceiling joists can be bearing. Walls parallel to joists usually aren't bearing unless they're outside walls.

Structural beams or girders are often visible below the ceiling. Sometimes they're built into the roof structure above the ceiling. If there's an attic above, you'll be able to see these beams or girders. Support must be maintained for *both ends* of such beams and girders.

If you find two or three studs grouped together in a wall, they're probably supporting the end of a beam or girder. If so, *don't take them out.* If necessary, cut access holes to find out what these studs are supporting. Make sure you don't disturb essential structural supports.

After you've determined what the hidden structural conditions are, you can decide how to deal with the situation. It may be necessary to change a beam or girder for a longer, larger one. Or a post may have to be inserted to transfer the beam's load from a wall you want to remove.

If your house has a basement or

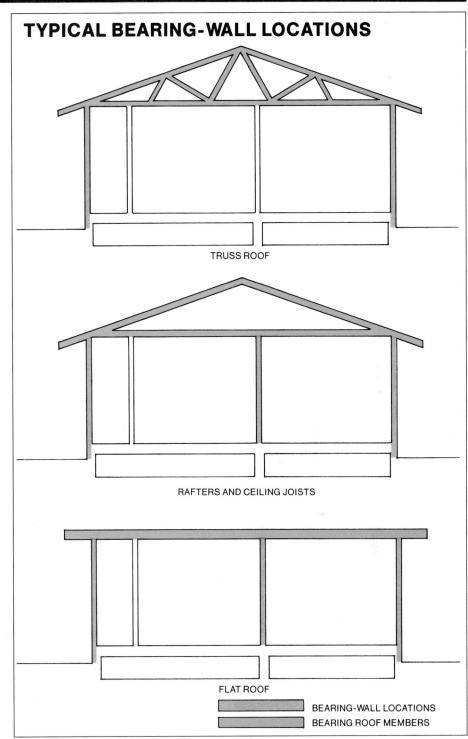

TYPICAL BEARING-WALL LOCATIONS

TRUSS ROOF

RAFTERS AND CEILING JOISTS

FLAT ROOF

BEARING-WALL LOCATIONS
BEARING ROOF MEMBERS

Bearing-wall locations will differ depending on structural requirements of the house. In all cases, exterior walls should be considered bearing. As shown here, pitched roofs with rafters and ceiling joists, and flat roofs, are usually supported near midspan by a bearing wall running perpendicular to joists.

crawl space, you can get clues to bearing walls there. All bearing walls will be supported from below by either a beam or by two or three floor joists grouped together. In the attic, basement or crawl space, use the access opening, a corner of the house, a vent stack or drain line, or recessed light fixture for a landmark. Don't try to judge which wall is which by eye. Unfinished spaces can be confusing, and you can easily misidentify a wall.

If a flat roof or the upstairs floor is above the walls in question, finding out which walls are bearing is more difficult because framing members are concealed. If you can't find bearing walls from the basement or crawl space, inspect the ceiling for clues.

Compression cracks where walls meet the ceiling indicate stress and may mean the wall is bearing. In plaster, the cracks may be on the wall a few inches *below* the ceiling. You may be able to spot a continuous drywall seam on the first-story ceiling. Or you can pull up some carpet on the second floor and look at the nailing pattern of the subfloor. These will indicate the direction floor/ceiling joists run.

Sometimes the only way to find out how the second floor is framed is to cut some small holes in the ceiling near the wall and look. If the upper-floor joists are lapped over the wall, or there's blocking between joists, it's a bearing wall. Check another wall or two that you can be fairly sure are not bearing. Most framers will block between second-story floor joists over beams and bearing walls, but not over non-bearing walls. Some framers will block above all walls *and* at midspan. If you've looked for all of the clues and you're still not sure whether the wall is bearing or not, treat it as a bearing wall.

SHORING

Bearing walls are built like other walls, but they hold up some part of the structure above. When you remove or modify a bearing wall, you must first brace, or *shore,* the structure it supports. The purposes of shoring are to prevent movement and possible collapse of the structure. Movement of structural members loosens up fasteners and pries off or cracks finish materials. Shoring can be rough and temporary, but it must be rigid, not flexible.

Shoring is most commonly used to hold up the ends of members like floor joists, ceiling joists, rafters or trusses that rest on a bearing wall. Leaving room to work between shoring and wall, tack a 2x6 or 2x8 to the floor and another to the ceiling directly above. Extend ends of these plates one or two joists beyond the bearing-wall area you're going to work on.

Then install studs or posts between

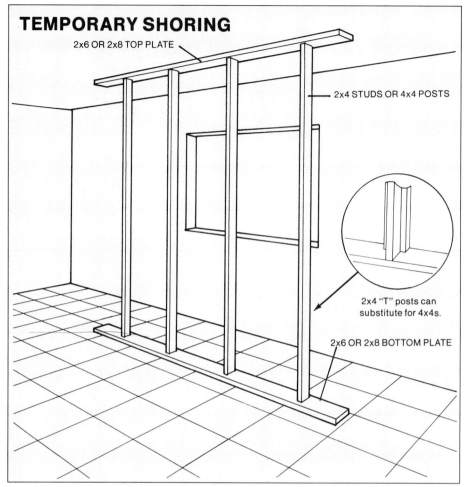

TEMPORARY SHORING

2x6 OR 2x8 TOP PLATE

2x4 STUDS OR 4x4 POSTS

2x4 "T" posts can substitute for 4x4s.

2x6 OR 2x8 BOTTOM PLATE

For light loads, use 2x4 studs spaced 2 to 4 feet apart. For heavier loads, use 4x4 posts spaced 16 to 24 inches apart. Alternative for 4x4 posts is 2x4s nailed in a "T" cross-section.

the plates to carry the load. Size, spacing and type of studs or posts is a matter of good judgment. If the load is heavy, or distance between floor and ceiling is large, use 4x4 posts or 2x6 studs spaced 16 to 24 inches apart. If load is light, use 2x4 studs spaced 2 to 4 feet apart.

If you're not sure of shoring requirements, consult the building department.

To make stiff and cheap shoring posts, nail two 2x4 studs together in a T cross-section. The post will be almost as stiff as a 4x4. Similarly, if you need to add stiffness to top and bottom plates, spike a 2x4 on edge to one or both edges of the plate. Toenail studs or posts in place with a nail or two—at the top only. Slip a pair of shim shingles under the bottom of each stud or post.

Wedge shoring into place to remove the load from the bearing wall. Tap shim shingles under each stud or post in turn until the load is transferred. Watch the corner where

wall and ceiling meet. If it starts to separate, you've shimmed too much.

You can sometimes tell the amount of load on a stud or post by tapping it with a hammer and listening. Tap a loose piece of 2x4 to get a representative sound, then tap the shoring as you drive in the shims. The sound will "tighten up" as the stud or post takes the load. If the stud makes a metallic ring, the load is excessive—ease off or add support on either side.

If members overlap the wall from both sides, such as a bearing wall in the middle of a house, shore both sides. Take additional load into consideration. In general, it's better to overbuild shoring than underbuild it. You can reuse shoring materials after you've removed the temporary shoring.

Before erecting shoring, check carefully to make sure the floor underneath will carry the additional load. You may have to brace the floor directly underneath the shoring to support the additional weight.

WALL FRAMING

The basic parts of a frame wall are a *bottom plate*, the vertical members called *studs*, and one or two *top plates*. Exterior walls and some interior bearing walls may have diagonal bracing. Members used in standard wall construction are usually 2x4s. In some cases, 2x6s are used for walls over 10 feet in height, or where extra depth is needed for plumbing lines. Some code jurisdictions allow 2x3s to be used for interior, non-bearing walls. In post-and-beam construction, framing members may be 4x4s or larger, depending on the original design of the house.

Framing Materials—Learn the difference between *actual* and *nominal* sizes of framing members. A 2x4 is rough-cut from the log at an actual 2 inches by 4 inches. This is its *nominal size*. It's then dried to a usable moisture level—usually 19% or less. After it's milled to a smooth surface and uniform size, the "2x4" measures 1-1/2 inches by 3-1/2 inches. This is its *actual size* when you buy it. *Green* lumber has been milled, but not dried. A green 2x4 measures 1-9/16 inches by 3-9/16 inches.

The chart at right shows nominal and actual lumber sizes. Keep these sizes in mind when planning and taking measurements. Green lumber can be used for landscape work, but should *not* be used for house framing. It has a tendency to warp and shrink as it dries out. To be sure you're buying dry lumber, check the grade stamp for the letters *KD*, the words *Kiln-Dried* or the letters, *S-DRY*.

The maximum allowable height for a 2x4 stud wall is 14 feet. In non-bearing walls, 2x4 studs can be spaced no wider than 24 inches on center. In bearing walls that support a ceiling and roof only, 2x4 studs can be spaced 24 inches on center, provided the wall is 10 feet tall or less. If the bearing wall supports a floor above, 2x4 studs must be 16 inches on center.

To increase the depth of a 2x4 wall to make room for plumbing, nail 2x2s to the existing 2x4 studs and plates. This will give you an extra 1-1/2 inches depth to run a 2-inch-diameter drain pipe through drilled holes, or to run a 4-inch-diameter stack vertically.

Maximum height for 2x6 wall framing is 20 feet. Any 2x6 wall can be spaced 24 inches on center, unless it is supporting a floor above. In that case, spacing must be 16 inches on center. Any wall thicker than 6 inches should generally be constructed as two separate 2x3 or 2x4 walls. See drawing above.

You're required to *fireblock* wall framing so that no vertical space exceeds 10 feet in height. Fireblocking consists of a continuous row of horizontal blocks nailed between the

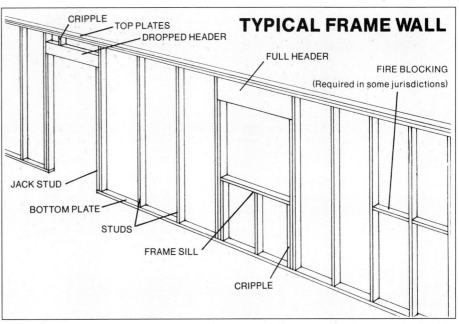

TYPICAL FRAME WALL

Walls are commonly framed with 2x4s, except for headers. Header size is determined by opening width and load on wall.

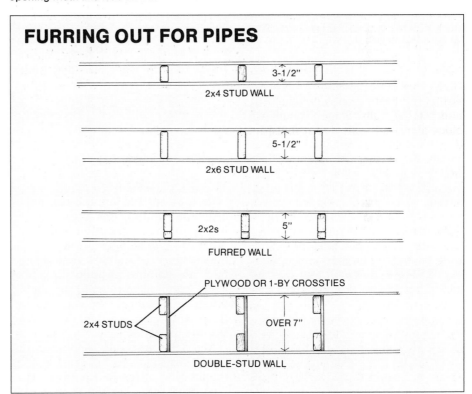

FURRING OUT FOR PIPES

Walls containing pipe runs must often be wider than standard 2x4 wall. Shown here are standard wall and three alternative framing methods.

STANDARD LUMBER SIZES

Nominal (inches)	Dry (inches)	Green (inches)
1	3/4	25/32
2	1-1/2	1-9/16
4	3-1/2	3-9/16
6	5-1/2	5-5/8
8	7-1/4	7-1/2
10	9-1/4	9-1/2
12	11-1/4	11-1/2

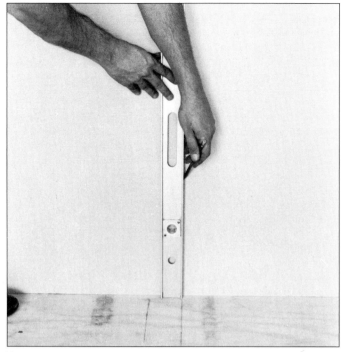

Use a chalkline to mark both sides of the new wall location. Then use a level to mark wall location on adjacent walls. Use chalkline again to mark ceiling.

To toenail stud, drive 16d nail partway into plate to hold stud end in place. Drive two 12d nails on other side, then two more alongside stop-nail. It's easiest to toenail top of stud first.

studs. Blocks must be the same width as the studs. You must also fireblock where soffits meet wall framing and in certain other situations, such as alongside stair stringers. Check local codes.

In some code jurisdictions, framing requirements may be stricter than those given here. This is especially true if your area is subject to earthquakes, high winds, heavy snows or other severe conditions. Check with your building department. The above recommendations only apply to framing lumber graded *Standard & better*, or *Stud*. You may be able to substitute the less-expensive *Utility* grade in your area and under your circumstances.

Don't use ungraded lumber. Most codes don't allow it. High-quality graded lumber is well worth the few extra dollars it costs. It's much easier and more satisfying to work with.

FRAMING A WALL

In new construction, wall framing is assembled on the floor, then tilted up into position. This is often impossible to do in remodeling because the ceiling prevents the wall from being tilted into an upright position. In most cases, you'll have to build the wall in place, first nailing the plates to the floor and ceiling, then toenailing studs to the plates.

Mark the new wall location on the floor, then snap a pair of chalk lines at the location of the new bottom plate. Be sure to allow for the thickness of wall-surfacing materials. For instance, if you're using 2x6 framing and 1/2-inch drywall, the total finished wall thickness will be 6-1/2 inches.

At adjacent existing walls, use a 4-foot level to continue the marks up the wall to the ceiling. If the end of the new wall is away from other walls, use a plumb line to transfer the marks to the ceiling. Then mark both sides of the new wall on the ceiling. Do not mark wall locations with center lines or the marks will be invisible under the plates. Also, don't mark only one side of the new wall location. It's too easy to get the wall on the wrong side of the line.

Cut to length one bottom plate and one or two top plates. Set the plates on edge across two sawhorses or on the floor. Position plates against each other with ends aligned. Use a pencil and square to mark stud locations across the top edges of both plates. Make sure the plates remain in alignment while you're marking so the studs will be plumb. From one end, mark every 16 or 24 inches, depending on the spacing requirements of the wall. These marks indicate the center lines of the studs. Mark locations for window and door framing. See pages 92-93 for details.

Once the plates are marked, align them to marks on the floor and ceiling and nail them to the existing framing. Use concrete nails to attach plates to concrete-slab floors; or use a masonry bit to drill holes, then install anchors and lag screws.

Measure between top and bottom plates for each stud. Mark each measurement next to the stud's marked location on the bottom plate. Don't just measure in one spot and then cut all the studs the same length. No structure is ever perfectly straight, and studs should bear evenly. So stud lengths will vary slightly.

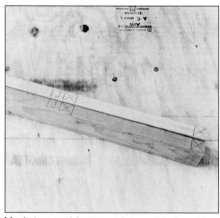

Mark top and bottom plates side by side with a small square. X indicates full stud, J indicates jackstud. Non-bearing walls need only a single top plate. Bearing walls should have double top plate.

After taking all the stud measurements, mark and cut the studs, one at a time. When cutting, start with the longest studs first, and work your way down to the smallest. That way a miscut stud can be trimmed for a shorter location. When cutting studs, cut to the outside of the marked line so the stud will fit tightly between the plates. The ideal fit for a stud requires a light tap or two to move it into position.

To attach studs, drive a 16d nail partway into the top plate and one into the bottom plate, 3/4 inch to one side of the stud center-line marks. The nails act as stops to hold the stud still while nailing it. Use two 12d nails to toenail the stud into the plate from the side opposite the stop nail. Drive the 12d nails partway into the stud before lifting it into position.

Toenail the stud to the bottom plate in the same manner. Remove the 16d stop nails. Then toenail each end from the other side—a total of four 12d nails at each end of the stud.

Blocking—Sometimes a new wall runs parallel to floor joists below but is not positioned over one. Install cross-blocking between floor joists under the new wall to help support its weight. Space blocking every 2 feet. The cross-blocking should be 2x6 or larger.

If trusses or ceiling joists are also parallel to the new wall, install cross-blocking every 2 feet so you will have solid backing to nail the plate to. In cases where there is no access to joists from above, you'll have to remove some of the ceiling material to install the blocking. If working from above, drive small nails through the ceiling on either side of the blocking so you can locate it from underneath when you nail the top plate to it.

Wall Problems—Out-of-plumb adjoining walls must be spotted early. If you have to build a wall perpendicular to an out-of-plumb wall, cut top and bottom plates to fit their locations. Tack the top plate temporarily into place. Use a plumb bob to get a reference mark on the top plate that's exactly above a similar mark on the bottom plate. When you position the plates side by side to mark the stud

If new wall runs parallel to floor or ceiling joists, install blocking between joists to attach top and bottom plates, as shown here.

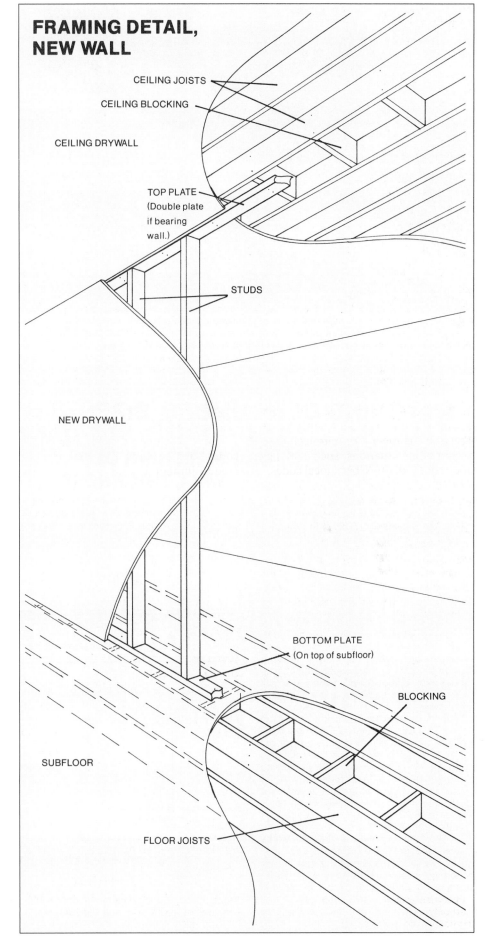

FRAMING DETAIL, NEW WALL

CEILING JOISTS

CEILING BLOCKING

CEILING DRYWALL

TOP PLATE
(Double plate if bearing wall.)

STUDS

NEW DRYWALL

BOTTOM PLATE
(On top of subfloor)

BLOCKING

SUBFLOOR

FLOOR JOISTS

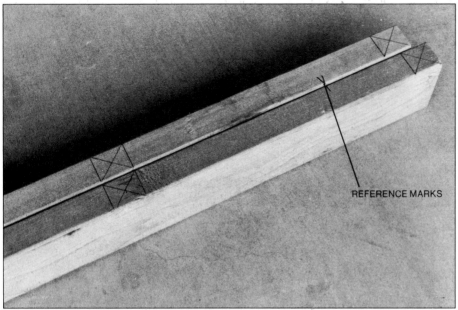

REFERENCE MARKS

When adjacent wall leans, tack ceiling plate in place and locate bottom plate. Use plumb line or stud and level to establish plumb reference marks. Line up plates for stud marking by plumb reference marks, not by ends. Start marking from end of *longer* plate.

center lines, make sure these *reference* marks are lined up, not the plate ends. That way the studs will be plumb.

When marking the stud center lines, measure from the wall-end of the longest plate. This ensures the first stud is 16 inches or less, or 24 inches or less, from the wall, but never more. Finish material will have to be trimmed to fit later on.

If an adjoining wall is curved, the end stud that lies flat against the wall should be warped into place roughly to follow the curve, and nailed there. If the wall is concave by more than 1/8 inch, reduce the distance to the first stud center line by the amount of the curve.

If the floor or the ceiling slopes, do not set the studs at right angles to the sloping surface. It's easier to set the studs plumb and trim the top or the bottom of the finish material.

MATCHING OLD LUMBER SIZES

Framing members in older houses usually aren't the same size as new members. Standard lumber sizes were introduced about 40 years ago. Since then, standards have changed several times, most recently in 1970. Houses built before this time are likely to have slightly larger framing members. Current standard sizes are listed on page 87.

It's usually impractical to search for lumber to match older house framing. A better course is to either build up the thickness of the next-smaller current size, or rip down the next-larger current size to match.

Furring out, or building up studs and plates to desired thickness, is only feasible if the old lumber size is the same as some combination of today's sizes. A standard 2x4 and furring strips cut from 1/2-inch plywood will match the full 4-inch studs used in many pre-1940 houses.

Plywood comes in thicknesses from 1/8 inch to 1-1/4 inches, making it relatively easy to match thicknesses of old studs. Also, scraps of lath or molding, rough or finish, work well as furring strips. If only a few studs need to be furred, using lath strips may be cheaper than buying a whole sheet of plywood. Continuous lengths are not needed for furring strips.

The same furring-out process works well for aligning the surface of a new drywall section with the surface of an adjoining plaster wall. Measure the thickness of the old wall in several places—plaster thickness can vary greatly. Subtract the thickness of the

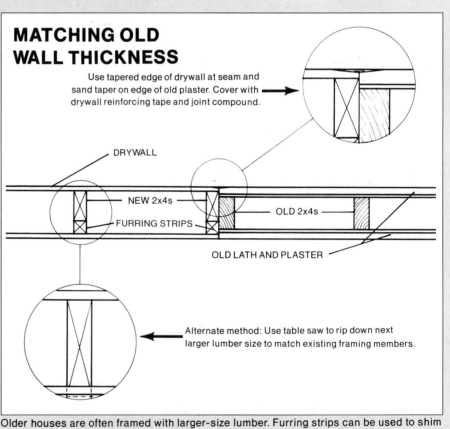

MATCHING OLD WALL THICKNESS

Use tapered edge of drywall at seam and sand taper on edge of old plaster. Cover with drywall reinforcing tape and joint compound.

DRYWALL

NEW 2x4s

FURRING STRIPS

OLD 2x4s

OLD LATH AND PLASTER

Alternate method: Use table saw to rip down next larger lumber size to match existing framing members.

Older houses are often framed with larger-size lumber. Furring strips can be used to shim out new framing members to match old ones, or larger members can be ripped down to fit old sizes.

drywall. Then fur out the new section of wall to the resulting dimension, centered on the old section. In some cases, you may need two thicknesses of drywall to match plaster thickness. If possible, leave existing lath in place.

NAILING TIPS

Nails have great strength if used correctly. When using nails to attach framing members, there are a few simple rules to follow.

Use Nails Correctly—When nailing a joint together, try to determine the stresses involved. The nail should be located crossways, or at least diagonally, to the direction of stress on the joint. If stresses on the joint are parallel to the nail direction, the nail will tend to pull out. Reposition the nail or rework the joint so the nail is crosswise to the direction of stress. If these methods are impractical, use a wood screw to attach the members. Nails have great *shear strength,* crossways to stress, but little resistance to withdrawal.

Box Nails vs. Common Nails—Two types of nails are commonly used for framing—*box nails* and *common nails.* Box nails have slightly thinner shanks than common nails. They are less likely to split the wood and are easier to drive. Also, you get more nails of a given size per pound.

On the other hand, box nails bend more easily. The wood in older framing members is often harder than in new ones. You may prefer to use common nails if you're working with older framing. Otherwise, to save time and money, use the smallest, thinnest nail codes and conditions will permit.

Splitting—Don't work with short pieces of wood if you can help it. There's no way to avoid splitting the piece. If you must nail near the end of a piece of wood and splitting is likely, look at the point of the nail. A nail point is made with four flat surfaces, but the surfaces don't form a square. They form a diamond. When the wide part of the diamond is parallel to the wood grain, the nail tends to wedge the wood fibers apart, causing a split. If you position the wide part of the diamond across the grain, the nail point tends to crush its way into the fibers instead of wedging them apart. In extreme cases, position the nail on a wood block with the point facing up. Then tap the point with your hammer several times to blunt it. This will inhibit splitting still more, again by permitting crushing rather than wedging.

Hammers—If you're constantly bending nails, don't be too quick to blame yourself or the nails. The problem may be your hammer. Replace any hammer with a chipped or worn face. Use the right-size hammer for the nails you're driving. A 20- or 22-oz. hammer is suitable for general framing purposes.

Also, don't use a hammer with a loose head or one with a crack in the handle. When using such a hammer, you may throw the head off the handle and injure somebody. Beyond that, some hammers just aren't correctly designed or assembled. These include most of the off-brand or "bargain" hammers. Buy the best-quality hammer you can find. Choose one that feels balanced and comfortable in your hand.

Pulling Nails—Don't pull a nail the way most people try to do it. The standard method of hooking the claws under the nailhead and using the hammer head as a rocker to pull the nail works fine for small nails. For large nails, drive the hammer claws onto the shank of the nail at the wood surface. Then use the hammer handle as a lever to bend the nail over sideways. You'll find that you've withdrawn about an inch of nail. Hitch the hammer loose, drive the claws onto the shank of the nail again, and bend it over again. Repeat this process until the nail is withdrawn.

Knots and Old Wood—Sometimes a piece of wood won't take a nail. This often happens when working with existing framing in older houses. The wood has become rock-hard over the years. Or, you may occasionally have to drive a nail near or through a knot. In either of these cases, substitute a fluted, hardened concrete nail for an ordinary one. These nails are unbendable and can be driven through almost anything.

When using concrete nails, wear safety glasses, a long-sleeve shirt and gloves. Hardened concrete nails will sometimes chip, or chip the hammerhead, and the fragment will have considerable velocity. This doesn't happen often, but when it does, you can be injured. Also, don't use your favorite hammer for this work.

Another option for hard-to-nail pieces is to drill a pilot hole and insert the correct-size flat-head wood screw.

NAIL SIZES AND AMOUNTS

Penny Size	Length	Number Per Pound
2d	1"	
Common		876
Box		1,010
Finish		1,351
3d	1-1/4"	
Common		568
Box		635
Finish		807
4d	1-1/2"	
Common		316
Box		473
Finish		548
5d	1-3/4"	
Common		271
Box		406
Finish		500
6d	2"	
Common		181
Box		236
Finish		309
7d	2-1/4"	
Common		161
Box		210
Finish		238
8d	2-1/2"	
Common		106
Box		145
Finish		189
9d	2-3/4"	
Common		96
Box		132
Finish		172
10d	3"	
Common		69
Box		121
Finish		132
12d	3-1/4"	
Common		64
Box		94
Finish		113
	3-1/2"	
Common		49
Box		71
Finish		90

Note: Nail lengths are designated by *penny size (d).* Use a nail three times as long as the thickness of the top board you're nailing.

WINDOW AND DOOR FRAMING

The horizontal load-bearing member at the top of the window or door opening is called a *header*. The horizontal member at the bottom of a window opening is called a *sill*. There are no horizontal framing members at the bottom of a door opening.

Vertical members for window and door openings consist of *full studs* that run from bottom plate to top plate on each side of the opening. *Jackstuds* are partial studs that support the ends of the window or door header. See drawing on page 87. For extremely large headers, building codes may require two, three or even four jackstuds supporting each end of a header.

The chart on page 94 shows rough-opening sizes for most standard doors and windows. For sizes not shown, call a window or door supplier for the information.

Once stud center lines are marked on the top and bottom plates, mark the exact locations of window and door rough openings. Adjust the locations—but not the rough-opening sizes—if you can, to line up with previously marked stud spacings. To the outside of the rough-opening marks, mark positions of full studs and jackstuds. Label outside-stud positions with an X for *full stud*, and inside-stud positions with a J, for *jackstud*. Nail in the full studs first.

Installing Jackstuds—The jackstuds holding a header must bear fully on the header and on the bottom plate or floor. Don't just measure one side of the opening and cut both jackstuds to the same length. If the floor slopes, the header will slope. To determine correct length, use a level to see if the floor slopes, and mark the rough-opening height at the high side of the opening.

Then use a level—and a length of straight lumber if necessary—to transfer the header height to the opposite side of the opening, as shown in the photo above right. Then measure down to get jackstud lengths. When the jackstuds are cut, mark them for location so you don't mix them up.

There are two methods of installing jackstuds. In the first method, jackstuds rest on top of the bottom plate. After the jackstuds are installed, the sections of plate within door openings are cut out with a handsaw. See *Method 1,* at right.

An alternate method is often used

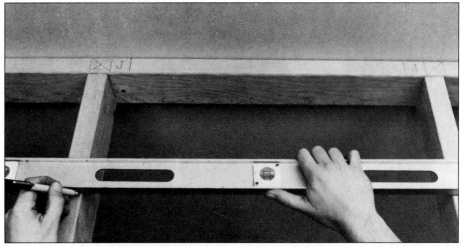

Don't measure from floor or ceiling to set header in openings unless they're known to be level. Find high side of opening at floor, measure and mark. Use level to transfer to other side. Measure jackstud lengths from marks.

for door openings. The wall is framed and the bottom plate is cut out at the door opening *before* the jackstuds and headers are installed. The jackstuds are then cut and installed so they rest directly on the subfloor. This method provides an uninterrupted surface for mounting the door jamb and makes a slightly stronger assembly. See *Method 2,* below right.

Always run a continuous plate across door openings, then cut out the section after the wall is framed and the bottom plates are attached to the subfloor. Do not drive nails into the plate within the door openings—the plate sections will be harder to

After framing is complete, cut out bottom plate at door openings. This preserves alignment across opening and helps prevent mistakes during framing.

remove. If you leave out sections of plate when framing the wall, you may save some material and time cutting the plates. But this can result in problems with wall alignment on opposite sides of the opening. A warped open-

INSTALLING JACKSTUDS

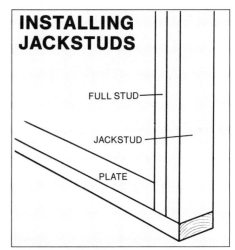

FULL STUD

JACKSTUD

PLATE

Method 1: Jackstuds are installed before plate is cut out at door opening.

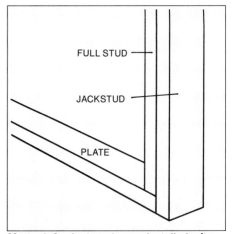

FULL STUD

JACKSTUD

PLATE

Method 2: Jackstuds are installed after plate is cut out at door opening.

INSTALLING A SILL

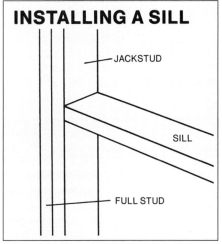

Method 1: Toenail sill between jackstuds in opening. This is weakest assembly.

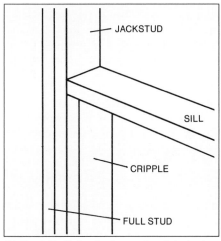

Method 2: Cut cripples and nail to jackstuds to support sill.

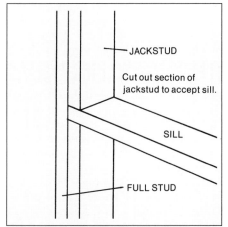

Method 3: Cut slot in jackstud to accept sill. Toenail sill into full stud behind.

HEADER DETAIL

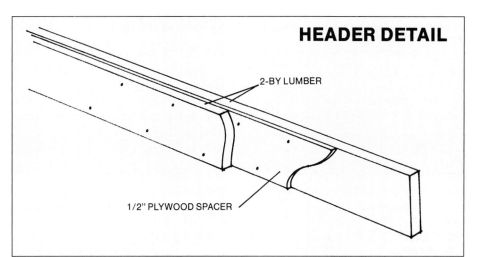

Instead of using 4-inch lumber for a header, nail two pieces of 2-inch lumber together, with 1/2-inch plywood spacer.

ing is harder to fix than a warped door.

Installing a Sill—There are three ways to install a sill at a window opening, as shown in the drawing above. As mentioned earlier, the sill is the horizontal framing member at the bottom of the rough-window opening.

Method 1 in the top drawing is the weakest assembly. The sill is cut to fit between the jackstuds and toenailed in place. *Method 2* requires cutting two *cripples* that are nailed alongside the jackstuds, as shown. The sill rests on the ends of the cripples.

Just as sturdy and more economical is *Method 3*. Before nailing in each jackstud, measure down from the top of the jackstud to the bottom of the rough opening and mark. Make a cut at the mark and another cut 1-1/2 inches below it. Nail the lower segments of the jackstuds to adjacent full studs, attach the sill, then nail in upper segments of the jackstuds. Then nail in the header.

Installing Headers—Headers for openings in 2x4 bearing walls are normally constructed of two pieces of 2-by lumber on edge with a 1/2-inch plywood spacer, or of 4-by lumber on edge. Headers for openings in 2x6 frame walls are usually three pieces of 2-by lumber with two 1/2-inch plywood spacers, or of solid 6-by lumber on edge. Codes require that a header meet the same load requirements as a structural beam. This means the header must be large enough to bear the weight of all structural members above it.

The following rule of thumb usually applies, as long as the header does not support any unusual loads, such as those described below. The header height in inches (nominal) should equal the width of the opening in feet, plus 2 inches. In other words, a 4-foot opening usually requires a 4x6 header, or two 2x6s with a 1/2-inch plywood spacer. An opening up to 6 feet would require a 4x8 or two 2x8s

with a 1/2-inch plywood spacer. Local codes may vary from this rule, so check header sizes with the building department before you start.

An example of an unusual load on a header would be a beam end resting on the header. The effect would be to add a large additional load to the normal load that the header would carry. Try to avoid complicated situations like this. If you're stuck with one, talk it over with a building official or, if necessary, a structural engineer.

Installing Cripples—Vertical members, called *cripples,* usually must be installed between the header and the top plate on window and door openings, and between the sill and bottom plate at window openings. Cripples take the place of studs. They distribute the load on a bearing wall onto headers across the openings. Cripples under windows provide nailing for finish materials.

In non-bearing walls, cripples are usually not needed if the vertical distance between the header and the top plate is less than 5 inches. Check local building codes. For larger spaces and in bearing walls, cut cripples to fit and nail them to correspond with the stud spacing on either side of the opening. This keeps the spacing consistent for the installation of finish-wall material.

Blocking—After you've framed the wall, inspect the framing for any places where the edges of drywall sheets or other finish material will be unsupported. Install blocks between studs to support edges and provide backing for nailing. Also make sure you have full backing for nailing where you plan to install moldings or trim.

If possible, measure actual door or window unit or get exact rough-in dimensions from supplier or manufacturer's literature. Prehung doors and aluminum-frame doors and windows come in standard sizes, so dimensions given here can be used for them. Wood-frame windows and sliding doors can vary by several inches in both dimensions, so consult supplier or manufacturer in every case.

Interior Swing Doors (No Threshold)

Door Opening	Rough Opening
2'-4"x6'-8"	2'-7"x6'-10"
2'-6"x6'-8"	2'-9"x6'-10"
2'-8"x6'-8"	2'-11"x6'-10"
2'-10"x6'-8"	3'-1"x6'-10"
3'-0"x6'-8"	3'-3"x6'-10"

Exterior Swing Doors (1" Threshold)

Door Opening	Rough Opening[1]
2'-8" single	2'-10-1/2"x6'-10"
3'-0" single	3'-2-1/2"x6'-10"
3'-6" single	3'-8-1/2"x6'-10"
5'-4" double	5'-7-1/2"x6'-10"
6'-0" double	6'-3-1/2"x6'-10"

[1]Based on standard 2-1/8" case molding or wider.

Aluminum-Frame Sliding-Glass Doors

Door Opening	Rough Opening
5'-0"x6'-8"	5'-1"x6'-9"
6'-0"x6'-8"	6'-1"x6'-9"
8'-0"x6'-8"	8'-1"x6'-9"

Aluminum-Frame Windows

Window	Rough Opening
2'-0"x2'-0"	2'-1"x2'-1"
2'-0"x3'-0"	2'-1"x3'-1"
2'-0"x4'-0"	2'-1"x4'-1"
2'-0"x5'-0"	2'-1"x5'-1"
2'-0"x6'-0"	2'-1"x6'-1"
3'-0"x2'-0"	3'-1"x2'-1"
3'-0"x3'-0"	3'-1"x3'-1"
3'-0"x4'-0"	3'-1"x4'-1"
3'-0"x5'-0"	3'-1"x5'-1"
3'-0"x6'-0"	3'-1"x6'-1"
4'-0"x2'-0"	4'-1"x2'-1"
4'-0"x3'-0"	4'-1"x3'-1"
4'-0"x4'-0"	4'-1"x4'-1"
4'-0"x5'-0"	4'-1"x5'-1"
4'-0"x6'-0"	4'-1"x6'-1"
5'-0"x2'-0"	5'-1"x2'-1-1/4"
5'-0"x3'-0"	5'-1"x3'-1-1/4"
5'-0"x4'-0"	5'-1"x4'-1-1/4"
5'-0"x5'-0"	5'-1"x5'-1-1/4"
5'-0"x6'-0"	5'-1"x6'-1-1/4"
6'-0"x2'-0"	6'-1"x2'-1-1/2"
6'-0"x3'-0"	6'-1"x3'-1-1/2"
6'-0"x4'-0"	6'-1"x4'-1-1/2"
6'-0"x5'-0"	6'-1"x5'-1-1/2"
6'-0"x6'-0"	6'-1"x6'-1-1/2"

DRYWALL INSTALLATION

Drywall, also called *gypsum board* or *Sheetrock,* has almost completely replaced lath and plaster as a residential-wall surface. Drywall consists of a layer of gypsum plaster between two layers of heavy paper. It's convenient for the do-it-yourselfer, because it's much easier to work with than lath and plaster.

Drywall is available in several types and sizes, depending on use. Most useful to the do-it-yourselfer is standard 1/2-inch-thick drywall in 4x8' sheets. Drywall also comes in 5/8-inch-thick sheets. 3/8-inch drywall is useful for resurfacing. Sheets also come in 12- and 16-foot lengths for special applications, but they are more difficult to work with and should be avoided if 8-foot sheets will suffice. The long sides of each sheet are tapered inward slightly so the drywall joints can be taped and finished without the seam showing.

MOISTURE-RESISTANT DRYWALL

A bathroom environment is hard on standard drywall. The main problem is water exposure, ranging from mild around the lavatory to severe over tubs and in the shower. Standard drywall can disintegrate quickly, even under a water-resistant covering such as ceramic tile. When the drywall disintegrates, the water-resistant covering goes with it. A special *moisture-resistant* or *water-resistant* drywall is used in water-prone areas. It is identified by light-blue or green coloring of the face paper. The name is often shortened to *MR* or *WR board.*

MR board should be installed on walls behind all plumbing fixtures, attached or freestanding. This includes lavatory and toilet, and the entire tub or shower enclosure, including ceiling. In smaller bathrooms, it won't cost much more to use MR board for the entire room. This makes sense because small bathrooms are more susceptible to steam and moisture condensation.

MR board can be cut and fitted like standard drywall, but there are some differences. All cut edges should be coated with special sealer—available from the drywall supplier—to preserve water resistance. All nails should be rustproof, not just rust-resistant. Hot-dipped galvanized nails are good. Drive nails just flush with the surface, and coat with the sealer. Seams must be covered with special materials, not regular joint compound and tape. Consult the supplier.

BACKER BOARD FOR TILE

In some parts of the country you can buy special backer board for use under ceramic tile. This material is a lightweight concrete product, installed with 1-1/2-inch galvanized roofing nails, directly over the wall framing. As with MR board, special joint and edge treatment is required. Because installation details vary, consult the supplier for specifics.

Because backer board is a concrete product, you should use a cement-base adhesive to apply the tile. You may need to apply a prime coat of adhesive or special primer recommended by the manufacturer.

INSTALLING DRYWALL

Drywall sheets come in pairs with the finish sides facing in. Sheets are held together with heavy paper tapes on the 4-foot ends. Because these pairs are heavy, you may want to pull the tape off the edges so you can move individual sheets to the work area. If you're buying much drywall, choose a supplier who will deliver and stack it near the work area, as long as the price is reasonably competitive.

Stack drywall against a wall, close to vertical to prevent warping. Do not stack it flat on the floor. Drywall is heavy. Do not put more than 8 or 10 sheets in one stack. Any more than this can weaken or collapse a floor or push a wall out of plumb. On wood floors, make sure the bases of stacks run across the floor joists, not parallel to them. Locate stacks convenient to the work area, but not where they will be in the way.

Cutting and Trimming—Most cuts in drywall can be made with a utility knife rather than a saw. A straightedge or a 4-foot level can be used as a guide, or cuts can be made freehand to a pencil line.

To make a crosswise cut on a sheet of drywall, measure and mark the sheet right on the stack. Then lock the straightedge on the marks with your foot at the bottom and your hand on the top, to guide the knife blade for the cut. To make lengthwise cuts, position the straightedge on the marks

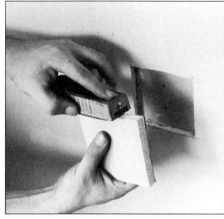

Drywall is easily trimmed with Surform tool. It works like a cheese grater. Several different models are made for various applications. Model shown, shaped like small block plane, is handiest for drywall and trim work.

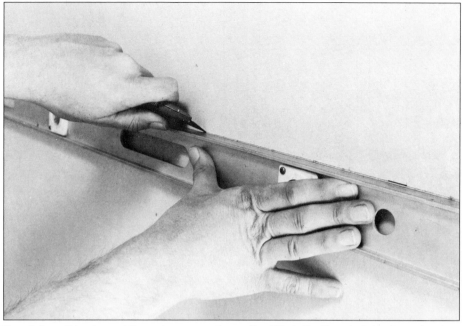

To cut drywall to size, cut through paper on face with utility knife. Use straightedge or level as a guide. Snap core, using back paper as hinge.

and have a helper hold one end while you cut.

After you make the cut on the front side of the sheet, pull the sheet away from the stack. Then hit the back side of the sheet with the base of your fist, or with a hammer handle, directly behind the cut. The core material will fracture, and the sheet will hinge neatly on the back paper. Be ready for it—the core breaks easily and the sections can get away from you and tear the backing paper or fall on the floor, damaging the sheet. Cut the backing paper along the fold, and the two pieces will come apart.

For narrow strips, cut the paper on both sides of the sheet and then break the core. If you want to keep the narrow strip, lay the sheet down on the floor with a length of rope or extension cord under the cut line. Push down on the strip with a length of wood to break the narrow strip cleanly. If you want the bigger piece and don't care what happens to the narrow strip, cut both sides and use your fingers to break off the narrow strip a foot or two at a time.

To trim a piece of drywall to fit, use a utility knife, or a *Surform tool.* This is a rasplike tool that is similar in principle to a cheese grater. Most useful for drywall and trim work is the palm-sized model, shaped like a small block plane. It will easily smooth ragged edges with a few strokes. The perforated cutting plates on Surform tools are replaceable.

To cut a hole in drywall for a projecting obstacle, such as a pipe stub or

electrical box, use a tape measure to locate the obstacle in relation to the floor and the last sheet of drywall you hung. Transfer the measurements to the drywall sheet, measuring in from two edges. Mark the outline of the obstacle. Or rub some colored chalk from your chalk line on the obstacle and place the drywall in position against the obstacle. Lightly tap the drywall to transfer the outline of the obstacle on the back side of the drywall.

Cut the marked side with a utility knife. Drive a nail at each corner of the cutout and cut from nail hole to nail hole on the other side. Make sure the cuts are deep. Then tap the piece out from the front with a hammer. For circular cuts you can use a *keyhole saw.* This is a saw with a replaceable, pointed blade.

Ceiling Installation—Because the edges of ceiling drywall should be supported by edges of drywall on the walls, hang the ceiling drywall first. Make sure edges at corners butt against the wall framing.

Ceilings are the biggest challenge you'll face in working with drywall. You'll need at least one helper to hang full sheets easily.

To hang more than a sheet or two, construct a *T-bar* from 2x4s for the helper to use in positioning the drywall. The vertical leg should be slightly longer than the distance from

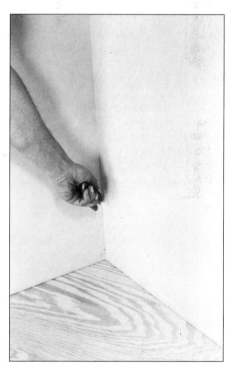

Slice through back paper to complete cut.

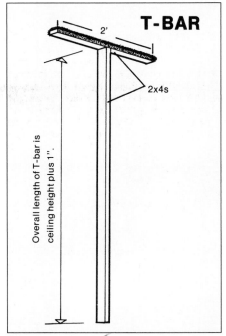

T-bar is used to pin drywall against ceiling while nailing. Carpet scrap on top of bar protects drywall from dents and scratches.

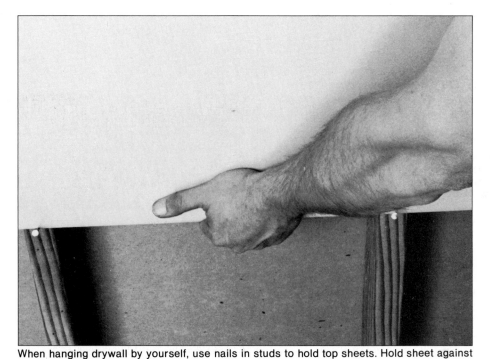

When hanging drywall by yourself, use nails in studs to hold top sheets. Hold sheet against studs until it's attached to the wall with several nails. Make sure hammer and nails are within reach before setting sheet up on nails, so sheet doesn't fall over on you when you bend to pick up hammer and nails.

floor to ceiling, minus 1-1/2 inches to allow for the thickness of the crossbar. The 2-foot crossbar should be centered on top of the vertical leg, as shown in the drawing above, and securely nailed on. Scrap carpet can be used to pad the crossbar to avoid damage to the drywall.

To hang ceiling drywall, carry the sheet to its approximate location. Then lift the sheet and balance it on your head while your helper positions the T-bar. Lift the drywall with the T-bar and set it loosely against the ceiling framing, bracing the T-bar to hold it there. Use a pry bar or hammer to make any final adjustments in the position of the sheet. Then the helper can pin the sheet solidly into position by kicking in the bottom of the vertical leg of the T-bar.

While the helper holds the T-bar to make sure the sheet stays in position, nail the sheet to the ceiling. If the ceiling is out of reach, rig a plank on two boxes or sawhorses. Position the plank so the top of your head is only 2 or 3 inches below the ceiling joists. This makes nailing easier, though nailing over your head is never really easy.

Wall Installation—Drywall on a wall can be hung by one person. But a helper makes work go more quickly. One person can cut and carry the dry-

wall to the location and tack it in place while the other does the finish nailing.

Drywall on walls is usually hung with the long dimension—and the tapered edges—horizontal. For small spaces, hang drywall whatever way produces the least amount of cutting and seams to be taped. Always start at the top of the wall with full sheets. Then fill in the rest of the wall, staggering the vertical joints.

Working alone, measure down 4 feet from the ceiling and drive three or four 8d nails into the studs. Angle the nails upward slightly to form a perch for the drywall. Then rest the sheet on the nails. Make sure you have your hammer and nails within reaching distance, because you'll have to hold the drywall in position once it's on the nails. Make sure that both ends or sides of the sheet are centered over a stud, and the top is butted tightly against the ceiling. Then drive a few nails in the top of the sheet to hold it in place, and do the rest of the nailing. Pull the 8d nails out of the studs and hang the next sheet.

Hang all of the top sheets in the room before starting the bottom ones. Position the first of the lower sheets. To raise a lower sheet into position below the upper sheet, slip the straight end of a flat pry bar or the

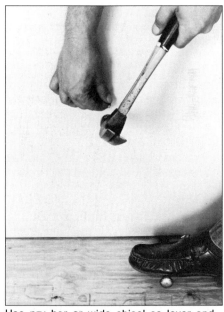

Use pry bar or wide chisel as lever and wood block as fulcrum to lift lower sheet of drywall into place for nailing.

blade of a chisel under the edge of the sheet. Then place a wood block under the pry bar or chisel for a fulcrum. Step on the outer end of the pry bar with one foot until the lower sheet butts tightly against the upper one. Hold the sheet in place with the pry bar and drive a few nails into the top of the sheet to hold it in place. Do not exert so much pressure on the pry bar with your foot that you crush the edge of the drywall sheet.

Drywall Nailing—Space nails 6 to 7 inches apart along all framing members. The best nails to use are 1-1/4 inch annular-ring nails, especially on ceilings. Nails should be rustproof, and have the correct heads for drywall. If you have difficulty getting the drywall to pull tight to the framing, drive nails in pairs, an inch or so apart.

Drive each nail so that the hammer head makes a slight dent in the drywall surface, but not enough to break the paper coating or the gypsum core. The dent provides a recess for the joint compound that will cover the nailhead.

When nailing both sides of a drywall joint, place nails opposite each other, on each side of the joint. If you stagger nails on adjoining sheets, you can introduce a waviness that will make joint finishing much more difficult.

FINISHING DRYWALL

Finishing drywall involves two operations, taping joints and covering nailheads. Tools required are a 6-inch taping knife, a 12-inch or 14-inch taping knife, and a *hawk* or pan to hold a working supply of compound. A hawk is a flat-blade tool with a handle on the bottom, in the center. Or, you can use a long, rectangular pan for the joint compound. Hawks and pans are available at drywall suppliers or building-supply stores. Or, you can use a deep, rectangular bread pan. The pan or hawk makes joint compound easier to work with, and helps keep compound in the bucket from getting contaminated with bits of dried compound on the knife.

Stiff scrapers or putty knives should not be used in place of taping knives. Drywall finishing requires a flexible blade with a straight edge and sides.

Drywall reinforcing tape and *joint compound* are available at drywall suppliers, home-improvement centers and paint stores. Premixed joint compound is much more convenient to work with than the dry powdered kind and costs about the same. Reinforcing tape is a roll of heavy, non-adhesive paper, usually perforated with tiny holes so joint compound will key into it.

As you're working, joint compound may squeeze out to the ends of the blade and drop off. To minimize this,

periodically clean compound from the ends of the knife blade. If any compound falls on the floor, wipe it up immediately and dispose of it. If you don't, someone may slip on it or track it through the rest of the house. Don't use your taping knives to pick up compound from the floor, and don't reuse the dropped joint compound. The knives will get nicked, and you'll pick up debris that will ruin the work.

Filling Nail Dimples—To get the feel of the tools, fill the nailhead dimples first. Use the 6-inch knife and hawk or pan. Put a small amount of joint compound on the edge of the knife, toward the center of the blade. Cover the nail dimple with a thick coat of compound. Make a second pass with the knife at right angles to the first to skim off excess compound. Use just enough pressure to level the joint compound. As you cover successive nail dimples, you'll develop a rhythm that will make the work move along rapidly.

If your knife touches a nailhead while you're filling nail dimples, you'll feel it. Drive the nail a bit deeper with a hammer and reapply the compound. Don't bother to clean the joint compound out of the nail dimple to do this—let it splatter. Drywall finishing is not a neat process.

Taping Joints—During the taping and finishing process, keep taping

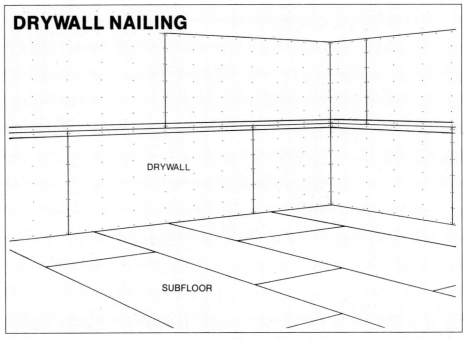

Shown is typical drywall installation on wall. It's usually easiest to run sheets horizontally. Nails are spaced 6 to 7 inches apart and driven in pairs at joints.

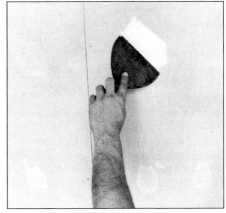

Fill nail dimples by applying heavy coat of joint compound. Strike off level at right angles. Second application may be needed to get level surface.

knives clean and joint compound uncontaminated. Dry bits of compound on the knife make it difficult to get a smooth finish surface. The same is true if debris or bits of dry compound get into the compound you're working with. If you have excess compound on the knife or hawk after finishing a section of drywall, don't put it back in the container with the fresh compound. Dispose of it.

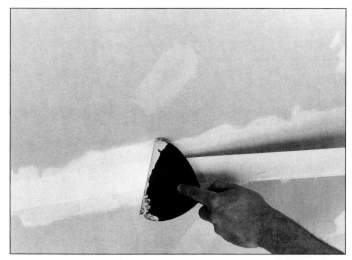

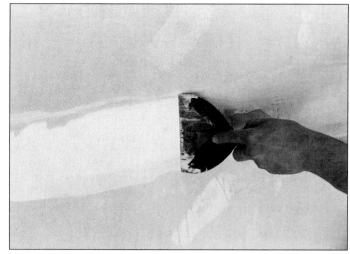

1. Apply reinforcing tape in a layer of joint compound, without causing bubbles or wrinkles. Immediately cover tape with another thin layer of joint compound.

2. After first coat with reinforcing tape is dry, apply second coat with 6-inch taping knife.

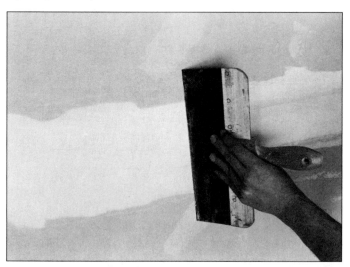

3. Apply top coat smoothly with 12-inch or 14-inch taping knife. Second top coat may be needed after first has dried, to compensate for shrinkage as joint compound dries.

4. Sand off any irregularities without roughing up exposed surface paper. Accidentally roughed-up paper should be skim-coated with joint compound and sanded level after drying.

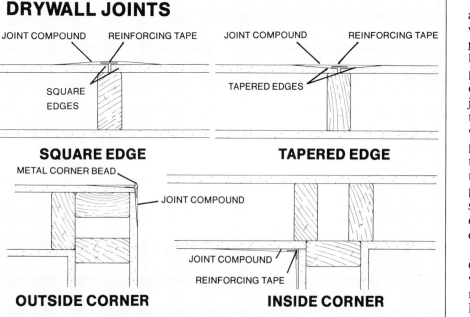

DRYWALL JOINTS

JOINT COMPOUND   REINFORCING TAPE

SQUARE EDGES

SQUARE EDGE

JOINT COMPOUND   REINFORCING TAPE

TAPERED EDGES

TAPERED EDGE

METAL CORNER BEAD

JOINT COMPOUND

OUTSIDE CORNER

JOINT COMPOUND

REINFORCING TAPE

INSIDE CORNER

For joints where the drywall edges are tapered, butter the joint liberally with joint compound. The object is to get a layer of compound in which to bed the tape, so be generous. Tear a piece of tape from the roll the length of the joint. Starting at one end of the joint, lightly embed the end of this tape in the compound. Cover the end with a small amount of joint compound. Then run the tape knife down the joint, lightly sticking the tape in the compound. Don't apply too much pressure, or the tape may slide or stretch. If the tape drifts off the joint or wrinkles, pull it loose and start over.

In dry climates, the tape may be too dry to stick properly. If so, the tape will begin to shrink and pucker a few minutes after it's applied to the joint. If this happens, remove the tape. Dip it into a bucket of water and remove excess compound before reapplying. Moisten successive lengths of tape before using them.

After the reinforcing tape is in place and before the bed coat dries, apply a thin, even coat of joint compound over the tape. Start in the middle of the joint and work toward each end. If the tape tends to slide out of position, hold it in place with your thumbnail while applying compound.

When the first coat of joint compound is dry, sand off any lumps or ridges with 120- to 180-grit sandpaper. Use a sanding block, or wrap the paper around a short piece of 1x2. If you have very much sanding to do, you'll save time if you use a *pole sander*. This tool looks somewhat like a sponge mop, except it has a pivoting head to which the sandpaper is attached. A pole sander is especially useful for sanding ceiling joints. Special sandpaper strips are available for the sander.

Voids or low spots in the joint compound can be filled with the second coat. Do not let the sandpaper cut into the reinforcing tape.

When all joints are sanded, apply a second coat of joint compound. Use the 6-inch knife to skim on a thin film of compound down the middle of the joint. Clean off the knife, then skim off any compound deposited outside the tapered area. Be careful not to remove compound inside the tapered area. See photo on page 98. Don't try to smooth out small ridges of compound on the tape when you're doing this. They can be sanded later.

When the second coat is dry, sand again. When sanding, carefully remove any ridges or high spots where the taper meets the flat drywall surface. Then use the 14-inch knife to skim a thin, even coat of compound over the joint. See photo on page 98. Run the knife along the full length of the joint, in one even, smooth pass. This should be the final coat, so take your time. The compound should go on smooth and level—any irregularities will have to be completely sanded out.

After the third coat is dry and sanded, check with a straightedge to see if the joint is completely level with the rest of the wall. If it isn't, add a fourth coat, using the 14-inch knife. Sand any irregularities.

Joints with Square Edges—Not all drywall joints have tapered edges adjacent to them. Joints at the 4-foot ends of sheets and joints between cut pieces will have square edges instead of tapered ones. Because the adjoining drywall edges aren't tapered, the reinforcing tape and drywall compound will be higher than the surrounding surface. You'll need to taper joint compound gradually away from the taped joint to hide this change in level.

Apply reinforcing tape and cover the same as for tapered-edge joints, page 98. Before applying the third coat, hold a straightedge alongside the edge of your widest tape knife. You'll find that the edge will probably have a slight bow to it. Use the side that most closely resembles the curve shown in the drawing on page 98. Gently warp the blade until it approximates the curve by putting fingers on one side of the blade and thumb on the other. Check frequently while you're working to make sure the curve is still there. The curve allows you to apply the third coat, or fourth coat if needed, over the tape and joint compound that beds it. Pay particular attention to these square-edge joints when finish sanding. Sanding across the joint helps smooth out any irregularities.

Finishing Corners—Taping and finishing corners is one of the most difficult and time-consuming parts of drywall finishing. There are special tools available for doing corners, but these are probably not worth the investment if you're doing one room or less. These tools also take getting used to.

There is an easy, though slow, way to finish corners so they come out looking as good as those done with specialized tools. The basic tool is a standard or somewhat modified 6-inch taping knife. The working edge of a standard knife is straight. On most taping knives, at least one of the sides will have a straight section at least 1 inch long. If yours doesn't, file or grind one side of the blade to provide a straight edge slightly less than 90° to the working edge.

If you file straight edges on both sides of the blade, it's helpful to have one that's just slightly under 90°, and the other with an angle between 60° and 75°. The second angle is useful for three-way corners, such as where two walls meet the ceiling.

Apply a bedding coat of joint compound to both sides of the corner.

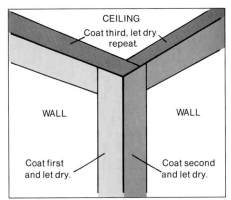

CEILING
Coat third, let dry repeat.

WALL

WALL

Coat first and let dry.

Coat second and let dry.

Where two walls and ceiling meet, use taping sequence shown here. Coat all corners with joint compound. Fold tape and apply to all three corners. Apply first skim coat to all surfaces, using sequence shown. When compound dries, sand lightly and repeat sequence.

Tear off a length of reinforcing tape to fit. You'll find an indented line down the middle of the reinforcing tape. Crease tape along the line so it forms a right angle. Be careful not to cut your fingers on tape edges while creasing it. Pat the tape lightly into the bed of joint compound. Use the 6-inch knife to apply a skim coat of compound to one side of the tape along the corner—side 1.

After a minute or two, go over side 1 with the tape knife. Apply enough pressure to remove the skim coat down to the reinforcing tape. This beds the tape solidly on that side. Don't disturb the reinforcing tape, or rough it up while doing this.

Before compound on side 1 dries, apply a skim coat to side 2. Position tape knife so the straight section on the side of the blade is riding on side 1. This prevents compound from building up a bead on side 1.

Let this coat dry thoroughly and sand off any irregularities. Then skim-coat side 1, the same way as side 2. Let dry, sand and skim coat side 2 again. Repeat process, adding skim coats to alternate sides of corner, letting coats dry and sanding them until the corner is done.

This technique produces perfect corners if you observe these precautions: Don't try to work on both sides of the corner at the same time. Sand off any ridges on both sides before you apply another coat of compound to either side. Where two walls and a ceiling meet, handle it as if you had a corner with three sides instead of two. The drawing above shows the correct taping sequence.

REPAIRING DRYWALL

Inspect existing drywall for damage and deterioration. If the paper surface is scraped or otherwise damaged, clean off any loose material. Then restore the surface with one or more skim coats of joint compound.

If the gypsum core is broken or disintegrating from water damage, remove damaged drywall and inspect the framing, and plumbing, if any. Fix any plumbing leaks and repair framing, if necessary. Put in a new section of drywall. If you have to remove drywall to gain access to plumbing or wiring, the following removal and replacement method works well.

First, locate the studs adjoining the area to be removed. To do this, remove a small section of the damaged area. Slide the end of a tape measure through the holes to locate the studs. If you'll be reusing the piece you take out, use a hammer and small nail to probe for the studs. Drive the nail through the drywall where you suspect a stud might be. If you don't find the stud, move about an inch left or right and try again. Don't move the nail more than 1-1/2 inches at a time, or you might skip over the stud.

After you've found adjoining studs, mark drywall along the stud center lines on either side of the damaged area. Use a framing square to mark perpendicular lines across the top and bottom of the area to be removed. This will make it easier to cut and fit

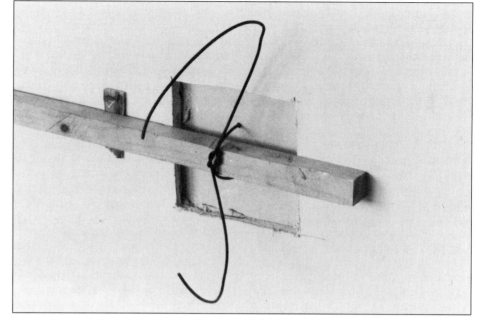

To repair small hole in drywall, cut out square. Use joint compound to glue in drywall backer square, holding in place with wire and stick until dry. Glue in face patch. Apply reinforcing tape on all four edges of patch. Apply joint compound over entire patch with wide knife.

replacement drywall. To remove drywall, score along the lines with a utility knife and a straightedge until you've cut through the drywall.

You may hit one or more nails with the knife as you work. As you find nails, chip the old joint compound off the nailheads. Drive the old nails into the stud with a pin punch or nail set, or pull them out. If you can't make the cuts along the middle of a stud, cut the drywall flush to the side of the stud that faces the work area. Then nail a length of 2x4 to the side of the stud to provide a nailing surface when you replace the drywall.

To save the cutout piece of drywall, gently pry it out with a chisel. Make sure you've cut completely through the paper backing or it will tear off when you remove the piece. If you're using new drywall for a patch, use the utility knife to smooth any rough edges around the cutout area.

To replace the piece you removed, cut a piece of new drywall to fit and insert it, or reinsert the old piece. Nail it in place. Then tape and finish the joints as described for square-edge joints on page 99.

To repair small holes in drywall, you can enlarge the hole to the nearest adjacent studs and nail in a patch, as shown in the drawing at left, or you can use the following method: Cut out the hole to an approximate square. Then cut a square backer of drywall

with sides that measure a little less than the diagonal measurement of the hole.

Punch two small holes close together in the middle of the backer, and loop a length of wire through the holes. Apply a coat of joint compound around the edges of the backer where it will contact the backside of the surrounding drywall. Insert the backer through the hole, and pull it into place with the wires. Then place a stick across the hole. Twist the wires around the stick to hold the backer in place while the joint compound dries.

Cut off the wires after the joint compound has dried and glued the backer in place. Cut a patch a little smaller than the hole. Glue this patch to the backer with joint compound. When this has dried, you can finish the patch.

REPAIRING PLASTER

Drywall materials and techniques can be used to repair plaster walls. First, remove all loose plaster, no matter how much of it there is. Don't try to cover over a disintegrating plaster wall—tear it all out if you have to.

If only the finish coat of plaster has loosened or been damaged, and the plaster undercoats and lath are still sound, one or more skim coats of drywall-joint compound will restore it. Add sand or fine sawdust to the compound to match the texture.

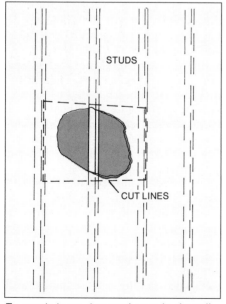

To repair large damaged area in drywall, cut back to framing members on both sides so you can nail in a patch.

Plaster that has loosened from the lath or deteriorated all the way through should be removed. Leave the lath and surrounding sound plaster in place. See *Drywall and Plaster Removal*, page 79. Then cut a piece of drywall to the size and shape of the opening and nail it to the studs, right over the lath. Edges of the drywall patch don't need to be supported by studs because the lath will hold them in place.

The patch does not have to be exactly the same thickness as the existing plaster, because it only forms a base for a skim coat of joint compound. Because plaster is often wavy, a flush patch can sometimes present problems at the edges. The patch should be about 1/16 inch lower than the surrounding plaster. If the plaster is thick, you may have to shim out the drywall patch, or even use two layers of drywall to get fairly close to the plaster surface.

After the drywall patch is in place, pack joint compound into joints so that it *keys* the plaster and the drywall patch together, locking both to the lath. Keying happens when the joint compound squeezes out behind the joint and hardens. Strike off this keying application flush and let dry. Tape the edges of the patch. Finish with one or more skim coats, feathering out onto the plaster at the edges.

MATCHING TEXTURES

You may have to match an existing textured wall finish after patching and repairs. Or you may decide to change the texture in the entire room. You can either buy a prepared texturing product, or you can mix your own. Textured paints work well, but the surface you're coating must be even and level. Textured paint will only hide small imperfections and won't make dissimilar materials match very well.

Mix Your Own—To mix your own wall texturing, start with drywall joint compound and thin to a consistency between mayonnaise and pancake batter. Instead of water, use liquid synthetic latex, available at ceramic-tile suppliers. Or use half water and half cheap latex paint. Prepare a thick mix for heavy textures, and a thinner mix for finer textures.

You can add a variety of materials to modify the texture of the basic smooth mix. For a medium texture, use No. 30 silica sand, available at masonry suppliers, or fine sawdust. For a coarse texture, you can use kitty litter. Do not use the kind with disinfectant additives. Many of these materials will take up moisture from the texturing mix, so you may have to add water.

The method of application also influences texture. A trowel, sponge or paint brush are often used. To cover large areas quickly, try one of the large, soft-bristle brushes used for applying wallpaper paste, or an ordinary broom. Anything at all can be used, from bare hands to a push broom. Experiment on a scrap piece of drywall or plywood until you find a mix and an application technique that matches surrounding walls, or one that produces a texture you like. Start and finish texturing strokes in the unfinished area, and then cover with succeeding strokes.

You may have to match a finish called *skip texturing*. Skip texturing is done by mixing several handfuls of No. 30 silica sand into a gallon of the basic smooth mix and applying the mixture with a 14-inch taping knife. The compound is applied in a quick skimming motion, with the knife blade almost parallel to the wall surface. This deposits compound in small, flat blotches across the surface of the wall. There should be very little material on the knife when doing this texture.

Wire whisk borrowed from kitchen works perfectly for mixing texture coatings. Wash promptly after use.

7

Floors

Changes in floor level, such as for this tiled step-up tub platform, require strong, rigid framing. Subfloor must be able to support weight of heavy floor materials, such as tile. *Photo courtesy of American Olean Tile Co.*

The first part of this chapter covers modifying and repairing existing floors. The second part deals with installing popular finish-floor materials.

The work to be done before installing a finish floor will depend on the type and condition of the existing subfloor and the type of finish-floor material you're installing. If you haven't yet chosen a finish-floor material, see pages 33-36.

Resilient floor coverings are popular for bathrooms. Installation procedures for resilient floors start on page 106. Instructions for wood floors start on page 113. Ceramic tile installation is covered in its own chapter, starting on page 152. Before you start reworking the subfloor, read the section on the finish-floor material you've chosen, then the section at right on floor repair and preparation. You can then

determine the type and amount of preparation required for the material you've chosen.

FLOOR REPAIR

A new finish floor can often be put down over an existing finish floor in good condition. But most old bathroom floors are so badly chewed up, rotted or otherwise deteriorated, that major repairs are needed. A sound floor is crucial to a successful remodeling job. Even on new work, good floor preparation is essential.

Wood-frame floors rarely have to be reworked structurally. Joists and beams that support the floor won't need repair or replacement unless the floor is seriously sagging or the members themselves are decayed. More often, you'll need to make repairs to the *floor underlayment* and sometimes the *subfloor* beneath.

Subfloor repairs may range from renailing a few loose boards or plywood joints to replacing whole sections of decayed or damaged subflooring. Wood decay caused by water leakage is the most common cause of bathroom floor damage.

You can fix many floor problems yourself, as described on the following pages. But rot or decay that has damaged the floor supports may require expert attention. Also, wood-frame floors may need additional blocking or bracing if they are to support a new wall or a heavy floor covering such as bricks, flagstones or heavy tiles.

Heavy fixtures like cast-iron bathtubs will sometimes need cross-blocking or even doubled floor joists to provide extra support. If you're unsure of the need for additional floor support or subfloor strength, check with the building inspector for advice.

Concrete-slab floors don't require much work unless they're badly cracked. Small cracks or low spots can be easily patched as described on page 105.

REPAIRING WOOD-FRAME FLOORS

If the existing finish floor isn't suitable as a base for the new one, remove it down to the underlayment. See page 78 in the chapter, *Preparing to Build,* for information on removing floor coverings. Depending on the condition of the underlayment and on the type of floor covering you're installing, some patching may be required to get a smooth, level surface. Different floor coverings may require different floor preparations.

If the existing underlayment is in bad shape, remove it. Examine the subfloor beneath. Probe with an ice pick or awl for soft, spongy areas. Closely examine areas around drain

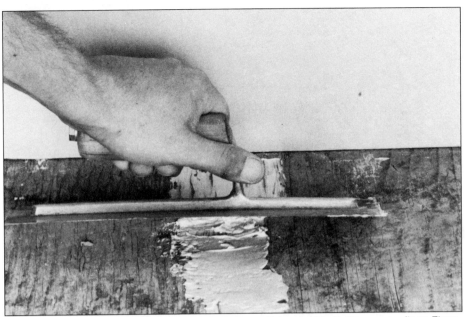

Patching imperfections in underlayment is an essential part of installing a new floor. Floor-repair compound can be sanded after it sets completely, if necessary.

lines and the toilet's floor flange. Slow leaks in old traps and supply pipes concealed by walls or cabinets can go undetected for years, causing considerable damage.

If you find any soggy or disintegrated sections of floor, rip them out with a pry bar. Use a tape measure to locate floor joists and mark their locations on the surrounding floor. You can often tell where joists are by the subfloor nailing pattern.

Remove all damaged subfloor materials back to the nearest sound joists, as described in the following text. Now is also a good time to make structural changes to the area to meet your remodeling requirements.

Fixing Damaged Underlayment—If the subfloor is sound but the underlayment needs patching, lay out a rectangular cutout. Center two of the cutout edges over the nearest sound floor joists adjacent to the deteriorated area. Use a framing square to square up the cutout. This simplifies cutting and fitting a replacement patch later.

If you have to repair the subfloor beneath, remove a section of underlayment that's one joist span larger each way than the repair section in the subfloor. In other words, the underlayment replacement patch should overlap the subfloor replacement patch so patch seams won't coincide. Or you can take up the entire sheet or partial sheet of underlayment affected.

Hidden nails can easily ruin an ordinary saw blade. Use a circular saw with a carbide-tip blade to make cutouts in underlayment. Wear safety glasses and gloves to protect yourself against flying nail chips. Set the blade only as deep as the thickness of the underlayment, so you won't weaken sound areas of subfloor beneath.

If the old underlayment is lumpy and torn, rip it up. Or you can install new underlayment directly over the old. Use 1/4-inch PTS (plugged, touched and sanded) plywood and annular-ring nails. Nail plywood into the joists.

If you're installing a resilient floor, underlayment in fairly good condition requires some preparation. Small imperfections in the underlayment surface can telegraph through and show up in the finish-floor surface. Redrive protruding nails and remove loose ones. Renail with annular-ring nails where necessary. Use floor-repair compound to fill cracks, dimples, plywood voids, hammer dents or splintered wood.

Occasionally you'll find that a *void* in the plywood underlayment has collapsed. A void refers to an area inside the plywood where a piece of one of the inside plies is missing. This forms a hollow, or indentation in the floor surface. Cut out the top ply over the void and fill with floor-repair compound.

JOIST REPAIRS

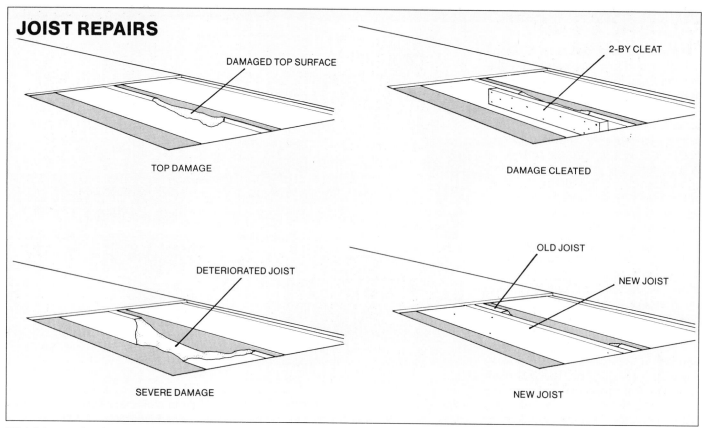

DAMAGED TOP SURFACE

TOP DAMAGE

2-BY CLEAT

DAMAGE CLEATED

DETERIORATED JOIST

SEVERE DAMAGE

OLD JOIST

NEW JOIST

NEW JOIST

If joist damage is minor, cleat damaged area to provide nailing surface for subfloor. If damage is severe, install new joist alongside old one.

Fixing Damaged Subfloor—After the underlayment is removed, mark joist locations on the subfloor. Lay out the rectangular subfloor cut inside the first one. Again, center the side lines of the cut over the joists. Use a circular saw with a carbide-tip blade and wear gloves and safety glasses.

Repairing Cause of Damage—After opening up the damaged area, find the cause of the damage. The damage may have been caused by plumbing or fixtures you've already ripped out. If not, track down the source and repair it.

It's a good idea to leave the cutout area open to dry for a day or longer. Areas that don't dry out during this time are clues to the location of a continuing leak. You may have to remove some sound flooring or part of an adjacent wall to find the leak.

Sometimes, floor damage is a result of inadequate ventilation under a house, or a leaky window, door, or wall that lets in water from the outside.

Repairing Damaged Floor Joists—If underlayment and subfloor have been damaged by water, the floor joists

may also be damaged. Check the joists with an ice pick or awl. Look for deterioration both on the top and bottom surfaces of the joists. Sometimes, water runs down a joist and accumulates on the bottom edges, causing decay of the bottom surface.

You can repair slightly damaged joists by nailing a length of 2x6 or 2x8 alongside the rotted portion of the joist. This provides a new bearing surface for the subfloor. If rot has structurally weakened the joist, replace it or install a new one alongside the old. It's often best to have a building official inspect the damage and recommend a repair procedure. If you follow the recommended procedure, the work is more likely to pass inspection.

Allow wet areas to dry completely before making repairs and patching the hole. To speed the drying process, direct a portable electric heater or fan into the area. If the underfloor area smells damp or musty after a day or two, check under the house for adequate ventilation, ground-water seepage or leaky plumbing elsewhere under the house. Other leaks can

occur at windows, doors, poorly placed downspouts or inadequate flashing around the house foundation, to mention a few sources. If you can't identify and repair the source of the leak, seek help from a qualified building contractor.

Replacing Underlayment or Subfloor—When any repair work and underfloor modifications are done, measure the thickness of the underlayment or subfloor. It needn't be replaced with exactly the same material, but the patch should be exactly the same thickness.

Due to its strength and durability, plywood is the best patching material. The face grain should run perpendicular to joists. Cut the patch to a size that allows 1/16- to 1/8-inch clearance around the edges. This provides for expansion and contraction of materials. Then nail the patch in place, using annular-ring nails.

Renailing Underlayment—Inspect the underlayment carefully, especially the nails. If some of the nails are backing out, don't just drive them in. Pull a few out and examine them. If they're smooth-shank and uncoated,

PATCHING A WOOD-FRAME FLOOR

When patching damaged underlayment and subfloor, center two of the cutout edges over the nearest sound joists. If both underlayment and subfloor are damaged, underlayment patch should be one joist wider on each side than subfloor patch. Patch seams should not coincide.

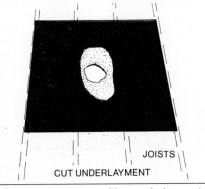

CUT UNDERLAYMENT

JOISTS

1. Damaged area with underlayment marked for cutting.

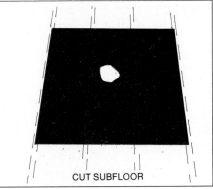

CUT SUBFLOOR

2. Underlayment cut and removed; subfloor marked for cutting.

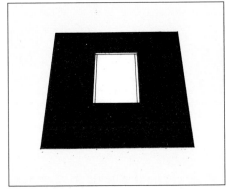

3. Subfloor cut, ready for patching.

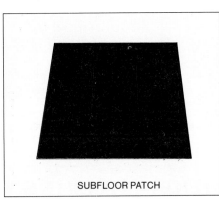

SUBFLOOR PATCH

4. Subfloor patch nailed in.

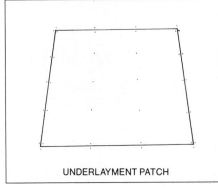

UNDERLAYMENT PATCH

5. Underlayment patch nailed in.

they'll keep backing out. This isn't a problem under certain types of finish floors, such as tile or brick; though loose nails can damage resilient-floor materials.

Plywood underlayment in good condition can be pulled up and reused. Remove the nails, and renail with annular-ring nails. Particle-board underlayment probably won't survive that much handling.

If particle-board underlayment is in good condition, pull loose or protruding nails with your pry bar or hammer. Or, use a nail set or punch to set loose nails completely through the particle board into the subfloor beneath. Renail with annular-ring nails. Patch nail holes with floor-repair compound.

REPAIRING CONCRETE FLOORS

Concrete-slab floors don't usually require much preparation. Remove floor covering, if necessary, as described on page 78. Examine the floor for defects. Chip off high spots and fill low ones with floor-repair compound.

Closely examine any cracks to determine their cause. If a crack is a

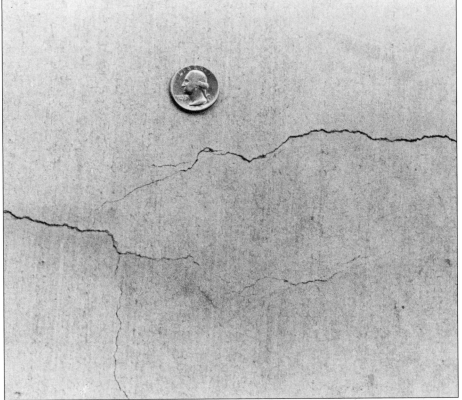

Minor cracks in concrete floor that begin and end nowhere in particular are usually shrinkage cracks from original pour. They can be filled or—under heavier finish materials—ignored. Larger or offset cracks indicate settling.

simple shrinkage or stress crack, it will not be offset vertically nor more than about 1/4-inch wide. These cracks can be filled with floor-repair compound.

If the crack is offset vertically, chop out the broken section of concrete to determine the cause of the crack. If the cause is a leaky pipe that has caused dirt to settle under the floor, fix the pipe and patch the concrete as described below. If major cracking has occurred over a large portion of the slab, consult a contractor.

To patch a hole in concrete, wet the dirt in the hole and tamp it down firmly. Use a length of timber such as a 4x4, 6x6 or railroad tie for tamping. Wet concrete edges around the hole. Make sure edges are free of dirt, dust or mud.

For small holes, use a concrete-patching compound. For large holes use mortar or concrete mix. Both are available at masonry suppliers or home-improvement centers. Follow instructions on package. Mix to a stiff consistency in a bucket or wheelbarrow. Dump the mix in the hole, adding wet chunks of the broken concrete to raise the mortar or concrete level even with the surface of surrounding concrete.

Use a board to strike off the patch surface. Allow patch to set up about an hour. Then use a mason's trowel to level and smooth-finish the patch. Don't walk on the patch for at least 2 days. Keep the patch damp so the mortar or concrete cures properly.

Check label instructions on any floor-covering adhesives. You may not be able to apply them over the patch for several weeks. Keep this in mind when sequencing your remodeling work. Make concrete repairs early so you can work on other phases of the project while the patch is curing.

If a concrete floor shows any signs of moisture, find the cause and fix it before installing the finish floor. To check for moisture, tape a piece of plastic wrap, on all four sides, over a small section of floor and leave it for 2 days.

If moisture condenses on the underside of the plastic, the floor is too damp to install the finish floor without some type of waterproofing. If you can't correct the moisture problem, find out from the flooring dealer what type of waterproofing is required for the floor material you're installing.

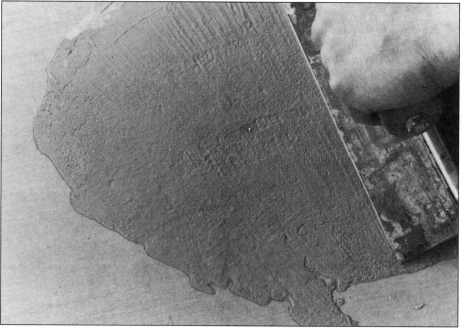

Major imperfections in concrete floor should be patched with new concrete or mortar mix. Make sure dirt below is well compacted, edges of hole are vertical and damp for good bond.

FLOOR-COVERING INSTALLATION

Installing the floor covering should not necessarily be left for last in a bathroom. The kind of floor covering determines when it should be installed. Thick, heavy or sloppy-to-install floor coverings should go down before *any* fixtures or cabinets go in. Floor coverings like brick and flagstone are in this category. Medium to lightweight floor coverings like ceramic tile or resilient materials should go down after the tub is installed. Any cabinets can be in place or not, depending on the job.

Under no circumstances should floor coverings go in after toilets, bidets or pedestal lavatories are installed. Such irregularly-shaped objects present too many fitting and sealing problems. Even if you're only installing a new floor in an existing bathroom, take out the toilet, and bidet or pedestal lavatory, if any. See pages 72-74. Then put them back on top of the new floor. It's *always* easier that way, even considering any repair work you might have to do in the process. Usually, the only cost is a new wax sealing ring for the toilet bowl. You may have to make some minor adjustments to the floor flange and connections to allow for the thickness of the new floor.

If practical, install floor coverings before applying any trim that contacts the floor, such as baseboard and door trim. The trim, prepainted or otherwise prefinished, will then cover most of the floor-covering edges. This way, cuts at edges don't have to be as precise.

RESILIENT FLOOR COVERINGS

Resilient floor coverings are those made of linoleum, asphalt, vinyl asbestos, solid vinyl and cushioned vinyl. Many are made in either *sheet goods* or *tiles*. General installation procedures for both sheet goods and tiles are covered in this section.

Each floor covering has its own specific installation procedures, recommended adhesives and seam sealers. Check with the dealer for specific instructions about the resilient floor covering you've chosen. He also can usually supply you with the right tools and materials for the installation. For more information on types of resilient floor coverings, see page 34.

INSTALLING RESILIENT SHEET GOODS

The stiffer sheet goods, such as heavy inlaid vinyl, cannot be unrolled in the bathroom and fitted directly. Fit stiff floor coverings by making a pattern and transferring the shape

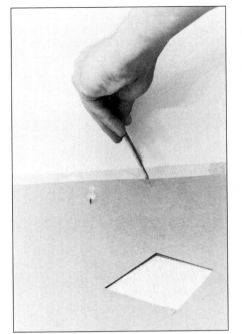

Square holes through overlaps in pattern paper keep sections in alignment. Keep paper in place with pushpins or thumbtacks on wood subfloor. On concrete slab, use tape at holes.

SCRIBING AT CURVED FLOORING EDGE

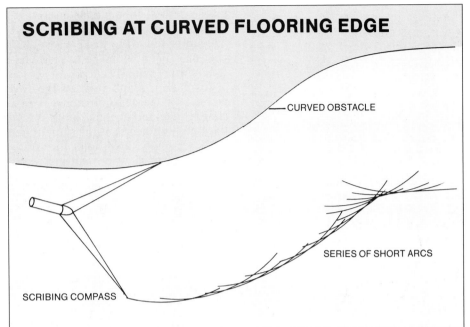

To transfer a complicated curved shape, use a compass to mark a series of short arcs on the pattern paper. These will not draw the shape of the curve directly. The curved shape will reappear when you use another series of short arcs to transfer the curve from the pattern back onto the flooring material.

SCRIBING COMPASS

Scribing compass for patterns can be made from readily available materials.

from the pattern to the floor covering. This technique also works for more flexible materials, especially on complicated cuts, and tight spaces. Some cushion vinyls can be trimmed to fit freehand—a few are as flexible as a throw-rug and rarely need a pattern.

Pattern-Making—Heavy flooring felt is the best material for making patterns. It looks like 15-pound building felt, but contains no asphalt. Any heavy paper will usually do, but it must lie flat on the floor, and not wrinkle or stretch out of shape.

Position pattern paper where the flooring will go, overlapping any seams about 6 inches. With a utility knife, trim the paper an inch or so back from all edges of the room. Then anchor the pattern paper to the floor.

If the floor is wood, use pushpins, thumbtacks or staples to tack the pattern paper down flat. On concrete floors, use a utility knife to cut out a 3- or 4-inch square every 3 or 4 feet along each piece of the paper. Then put a strip of strapping tape or duct tape across each hole to stick the pattern paper to the floor.

To align overlaps, cut another row of squares every 3 or 4 feet along each overlap. These squares should be cut with the utility knife blade held at 90°, so you can use the cut edges to realign the pieces of pattern paper. Number the pieces if you need to, and put an

up arrow on each one.

Use a *scribing compass* to mark the pattern. A scribing compass is an adjustable compass with a sharp point on each end, available at floor-covering dealers and hardware stores. Try to find one with a locking adjustment. If you can't find a scribing compass that locks, set the points at some convenient spacing, such as 2 inches. Check frequently to make sure the adjustment hasn't been disturbed. Or you can make a nonadjustable scribing tool from a wood dowel, thumbtack and finish nail, as shown in the drawing above.

Hold the compass at exactly 90° from the wall. Pull it along the wall to make a scratch on the pattern paper. The vertical position of the scribing

compass doesn't matter. You can tip it in any convenient direction, but keep the points perpendicular to the wall.

Where the floor covering meets pipes, cabinets, doorways or other obstructions, use the same technique. Check any scribe mark you're unsure of by holding the point at the wall stationary and swinging a radius on the pattern paper with the scratching point.

The radius should just touch the scribed line. Wherever you drift off 90°, the pattern will come out too big. You'll then have to trim excess material to fit. But you can't cut the floor covering too small unless you let the scriber point move away from the wall.

To follow a complicated shape, move the point at the wall 1/8 inch at a time and make a series of radii to transfer back from later. See drawing above.

Cut to the Pattern—Unroll the floor covering on a flat, clean surface such as the floor in an adjacent room. Let the floor covering relax until it's completely flat and at the same temperature as the bathroom. The dealer can tell you if there are steps you need to take to acclimate the material to its new location. If the floor covering won't relax completely, roll it *gently* in the opposite direction and leave it that way for a few hours.

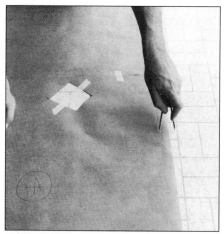

To get a perfect fit, work carefully as you transfer scribe line from pattern to sheet-floor covering. Any slips here are likely to show.

Take up the strips of pattern paper and reassemble them on top of the floor covering. To install floor covering in multiple pieces, rough cut the pieces and lay them out side-by-side with the design matched. Position the pattern paper on the floor covering so the design is straight and symmetrical. Tape the pattern in place at the holes.

Transfer the scratch line from the pattern paper to the floor covering with the scribing compass. The distance between compass points should be the same as when lines were scribed on pattern paper. *Keep the scribing compass exactly perpendicular to the line you're transferring.* If you let the compass get off 90°, your final cut will be slightly too small. See photo above.

After marking the floor covering, cut along the line with a utility knife. Where possible, use a steel straightedge as a guide. Take your time and make short, straight cuts. If you drift off the line, be sure you drift to the outside, into the scrap area. To fit the floor covering around isolated objects such as pipes, use the steel straightedge and make a cut to the nearest edge. Try to place the cut in an unobtrusive location.

Pull the pattern off the floor covering. Loosely roll up the floor covering and carry it into the bathroom. Unroll the floor covering into place. Trim or sand the edges to fit tight spots.

Cut in Seams—On some sheet-floor coverings, the design runs all the way to a precision-cut edge. All you need do is butt the edges together and line up the design. Others have either one or two unpatterned *selvage edges* that have to be cut off to make a seam. Or you may need to make a seam between two previously cut edges.

To make a seam, overlap the two pieces until the design matches. Use a straightedge and a utility knife to cut through both pieces at the same time. Work carefully and hold the knife exactly vertical when cutting. You only get one try at this. It's OK if the knife wanders from the cut line, as long as it's held exactly vertical. Use weights or have several helpers stand on the material to anchor the two pieces so they don't shift while you're cutting. Remove scrap from underneath and the seam should drop into place.

If the floor covering is too thick or heavy to cut two layers at once, cut or score and snap one layer with a utility knife and a straightedge. Put this piece underneath and use it as a guide for a marking tool called an *underscriber*. When the underscriber is correctly adjusted, it makes a mark on the upper layer that exactly corresponds with the edge of the lower layer. Then cut the upper layer to the scribed line.

If you don't have an underscriber, cut one thickness with a utility knife and straightedge as before. Put the cut piece *on top* of the uncut piece. Then cut the second piece, using the edge of the cut piece as a guide. Hold the utility knife at 90°, with the blade flat against the edge of the cut piece.

Attach Floor Covering—Follow manufacturer's recommendations for attaching the floor covering to the floor.

Some coverings require an adhesive or *mastic* over the entire floor surface, others just around the perimeter. Some can be attached with double-face tape or staples. Some materials can be loose-laid, though for safety reasons you should secure any exposed edges such as at doorways. The floor-covering dealer can advise the best fastening methods for the floor covering you've selected.

Remove all debris from the floor before laying the floor covering. This includes removing crumbs, chips and other lump-makers. Then apply adhesive, if you're using it, and attach the floor covering.

Trial-fit the floor covering before applying adhesive. If you don't, you'll have no time to make corrective cuts before the mastic sets. Also, once the floor covering is down, you can't take it up to rework it. The following methods are most commonly used to adhere sheet flooring:

Double-face tape can be used instead of adhesive to attach some types of floor coverings. To attach floor covering with double-face tape, start at the seams. Lift one edge of the seam and draw a pencil mark along the floor, using the other side of the seam as a guide. Then lift the other side of the seam and put a strip of tape on the floor centered on the pencil line.

Two-inch tape works well for seams. Peel the release paper from the top of the tape and lower the two sides of the seam into contact. Smooth out bubbles or waves in both pieces of floor covering. Press down or roll the seam to get a good bond.

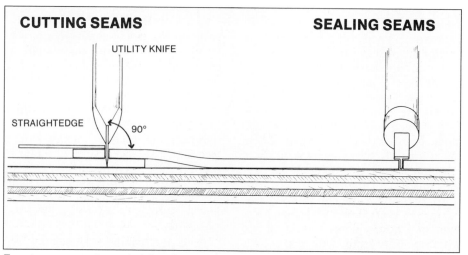

To cut seams, overlap material until pattern matches. To make cut, use straightedge and utility knife held exactly vertical. Seams are sealed with a clear-liquid seam sealer, using a special applicator, as shown at right.

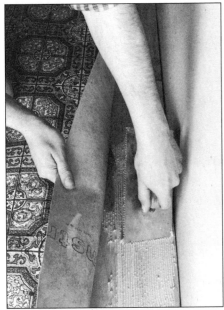

Some floor coverings require only a 6- or 8-inch strip of adhesive at seams and edges.

If manufacturer calls for it, staple every 3 or 4 inches at perimeter of floor coverings. Stapling should be done after seams are adhered. Place staples so trim hides them.

Fasten edges with 1-inch or 1-1/2-inch double-face tape. Roll back the edge, stick the tape to the floor, remove the release paper and press down the edge.

Staples are often used to attach thinner floor coverings at the edges. Drive staples where they will be hidden by moldings, 2 or 3 inches apart. Stapling is usually combined with a special adhesive for seams and exposed edges.

Perimeter adhesive is applied around edges and at seams. Do the seams first. Fold back edges of adjoining pieces and apply a strip of adhesive about a foot wide, stopping 6 or 8 inches from walls at either end of the seam. Adhesive should be applied with a notched spreader or trowel. The notches should be the size recommended on the adhesive can or in the floor-covering manufacturer's installation instructions.

After seams are done, do the edges. Lift one edge at a time and put down a 6- to 8-inch-wide strip of adhesive along the wall. Make sure the floor covering lies completely flat. If adhesive instructions call for it, use a floor roller to bond the floor covering to the adhesive. The floor-covering dealer should be able to supply a floor roller if you need one.

Full adhesive application may be required for some floor coverings. For this method, fold back half of a piece of floor covering and apply an even coat of adhesive to the floor surface. Use a notched trowel or spreader of the recommended notch size. Be careful not to step or kneel on the fold.

Lay the floor covering back down and bed it in the adhesive. Then do the other half of the same piece. Roll if required before laying the next piece of floor covering. Use a floor roller or a heavy push broom to work out any bubbles. Push bubbles toward an edge and out. If you have several pieces of floor covering, it's generally best to work out bubbles from a wall to a seam, then from seam to seam, then to the other wall.

Unless you walk on or roll a piece of floor covering, you can slightly adjust its position during the *open time* of the adhesive. Open time is the time between application of adhesive and when it dries or sets. Open time for an adhesive is usually given on the container label. After it's walked on or rolled, the floor covering is down to stay, so make sure seams are aligned first.

After adhesive work is done, promptly clean up any drips with solvent specified on the adhesive can. Then seal the seams.

Seal Seams—After the seams are cut and floor covering is adhered, seal the seams. For most floor coverings, clear-liquid seam sealers in special applicator bottles are available. Fit the little guide on the applicator tip into the seam. Lay down a bead of seam sealer to bond the two pieces together.

Attach Trim Strips—Many types of strips are available from your floor-covering dealer, in an array of colors, widths and offsets. The last step in installing sheet-floor covering is finishing doorways and other exposed edges. If the floor covering meets another hard-surface material, you can put down a metal trim strip with screws or tacks.

If the new floor covering meets carpet, lift up the carpet edge and run the floor covering an inch or two under it. After everything else is done, slide a piece of clamp-down metal carpet trim under the edge of the carpet and nail it to the subfloor. Then use a hammer and a wood block to bend the free edge of the clamp-down strip to anchor the carpet. On deep-pile carpets, trim the pile along the carpet edge so the clamp-down strip won't trap too much of it.

Freehand Fitting—Some more flexible sheet-floor coverings can be installed directly over the floor. This involves a process similar to carpet installation. The floor covering is trimmed to fit by creasing it at the walls and cutting along the crease.

Measure the floor and roughly cut the floor covering to size and shape. Allow 1 to 2 inches extra around the room perimeter. Roll out the floor covering in the room, so the edges run up the walls on all sides.

If one of the room walls is fairly straight, and in the right place, you may be able to butt one factory edge of the floor covering against it and start from there. Otherwise, start at a long wall and trim both ways from the center, a little at a time.

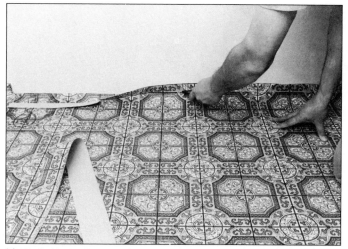

It's easy to crack sheet-floor covering when cutting in freehand, so don't crease too hard at the wall. Make several cuts to approach a fit by stages.

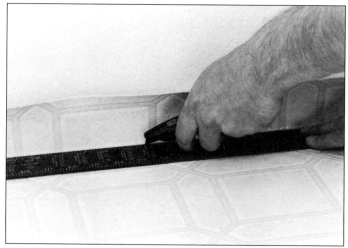

Some flexible floor coverings are designed to be cut directly into place, using framing square as knife-guide. Check with dealer to be sure before trying this.

Push 4 to 6 inches of the floor-covering edge into the angle between floor and wall. It probably won't bend to a right angle, but make as small a radius as you can. Then cut along the top of the radius with your utility knife. Don't cut in the middle of the radius or remove too much surplus material at a time. See photo above.

After the first cut is complete, go back and make a second, tighter cut. You'll be able to make a smaller radius at the wall this time. The radius size and the position of the cut on the radius varies for different floor coverings, depending on thickness, composition, and even the temperature and humidity.

Work down the curve of the radius until you find the right cutting location. Note that the bending characteristics of your floor covering may be different in one direction than in the other.

When fitting floor covering in a corner, first cut out a square at the corner. Make sure the inside corner of the square doesn't reach below the level of the floor.

When trimming the floor covering, don't try to cut away all the surplus material at once. Make many small passes with the knife, each coming a little closer to a tight fit. After all pieces are fitted, cut in the seams, if any, as described on page 108. Then fasten down the floor covering.

One line of floor coverings made by Armstrong is so flexible that the manufacturer recommends going directly to a finished trim cut. They suggest that you lay out the floor covering in the room and align any

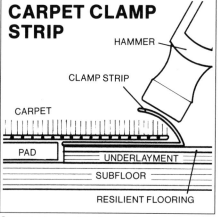

CARPET CLAMP STRIP

HAMMER

CLAMP STRIP

CARPET

PAD

UNDERLAYMENT

SUBFLOOR

RESILIENT FLOORING

Carpet clamp strip is used where carpet meets resilient flooring.

seams. Then use a framing square to push the floor covering squarely into the angle between floor and wall. Using the framing square as a guide, cut the floor covering with a utility knife held at a 45° angle. The floor covering should drop into place with only one guided cut. Use this method only if it's specifically recommended for the floor covering you've selected. Less-flexible material will crack.

RESILIENT TILE

Start by marking out the layout lines for the tile, as shown on page 151. Unless you're using self-stick tiles, apply the recommended adhesive, following label instructions. Lay the whole tiles first, then the cut ones. Resilient tiles should be at room temperature when they're laid.

Butt one side of the tile against a tile already in place, line up the corners, and lower the tile onto the floor. As you lower the tile, warp

down the corner toward the adjoining tile just enough so the edges don't catch. Work along, then outward from, your layout lines. Don't slide tiles into position or adhesive will pile up at the seams.

Don't use up one box of resilient tile and then start the next, even if the boxes have the same lot number. There can be slight changes of color or reflectivity from box to box. Mix up tiles from two boxes as you work so variations are disguised. A good method is to use the first half of the first box. Then alternate the second half of the first box with the first half of the second box. Then alternate the second half of the second box with the first half of the third box, and so on.

Cut and Fit Tiles—The thinnest resilient tiles can be cut with scissors. Most self-stick tiles are of this kind. Thicker and more rigid tiles can be cut with a utility knife. The thickest and most rigid tiles can be scored repeatedly with a utility knife and a straightedge, then snapped apart.

Fit partial pieces of tile along walls using the following technique: Place a loose tile on the full tile adjacent to the space you want to fit. Position the loose tile to match the pattern you're creating. Don't align the loose tile to the one it's on—position it for the space you're filling. See drawing on page 111.

Place another full tile on top, pushed against the wall. Use the edge of this second loose tile to mark the first loose tile. When you cut on the mark, the piece farthest from the wall should fit the space perfectly. If you've laid out the floor correctly, the

Continued on page 112

TILE PATTERNS

Some tiles have a directional pattern, even if they're a solid color. The pattern may be subtle when comparing individual tiles, but will show up in the finished floor. Check information on or in the box, or any markings or arrows on the back of the tile itself.

You don't have to lay tiles all in one direction. You can vary the pattern by laying one row of tiles straight and the next row 90° to the first, alternating the rows. Or you can alternate the directions of successive individual tiles. Another choice is to alternate tiles or rows straight, 90° right, reversed, then 90° left. If you do any of these rotations, lay them out before adhering them to the floor. Then look at the layout under a strong light.

As you lay tiles, be alert for mixed pattern directions within the same box. If you're rotating pattern directions, stagger the rotation when you start a new row. If the change in pattern direction is hard to see, indicate direction with a grease pencil along edges of whole tiles where they meet partial tiles. This will help you orient partial tiles when you cut them.

Marbled Tiles—As a rule, marble-pattern tiles are never laid in one direction. That doesn't mean you have to lay them in the traditional checkerboard pattern. Tile can be laid in alternating rows, in a herringbone pattern, or in a chevron pattern. Experiment with loose tiles to find pleasing patterns.

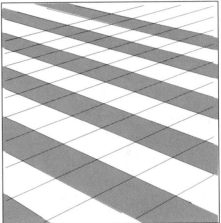

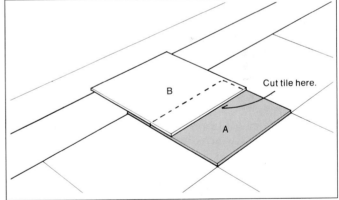

CUTTING TILES

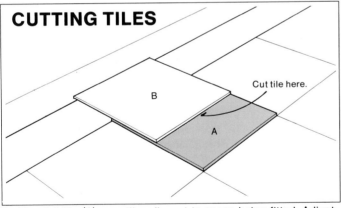

Position full tile (A) over tile adjacent to space being fitted. Adjust tile right or left to align with space, if necessary. Place another full tile (B) over tile A in position shown. Mark and cut tile A as indicated.

To cut partial tile to fit space, first position partial tile (A) over tile adjacent to space being fitted. Place second full tile (B) over tile A. Exposed piece of tile A will fit cut location.

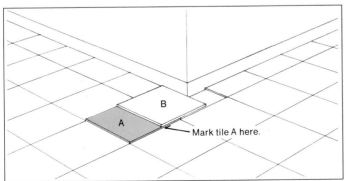
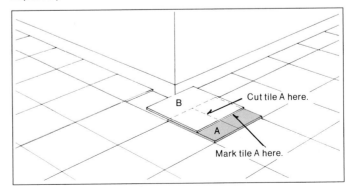

Fitting to outside corner is done the same as fitting cut tile in top drawings, only in two directions.

Continued from page 110

cutoff piece will be less than half a tile, and you can throw it away. If you have a few cut locations that are less than a half tile in size, you may be able to use the cutoff pieces in those locations. This can be done by placing the cut piece on the far edge of the adjoining full tile. Mark and cut as shown on page 111.

Cuts such as inside and outside corners are made by a variation of the same technique. Place the tile you're fitting on one adjacent whole tile and then on the other adjacent tile until you've transferred all of the necessary measurements. Then cut the tile to fit. See drawing on page 111.

Fitting Irregular Objects—When fitting irregular objects such as pipes, you may have to make a paper pattern. Grocery-bag paper works well. When the fit of the paper pattern is satisfactory, transfer the pattern to the tile. Cut out the shape with a utility knife using short, firm strokes.

If you find stiff or thick tiles difficult to cut, warm them in the oven at a low temperature for a few minutes. This makes them easier to cut. When making complicated cuts in inlaid-vinyl tiles, small segments of the pattern may fracture. Segments can be cemented in separately, if necessary.

If an irregular object such as a pipe is away from the wall, cut a straight slit from the object to one edge of the tile. Place the slit in the most unobtrusive place you can.

BRICK FLOORS

Brick for floors is installed similarly to ceramic floor tile. Don't construct brick floors of any brick other than *pavers*. Pavers are specifically made for the heavy wear of flooring use. They're available either full thickness, or half thickness, called *split pavers*.

Brick floors are heavy and thick. The weight doesn't create problems on a concrete slab, but wood-frame floors must be strong and rigid enough to support the brick.

If the subfloor is at all springy, a brick floor can cause a permanent sag. A subfloor can be springy and more than strong enough, or it can be rigid but weak.

If there is a crawl space or basement below, additional girders or joists can be installed to add rigidity or strength. An additional layer of 5/8- or 3/4-inch plywood can be installed to compen-

sate for flex in the subfloor itself.

Flexibility can be detected by jumping up and down on the floor while another person stands nearby to feel how the floor reacts. Strength can be determined by noting the size, spacing and span of all subfloor members. From that information, your local building department should be able to tell you if you can safely install brick on the existing floor structure, or if additional bracing is needed. Most building departments have charts that prescribe the type of subfloor required for loads of various weights.

The additional thickness of a brick floor can cause problems where the bricks meet other floors. If you're building a new floor structure, you can lower the brick areas to compensate. Or, if the ceilings are high enough, you can build a platform to raise the brick—and the bathroom—a full step up from surrounding floors.

The platform solution mentioned can be useful if you have to cope with problems of floor strength or excessive flexibility. Properly designed, the platform can add enough strength or stiffness to make brick feasible. Like any thick flooring material, it's best to put brick down before any fixtures and cabinets are installed.

Dry-Laid Brick—The simplest brick floor is laid dry. No mortar is used, so the subfloor must be smooth and level before you start.

Put a layer of 30-pound building felt over the entire floor. Do not overlap the seams and do not wrinkle the felt. Use a few staples or small dabs of construction adhesive to keep the felt from moving around underfoot. Set up your layout lines on the building felt as you would for any kind of block flooring. See page 151.

Put down all whole bricks, pushed tightly together, working outward from the layout lines.

There will probably be a slight variation in the dimensions of the bricks. Undersize or oversize bricks can be segregated and used together to avoid gaps. One advantage to dry-laying brick is if a section doesn't look right or you make a mistake in the pattern, you can take the bricks up and start over.

After the whole bricks are in place, mark and cut the partial bricks. Brick is an unglazed-clay product and is cut much the same as quarry tile or Mexi-

can tile, pages 148-149. In non-critical areas such as under cabinets, cut bricks by scoring and splitting with a hammer and brick set.

When all bricks are in place, sprinkle the floor with fine sand and sweep the sand into cracks. After the floor has been in place for a few days, it is sealed or finished as described on page 157 for unglazed tile.

Laying Bricks in Mortar—If the subfloor is uneven, lay brick in a mortar bed. Over wood subfloors, the mortar bed should be put down on 15- or 30-pound building felt, and should be a full 1-1/2 inches thick. On a clean concrete subfloor, the mortar bed need only be 1/2-inch thick. The mortar mix used is 3 parts sand to 1 part Portland cement, with up to 10% hydrated lime added to improve plasticity.

Starting from the layout lines, put down about 2 square feet of mortar. The area covered does not have to be precise. Then seat a row of bricks along one layout line. Use a level to get the top surfaces even and level. To level a brick, just push or tap it into the mortar bed.

Clean excess mortar from edges you won't immediately be adding bricks to. If you're allowing for mortar joints between the bricks, space them apart with small strips of wood.

Continue the above process until all whole bricks are laid. As you work, remove mortar from locations where cut bricks will go. Make all cuts in bricks at one time, so you can use extra pieces. Then use a narrow trowel to lay a mortar bed in the cut-brick locations.

Remember, if you lay brick without mortar joints, there's no place for the mortar to squish out as you level the cut pieces. Make sure you put down the right amount of mortar under the cut pieces.

Avoid walking on mortared bricks until the mortar has set. If you have time, lay all whole bricks in mortar and allow the mortar to set for a day or two. Then set the cut pieces. If you have work over freshly laid bricks, wait several hours for the mortar to take an initial set. Use large pieces of plywood or hardboard to distribute your weight as you work.

After laying the brick, keep it wet for a day or two, to allow mortar to cure completely. If the floor has no mortar joints, sweep fine sand into

LAYOUT FOR PARQUET FLOORING

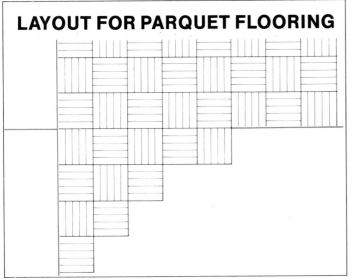

Blocks are laid out in step fashion from intersection of layout lines. Complete each quarter of floor before starting next.

Allow a 3/8- to 1/2-inch gap at all edges of any wood flooring for expansion and contraction. Here, removable plywood strip was used to provide even spacing. Trim will usually cover gap. The floor dealer can supply cork filler strips to fill any gaps that show.

the cracks. If the floor will have mortar joints, grout and seal them the same as for unglazed tile. See page 157.

WOOD FLOORS

Wood flooring materials come in strips, planks, and in blocks, also called *parquet.* Wood flooring materials are available prefinished, sanded and unfinished, and unfinished requiring sanding. A more complete description of the flooring types appears on page 35.

PARQUET INSTALLATION

Parquet flooring requires a subfloor that is sound, tight, smooth and dry. Repairs to subfloor and floor underlayment are described on pages 102-104. If you're laying parquet over a concrete-slab floor, check with the flooring dealer for subfloor requirements. Also, check carefully for moisture, as described on page 106.

Set up layout lines as for other block flooring, page 151. Trowel on as much adhesive as you can cover during the adhesive's *open time.* The open time, or *setting time,* is shown on the adhesive can.

At the intersection of your layout lines, put down a row of six or eight blocks along one line. Some parquet blocks have tongues on two edges and grooves on another two. This allows them to interlock. Carefully align the face of the block, not the tongue, with the layout lines. Fit the blocks together hand-tight. The corners of the blocks should line up exactly.

Then start the next few rows on one side, step fashion. Keep applying adhesive and setting blocks in the steps until the first quarter of the room is done. The stepped blocks enable you to back your way out of the corner, fitting cut blocks as you go along. There's a knack to seating the blocks without sliding them on the adhesive, despite the tongue-and-groove edges. With practice you'll be able to slide the tongues and grooves together while you drop the block flat into position.

When several blocks are in position, use a hammer and a padded wood block to bed them solidly into the adhesive. Doublecheck intersections of block corners before you bed the blocks. This is where any misalignment will show up. If necessary, realign blocks before bedding.

Cutting and Fitting Parquet—You should allow clearance for expansion and contraction of blocks around the floor perimeter and at any obstructions. Cutting and fitting perimeter blocks is simpler than with other materials. Use a removable spacer strip of 1/2-inch plywood along any walls and around obstacles. Then cover the expansion gaps with moldings.

With the spacer strip in place along a wall, place the block to be cut exactly on top of the adjacent whole block. Use another block with the tongue trimmed off as a gage to mark the loose block for cutting. You'll find the exposed piece beyond the gage block will fit the space. Use a fine-tooth

handsaw or saber saw to cut the block. If you use a table saw or radial-arm saw, use a finish blade.

Irregular pieces can be fitted by making a paper template. Cut the paper template to fit the space. Pencil the shape of the template onto the block for cutting. You may have to cut a block in two pieces to make a cutout for a free-standing obstacle. It's often easier to detach the obstacle, drill a hole in the block, install it and replace the obstacle.

Finishing—Many parquet-flooring products are prefinished. All that's needed is a coat of any good paste wax. If you're working with unfinished parquet, use finishing techniques discussed on page 115 for strip flooring. Parquet should be sanded on alternate diagonals because of the mixed grain directions.

WOOD STRIP INSTALLATION

Try to install wood-strip flooring in a way that requires the least cutting and fitting, usually longwise. If the strip pattern is visible from doorways and other rooms, make sure the strip direction gives you the desired space illusion.

If you're laying wood-strip flooring over a concrete-slab floor, check with the flooring dealer for subfloor requirements. Do not put wood flooring over concrete floors that show signs of moisture unless the floor can be waterproofed.

On wood-frame floors, you may be able to run wood-strip flooring in any direction you want to without reference to joists beneath. It depends on the strength and stiffness of the subfloor material. Thin strip flooring will require a sturdy subfloor of 1-inch plywood or 2x6 tongue-and-groove subflooring. If you're using 2-inch (nominal) planks for the finish floor, a subfloor may not be required at all, but flooring must run perpendicular to the joists. If you're in doubt, consult the building department.

Application—If possible, start laying wood strips from a wall that's close to parallel to your central layout line. Sort out the short pieces in the flooring bundles and save them for use under cabinets and for cut pieces. Put down a layer of *resin paper* (available at the flooring dealer) or 15-pound flooring felt. Snap a chalk line 1/2 inch from the wall, parallel to the layout line. Align the first strip to it. This will allow room for the flooring to expand and contract.

Snap a line 1/2 inch from the adjacent walls. Align flooring-strip ends to this line as you lay them. Face the tongue on the first strip away from the wall. Drive nails through the top surface of the strip, along the back edge, so the nails will be covered by molding. This procedure is called *face nailing.* See drawing at right.

Nail size and spacing will vary with to the type of wood-strip flooring you use. If nailing instructions aren't provided with the flooring bundles, ask the flooring dealer.

Maintain the 1/2-inch spacing at the end wall. Keep adding pieces until you reach the wall opposite the starting point. Mark and rip a piece to close out the run. Ends of flooring pieces will often have tongues and grooves the same as the edges. This is called *end-matched* flooring. With end-matched flooring, use the cutoff piece from the end of the last run to start the new run.

After the first strip in each run is face nailed, *blind nail* remaining strips until you get near the opposite wall. Strips are blind nailed through their tongues, so nails won't show. This can be done by hand—carefully—if the floor area is small. For large areas, use a *hammer-actuated nailer.* This device hooks onto the tongue-edge of the strips and is loaded with strips of nails or special staples. When you hit the plunger with a special hammer, the strip of flooring is driven tight and nailed through the tongue.

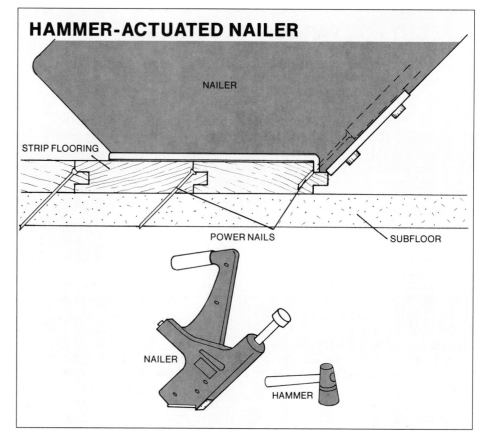

HAMMER-ACTUATED NAILER

NAILER

STRIP FLOORING

POWER NAILS

SUBFLOOR

NAILER

HAMMER

A hammer-actuated nailer is one of the specialized tools you'll need to install wood strip floors. The dealer who rents or sells you the nailer will also be able to provide the special nails that go with it.

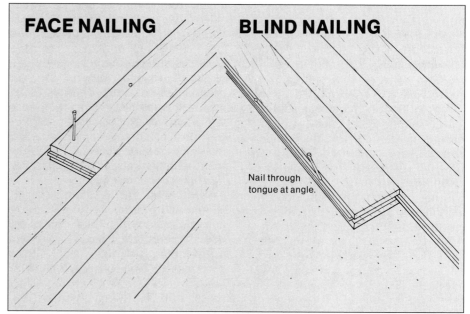

FACE NAILING

BLIND NAILING

Nail through tongue at angle.

End rows of wood strips at walls must be face nailed. Rest of strips are blind nailed, as shown.

You can rent a hammer-actuated nailer from the flooring dealer or a tool-rental company. Get a supply of the special nail or staple strips and the special hammer for the nailer.

If the flooring is running across the joists, try to catch the joists as you nail. An occasional miss doesn't matter, but a large area of flooring that isn't solidly nailed to underlying joists is prone to squeak.

If you find any warped strips in the

bundle, put them aside. You can use them later for cutting shorter, straight sections.

The last few strips will be so close to the wall that a hammer-actuated nailer won't fit between the flooring and the wall. If strips are fairly wide, you may be able to blind-nail the next-to-last strip with an ordinary hammer. Otherwise, face-nail the last few strips as unobtrusively as possible.

Set any exposed nails below the floor surface. Fill nail holes with a wood filler that matches the wood color. Maintain the 1/2-inch expansion clearance on the last wall. Use a pry bar and a wood block to wedge the last few strips in place.

Finishing—If you've installed prefinished wood-strip flooring, apply a coat of any good paste wax. If you've installed unfinished flooring or are reconditioning an old wood floor, use the following procedure. The only difference is that a new unfinished floor won't require as much sanding as an old one.

You'll need two rented tools to sand a wood floor—a large *drum sander* and an *edger*. The drum sander looks like a large lawnmower with a handle on the back. The edger is either rotary or a variation of a belt sander. Of the two types of edgers, the belt type is preferable. In a small bathroom, you may be able to get by with just an edger.

The tool-rental company or flooring dealer should also carry sandpaper belts for the machine you rent. You'll need belts with coarse, medium and fine grits for the drum sander, and medium and fine grits for the edger. If the machines don't have decals showing how to load the sandpaper, ask the people at the rental company or flooring dealer how to do it. The machines vary.

Before sanding, use a nail set or punch to set all nails well below the floor surface. Remove or glue down splinters and renail loose spots in the floor.

Start with coarse paper in the drum sander. Position the sander close to one wall and turn it on. Hold the drum clear of the floor until it reaches full speed. Gently and smoothly lower the drum into contact with the floor.

Let the moving drum guide you and the machine across the floor, parallel to the grain. At the other wall, gently and smoothly lift the drum off the floor and pull the machine back to the far wall. Try to keep the drum from notching the floor or cutting ridges in it. Keep the sander moving in a straight line along the grain of the wood. Move the drum sander just slowly enough to remove irregularities in the surface and offsets between boards. Don't move too slowly, or you'll remove more wood than you need to.

The second pass with the drum sander is more difficult than the first. Lap the drum a few inches over the previous pass and move across the floor *at the same speed as the first pass.* If you go faster or slower, the second pass will remove too much or too little wood, making a ridge. Keep a measured pace as you work. Speed becomes less critical with fine-grit sandpapers, because ridges are smaller and more easily sanded out.

After you've sanded the whole floor with the drum sander, reverse the machine direction and carefully sand the strip along your starting wall. Stay with the grain. Then repeat the entire sanding process, using medium-grit sandpaper.

Park the drum sander in the middle of the room with the drum elevated. A hot drum resting on the floor can cause a scorch mark. Use the edger to sand the border where the drum sander couldn't reach, with medium, then fine paper. Sand along the grain, where possible. Sand all edges level with the main surface. In tight locations such as corners, you may have to sand by hand.

When you've sanded the entire floor with medium-grit sandpaper, fill any imperfections with wood filler. If you're going to stain the floor, the filler should match the stain color. To make your own filler, mix some of the sanding dust with a 1-to-1 mixture of white glue and water. To match the filler color to the wood, add a small amount of water-base or alcohol-base wood stain to the mixture. Let the filler dry before final sanding with fine-grit paper.

During final sanding, try to keep dirt and stains off the wood. Wear socks over your shoes, clean your knees, and make sure tools don't leave metal marks. Vacuum up any sawdust that escaped the bags on the sanders.

If your vacuum cleaner has a metal nozzle, wrap it in masking tape to protect the floor. Use a brush attachment if your vacuum has one. Frequently empty the vacuum-cleaner bag. Marks, dirt or imperfections left on the floor will show under the finish.

Apply Finish—The actual finishing procedure you use for your new or reconditioned floor is largely up to you. If you want the finished floor to be darker than it is now, you can stain it. To see the true color of the wood, moisten a cloth with some paint thinner—water will raise the wood grain—and wipe a spot on the floor.

Until the paint thinner dries, the spot will be the color of the floor with a clear finish. If you like the color, you don't need to stain. If you want a lighter floor color, you'll have to bleach the wood before you apply the finish. Wood bleaches are available at paint stores.

When selecting a stain for a wood floor, take a piece of leftover flooring to a paint store or flooring dealer and try on various stains. Stain can be applied separately, or as part of the finish. If you've sanded an old wood floor, the old finish may still show in cracks between boards. You can hide color difference by staining the whole floor the same shade or darker than it was. Open-grain wood species such as oak require filling before applying stains and finishes. Other species require sealing before staining to prevent uneven stain absorption.

There are a number of penetrating sealers, sealer-waxes and surface finishes that can be used on wood floors. Because there are so many combinations of wood species, colors, and finish-material systems, no specifics can be given here on finish application. The finish supplier and manufacturer can give you detailed instructions for your particular set of circumstances.

In any event, make sure—by testing if necessary—that the finish you've selected is completely water resistant.

Avoid the old-fashioned natural varnishes, such as those based on linseed oil. They're waterproof, but not very durable under repeated water exposure, and not very resistant to wear. The modern synthetic varnishes work well and are made in several surface glosses ranging from high-gloss to matte. For most wood floors, several coats of a polyurethane finish will adequately waterproof a wood floor. Polyurethanes come in gloss and satin finishes.

8

Plumbing

Installing this much exposed plated pipe requires care. Use smooth jaw wrenches. Check for burrs on the jaws before you start. Wrapping wrench with adhesive tape is another way to protect plated surfaces. "Antique" plumbing fixtures are modern reproductions. *Photo courtesy of Kohler Co.*

The first part of this chapter describes how to modify existing plumbing systems to suit new or relocated plumbing fixtures. This work is referred to as *rough plumbing.* It includes all work done to water-supply and drain pipes to the point where they emerge into the room. At this point, the pipes are *stubbed out,* or capped off, until you are ready to install and hook up the bathroom fixtures. Fixture installation and hookup, called *finish plumbing,* is cov-

ered in the second part of the chapter, starting on page 128. Read both sections before you do any work.

ROUGH PLUMBING

Most building departments allow homeowners to do their own rough plumbing, provided correct permits are obtained. In a few localities, certain plumbing work must be done by a licensed plumbing contractor.

The first step in changing any

plumbing system is to locate existing pipe runs, then lay out the change and make a materials list. Working from your scale drawing, page 60, measure and mark on the wall and floor the centerlines of all proposed plumbing fixtures and their rough-in dimensions. Have the supplier give you the rough-in dimensions for bathroom fixtures you're installing. Make sure the wall framing includes adequate blocking for installing the fixtures. Then determine the types and amounts of pipes and fittings you'll need to make the changes.

DRAINING THE SYSTEM

Before you do any plumbing work, shut off and drain the system. Especially on older systems, things can go wrong—such as a cracked pipe or a failed fitting—on even small repairs. If the water is on when this happens, a lot of it can leak out before you can reach and turn off the main shutoff valve.

Turn Off Water—First, locate the main shutoff valve. This is a hand-operated valve that turns off water to the entire house. If you don't know where the shutoff valve is, start by finding your water meter. The meter is usually in a concrete or metal box recessed in the ground near one of the property lines. A hand-operated shut-off valve may be there. If there isn't one in the box, check along the house foundation on the side toward the meter. In warmer climates, the main water pipe often exits the ground near the foundation and enters the house above ground level. The shutoff valve is often there, usually along with a hose bib that can be used to drain down the system after the valve has been shut off.

In colder climates, look for another box like the water meter's, near the house foundation. The main valve may be there. This setup is sometimes used in colder climates for houses with crawl spaces or slab floors.

If the shutoff valve is in none of these places, look inside the house. Check in the basement or crawl space, especially along the foundation wall toward the water meter. Also look in the utility room or garage, if they're on the side of the house toward the meter.

If you can't find the shutoff valve, your plumbing system may not have one. As a last resort, call the water company for help. You can make arrangements with the company to shut off the water at the meter for a few hours, so you can install a shutoff valve, or repair or replace a frozen one.

After shutting off the water supply, drain the system below the level of the sections you'll be working on. Open a low faucet, such as a hose bib, to let out water and a high one such as a sink faucet, to admit air.

In many parts of the country, you'll find shutoff valve in meter box. If valve is on streetside of meter, check with water company before using shutoff—it belongs to them.

Water Heaters—Your water heater can be damaged if it's allowed to operate without water. If there are valves on both inlet and outlet sides of the water heater, close them both before draining the rest of the system. Otherwise, turn off the water heater and let it drain along with the rest of the system.

ACCESS TO PIPES

Modifying or repairing existing pipes, or installing new ones, requires working access. If the area you're working in is already stripped to the bare framing, no special measures are needed. But if the wall-finish material is in place, some cutting will be needed. Detailed information on cutting and patching drywall and plaster is on page 100.

Where most or all of the pipes are in one wall, it may be easier to completely remove finish material on one side of the wall. You can complete the plumbing work—and any electrical changes—and then close the wall in again.

Access Openings—Especially behind the head of a tub or the fitting wall of a shower, it's good to provide some means of permanent access for future repairs. An access panel can be installed in an adjoining closet, if there is one. But you can install an access panel in any wall, if it's in an unobtrusive location. The panel and trim can be painted to match the wall, or made nearly invisible by paneling or papering to blend in.

To make an access opening, cut out

a patch of drywall or plaster opposite the fitting and tub drain, if there is one. The patch shouldn't extend to the floor, but should end a few inches above the baseboard. The vertical edges of the patch should be centered on studs. Cut and toenail in 2x4 blocking to support the top and bottom edges of the opening.

Use the piece of drywall you cut out to make the panel itself, or cut a piece of plywood or new drywall to size. Glue and staple a small molding to the edges of the panel. You can use molding to match other trim in the room. Door-stop molding works well. Secure the panel in the opening with two or three flat-head wood screws in each vertical edge, through the molding and into the stud.

If you're installing new drywall and putting in an access panel, it's a nice touch to edge the hole with metal J-channel on all four sides. The J-channel helps prevent edge damage during future plumbing repairs.

Floor Access—When you need to work on pipes in the floor, first try to gain access from underneath. If there's an unfinished basement or crawl space below, work from there.

If there's a finished ceiling below, consider installing an access panel in the ceiling. You can use the same technique as described above for wall-access panels, but more screws may be needed to support the weight of the panel. If there's no way in but from the top, cut an opening in the floor as shown on page 105.

The toughest access problem you'll encounter is getting to pipes under a concrete slab. Heavy tools are needed, depending on the thickness of the concrete and the amount that must be removed. A heavy-duty hammer-drill with a masonry bit will work for small areas. Larger areas or tougher concrete call for a rotary-impact hammer, either electric or pneumatic. These tools are available at tool-rental companies. If over a square yard or so of concrete has to be removed, rent a jackhammer and compressor. For removing long, narrow strips of concrete to lay pipe runs, rent a concrete saw. Make two saw-cuts. Then break out the strip of concrete between the cuts, using a 3-pound, short-handle hammer and large mason's chisel.

The removal technique is tedious but similar, no matter what tools you use. Mark the limits of the cut with pencil or chalk. Cut or break out a manageable-size piece, work it loose with a pry bar and drag it away.

When removing concrete, full safety precautions are mandatory. There will be noise, flying chips and chunks, and sparks from tools. If there is metal reinforcing in the concrete, you may have to cut the chunks loose with sheet-metal shears, diagonal wire cutters or a hacksaw.

Near the edges of the cut, break the concrete off the reinforcing so some of the reinforcing extends into the patch area. Then wire in similar reinforcing material before patching. Concrete patching is covered on pages 105-106.

As you work, be alert for pipes in or directly below the concrete. Pipes are usually buried deep enough to avoid damage when concrete is removed, but sometimes not.

When you're working alongside a wall, you may find the concrete slab is thicker under the wall. This means the wall is bearing, and the thick section is part of the house foundation. Don't cut all the way through that thickened section. You can remove small portions of it for clearance if you need to, but plan on running new pipes alongside or underneath.

WATER-SUPPLY SYSTEM

Most existing water-supply systems are either *galvanized pipe* or *copper pipe*. A few systems installed within the last decade use plastic pipes and fittings. These include *polyvinyl chloride* (PVC), *chlorinated polyvinyl chloride* (CPVC), or *polybutylene*. These systems are not yet common.

In most code jurisdictions, plastic pipe has only recently gained acceptance for use in indoor water-supply systems. A few jurisdictions still prohibit its use. Plastic pipe is more commonly used for drain systems and trap assemblies.

When modifying an existing system, it's best to use pipes and fittings of the same material. You can often add plastic pipe to a metallic-pipe system, but special adapters are required. Mixing two kinds of metal pipe can lead to *electrolytic corrosion*. This can result in rapid failure of pipes or fittings.

Dissimilar metal pipes, usually

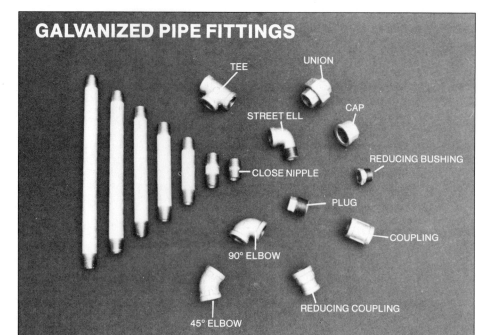

GALVANIZED PIPE FITTINGS

TEE
UNION
STREET ELL
CAP
CLOSE NIPPLE
REDUCING BUSHING
PLUG
COUPLING
90° ELBOW
45° ELBOW
REDUCING COUPLING

copper and galvanized, should be connected with a *dielectric union.* This connector looks like an ordinary union, but it electrically insulates the two metals from each other. Without current flow there's no electrolytic corrosion.

Adapters—There are adapters to connect practically anything to anything in a plumbing system. Some situations may require you use two adapters together. For example, if a former owner has used *flare connections* in a copper system, you can use adapters to convert to pipe threads and then to copper *sweat connections.*

Describe connectors accurately when you go to buy them. Always write down the description of the adapter itself, as in *1/2-inch male IPS x 1/2-inch female CPVC.* IPS stands for *Iron Pipe Size.*

First, look at the existing pipe end and write down what connects to it. That describes one end of the adapter. Then decide what you want to connect to the adapter and write down what fits that. That describes the other end of the adapter.

Galvanized Pipe—Iron or steel water-supply pipe is usually coated, or *galvanized,* with zinc to increase resistance to corrosion. Standard sizes of galvanized pipe are listed in the pipe sizing chart on page 124.

Galvanized pipe and fittings are threaded together. The pipe threads are tapered and fittings have the reverse taper. These threads are dif-

ferent from machine threads, which are straight. Never try to combine machine and pipe threads, even though some sizes seem to be identical.

The tapered threads and malleable fittings make galvanized-pipe systems leakfree in the face of vibration and changes in water temperature. As the pipe and fitting are threaded together, the taper forces the fitting to stretch to accommodate it. The heavy band at the end of the fitting remains in tension, squeezing the threads and preventing leaks.

Though galvanized pipe is not as corrosion resistant as copper or plastic pipe, it's still the most common pipe you'll find in an older home. Until recently, it was the least expensive pipe available.

Have the plumbing supplier cut galvanized pipe to length and thread it when you buy it. Threaded pipe nipples come in standard lengths from 1 to 12 inches, sometimes longer. You can buy galvanized pipe in lengths up to 21 feet, but you usually must thread cut lengths yourself or have the plumbing supplier do this.

To do your own cutting and threading, use a hacksaw, a sturdy vise and a *pipe threader.* This tool has a threaded cutting head, called a *die,* attached to a long handle. The die is positioned over the pipe end and rotated to cut the threads. Pipe threaders come with interchangeable dies for different pipe sizes and can be rented at most tool-rental companies or purchased at most plumbing suppliers.

Several tools are used for assembling and taking apart galvanized pipe. *Vise-grip pliers* and *Channel-lock pliers* can be useful in tight spaces. But if you're removing or adding much galvanized pipe, use the right-size *pipe wrenches.* Also called *Stillson wrenches* after their inventor, pipe wrenches are self-tightening as long as they're facing in the right direction. The movable jaw of a pipe wrench swivels to lock the teeth of both jaws solidly into the pipe or fitting. Be careful when using pipe wrenches. The jaw's swivel action develops enough force to distort a fitting or pipe end so severely that it won't mate with other threaded pieces.

Always work with pipe wrenches in pairs. Use one to hold back against the other, one wrench on either side of the joint. This concentrates the force on just the one joint you're working on.

If additional force is needed to loosen a threaded connection, position the handles of both wrenches vertically and slightly apart from each other. Use both hands to squeeze handles together as you would a pair of pliers. Be careful not to pinch your fingers between the handles.

If even more force is needed to break a joint loose, slip a length of pipe over each wrench handle to increase leverage. If a pipe connection appears to be frozen tight, apply a squirt of penetrating oil or WD-40 to the connection before trying the above methods.

When tightening threaded connections, don't overdo it. Tightening a connection too far risks splitting the fitting or stripping threads. When you have to apply heavy pressure with the pipe wrench to get another quarter turn, the connection is tight.

Use *pipe-joint compound* on all threaded connections unless pipe manufacturer's assembly instructions say otherwise. Pipe-joint compound does not act as a sealant, except where pipe threads are poorly cut or damaged. It's used to lubricate pipe threads, allowing a connection to be tightened beyond where it would if the threads were dry.

Many years ago, white lead ground in oil was used for pipe-joint compound. White lead is highly toxic. If you find an old can of white-lead compound among your supplies,

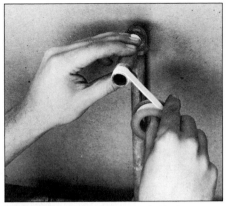
Wrap pipe-thread tape clockwise, as shown.

don't use it—dispose of it safely. This also applies to any unmarked bags of dark red powder, which is probably *litharge,* or red lead. This toxic substance was also used as a pipe-joint compound, mostly on boilers and steam-pipe fittings. If you find white or red lead has been used on the pipe joints you're working on, clean it off with a wire brush and solvent. Use modern pipe-joint compound for reassembly.

Today, anything a plumbing supplier has on the shelf labeled "pipe-joint compound" is safe and will do the job. But the easiest and cleanest product for the do-it-yourselfer is a roll of *Teflon pipe-thread tape.* One popular brand is called *Tape Dope.* Like pipe-joint compound, the tape acts as a lubricant. It has no adhesive.

To apply the tape, wrap it tightly onto the male threads of the pipe connection. The tape should take on the form of the threads. Wrap tape clockwise around the threads, as shown in the photo above. Two or three layers of tape will suffice. Don't be alarmed if you take apart one of these connections and find the tape has smeared. This is the way it's supposed to work. Apply another layer or two of tape and reassemble the connection.

A special lubricant is available for the tape, but you don't really need it, except on large pipe sizes. On small pipe sizes, a drop of light oil or squirt of WD-40 can be used, if necessary. Pipe-thread tape makes the threads slick, so don't overtighten. One advantage of the tape is that it won't harden or dry out. This makes future dismantling easier.

If possible, start dismantling galva-

nized pipe at the *downstream end* of the pipe run you're working on, or at a nearby *union.* The downstream end is the last fixture in the pipe run. The point where the water enters the house is called the *upstream end.* A *union* is a fitting that allows you to disconnect the pipe on either side of it.

Unless there is a union nearby, it's hard to dismantle sections in the middle of a pipe run. If there's no union nearby, find a short piece of pipe in the run or a fitting in a convenient location. Cut the pipe or fitting with a hacksaw. Then unscrew the cut ends. You can dismantle the pipe run in either direction from there. If you cut a short pipe length, called a *nipple,* it can be replaced with two shorter nipples and a union.

To make a new connection, cut and remove a length of pipe, then substitute two shorter lengths with a *tee* in the middle. An easier way is to find a convenient elbow or coupling. Remove it and substitute a tee.

You can't *always* make additional connections to existing pipe runs. Fixtures already connected to that run may have used up all of its legal or actual *flow capacity.* Flow capacity is the amount of water a pipe can carry. If too many fixtures are being used at the same time, and the pipe is not

If you have trouble getting into a galvanized-pipe system to make changes, pick a convenient short length of pipe. Cut with a hacksaw, and later replace with two shorter pipe nipples and a union.

large enough to handle them, the water at each outlet will be reduced to a trickle. To make an additional connection, you may have to increase the pipe size upstream of the new connection. Refer to the pipe-sizing chart on page 124 for flow requirements for various bathroom fixtures.

Copper Pipe—There are two kinds of copper pipe—hard and soft. The only real difference between hard- and soft-copper pipe is that soft copper is bendable. Soft-copper pipe has several advantages over hard-copper pipe. You can carry it home in a coil, rather than in straight 20-foot lengths. You don't need as many fittings, because you can bend it around corners. Soft-copper pipe easy to thread into existing walls and floors. Also, the pipe can be bent to align to fittings and fixtures.

In some cases, soft-copper pipe is harder to work with than hard-copper pipe. Bending soft-copper pipe isn't as easy at it may seem. Bends must be gradual and free of kinks. This requires a tool called a *bending spring.* This is a length of steel spring that slips over the pipe so it stays round and doesn't kink.

It's difficult to straighten out curves at the ends of a length of soft-copper pipe. Because soft copper is malleable, you must be careful not to deform pipe ends when cutting, bending and handling. It's hard to get leakproof solder connections if pipe ends are out of round. See *Soldering Joints* on page 121.

Hard-copper pipe is easier to work with, provided there is adequate access. Because this pipe is less likely to deform, it's easier for the novice to cut, and to make good solder connections. Hard-copper pipe is slightly less expensive than soft-copper pipe.

If you don't have a way to transport 20-foot lengths of this pipe, take your measurements and a pipe cutter with you. Cut the pipe into convenient lengths before hauling it home.

You can buy copper pipe in three wall thicknesses. The heaviest is *Type K*, available in hard and soft pipe. Type K is identified by a green stripe or green lettering. *Type L* is medium weight, available both hard and soft, and identified by a blue stripe or lettering. The lightest is *Type M*, available in hard pipe only. It has a red stripe or lettering. The difference between the types is primarily in their

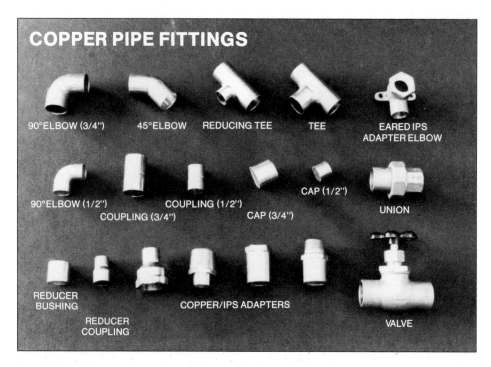

COPPER PIPE FITTINGS

90°ELBOW (3/4")   45°ELBOW   REDUCING TEE   TEE   EARED IPS ADAPTER ELBOW

90°ELBOW (1/2")   COUPLING (3/4")   COUPLING (1/2")   CAP (3/4")   CAP (1/2")   UNION

REDUCER BUSHING   REDUCER COUPLING   COPPER/IPS ADAPTERS   VALVE

bursting strength, but even the lightest is safe for residential use. Still, local building codes may dictate which type you can use.

Copper pipe for rough plumbing is usually assembled by *sweat-soldering* the joints. This technique is described on the facing page. Copper pipe can also be connected with *flare fittings*, or *brass compression fittings*, as described on page 129. These fittings should not be used on plumbing inside a wall or under a floor. It's possible for flare and compression fittings to loosen and leak. To tighten them would require tearing into the wall or floor.

Plastic Pipe—In many jurisdictions, you can use PVC (polyvinyl chloride) and CPVC (chlorinated polyvinyl chloride) plastic pipe for residential plumbing systems. Of the two, CPVC is much more resistant to heat, so use PVC on cold-water lines only. Both types are usually rigid, although there are somewhat flexible versions for special uses. Fittings for plastic pipe are socketed much like sweat fittings for copper pipe, but plastic pipe is solvent-welded rather than soldered.

Cleaners, primers and solvent-weld cements are entirely different for PVC, CPVC and polybutylene. If you have more than one kind of pipe on the job, don't mix up either the pipe and fittings, or the cleaners, primers and cements.

Plastic pipe is easy to assemble. Cut pipe to length with a fine-tooth handsaw and remove all burrs with sand-

paper or a utility knife. See photos on page 125. Clean pipe ends and inside of fitting with the appropriate cleaner, available from the pipe supplier.

If required, apply a thin coat of primer to pipe and fitting and let dry. Though PVC and CPVC cleaners and solvents are usually clear, the primer is often tinted a color. The reason for this is that the application of primer is required in some code jurisdictions. If this is the case where you live, apply additional primer to the pipe an inch or two beyond the fitting so the building inspector can see that you've used it.

Work quickly with solvent-weld cement—it sets up fast. You must position pipe and fitting correctly on the first try. Use index marks across the joint if you need them. Coat the pipe end and inside of the fitting with cement. Insert the pipe end into the fitting with a continuous, smooth twisting motion. After the pipe bottoms out in the fitting socket, give it another 1/4 to 1/3 twist, stopping with the fitting in its correct position. In a few seconds the fitting will freeze there. Leave the joint undisturbed for a few minutes to set up.

Work carefully with plastic pipe. An error on one joint creates at least one extra cut and three extra joints. If you make a mistake, don't try to readjust pipe and fitting. You'll create a leak. Let solvent cement set up a few minutes so you don't disturb nearby joints. Saw off the pipe a few inches

Continued on page 122

SOLDERING JOINTS

The basic technique for connecting copper pipes and fittings is called *sweat-soldering*. Melted solder is drawn into the thin space between pipe and fitting by capillary action. This process is made possible by the high quality control standards of today's pipe and fitting producers. The outside diameter of copper pipe and the inside diameter of the fittings are carefully controlled.

You'll need a propane torch, a pipe cutter, emery cloth, soldering flux and solid-core solder.

Clean, Flux, and Assemble—Clean pipe end and inside of fitting with emery cloth. All traces of oxidation and foreign substances must be removed. A few twists of the emery cloth are all that's needed. Don't use steel wool—the particles left behind oxidize when heated, contaminating the joint.

Coat both surfaces with flux, either paste or liquid, to prevent new oxidation. Plug pipe all the way into the fitting socket. On most jobs, several joints can be prepared, and then soldered one after the other.

Heat—After pipe assembly is lined up correctly, light propane torch and adjust it. For small pipe sizes, the blue inner flame should be about 3/4-inch long, for large pipe sizes, 1-1/2 inches long.

If there is any white or orange in the flame, the torch-tip air openings are partially plugged. Shut off torch and *let it cool*. Remove torch tip and clean it.

Position tip of blue inner flame against side of joint. Move torch back and forth to distribute heat evenly. The flux will melt and then start to bubble and smoke a little. Test heat by touching pipe with the end of the solder. The joint is hot enough when solder melts after a second or so from heat in the joint, outside the torch flame.

Solder should spread freely, and have a shiny surface. If melted solder bubbles and becomes dry and porous-looking, the joint is too hot. Remove torch and pull joint apart carefully—it's hot. Reclean, reflux, and start heating again.

Feed Solder—Once the connection is heated to the correct temperature, start feeding solder. Use the somewhat cooler flame beyond the blue flame to compensate for heat the solder absorbs. Feed melting solder into joint from the top.

When melted solder starts to run off the bottom of the joint, move flame away from the joint, but keep feeding solder. As the joint cools, some of the melted solder will seem to disappear. It's being drawn into the joint. Keep feeding solder until enough heat has dissipated that the melting rate has slowed to almost nothing.

As you feed solder, slide the melting end around the joint, to form a small radiused surface of solder covering the joint opening. Wipe off surplus solder with a damp cloth before it completely

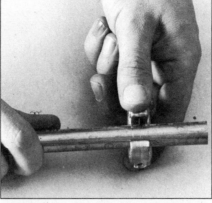
1. Use pipe cutter to make clean, square end.

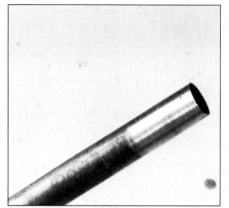
2. Clean pipe end and inside of fitting with emery cloth.

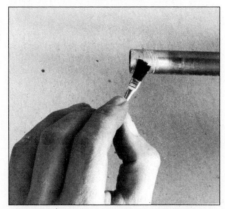
3. Apply flux to pipe end and inside of fitting.

4. Attach pipe to fitting and heat until solder melts when touched to joint.

5. Feed solder into joint from top, using outer cone of torch flame to maintain temperature. Continue to feed solder as joint cools.

6. Unbroken radius of solder around joint indicates it is completely sealed.

sets up. After the joint cools, clean off remaining flux.

Did It Work?—That radius of solder indicates the joint is completely sealed. If you cleaned the joint correctly, saw the solder draw in, and have a complete radius, you've got a good solder joint.

Safety—Whenever possible, do your soldering in the open. When you have to solder pipes in a wall or near framing members, protect them with a piece of sheet metal or 1/4-inch asbestos board, if you have it. If these aren't available, use a piece of 1/2-inch drywall. Wet the paper on the side toward the flame so it won't catch fire, and keep rewetting it

periodically. Keep a fire extinguisher or a bucket of water handy.

The melting point of plumbing solder is fairly low, but melted solder can produce a burn on bare skin. Dripping solder won't ordinarily burn or set fire to clothing or shoes, but it does fuse and damage nylon, polyester and a few other synthetic fabrics. Solder spatters can be peeled off most fabrics after they cool. Remove solder spatters before putting clothes in the washing machine. The solder can damage the washer's pump.

When soldering, wear gloves to protect hands and safety glasses to protect eyes.

NOISE CONTROL

Bathrooms and their equipment and plumbing often create noise problems. Such noise can be controlled or reduced—it can rarely be eliminated completely. First you should analyze the problem, so you can correctly apply the solutions described here.

Bathroom noise can be a complicated problem. The source of the noise can vary, so you need to locate it before you cure the problem. Bear in mind that your bathroom can have more than one noise problem.

Sometimes bathroom noise is bothersome only to the user, but more often the noise filters into other rooms or through the house. Noise generated in or near the bathroom can leak to the rest of the house, such as through the gap under a door. Or noise can be transmitted through surfaces, such as walls or doors, such as when someone knocks on the other side of a wall and you hear it on your side.

The principal noise sources are noisy fixtures and pipes. But a noise that seems to be caused by a fixture can be originating in the pipes, and vice versa. Noise problems and solutions described here are categorized by the normal *apparent* source. Bear in mind that you may have to take more than one of these measures to finally solve the problem.

Controlling Fixture Noise—One of the most frequent noise complaints is noise when a toilet is flushed. Installing a toilet that flushes more quietly may or may not solve the problem. The objectionable noise might actually be caused by the flushed water flowing through the drain lines. Or a constriction in the water-supply line may be causing noise during flushing and refill. If any of those noisy pipes are in solid contact with the house framing, the noise will be amplified and transmitted to other locations in the house.

If any fixture, including a toilet, chronically produces a lot of glugging and gurgling noises, check the vertical stack that goes through the roof. It may be blocked, forcing the fixture to vent through the trap. Or the vent may be too small. Suspect venting problems first if *all* the fixtures glug and gurgle.

A toilet that whistles or *sings* while the tank is filling can often be corrected by replacing the *ballcock*, or fill valve, with a quieter one. Before replacing the ballcock, though, check to make sure the supply valve is all the way open and the supply riser isn't kinked.

Some tubs drum loudly from the impact of the water while they're filling. Filling most of the space under the tub with insulating foam will not only deaden noise, but will insulate the tub so the bath water doesn't cool down as fast.

Foam made without formaldahyde is now available in aerosol cans, making the job a simple one. If the wall-finish materials are already in place, you may have to poke a few holes for the nozzle of the aerosol can. Don't entomb the piping and drain lines so thoroughly that any future repair work would be difficult.

Controlling Pipe Noises—Pipes produce two kinds of noise—gurgles produced by water flow, and banging noises when water flow starts and stops, called *water hammer*. Pipes can transmit such noises a surprising distance.

Singing and whistling is a sign of excessive water-flow velocity somewhere in the plumbing system. Sometimes, excessive velocity will produce a low rumbling from a type of extremely turbulent flow, called *cavitation*. The remedy is to locate and remove the constriction that produces the excessive flow velocity. Sources include blockages due to scale formation, bent or pinched pipes, and undersized pipes or fittings.

After pinpointing which fixtures produce the noise, check for a pinched supply pipe or for a partially closed supply valve. If all the fixtures cause the noise to start up, one or more pipes to the bathroom are probably partially clogged, or were undersized to begin with.

Blockages inside pipes can be difficult to pinpoint. One fairly successful method of locating the blockage source is to use a short length of rubber hose as a "stethoscope." Listen through one end of the hose while moving the other end along the pipes in question. This method is often used by auto mechanics to locate engine noises.

Check the chart on page 124 to verify pipe sizing. Also check all valves and fittings to make sure they're correctly sized and fully open.

Water Hammer—This is a banging noise that occurs when water is turned on or off. If the noise appears to be right at the fitting you're operating, the remedy is a device called an *air chamber*. If the noise seems to be elsewhere, such as inside the wall, a pipe is probably not adequately strapped down and is free to knock against something else. An air chamber on the line may help a pipe-knock, but often the only solution is to get inside the wall and securely strap the pipe.

An air chamber is a length of pipe installed vertically, capped at the top and connected to a water line at the bottom. A small quantity of air is trapped in the air chamber and dissipates any shock waves generated in the water line. That's because air is highly compressible; water is difficult to compress.

You can make your own air chambers, or buy ready-made ones at a plumbing supplier. Air chambers are normally installed inside the wall. If you need to correct a water-hammer problem on an existing fixture, dismantle the supply pipe and remove the stop. Then install the air chamber on a tee where the stop valve was, add a short length of pipe, and reinstall the stop valve.

Drain-Line Noise—This problem is more common in ABS plastic drain lines than in cast-iron ones. The sheer mass of cast-iron drain pipe more effectively absorbs water noises. One of the advantages of ABS—its light weight—works against it from the noise standpoint. Drain-line noise can be reduced by covering pipes with an aerosol insulating foam.

Continued from page 120

back from the fitting, and discard the fitting. Install a coupling and a short length of pipe, and a new fitting.

Testing the System—After you've made all changes to the water-supply system, cap all the open pipe ends. Then *slowly* turn on the water. Have a helper watch the new connections while you do this—there may be a joint you forgot to cement, solder or tighten, which can spew a lot of water in a short time.

Check the entire system for leaks. Leave the system under pressure for an hour or so, then recheck. This allows air in the system to escape and water to drip from any small leaks. If you find any leaks, drain the system, fix the leaks, then retest.

DRAINAGE SYSTEM CHANGES

Drain-line modifications can be laid out in pencil on walls and floor the same as for water lines. Two main rules for drain lines must be observed at all times: *1. Sewage always runs downhill.* This means all lines must be sloped away from the fixture or inlet, at least 1/4 inch per foot. *2. All drainage systems must be vented to the atmosphere.*

Vertical runs, called *stacks,* should extend up through the roof for venting. There are limits on how far you can run a horizontal drain line without providing a stack. Use the table on page 124 as a general guide. Drain lines for island lavatories require a loop to serve as an air break. Check with your local plumbing inspector for specifics and any local code variations.

Slope is usually no problem if you're relocating a drain line closer to the present stack. If you use the original stack opening, the slope for the new run will be even steeper than that of the original run, provided the new drain inlet is at the same level as the old drain inlet.

It's sometimes more complicated if

If you have a noisy drain line running across the dining-room ceiling and down the wall, poke a few holes in the finish material and foam the airspace around the pipe in both places. If you're installing new pipes or otherwise have the wall opened up, you can foam the pipe in the stud bay before closing up the wall. After the foam sets, saw off any excess with a serrated bread knife.

Amplified Pipe Noise—In many cases, the source of a noise is quite small, but amplified by contact between the pipes and a larger resonating surface, such as drywall. This is the same principle as when the tiny sound produced by a violin string is transmitted to the box of the instrument and amplified. The effect is more pronounced with high-frequency noises than with low-frequency ones. You can recognize this kind of noise by the fact that it doesn't seem to come from one specific place. The noise seems to come from a whole surface at once. The only cures are to separate the pipes from the resonating surface—wall, floor, or ceiling—or to change the resonating behavior of the surface.

If you can get to the noisy pipe, isolate it. Use short lengths of pipe insulation, fiberglass insulation, or even a couple of thicknesses of 15-pound building felt. Building felt is a particularly good approach for pipes running through holes in studs, where the holes are only a little larger than the pipes. Don't forget the holes where pipe stubs come through the wall.

If it's not feasible to get to the pipes, you can try changing the resonating surface instead. Anything you do to increase the mass, size or thickness of the resonating surface is likely to reduce noise. Often the most practical method is to apply an extra layer of drywall, laminating it to the wall surface with a thin layer of joint compound before nailing.

Sound Leaks—A house structure leaks noise quite readily. Any small hole or crack provides a transmission path for plumbing noises. Heating and cooling

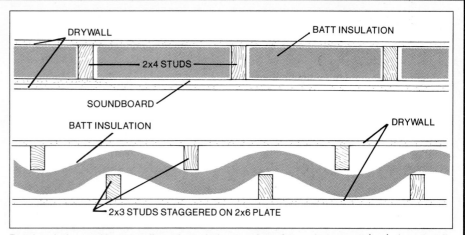

Batt insulation and/or soundboard can help soundproof an existing wall (top). A new wall can be soundproofed by staggering studs (bottom). This prevents sound from being transmitted through the studs themselves.

ductwork channels sound. Sounds traveling through ductwork can usually be deadened by lining the first few feet of duct behind the registers with rigid-fiberglass insulation board. Be sure the insulation board you use is specifically approved for use *inside* ductwork.

Finding sound leaks will require some detective work, depending on the problem and how much work you're doing on the bathroom. Any opening in the wall, floor or ceiling surface is suspect. Seal all openings around pipes and electrical boxes with caulking compound or insulating foam from an aerosol can. Pull off any baseboard and caulk the line where the wall meets the floor. Back-to-back electrical boxes and adjoining recessed medicine cabinets transmit almost as much sound as an open hole in the wall—consider reworking them to eliminate the sound path.

Loose-fitting bathroom doors provide sound-transmission paths. In many homes with warm-air heating systems, the bottoms of doors are cut off an inch or more above the floor to allow for air return. Standard exterior weatherstripping and bottom sweeps can help reduce sound. Other arrangements for

air return can be made that conduct much less sound.

Structural Noise Control—You can take many steps to control noise, starting in the planning process. Try not to locate a bathroom door so it faces another room door. Locate closets—in the bathroom or adjacent rooms—so they serve as additional sound buffers. Arrange ductwork so there's room for sound-absorbent material around the duct, between the bathroom register and any others.

Walls can be built so they reduce noise transmission. Several kinds of sound-absorbent wall coverings are made, commonly referred to as *soundboard*. Soundboard is attached to the studs, under the drywall. If you're planning to use soundboard, be sure to allow for the additional thickness.

Installing batt insulation in an otherwise empty wall space does little to control sound transmission. Air transmission of noise inside the wall is cut down, but noise still travels through the studs. If you build the wall so the studs don't extend all the way through it, batt insulation can do quite a bit of good in suppressing noise. Construction details for this sort of wall are shown above.

you're moving the inlet farther away. First check to see if there was enough extra slope in the original installation to permit you to get an acceptable amount of slope in the new run. Check slope by using a level or by measuring from the floor the heights of stack opening and new drain inlet. Adjust for any slope in the floor when you take measurements.

Divide the height difference between openings, in inches, by the horizontal pipe run in feet to get the number of inches drop per foot of run. As mentioned, you'll need a minimum of 1/4 inch slope per 1 foot of run. Any less will cause slow drain-

age or clogs in the drain line. Level or upsloped drain lines won't drain at all.

If there isn't enough slope, raise the inlet at the fixture, if you can. Otherwise, rework the stack to lower the opening.

Cast-Iron Pipe—You may have any of several different types of cast-iron drain pipe, depending on the age of the system. *Belled cast iron* was used in the earliest systems. The pipe was made in sections 3 or 4 feet long, with a bell-shaped hub on one end. The straight end of one length was inserted into the belled end of the other. Then the bell was stuffed with a tarred ropy material called *oakum* and tamped.

Finally, melted lead was poured into the joint, allowed to cool, and tamped tightly into place with a blunt chisel, called a *caulking iron*.

Belled cast-iron pipe is difficult to modify. Replacement lengths and fittings are not readily available today. Also, because of the belled ends, you often have to take the system apart from the top end of the stack. When you must rework such a stack, it's best to dismantle it down to the stack opening, then replace the stack with ABS-plastic drain pipe to suit the new layout. See pages 125-126. There's an adapter that fits into a cast-iron hub and accepts standard ABS pipe.

DETERMINING MINIMUM PIPE SIZES

1. Make a list of fixtures on water line in question. Refer to chart and add up fixture units for each fixture. Left column is for sizing main pipe between hot-water heater and street service. This pipe carries combined hot- and cold-water demand for each fixture connected to it. Right column is for sizing individual hot- and cold-water branch pipes. In most cases you'll be working with branch pipes. See below.

FIXTURE UNITS

	Main pipe	Branch pipes
BAR SINK	1	.75
BATHTUB	2	1.5
DISHWASHER	2	1.5
HOSE BIBB	3	3.0
KITCHEN SINK	2	1.5
LAUNDRY SINK	2	1.5
LAVATORY	1	.75
SHOWER	2	1.5
WASHER	2	1.5
TOILET	3	3.0

2. Find the approximate total length of the water line you're sizing from the chart below. Then find the next-largest number that exceeds your total fixture-unit count, in the appropriate column below. The pipe size at the top of the column is the one to use.

TOTAL FIXTURE UNITS

Pipe Size	1/2"	3/4"	1"	1-1/4"	1-1/2"
Maximum Pipe Length					
40'	9	27	60	168	270
60'	8	23	47	130	225
80'	7	19	41	106	193
100'	6	17	36	89	167
150'	5	14	30	66	128

Note: These figures are based on pipe of average interior roughness, and normal water pressure (46 to 60 PSI delivered to the house). It is also assumed that water meter and street-service line are at least as large as the pipe you're sizing. There may be local code variations.

MAXIMUM HORIZONTAL RUN FROM TRAP TO VENT

Pipe Size	Maximum Run
1-1/4"	2'-6"
1-1/2"	3'-6"
2"	5'-0"
3"	6'-0"
4" and over	10'-0"

DRAIN LINE SLOPE

LEVEL   1/4" per foot minimum

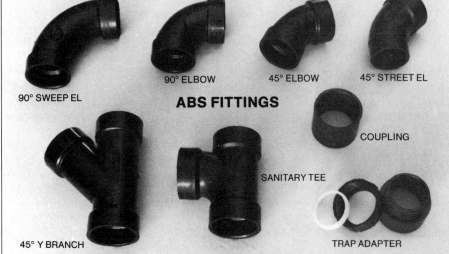

ABS FITTINGS

90° SWEEP EL   90° ELBOW   45° ELBOW   45° STREET EL

COUPLING

45° Y BRANCH   SANITARY TEE   TRAP ADAPTER

Later cast-iron systems used the same belled-end pipe, but with neoprene gaskets instead of lead and oakum. These gaskets usually disintegrate if disturbed. Replacements are hard to find.

Also, you need a special tool to make connections. The tool is attached on either side of the joint with chains. A compound linkage then draws the two parts of the joint together. Again, it's usually easier to dismantle the stack and replace it with ABS drain line.

If you want to use the same kind of pipe for replacement, try to find an older plumber who has the tools and has worked with this kind of pipe. Many younger plumbers won't know how to do this work.

More recent cast-iron systems use *no-hub pipe.* Straight lengths of cast-iron pipe are joined with couplings made of neoprene with a stainless-steel jacket and two integral clamps. Because pipe sections butt together instead of interlocking, a section can be removed at any point in the run and modified.

Securely support upper sections of a vertical stack before you remove a section from it. Use any method of support you're sure will work. Methods of support vary with stack location. One method is to tack a length of 1x4 or 2x4 between the studs in front of the stack. Then fasten the stack to the crosspiece with perforated-metal strapping tape. Another method is to fasten a length of perforated-metal strapping tape to the stack with a worm-drive hose clamp, then nail the other end of strapping tape to a stud.

The neoprene-lined couplings should not be reused—buy new ones. Band tension is critical to permanent sealing of couplings. You'll need a special T-shaped torque wrench. Torque wrenches should be available where you buy the couplings.

Cutting Cast Iron—If you only need to make one or two cuts in cast-iron drain line, you can use a hacksaw or a hammer and cold chisel. You can also use a metal-cutoff blade in a portable circular saw. To cut with a hammer and cold chisel, mark a line all the way around the pipe. Make a light cut with the chisel along the cut line. Keep chiseling around the pipe, gradually deepening the cut, until you've cut all the way through. To avoid breaking the pipe, do not use heavy blows.

BELLED CAST-IRON PIPE

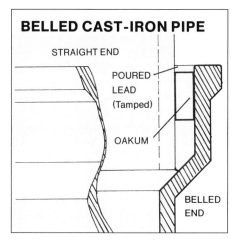

STRAIGHT END

POURED LEAD (Tamped)

OAKUM

BELLED END

GASKETED CAST-IRON PIPE

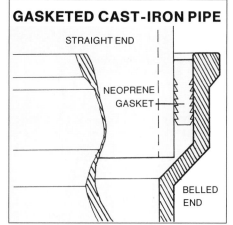

STRAIGHT END

NEOPRENE GASKET

BELLED END

NO-HUB CAST-IRON PIPE

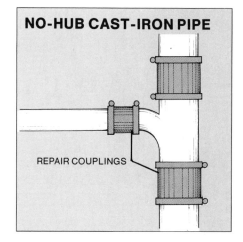

REPAIR COUPLINGS

To make many cuts in cast-iron drain line, rent a device called a *squeeze cutter*. It looks like a large chain wrench, but the chain is lined with cutting wheels. The chain is wrapped around the pipe and gradually tightened until the pipe fractures, making a clean cut.

ABS-Plastic Drain Line—Most new residential drainage systems are built with *ABS* (acrylonitrile butadiene styrene) plastic drain line. ABS is easily modified and installed. The joints are solvent-welded, similar to other kinds of plastic pipe. See photos at right. Once assembled, the separate parts form a single unit. ABS systems do not depend on mechanical joints.

Cut ABS-plastic drain line with a fine-tooth handsaw. Don't use a hacksaw—the teeth clog up with plastic particles. Also, don't cut ABS with a power saw. Heat generated by the fast-moving blade can cause the plastic to melt and stick to the blade.

To modify ABS drain lines, use *repair couplings*. These fittings look like standard couplings, but do not have an internal ridge to serve as a pipe stop. You can slide a repair coupling all the way onto one piece of pipe and slide it back down over the joint. If your plumbing supplier doesn't stock repair couplings, file the internal ridge off a regular coupling and use that.

To raise or lower a fitting in a vertical stack, make cuts in the pipe several inches above and below the fitting. Then cut off part of the loose piece and reattach the shorter piece with a repair coupling. Cut a piece of pipe to fill the gap at other end, or use the piece cut from the opposite end of the section. Use two repair couplings to complete the modification.

To insert a fitting in a run of plastic pipe, determine the location for the fitting. Mark on the pipe the location of the bottoms of the hubs of the new fitting. Mark and cut 6 or 8 inches beyond the hub marks, to free the section of pipe. Cut the free length at the hub marks, and cement in the fitting. Then replace the assembly in the pipe run, using two repair couplings to attach it.

Copper Drain Line—These are excellent systems, but not used much in residential work because of cost.

They're much more common in commercial applications, so pipe and fittings should be available.

Copper drain lines are cut and connected exactly the same as copper water-supply lines, described on page 120. You may need a large torch if you have to solder these larger pipe sizes.

Testing Drain Lines—Like water lines, drain lines are subject to inspection and testing. Testing requirements for a complete new drain system are the same in most

Basic steps common to all plastic pipe are shown here: 1. Cut square, clean off burrs. 2. Apply cement to fitting. 3. Apply cement to pipe end. 4. Join with a 1/4-turn. Cement sets within a few seconds, so you must work quickly. Some kinds of pipe require cleaner or primer before cementing. Check with the pipe supplier.

To relocate a fitting in plastic drain line, follow the steps shown here: 1. Cut drain line. 2. Cut stack. 3. Modify stack. 4. Replace modified stack using repair couplings. Technique for installing a new fitting is similar. Finally, patch cut made in drywall.

jurisdictions. All openings in the system are capped or plugged. An air compressor is then used to increase air pressure in the system. If the air pressure holds for a specified period of time, the system is tight. Then the plugs or caps can be removed and the system can be connected.

Testing requirements vary when you've only changed part of the

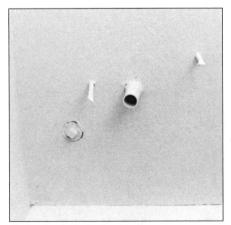

Correct rough-in for lavatory is capped hot and cold water stubs, capped drain stubs. Stubs should be located so they don't interfere with later work such as cabinets. Keep holes in wall finish material small enough that escutcheon covers them.

system. The only way to find out what's required is to discuss the work to be done with the building inspector. Small changes can often be approved on the basis of a simple visual inspection. If so, keep the work neat and tidy—it helps.

Plastic drain systems are the easiest to cap for pressure testing. The fitting manufacturers make simple plugs that cement into open pipe ends. After testing the system, plugs are broken out with a screwdriver so you can make finish connections. Inflatable plugs and screw-on caps are used to close off the openings on copper and cast-iron drain systems. Inflatable plugs, pressure gages and air compressors can usually be rented from a tool-rental company.

ROUGHING-IN FOR FIXTURES

All of the rough plumbing for fixtures should be complete before any finishing work is done in the bathroom. The construction sequence chart on page 69 details the recommended working order. This involves running and stubbing out hot and cold water-supply lines and drain lines, and installing required blocking. If possible, get the roughing-in sheets

from the plumbing supplier for the exact make and model of each fixture you'll be installing.

Stubs and Caps—Generally, pipes stubbed out of the wall should extend 4 to 6 inches beyond the finish-wall surface. Any excess can be cut off as you do the finish installation. But if the stub is too short, you'll have to cut into the wall or floor to lengthen it.

How you cap off a stub depends on the kind of pipe you're working with, and how you're going to connect the fixtures to it. If you're using threaded connections, install the correct-size male-thread adapter to the stub, and use a threaded cap. For sweat-soldered, cemented or compression connections, make the stub an inch or two longer and solder or cement on the appropriate size cap. When you attach the finish connections, all you need do is cut off the caps along with an inch or so of pipe. This is also the best approach if you don't yet know what the connection method will be.

Vanity-Top Lavatory—All that's needed is hot and cold water lines, and drain line, stubbed out and capped. See photo below.

Wall-Hung Lavatory—Water-supply and drain-line stubs are similar to those for a vanity-top lavatory. You'll also need to install a horizontal mounting block of 1x6 or 3/4-inch plywood to provide anchorage for the bracket that supports the lavatory. The mounting block should be recessed flush with faces of adjoining studs, and should be securely attached with countersunk flat-head wood screws.

If you prefer, 2x6 blocking can be cut to fit between the studs. To attach, toenail 16d nails through top and sides of block into studs, or into block from other side of studs, if enough wall covering was removed for access.

Floor-Mounted Toilet—The water-supply line for a toilet can be stubbed out from the wall or the floor. The drain line requires a special fitting called a *floor flange*, which must be positioned the correct distance from the wall. See drawing on page 128.

Almost all standard toilets are designed for the centerline of the floor flange to be 12 inches from the wall. This flange setup is referred to as a *12-inch rough-in*. If you're planning to install an older toilet, measure it to make sure you have enough clearance. Some were made for 10- or

14-inch rough-in, and some antiques have completely odd rough-in dimensions. Incidentally, a few toilets are still made for 10 and 14-inch rough-ins, to serve as replacements for older toilets. One of these can save a lot of extra work if you rough in wrong, or don't want to move an old 10- or 14-inch drain setup.

The floor flange is attached to the drain pipe much like any other fitting. It's cemented onto ABS pipe, soldered onto copper pipe, lead-jointed or clamped in place on cast-iron pipe. Make sure you get the correct floor flange for the type of pipe you're using.

The outer lip of the floor flange should rest on the floor, and should be tightly fastened with screws to the subfloor. Position the bolt slots so the bolts can be slipped in and located to line up with the bolt holes on the bowl. To keep debris out of the drain line, cap or plug the floor flange after roughing in. The toilet is installed after all finish work is done, including painting, trim work and floor-covering installation.

Wall-Mounted Toilet—A sturdy carrier must be installed in the wall to hold up a wall-mounted toilet. The thickness of the carrier usually dictates at least 2x6 studs in the wall. Carrier mounting in wall, connection of carrier to drain system, and assembly of toilet to carrier are all critical, and all variable. When you buy carrier and toilet, make sure that all parts are compatible, and get the detailed installation instructions. Follow them to the letter, especially with regard to any special sequence of bolt tightening.

The carrier is installed in the wall and connected to the pipes at the rough-in stage, before drywall or other wall-finish material is in place. The toilet itself is installed after all the finishing work is done.

Bathtub and Drain—Almost all built-in bathtubs install to the framing, not to the surface of the finish material—as shown above. So the bathtub and its drain must go in early, before the walls are closed in. It should also be installed before any other bathroom fixtures or cabinetry. Installation procedures for prefabricated shower units are much the same. Other fixtures are installed in the finish-plumbing stage, pages 128-133.

You must take steps to protect the

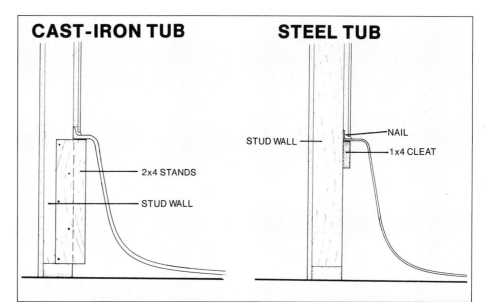

CAST-IRON TUB

2x4 STANDS
STUD WALL

STEEL TUB

STUD WALL
NAIL
1x4 CLEAT

Cross-sections of cast iron and steel tubs show how they fit against framing. Heavier cast-iron tub requires 2x4 stands or tub hangers for support. Cleats and nails support steel tub.

tub while the rest of the work goes on. So when you get the tub, get an inexpensive device called a *tub protector*. This is a molded-plastic cover that takes the abuse so the tub doesn't have to. Some fiberglass tubs are shipped in cartons that are marked for cutting up and reworking into a tub protector.

Before installing the tub, double-check the dimensions of the opening against the dimensions of the tub. The tub shouldn't be a force-fit, but there shouldn't be more than about a 1/4-inch gap where the tub meets the walls.

Fix or replace any bowed or mislocated studs. You may have to adjust wall locations slightly, and it's easier to do before the tub is in place. Also check the opening for squareness, using a framing square.

Now for the big job: Uncrate the tub and move it into place. Recruit as many helpers as tub weight dictates. All tubs are delicate before they're in place, and a big cast-iron tub can weigh as much as 1,100 pounds. Treat any tub like a giant hard-boiled egg—the object is to avoid cracking the shell. Use a dolly, and blankets and pads when necessary, to prevent damage.

The strategies for getting a tub into place vary with the circumstances. No one approach will work in every bathroom. The problem is similar to removing a tub, so much of the information about removal, starting on page 74, will be helpful. Be especially

careful for potential damage sources like nailheads or pieces of debris that can scratch or chip the tub when it's installed. If you scratch or ding the old tub in the process of getting it out, it doesn't matter much. The new tub must be protected more carefully.

After the tub is in place, carefully inspect it for any signs of *stress cracking*. This is fine cracking or crazing in the tub's finish surface, caused by overflexing the tub shell during installation. Edges and corners are the most-common problem spots.

Fiberglass tubs and shower enclosures with integral surrounds, like the kind shown on page 44, are prone to crazing where the end panels of the surround meet the top of the front apron. If you've cracked, chipped or otherwise damaged a tub or shower enclosure during installation, consult the supplier about the possibility of repairing it in place.

Don't lock in the tub or shower with wall-finish materials until you have the damage taken care of. You may have to pull out the tub or shower enclosure and replace it.

To avoid future problems keeping a good seal between tub and wall, the rim of a tub must be anchored in place and supported. A leveled 1x4 cleat on all three sides is good for enameled-steel and fiberglass tubs. The edges of a cast-iron tub are often too irregular for a cleat. If the tub supplier can furnish them, use metal hooks and brackets, called *tub hangers*, that mount on the studs. These are adjust-

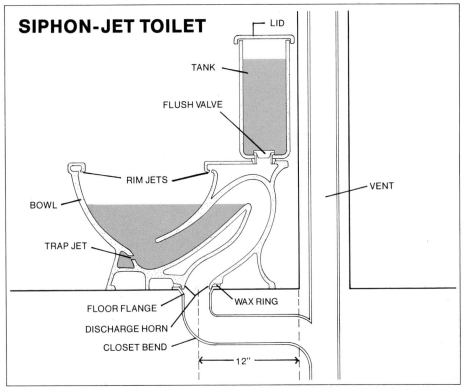

SIPHON-JET TOILET

- LID
- TANK
- FLUSH VALVE
- RIM JETS
- BOWL
- TRAP JET
- FLOOR FLANGE
- DISCHARGE HORN
- CLOSET BEND
- WAX RING
- VENT
- 12"

Floor flange for all modern toilets is centered 12 inches away from wall. Flanges for older toilets may be on 10-inch or 14-inch centers.

able and transfer some of the weight of the tub to the studs.

If you can't get tub hangers, shim the cast-iron tub so the rim is level all the way around. Then cut and insert 2x4 blocks to support the back apron of the tub on the bottom plate of the wall behind, as shown on page 127. Depending on the weight of the tub, two or three hangers or 2x4 supports along the back edge of the tub are sufficient.

Some enameled-steel tubs and most fiberglass tubs and shower enclosures will have slots or perforations along the rim for nailing. Nail through slots at each stud with a 1-1/2-inch galvanized roofing nail. Drive nails carefully, so you don't crimp or deform the tub, or hit it with the hammer.

Cast-iron tubs generally need no nailing. If an enameled-steel tub doesn't have nail perforations or slots, drive a nail at each stud anyway, just above the tub flange. Trap the flange against the stud with the head of the nail.

The tub drain assembles and connects to the drain pipe by means of slip joints. Consult the instructions packed with the drain for assembly specifics on gaskets and washers at drain and overflow openings. Loosely

assemble the drain, and trim any parts necessary to fit everything together. Then tighten one connection at a time, starting at the drain and overflow openings and working down to the drain-line connection.

Tub/Shower Fitting—All tub and shower fittings can be divided into the *trim parts* and the *body* of the fitting. Some manufacturers may package body and trim separately. The body is installed at the rough-in stage. Put the trim parts aside for finish installation.

The rough-in dimensions shown in the drawing on page 76 are the *usual* ones for height of shower head, fitting body and tub spout. Adjust up or down to suit yourself. You can also install two showerheads, one high and one low, with a selector valve between. This is especially helpful if some users are short, and others tall.

The fitting body connects to the hot and cold supply lines, either by direct sweat-soldering, direct IPS thread, or by a ground-joint connection. You'll have to adapt the supply pipes you're using to fit the inlet connections. Then run lines from the outlets to spout or shower-head locations. On the lines to spout or shower-head locations, use an *eared* elbow to turn the last corner. This provides a way to anchor the pipes.

Some manufacturers use the same fitting body for shower, tub/shower and tub use. A plug is provided for the unused opening in the fitting body. Be sure you thread in and tighten this plug during the rough-in stage, if it's needed.

Now that the fitting body and outlets are in place, cut blocks of 1x6, 2x4 or 3/4-inch plywood to fit across the stud bay you're working in. You'll need a block for the fitting body and one for each outlet.

Nail each block in place, then nail through the ears on the fitting body and on each eared elbow into the block. The fitting body will usually be marked so you can tell how far in or out of the wall it should be. Some fittings are shipped with plastic guards attached, marked for positioning. Remember, the fitting or outlet will be where you put it now, for a long time. Make sure everything is straight and lined up where you want it.

Other Fixtures—This section has covered rough-in for the most common bathroom fixtures. There are many more, in all sorts of sizes and shapes. For special or unusual fixtures, consult the manufacturer's literature or the supplier for the details of rough-in requirements and installation sequence. This applies especially to hydromassage tubs. They require not only a supply and drain rough-in, but an electrical hookup and access for occasional servicing and inspection.

FINISH PLUMBING

Installing and hooking up fixtures, called *finish plumbing*, can be one of the final phases of your remodeling project. After the rough plumbing is done, you can install the finish floor and walls, and the cabinets and countertops. Then do the remaining finish work, including plumbing-fixture installation. Before you start any finish work, make sure required rough-plumbing inspections have been made and approved.

Generally, the best approach to finish plumbing is to prepare the water-supply lines and drain lines for connection before you mount the fixtures. Then install lavatories and fittings and connect them, including traps. Trim out the tub or shower fitting next. Finally, install and connect toilet. Test all fixtures.

SUPPLY PIPE INSTALLATION

Shut off and drain the water system. Then remove caps from water supply-pipe stubs. On a galvanized-pipe system, just unscrew the caps. On capped copper or plastic, cut the pipes just behind the soldered or solvent-welded caps.

Most supply pipes come in two parts, the *stop valve* and the *riser.* These parts are sold separately, so you can custom-make an unconventional supply pipe if you have an unusual situation. First install the *escutcheon* and then the *stop valve,* as shown in photos at right.

On a galvanized-pipe stub, unscrew the cap, apply pipe-joint compound and thread on the stop valve. Use a smooth-jawed wrench to avoid marring plating on the stop valve. For a completely exposed installation, use a chrome-plated supply nipple. Unscrew galvanized nipple from outlet and install the plated one. Then install escutcheon and stop valve.

On copper and plastic systems, stop-valve installation depends on how you capped off the rough plumbing. If you finished off the stubs with a *threaded adapter*—1/2-inch female sweat x 1/2-inch male IPS, for example—unscrew the threaded cap on the adapter. Apply pipe-joint compound, and screw on the stop valve. This is also the best way to connect a plastic-pipe system.

If you soldered caps on copper pipe stubs, cut off each pipe about 1/2 inch behind the cap. Solder on the stop valve, or use a stop valve with a *compression connection,* as shown in the photos at right.

To install a compression-type stop valve, put the *escutcheon* and the *compression nut* on the stub. Then put the *compression ring*—also called a *ferrule*—on the stub. Slide the back of the stop valve onto the stub until it bottoms out. Then thread and tighten the compression nut. Don't worry about the outlet position on the stop valve while tightening. Just make sure the stub stays bottomed. Then back off the compression nut until you can swivel the stop valve, position it, and retighten.

After installing compression stop valves, shut off the stop valves, turn on the water and check for leaks. If the compression connection leaks, turn off the water, unscrew the com-

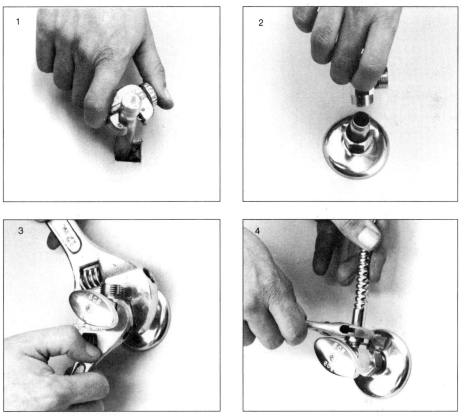

Easiest supply valve to use on copper pipe is compression type. Assembly steps are as follows: 1. Cut end of stub square and remove any burrs. 2. Put on escutcheon, compression nut, compression ring. 3. Seat valve body on end of pipe, tighten compression nut to seat ring on pipe. 4. Fit riser with slight bend, assemble and tighten connections at both ends.

pression nut and remove the stop valve. Wrap about two thicknesses of pipe-thread tape onto the compression ring, and reassemble. Don't overtighten, and don't try to slide the compression ring once you've made the connection.

Riser Assembly—The risers are usually connected to the stop valves and fixture with rubber-cone washers. Before assembling the end connections on the riser, trial-fit each one. Trim the riser to length and bend to align with the stop valve and with the fixture connection. Make sure each end of the riser enters the socket straight, not at an angle.

It's better to have a slight curve in the riser, rather than a straight run. The curve provides some flex to absorb small stresses without disturbing the end connections. See photo above. Swivel the stop valve slightly to one side to get a curve or to use up surplus riser length.

Assemble end connections on the riser, thread and tighten. When bending risers, work carefully. They're easy to kink and not easy to unkink. If you do kink the riser, it's better to replace it than try to unkink it.

WALL-HUNG LAVATORIES

Blocking to support the lavatory should already have been installed in the wall during the rough framing stage. Determine the offset between the top of the wall bracket and the top of the lavatory. You can get the offset either from a roughing-in sheet, or by fitting the bracket to the lavatory and measuring. Measure up the wall and mark on it the height of the lavatory. Then measure the offset from the height mark to mark the height for the wall bracket.

Measure and mark the centerline of the lavatory, according to your original plan. Then use a level to draw a horizontal line through the offset height mark, to serve as a positioning reference for the wall bracket.

Hold the wall bracket on the reference line and center it. Mark the screw holes on the wall with a pencil. Remove the wall bracket and drill pilot holes to fit the screws, usually provided. Install the bracket. If screws aren't provided, check the roughing-in sheet for correct screw size and type.

Before hanging the lavatory, install the faucets and drain fitting on it, as

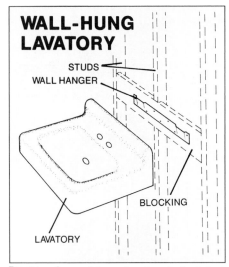

WALL-HUNG LAVATORY

STUDS
WALL HANGER
BLOCKING
LAVATORY

Blocking for wall-hung lavatory is installed when wall is framed.

Attaching clips are used to mount self-rim lavatory to top from underneath.

described on page 131. It's much easier to do at this stage. Don't install the pop-up or strainer assembly now—it's easy to get at later.

Pick up the lavatory and lower it into place on the bracket. If the lavatory doesn't go onto the bracket smoothly, lift it back off. Coat the inside of the bracket and the surrounding wall surface with wax from a candle stub and reinstall the lavatory.

When you're sure the lavatory is seated completely in the bracket, install any anchoring screws, hook-bolts or other anchoring parts that came with the lavatory. Finish by sealing the joint between lavatory and wall with tub-and-tile caulk.

PEDESTAL LAVATORIES
Pedestals for today's lavatories are not usually supporting, they're cosmetic. The lavatory is wall hung as described on page 129. There are a few exceptions—some hospital and commercial fixtures are still made to be free-standing on a pedestal. Also, you may be installing an older—or antique—free-standing pedestal lavatory. Such free-standing lavatories are easy to spot. They're almost always cast iron, the pedestal is large and flared at the base, and the back of the lavatory has no provision for a wall bracket or screw-mounting.

If you're installing such an antique or specialty unit, first install the pedestal. Use a level to be sure it's plumb, shim if necessary, and securely screw it to the floor. Then set the lavatory and fasten it to the pedestal by whatever means are provided. Use a

level on the top of the lavatory to make sure it's level in all directions. The rest of the hookup is essentially standard.

For the current wall-mounted pedestal lavatories, you *must* have a roughing-in sheet for the fixture. If there isn't one in the box with the fixture, get the roughing-in sheet from the fixture supplier. The roughing-in sheet will give you the setting height for the wall bracket to suit the height of the pedestal.

If you want the lavatory higher than standard, you can adjust the bracket height and other roughing-in dimensions accordingly. You must then use a spacer of some kind under the foot of the pedestal. Otherwise, installation is the same as for any other wall-hung lavatory, covered above. The pedestal usually bolts into place after all the pipes are connected.

VANITY-TOP LAVATORIES
There are two types of lavatories that drop into a vanity top. The *self-rim* type comes with an integral mounting lip. The other type uses a separate metal mounting rim. The self-rim type looks neater and more streamlined, and is easier to clean, so it has all but replaced the separate-rim type.

To install a self-rim lavatory, first mount the fitting body, as described on page 131. Leave off the strainer or pop-up assembly. Apply a ribbon of tub-and-tile caulk around the underside of the rim, and lower the lavatory into its cutout. You can use the fitting as a handle, and hook two fingers of your other hand through the drain hole in the bottom. Use a tape measure to position the lavatory and square it up. From underneath, slip the attaching clips into position and tighten until the lavatory is pulled down to the vanity top. Wipe off any extruded caulk with a wet paper towel.

If you're installing a self-rim lavatory in a ceramic-tile vanity top, you might want to omit the tub-and-tile caulk in the directions above. Prepare some matching grout after the lavatory is in place, and use it to seal the seam between the lavatory rim and counter.

To install a lavatory with a separate metal rim, proceed as above but apply caulk to both lips of the rim before dropping it over the lavatory. The rim should be on the lavatory before you

Self-rim lavatory is simple to install in a vanity top. Caulk is used to seal lavatory to top.

lower it into the cutout. Some metal rims clip to the lavatory, so you can treat the assembly like a self-rim. On other rim types, you'll have to hold the lavatory and rim assembly in place while a helper slips the anchoring clips into place and tightens them.

UNDERCOUNTER LAVATORIES

Looking like china mixing-bowls with a hole in the bottom, under-counter lavatories are an exception to the general rule that the finish plumbing should go in after everything else. Undercounter lavatories should be installed in the vanity top before it's attached to the vanity.

Plastic-laminate or synthetic-marble tops should be completely finished before the lavatory is installed. If the vanity top is to be surfaced with ceramic tile, it's best to install undercounter lavatories in the rough top, and work the ceramic tile to the lavatory.

Turn the vanity top upside down on cardboard boxes or padded saw-horses. Apply a bead of tub-and-tile caulk to the rim of the lavatory and drop it into place over the cutout. The overflow on the lavatory should be toward the front edge of the top. Feel or look underneath the top and make sure the lavatory is centered in the cutout, and correctly lined up.

Position the attaching clips around the lavatory rim and screw fast to the underside of the top. Check the screw lengths against the thickness of the top, to be sure they don't come through the finish side. Turn the top right-side up and clean up any squeezed-out caulk with a wet paper towel.

LAVATORY FITTINGS

Holes for mounting faucet and drain fittings will be molded or punched into most lavatories. If the fitting mounts in the vanity top, you should have marked and drilled the holes when you were making the top.

If the fitting has a base gasket, drop it into place. If not, apply a ribbon of tub-and-tile caulk around the base of the fitting. Place the fitting and loosely assemble the attaching parts from underneath. The fitting body will be attached by nuts and washers, either on threaded shanks that also serve as water connections, or on captive mounting bolts. Square up the fitting,

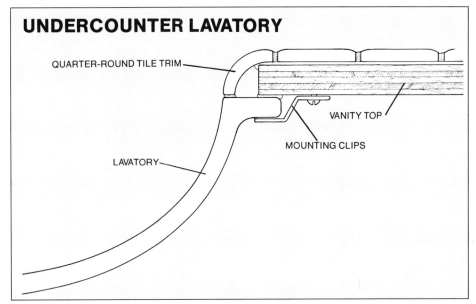

Undercounter lavatory is attached with mounting clips to underside of vanity top.

using a tape measure if necessary, and tighten the attaching parts. Clean up any extruded caulk.

Finish fitting the supply risers to the water connections on the faucet fitting and tighten them up.

To install the strainer or pop-up, apply a bead of tub-and-tile caulk to the rim of the part that fits in the bottom of the lavatory. Press it into place and assemble the rest of the parts from below. The drawing at right shows a typical pop-up assembly.

The lower body of a pop-up will have a connection for the operating rod from the fitting body. This connection should be pointed directly at the centerline of the fitting. Assemble the pop-up mechanism and its rods,

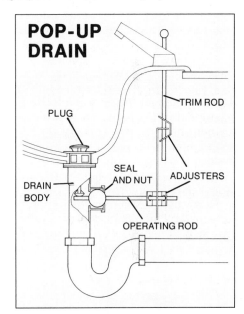

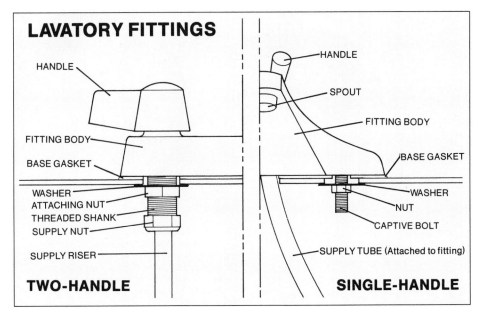

and adjust. Thread the tailpiece solidly into the bottom of the strainer or pop-up, and install the trap, as described below.

TRAP INSTALLATION

Traps are available in both metal and plastic. Either type can be used on any drain system. If plastic traps are code-approved in your jurisdiction, they are preferable to the metal ones. They're non-corroding and the smooth interior does not collect debris or scale. Both types install similarly. A male-thread trap adapter is required on the wall stub. Remove the cap from the drain-line stub and install the appropriate adapter.

Loosely assemble the trap with its nuts and washers in place and trial-fit it. Cut off surplus pipe at the outlet end of the trap. If the outlet arm of the trap does not slope downward, reposition the parts. Or, remove the strainer tailpiece and cut some off.

Leave plenty of overlap at the various slip joints in the trap assembly. Hand-tighten all the nuts and recheck alignment of the parts. Then wrench-tighten the nuts, if necessary. Do not overtighten nuts or the trap will be harder to dismantle for future servicing. Some plastic traps require only hand tightening.

Don't use plastic traps that require solvent-welding. This type is easy to put in, but alignments of strainer and drain-line stub are critical. Also, you can't service the trap without cutting it apart with a saw and replacing it with a new one.

Before turning on the water to check your work, remove the *aerator* from the faucet, if it has one. The aerator is usually a small screw-on assembly in the end of the faucet spout. Then you can flush out any debris in the lines without clogging the aerator. If you do this before you install the drain or trap, put a bucket under the sink.

TUB AND SHOWER FITTINGS

Finishing the installation of a tub or shower fitting is largely a matter of applying the trim parts you put aside when the fitting was roughed in. Remove any guards or other protective devices, and put on the trim parts. Install any gaskets provided, and make liberal use of tub-and-tile caulk where it's needed to keep water out of the wall.

Tub spouts deserve special attention because they can be confusing to install. As you can see from the drawing below, the spout threads are at the front, not the back. So when it's installed, the back edge of the spout has to contact the wall when the threads come up tight. If the fit is too loose, water will leak into the wall. If it's too tight, the threaded water connection won't seal.

The best way to get an exact fit is to thread an overlength pipe nipple into the spout you'll be installing. Hand-tighten it and measure the amount of leftover nipple sticking out of the back of the spout. Comparing this to the overall length of the nipple will give you an exact length for the stub sticking out of the wall.

If the spout stub is copper, cut it off so when you solder on a male-thread adapter, the measurement will come out right. If the stub is threaded pipe, tighten it and mark it even with the face of the wall. Then unscrew the pipe nipple, measure the part inside the wall, and add the measurement to the measurement arrived at above. Then select a pipe nipple to fit. You may have to get a nipple made to fit an odd measurement.

Don't use a wrench to tighten the spout. It will damage the chrome plating. Use a screwdriver handle in the open end of the spout to thread it. If the spout resists threading, use a web strap or web belt. Double it around the spout, and fold it back on a flat metal object—see photo below. The blade of a chisel or a flat pry bar will do. Use the chisel or pry bar as a lever to tighten the strap to thread the spout.

FLOOR-MOUNT TOILET INSTALLATION

Connect the supply valve to the

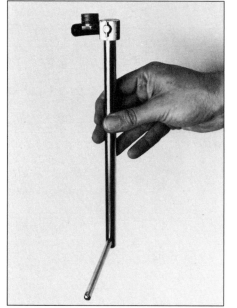

A basin wrench is useful for attaching fittings to underside of lavatory and other tight spots.

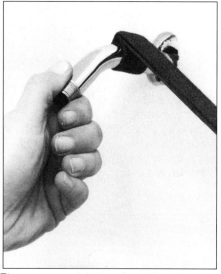

There are special strap wrenches for installing finish parts without marring. You can improvise one with a web belt or other piece of webbing, and a flat piece of metal. Pinching the webbing with vise-grip pliers also works.

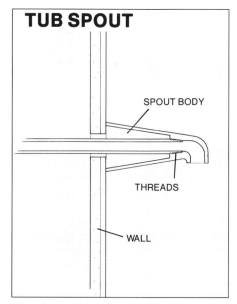

TUB SPOUT

SPOUT BODY

THREADS

WALL

Threads for attaching tub spout are at front of spout. Water-supply nipple must be carefully measured so spout fits correctly.

stub as described on pages 128-129. Remove the plug or cap from the floor flange, and insert the flange bolts in their slots. Unpack the toilet parts and check them. If bowl and tank are separate, assemble them. There should be a package containing a sponge ring and bolts and washers inside the tank. Assemble according to the instructions but don't over-tighten—you can break the tank or bowl. *Note:* there are some cases where it makes better sense to set the bowl and then install the tank. If you run across one of those cases, do it that way. But it's usually easier to assemble tank and bowl first.

Carefully roll the assembly over onto an old rug, blanket or newspapers so it's standing on the top of the tank and the front of the bowl rim. Apply the seal ring—usually wax—around the discharge horn on the bottom of the bowl, and make sure it sticks there. Peel off the paper on the seal ring. Apply a bead of tub-and-tile caulk around the perimeter of the underside of the bowl.

As long as your back is in good shape, the easiest way to handle and set a toilet is all by yourself. From the upside-down position, roll the toilet up on the nose of the bowl, and slowly move it over toward the upright position. Keep complete control of the toilet at all times—it is chinaware and extremely fragile.

Spread your knees and walk right in over the bowl, taking a grip on both sides of the web between tank and bowl, about where the seat bolt holes are. Rest your forearms on your legs, just above the knees. Lift the toilet a few inches off the floor by slightly unbending your knees. The whole assembly will swing a time or two and come to rest. You can raise or lower it by straightening or bending your knees slightly. You can keep the assembly suspended this way as long as your wrists hold out.

Duckwalk yourself and the toilet into position, and line up the bolt

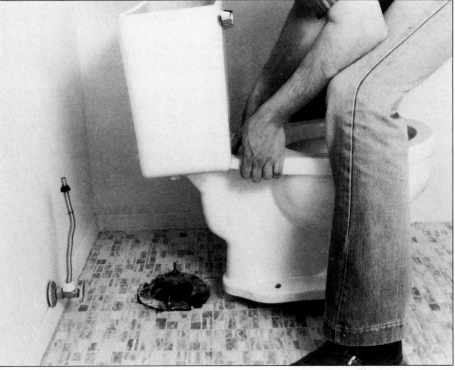

The easiest way to set a toilet is by yourself. The technique isn't as hard on your back as it looks. All the weight is on knees, through forearms. The secret is to keep the toilet balanced.

holes to the flange bolts. Lower the toilet smoothly into position. If the bowl doesn't sit all the way down onto the floor, the discharge horn hasn't seated in the flange. Lift slightly and move the toilet around until the discharge horn lines up with the flange, then lower again. You might want to first practice this maneuver while the toilet is upright, before seal ring and caulk are put on.

Drop the washers onto the flange bolts and attach the nuts. Tighten gently, alternating sides. Do not over-tighten bolts, or you risk cracking the toilet base.

Some toilets have plastic bolt caps that snap onto ears on the washers. If you're installing these, line up the washers as you tighten the nuts. Then snap on the bolt caps. Set conventional ceramic bolt caps by partially filling them with a blob of tub-and-tile caulk, then pressing them onto the

bolt and nut. Clean off any extruded caulk at bolt caps, and along the bottom edge of the bowl.

Connect the water-supply line, then put on the tank lid. Finally, install the toilet seat by inserting the threaded shanks through the bolt holes and tightening the nuts.

WALL-MOUNT TOILET INSTALLATION

Don't try to install a wall-mount toilet without a couple of helpers. The installation sequence varies considerably for different models, so no general instructions can be given here. Detailed instructions should be packed with the toilet. Be sure to check all parts and gaskets before you start. Keep any required wrenches within easy reach. Follow the installation instructions exactly—don't improvise, and don't overtighten bolts.

9

Electrical Work

Wiring for whirlpool bath like this one must be protected by a ground-fault circuit interrupter (GFCI). In some code jurisdictions, wiring for whirlpool baths and spas must be done by a licensed electrician. Housings for recessed light fixtures, such as those shown here, are usually installed during rough-framing stage. *Photo courtesy of American Olean Tile Co.*

Electrical systems are complex and carefully regulated by codes. In some jurisdictions, all electrical work can only be done by a licensed electrician. In most, you can do some or all work yourself. This chapter does not cover everything you need to know to rework your electrical system. It does cover basic circuit design and circuit installation. It also covers basic light-fixture installation.

Information in this chapter is based on the *National Electrical Code,* and therefore is applicable anywhere in the United States with only minor local variations. In Canada, each province has its own master electrical codes. Local variations apply. Check with your local building department before making any changes to your electrical system.

ELECTRICAL REQUIREMENTS

The minimum code requirements for a bathroom are simple in most localities. A fixed light must be installed, controlled by a switch near the door. There must be a convenience outlet near the lavatory, protected by a ground-fault circuit interrupter (GFCI). A ground fault circuit interrupter compares the current on both sides of the circuit and shuts off if even a small amount turns up missing.

An exhaust fan is required if there is no natural ventilation, such as an operable window, or not enough to meet code requirements.

Usually, one 15-amp circuit will

handle all of the needs of a fairly small bathroom—a large one may require two circuits. Permanently wired appliances such as fans and 120-volt heaters can be combined with outlets and light fixtures on a circuit. Any appliance over 12 amps must be on a circuit of its own. 240-volt heaters will require a separate circuit. Heaters should be figured into the current load at 125% of their rated amperage.

CIRCUIT DESIGN

The steps involved in designing electrical circuits for your new bathroom are to make a sketch of the bathroom and then pin down the location and size of each electrical demand. You can then plan the new circuitry.

If the specifications for a piece of equipment indicate wattage, divide the wattage by the voltage to get the amperage. For example, 1,000 watts divided by 120 volts equals approximately 9 amps.

Figure convenience outlets at 1-1/2 amps each. No allowance is needed for switches. Figure light fixtures at the actual maximum wattage, but never less than 1 amp. If you haven't selected all equipment yet, or don't have information on what you've selected, ask your electrical supplier to get the figures for you.

MAKE A MAP

Start by mapping existing electrical connections, not only in the bathroom, but in adjoining areas. Some circuits may serve more than one room. Draw in outlets, fixtures and switches you can see in the bathroom and adjoining rooms.

To isolate a circuit, remove a fuse or shut off a circuit breaker that serves some part of the bathroom. In many cases, the entire bathroom is served by one circuit. Mark the circuit number on the sketch next to each electrical connection that's inoperative. Use a switched-on lamp to find outlets that are on that circuit. Be sure to check outlets in adjacent rooms.

After you've tracked down every outlet, light and permanently wired device on that circuit, turn on that circuit and turn another one off. Keep going until you've determined the location and the total load on each circuit you're concerned with.

It's a good idea to keep checking circuits until you have the entire house mapped. Such a map can make future repairs and changes easier. If existing circuits aren't numbered at the panel box, number them with a felt-tip marker before you make any electrical changes. A circuit map for a typical bathroom is shown above.

LIGHT FIXTURES AND SWITCHES

Mark a small "3" on your map next to any switches you know to be the *three-way* type. A three-way switch allows a light to be controlled from two different points. See drawing above. On switches that are not three-way, remove the cover plate and see how the switch is wired.

Ignore wires that are not connected to the switch. If a pair of wires from a single cable are connected to the switch, power for the light is fed in at the light. If one wire each from two different cables is attached to the switch, the power feeds to the switch, and from there to the light. See drawing above.

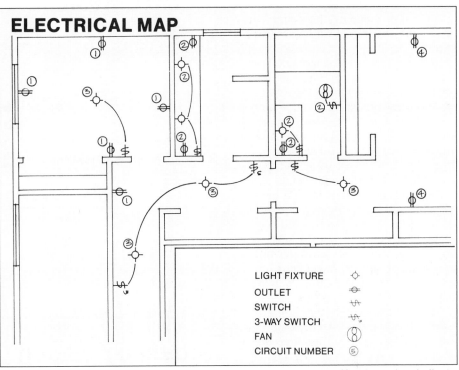

ELECTRICAL MAP

LIGHT FIXTURE	◇
OUTLET	⊖
SWITCH	⌇
3-WAY SWITCH	⌇
FAN	⊗
CIRCUIT NUMBER	⑤

Circuit map shows locations of all fixtures, switches and outlets. Use legend to indicate types.

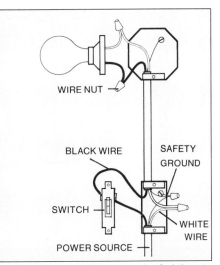

In this light circuit, power is fed in at switch.

In this circuit, power is fed in at light.

INSPECT EXISTING SYSTEMS

As you're mapping the system, inspect the wiring. Conductor wires should be free of corrosion and should be at least 14-gage *solid* wire, not multistrand wire. The insulation should be intact and flexible, not brittle and deteriorated. Cables containing the wires should be firmly attached where they enter junction boxes. Junction boxes themselves should be free of rust and corrosion and firmly anchored to the framing.

Switches and outlets should be serviceable and free of cracks, corrosion, brittle insulation, paint and accumulated grime. Very little bare wire should be visible at screw terminals and none at splices, except for safety ground wires. These are often bare copper for their entire length.

Taped splices within junction boxes were, and in some instances still are, permitted by code. But the wires should be solidly connected. The tape should still be flexible, firmly in place, and covering all of the splice. Splices *outside* junction or fixture boxes are *not allowed* by any code and should be enclosed in a junction box. All connections should be protected from mechanical strain and damage.

If the existing system has problems, correct them as you remodel. A worn-out or improperly wired electrical system is dangerous and probably illegal.

LAY OUT NEW CIRCUITS

Working from the map of your existing electrical system, add up the amperages on each circuit and compare the total to the amperage of the fuse or circuit breaker for that circuit. If any circuits are overloaded, you'll need to reduce the load.

Laying out new or revised circuits is a trial-and-error process. Put a piece of tracing paper over your floor plan. Start by noting the location of the main-panel box or fuse box. Then work out the shortest and least destructive path for any required new wiring. This will tell you where the new circuit wiring should arrive at the bathroom.

Your floor plan is two-dimensional, but your house is three-dimensional. So use the appropriate notes for any locations where you'll have to run cable up or down a wall. This will help you estimate the amount of cable you'll need.

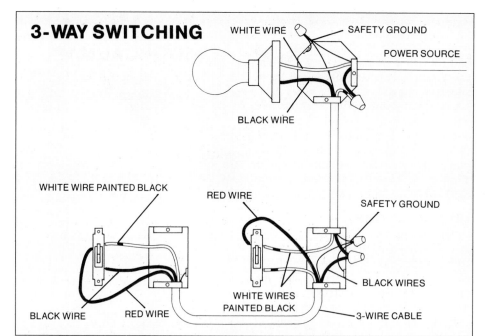

3-WAY SWITCHING

Three-way switching allows you to control light from two separate locations.

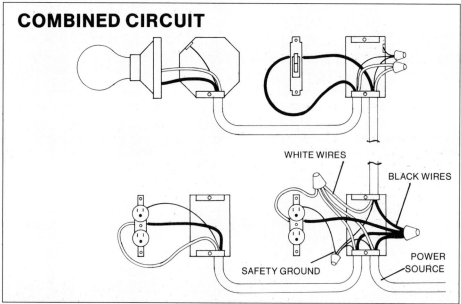

COMBINED CIRCUIT

Combined circuit for typical bathroom provides light fixture and two convenience outlets. Outlets should be three-hole type, connected to safety ground.

The object of the circuit-design process is to divide the electrical load equally among the circuits available. Keep trying different patterns until you find one where the load on the various circuits is almost equal. The layout you want is the one that uses the least amount of cable and requires the least amount of reworking and chopping out for access. As mentioned, all 240-volt equipment and 120-volt appliances over 12 amps must be on circuits of their own.

WIRE TYPES

In most jurisdictions, you can use non-metallic cable for residential applications. A cable is a group of insulated wires wrapped together in a casing. Non-metallic cable is encased in a jacket of insulating material, usually plastic. Metallic cable uses a flexible, metallic spiral jacket to encase the wires.

The most common non-metallic cable types are type NM, type NMC, and type UF. Type NM is approved for clean, dry locations only. Type NMC is also approved for wet or corrosive locations. Type UF can be used in wet or dry locations, and is also approved for direct underground burial.

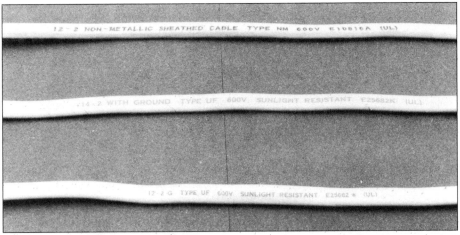

All non-metallic cable is marked for easy identification. Type NM is suitable for dry locations only, NMC for wet or dry, UF for wet, dry, or buried directly in the ground. First number indicates wire gage, followed by /. Next number after / indicates number of wires in cable. If there's a safety ground in cable, it's also indicated.

There are many other cable types for different applications, and also a separate coding system for single wires. Your electric supplier or local building official can tell you which types your local jurisdiction permits. Printing on the cable jacket will tell you wire type and gage, and the number and kind of wires. For instance, a cable marked "14-2" contains two 14-gage wires, one with black insulation and one with white.

If the cable is marked "-3" after the gage number, it contains a black wire, a red wire and a white wire. If the cable is marked "with ground" after the gage and the number of wires, as in "12-2 with ground", the cable also contains a bare copper wire or a wire with green insulation. It is used for safety grounding.

WIRE SIZES

Minimum wire size in most jurisdictions is 14 *AWG*—American Wire Gauge. Only solid wires can be used, except for connection leads in a light fixture. Correct wire size for a circuit depends on two factors. The first is the current-carrying capacity of the wire. Because current is measured in amps, this is the amperage capacity of the wire, called *ampacity*. The table at right shows the ampacities of the smaller wire sizes.

The other factor in correct wire size is the resistance of the wire to electrical flow. The larger the wire, the less resistance. Resistance causes voltage to drop at the end of the wire. Some electrical energy is dissipated along the way, as heat, to overcome the resistance in the wire.

If a wire is long enough or small enough, no voltage at all will be available at the other end. Codes generally limit this *voltage drop* to a maximum of 5%, but for economical operation, it should be kept below 3%. The table below shows maximum length for each wire size for an acceptable voltage drop.

Wire sizes should meet minimum requirements for both ampacity and voltage drop. Overload current protectors, either fuses or circuit breakers, should be sized *no larger* than the total ampacity of the circuit they protect.

WIRE COLORS

Wire colors are part of a coding system to help you keep track of wires in the electrical system. Black wires are always *hot,* or on the electrically charged side of the system. Black wires are always connected to brass-colored terminal screws. White wires are always on the neutral side of the system, and are always connected to silver terminal screws.

Red wires, if any, can be thought of as extra black wires. The two primary uses of a red wire are in three-way switch circuits and in three-wire, 240-volt circuits. Green wires and bare copper wires are always used for safety grounding, discussed below.

You may not be able to get a piece of cable with the particular combination of wire colors you need, and you don't have to. Use a cable with the right number of wires, and as close as you can get to the right colors. Then paint or tape the wrong-color wires with the right color, *at both ends.*

SAFETY GROUNDING

Bare copper wires or green wires are used exclusively for safety grounding. The white wire that's part of the cable, called a *neutral* wire, grounds the circuits. In addition, every metal part in an electrical system must be independently grounded.

The safety ground is not part of the circuit. It grounds every metal junction box, every appliance and all metal parts that might become charged. The safety ground also connects to the third hole in convenience outlets, effectively grounding metal parts of any tools and appliances with

WIRING AMPACITY AND LENGTH

Wire Size (AWG)	Ampacity[1] (amperes)	Wire Length[2,3] (One way @ maximum amps @ 120 volts.)				
		VOLTAGE DROP				
		1%	2%	3%	4%	5%
14	15 amps	15'	30'	45'	60'	75'
12	20 amps	18'	36'	54'	72'	90'
10	30 amps	18'	36'	54'	72'	90'
8	40 amps	22'	44'	66'	88'	110'
6	55 amps	25'	50'	75'	100'	125'
4	70 amps	32'	64'	96'	128'	160'
3	80 amps	35'	70'	105'	140'	175'
2	95 amps	38'	76'	114'	152'	190'

[1]Information is for copper conductors only, with not more than 3 conductors per cable. Also assumes maximum 140F conductor temperature, maximum 86F ambient temperature. Some insulation types may have higher ratings, but none lower.

[2]Double lengths given for 240-volt applications.

[3]Amperage and voltage drop are proportional—lower amperage through same size wire means less voltage drop. Example: 8-gage wire at 40 amps/120 volts loses 2% voltage in 44 feet; 8-gage wire at 20 amps/120 volts loses only 1% in 44 feet.

a three-prong plug. Codes may require that convenience outlets in bathrooms be the three-hole, grounded type.

Safety grounding has prevented many accidents and saved many lives. Before it was introduced, a loose wire or a frayed spot in insulation could make any metal object part of the circuit, causing serious shock. The safety ground helps prevent such accidents.

It isn't necessary or required that you tear into walls and add safety grounding to an older electrical system. But the electrical inspector will require it on all new circuits. Always use cable with a ground wire. Connect every piece of metal in the system to the safety ground. Terminal screws and clips are color-coded green. Connect the safety ground to a good main ground.

A water pipe will usually do for a main ground, if it's metal all the way to the underground street piping. The best ground, if you can get to it, is the grounding strip in the service-entrance panel box. The grounding strip won't be hard to find—all the white wires are connected to it.

If you're in doubt about the adequacy of a ground connection, check it with the electrical inspector on one of his inspections. Many electrical inspectors carry instruments that directly measure how well a ground connection is working.

ALUMINUM WIRING

The wiring in most electrical systems is made of copper. Cable with aluminum conductors has been used in the past and is common in the largest wire sizes. Aluminum wiring can be perfectly safe, but specific installation techniques must be used.

When first introduced, aluminum wire and copper-coated aluminum wire were substituted for copper wire. Aluminum wire was on the market several years before the need for special installation techniques was discovered. If your house has aluminum wiring in the branch circuits, it is strongly suggested you have a competent electrician check the entire system. He can quickly tell you if the system has been installed safely, or if it's a fire hazard.

If the system isn't safe, it can be made safe by replacing existing connection devices with the right ones, and installing them correctly. The

Cables running into non-metallic boxes like this must be anchored to framing within 8 inches of box. Metal boxes have cable clamps mounted on box to secure cable.

wiring itself does not have to be replaced. Do not try to do this work yourself. Also, all new wiring should be copper.

CONNECTION DEVICES

The three basic connection devices in an electrical system are the *switch,* the *outlet,* and the *wire nut.* Switches and outlets should be marked with the Underwriters Laboratories stamp or label. They should not be operated at a voltage exceeding that marked on the device. The standard switches and outlets shown in this chapter should not be installed on circuits over 20 amps. Other types of switches are available for higher amperages and for 240-volt circuits.

Switches are always installed in the black-wire side of the circuit (black-black) or the red-wire side (red-red). Never install a switch in the white (neutral) side. Crossing colors will create a short circuit when the switch is turned on. Three-way switches are a special case, shown on page 136.

120-volt outlets are always connected from black to white or from red to white, never from red to black. On some outlets, wire colors are indicated next to the terminal screws.

Use wire nuts to connect a wire to one or more other wires. These plastic devices are lined with molded threads or with a small, conical metal spring. For more on installing switches, outlets and wire nuts, see page 140.

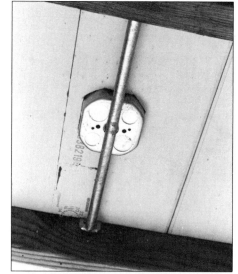

All ceiling-mounted light fixtures that weigh over a pound or two should be supported by a hanger strap attached to ceiling joists.

WIRING FOR NEW ELECTRICAL CIRCUITS

If possible, install new wiring while framing is still exposed. It's much easier that way. The installation sequence of rough wiring varies, depending on whether the wall framing is exposed or covered.

ROUGHING-IN WITH EXPOSED FRAMING

Working with exposed wall framing, first install the switch and outlet boxes at the appropriate locations. The easiest boxes to install are ones that come with the attaching nails mounted on the box. Place the box alongside a stud and drive in the nails to anchor the box in place. Boxes should project by an amount equal to the thickness of the wall-finish material.

Switches are normally 44 to 48 inches from the floor, outlets 12 to 15 inches above the floor. The exception is switches and outlets above counters. Light fixtures on walls can usually be mounted on an outlet box, but ceiling fixtures are installed differently. Remember, the ceiling box must also physically support the fixture, and some fixtures are quite heavy. Stamped-metal hanger straps are available to fit between ceiling joists on both 16- and 24-inch centers.

The hanger strap is first nailed into

place between the joists. An octagonal fixture box is then attached to the hanger strap's threaded stud using the nut provided. Again, the box should protrude beyond the framing enough to line up with the finish-ceiling surface. You can also use hanger straps in walls when you're forced to locate a switch or outlet between studs.

Determine where cables will run inside the wall, floor and ceiling framing. Bore holes in framing members wherever it's necessary to run the cable across one. Hole diameter in studs should not exceed 40% of the width of the stud.

Holes in floor or ceiling joists must be at least 2 inches away from the top or bottom edge of the framing member. The diameter of a hole cannot exceed 1/3 the depth of the member. If any hole is less than 1-1/4 inch from the edge of a stud, the wiring must be protected from nail penetration. Special 1/16-inch-thick steel protective plates are available for this purpose.

Try to avoid notching for wiring. Notches provide a starting point for splitting of the framing member. Double-check with the building department before drilling holes in floor or ceiling joists—permitted hole sizes and locations vary in different localities.

Pulling Cable—Run the cable through the holes and into the boxes without cutting it. At boxes in the middle of a cable run, loop the cable into and back out of the box—about an 18-inch loop. Leave about 12 inches of cable at the last box. This may seem like a waste of expensive wire, but the code requires a minimum of 6 inches of each wire inside the box. The rest of the cable in the box will be used as you anchor the wires in place.

Cables should not hang loose inside the framing. Working backwards from the last box, use *cable straps* to anchor the cable to the side of the framing members. Space straps at 4-1/2-foot maximum intervals. Cable straps are available at electrical-supply stores. Turn any corners with a gentle radius and make sure there is no stress on the cables. Don't stretch, crush or kink cable while you're installing it. You may damage the wires and insulation inside. On metal boxes, tighten the clamps on the cables at box

When running new wiring behind existing wall finish, first cut all access holes. Then drill holes for wires as flat as possible.

entrances. Cable should be anchored to framing within 8'' of any non-metallic boxes.

ROUGHING-IN
WITH FINISHED WALLS

With finish-wall material already in place, start with the wiring instead of the boxes. Route wires so any cutting and patching done to walls will be hidden, or at least unobtrusive.

First, mark the location of all switch, outlet and fixture boxes, using the boxes as templates. Cut the box openings in the walls and ceilings. Before you cut, check the cover plates to make sure they will conceal the cutouts when the box is installed.

It helps to draw the circuit layout on the walls and ceiling as you figure it out. When possible, run wiring parallel to the framing members to a location where access holes in the finish-wall material will be concealed. After you've decided where cables have to run, cut access holes as shown above. Extend the access hole in the finish-wall material 2 or 3 inches either side of the framing member. Through the access hole, drill a hole crosswise through the framing member on an angle.

Turning Corners—If the cable must turn a corner, such as at the junction of a wall and ceiling, cut two access holes. Position one in the wall and one in the ceiling, extending out 4-6 inches from the corner.

Drill a slanted hole up through the top plates of the wall. Be careful not to drill through nails attaching framing members. Then double over the end of the cable and push it up through the hole. Snag the doubled-over end and pull it into the ceiling. The hooked end of a wire coat hanger

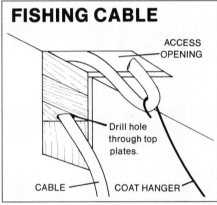

FISHING CABLE

ACCESS OPENING

Drill hole through top plates.

CABLE   COAT HANGER

Coat hanger works well for fishing cable where wall meets ceiling.

works well for this if you can't get your hand in to pull the cable. The same technique works at corners where two walls meet.

Fishing Cable—Work the cable into walls and ceiling through the access holes, leaving 12-inch tails or 18-inch loops at each box location. Because cable is not very rigid, there will be times when you can't push it from one access hole to the next. In that case, use a *fish tape*. A fish tape is a roll of spring-tempered flat steel that is much more rigid than cable, but also bendable. It has a pulling loop on the end, so you can force it past obstacles and around corners, and then pull cable back through with it.

The fish tape can also be used to run cable across sections of exposed wall without having to cut into finish material. Cut an access hole in an adjacent concealed location and look for existing cable or pipe runs across the section of exposed wall. If you find such a run, work the fish tape through the holes alongside the existing run. Then connect the end of the new cable to the fish tape and pull it back through the holes.

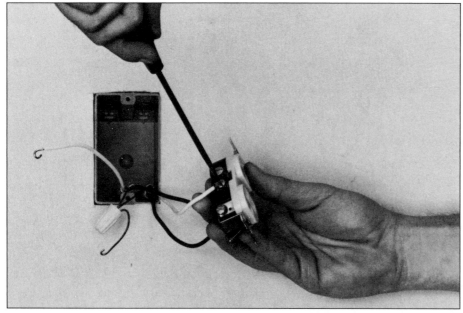

Most outlets and switches have simple push-in connections in addition to terminal screws. Little slot beside push-in hole admits screwdriver to release wire, if necessary.

Wires are connected to terminal screws on outlet. Make loops in wires with needle-nose pliers. Loop should point clockwise around screw. Do not overlap wire on screw. Do not overtighten.

Box Installation—Boxes for outlets, switches and fixtures are installed after the wiring is in the wall. There are a variety of special boxes for use in existing finish walls. Most are anchored to the finish material by U-clamps or expanding clips. These special boxes are convenient because they reduce the risk of losing the box and the cable ends inside the wall.

But it's preferable to position the boxes adjacent to framing members, the same as in new work. Then anchor them by drilling two holes in the side of the box and driving in two screws. Mount boxes so the front edges will be level with the finish-wall surface, or slightly behind it.

FINISH INSTALLATION

Finish parts of an electrical circuit can be installed after all rough wiring is done and wall-finish materials are installed. What's involved in finish electrical work is the installation of outlets, switches and light fixtures. Then you can hook up the circuit and test it.

OUTLETS AND SWITCHES

Wire preparation at all electrical boxes is essentially the same. Strip the cable jacket back to within an inch or two of where cable enters the box. Trim wires to approximately 6 to 8 inches in length. You now have a choice of connection methods for switches and outlets. All modern switches and outlets still have tradi-

tional terminal screws on the sides. Most also have simple push-in connections on the back.

Screw Terminals—To connect to a screw terminal, strip enough insulation from the wire to make a loop 3/4 of the way around the screw shank, but not more than once around. Don't overlap the wire under the head of the terminal screw. Form the loop with needle-nose pliers.

Hook the loop over the shank of the terminal screw and pinch it into place under the screw head with needle-nose pliers. The end of the loop should go clockwise rather than counterclockwise, so that tightening the screw will tighten the loop rather than expand it. Then snug down the terminal screw. The screw should be tight enough so you can't unscrew it using the wire as a lever. Don't tighten the terminal screw enough to substantially deform the wire.

Do not connect two wires to the same terminal screw. A loop formed in a continuous wire will achieve the same result.

Push-In Connections—Far simpler and faster is to use the push-in connections in the back of the box. Strip the insulation off the end of the wire. There's a handy strip-length gage molded on the end or backside of push-in switches and outlets. Then push the wire into the appropriate hole in the back of the switch or outlet. If you get it wrong, push a small screwdriver into the slot next to

the wire hole and the wire will come free.

Mounting Procedures—Don't try to force the switch or outlet into the box on top of all the surplus wire. Fold the extra wire length a few times so it accordions neatly into the box without straining the connections.

Start the top and bottom screws on the switch or outlet into the threaded holes in the box. Tighten the screws to pull the device down until the *plaster ears* on the device are resting firmly on the finish-wall surface.

Adjust the switch or outlet so it is vertical, whether the box is vertical or not, by means of the slotted screw holes. Then position the cover plate and snug down the screw or screws. Don't overtighten cover-plate screws. The thin plastic plate is easy to break.

Wire Nuts—Connection of one wire to another is most easily done with a *wire nut.* Strip approximately 1 inch of insulation from the wire ends. Twist the ends together with pliers and snip off square. Screw on a wire nut of appropriate size. If any bare wire still shows, unscrew the wire nut and clip a little more off the end of the wires. Then reapply the wire nut.

It's easy to tell if you're using the right-size wire nut for the number and size of wires to be joined. If the wire nut is too large, the wires will bottom out at the end of the nut but will not anchor. If the wire nut is too small, the wires won't thread very far into the wire nut, or may not start to thread in at all. If you're in doubt of the connection, try the next size nut.

FIXTURES

Fixture wires are generally connected to the circuit wires with wire nuts. Unpack the fixture and make sure all the pieces are there and intact. There will usually be an assembly sheet and a package of attaching hardware, including wire nuts. Fixtures are usually attached to the junction boxes by means of screws or a threaded center stud. Recessed fixtures are somewhat different.

Screw-Mounted Fixtures—The parts bag that comes with a screw-mounted fixture will usually contain a flat mounting strip with two threaded holes and two slotted holes. Slip the mounting strip over the machine screws on the face of the junction box and tighten down. Then assemble and wire the fixture, according to the instruction sheet. Insert finish screws from the parts bag through the canopy of the fixture and thread them into the threaded holes in the mounting strip.

Adjust the fixture canopy so it is centered over the junction box and completely covers the wall or ceiling opening. Then tighten the finish screws until the canopy of the fixture contacts the wall or ceiling surface. Don't overtighten, or you'll crush the canopy or pull the screws through it.

Stud-Mounted Fixtures—The flat mounting strip for a threaded center-stud fixture will have two slotted holes for the junction-box screws, and a large threaded hole in the center. In some cases, the threaded center stud will be tubular and will serve as a conduit for the fixture wiring. In other designs, a decorative cap or hook goes on the end of the threaded center stud. Consult the assembly sheet for specifics. In any case, start the threaded center stud into the flat mounting strip, connect the wiring, then attach the fixture to the center stud. Add any additional parts to the threaded center stud that holds the fixture in place.

Heavy Fixtures—Large, heavy fixtures can sometimes exceed the strength of the box screws. Hanger straps, described on page 138, are mandatory for such fixtures, even if the junction box is attached to a framing member. Then the hanger strap's threaded mounting stud can be used to support the fixture independent of the box itself.

Recessed Fixtures—Recessed fixtures can't be ignored until finish

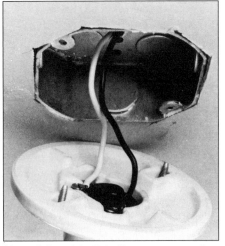
Many lightweight light fixtures mount with screws, directly to the electrical box.

installation, as can other fixtures. In most cases, you must install some part of the recessed fixture, usually a sheet-metal housing, when you install the rough wiring.

The rest of the fixture is installed after the finish-ceiling material is in place. Make sure the finish parts of the recessed fixtures are kept in the original boxes, stored safely, and are marked as to location. Recessed fixtures are so varied in their construction that no assembly specifics can be given here. Be sure to keep the assembly sheet with the rest of the finish parts.

Ceiling insulation placed directly on top of a recessed fixture can cause a potentially dangerous heat buildup. Either clear away such insulation, or make sure the fixture is marked *I. C.,* for *Insulated Ceiling,* on the UL label.

SPECIAL ELECTRICAL HOOKUPS

Because of the hazards presented by water and grounded metal fixtures, extra care should be taken hooking up special equipment in and around a bathroom.

Sauna heaters, steam generators, hydromassage pumps and heaters, and demand-type water heaters can all be classed as special equipment. Such devices often use fairly large quantities of electricity, and are connected with heavy-gage wiring and high-capacity overload protectors. Study the manufacturer's installation instructions carefully, and follow them to the letter.

Circuit requirements are dictated by the equipment—check the manufacturer's literature. 120-volt equip-

Heavier fixtures are usually hung on tubular center stud. Other mounting methods are also used. Check directions that come with fixture.

ment 12 amps or under can be connected to a 15-amp circuit with other loads. 120-volt equipment over 12 amps should be on its own circuit, appropriately sized.

Every piece of metal on the equipment, exposed or not, should be solidly grounded. Grounding can be checked with a small battery-powered continuity-tester. These are inexpensive and available at any electronics store, and most hardware and auto-parts stores. Connect the clip to a good ground and touch every piece of metal in sight with the probe. If the light comes on, the part is grounded. If you find any parts that aren't grounded, find a way to tie them to a grounded part with a length of solid copper wire. Paint film under screws or other fasteners will sometimes prevent grounding. Try loosening and retightening screws and bolts to cut the paint film and get a good ground.

If you have an ohmmeter or multitester, you can use it to check grounding. If you have either one, you should already know how to use it. More than a small fraction of an ohm between any part and ground indicates resistance, which means the ground is not sufficient.

Plug-and-cord hookups are preferable anytime the equipment manufacturer or codes don't prohibit them. They provide an easy means of removing equipment, and an extra, positive disconnect when you're servicing it. Switches or circuit breakers can fail or short across, or accidentally be turned back on—a pulled plug can't.

Heating & Venting Systems

Small sections of electric baseboard can provide heating in smaller areas, no matter what the main heating system is.

Heating systems are complicated and can be delicate. Substantial modifications can disrupt the performance of the whole system. You won't be aware of problems under normal circumstances, but under the most extreme ones, such as the first heat wave or cold snap—no time to start fixing things.

Many bathrooms are underheated to begin with. Bathroom remodeling often requires changes to the present systems. Some changes are safe and easy. Lengthening or shortening a duct by a foot or two, or moving a length of baseboard convector a few feet, usually won't affect the system enough to matter. For major modifications to heating and cooling systems, call a heating-and-cooling contractor.

HOT-WATER HEATING SYSTEMS

In hot-water heating systems, a central boiler generates hot water. A pump circulates it through baseboard convectors or radiators to deliver heat to the rooms, and back to the boiler.

Hot-water heating systems can be modified using the plumbing techniques described in the chapter, Plumbing, pages 116-133.

If you're not familiar with the design and construction principles of your hot-water heating system, consult a plumber or heating contractor on any modifications. A knowledgeable contractor is a must for changes to a steam or vapor-vacuum system. If you have a working knowledge of your hot-water system, you can follow the guidelines here.

Pressure drop and *flow rate* should closely approximate that of the original. Make sure pipe length and size remains about the same, including pipe inside the baseboard unit. Also make sure the modified section contains the same number, size and type of fittings.

Some hot-water systems circulate water directly from one baseboard unit or radiator to the next. Others use a *main,* a large-diameter circulating pipe, and move hot water into the baseboard units or radiators through a

diverter tee. This is a tee with a small vane inside that redirects part of the water flow. If you have to modify the main, reinstall the diverter tee in the same relationship as it was before.

If you've added any extra windows or doors, or enlarged the bathroom, you may have increased the heat loss. To compensate, you may have to increase the amount of *finned element* in the bathroom baseboard convector. This may upset the balance of the system, requiring adjustment of the balancing dampers on all the baseboard units.

If the units don't have balancing dampers, balance them by using heavy-duty aluminum foil. Pull the cover off and wrap foil around part of the finned element. The foil blocks some of the air flow around the elements and reduces heat output.

If you've added finned elements to the system and the overall output doesn't seem adequate, check the limit-control settings on the boiler. It's possible that the *operating*-limit control, *not* the safety high-limit, is

HOT-WATER HEATING SYSTEMS

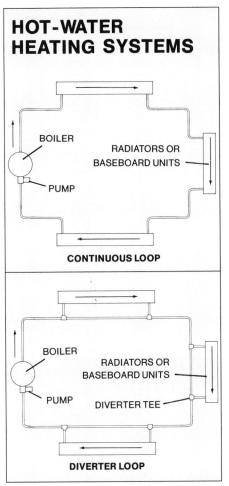

CONTINUOUS LOOP

DIVERTER LOOP

On continuous-loop system, hot water runs directly through heating units. On diverter loop, flow is directed through units by diverter tees.

set fairly low and can be moved up 5 to 10 degrees. If the boiler operating temperature is set fairly low—in the 160F to 180F range—it's possible to increase operating temperature.

If operating temperature is in the 205F to 210F range, you can't get any more heat out of the boiler. *Note:* If you're not *completely* knowledgeable about boiler controls, have a competent serviceman make any needed adjustments.

If you've reduced heat loss, you can turn the boiler operating temperature down a few degrees. If your boiler is oil-fired, a serviceman will often be able to install a smaller-size nozzle to reduce capacity.

If your present hot-water heating system won't handle additional heating load, consider adding an electric heating unit with its own thermostat.

ELECTRIC-HEATING SYSTEMS

Electric-baseboard systems are easy to modify, because each room's heating unit and thermostat is separate. Both can be relocated like any other electrical fixture. See chapter, Electrical Work. Or a larger or smaller baseboard unit can be substituted.

If possible, baseboard units should be located under or near the window, or at least on an outside wall. The thermostat should be located away from drafts and heat sources, on an inside wall. Recessed electric wall heaters should be located on an inside wall, so heat doesn't leak out the back.

If you have a problem finding an open stretch of wall for an electric-baseboard unit, try using a recessed wall heater or a fan unit instead.

Wall and Ceiling Heaters—Many different kinds of supplementary electric heaters are made. Most resemble recessed light fixtures in basic construction. Some, like infrared heatlamps, *are* recessed light fixtures, and are installed as shown on page 141.

Others combine the function of light, heater and fan. If there's a fan involved, installation is similar to a fan, page 149. Install the rough housing and duct at the rough stage, install the working parts and trim during the finish stages.

WARM-AIR HEATING SYSTEMS

Warm-air heating systems typically generate warm air in a central furnace and circulate warm air through a system of ducts. The duct network for central cooling systems is much the same, and the two systems often share the same ductwork. Most ductwork is made of sheet metal. A few systems are fiberglass board, or flexible heat-resistant plastic tubing. Fiberglass-board duct is difficult for the owner-builder to modify, because special fabricating equipment is required. Flexible plastic ducts can easily be moved to new locations.

A sheet-metal duct system is relatively easy to modify. Remove any registers in the area you're working on. If the ducts haven't already been exposed by other work, you'll have to remove as much finish material as needed to provide access. In some

ELECTRIC — BASEBOARD UNIT

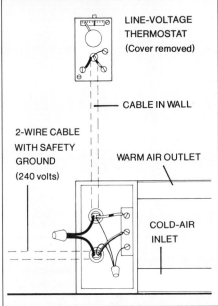

Electric-baseboard heaters can be installed independent of main heating system. Most are wired at 240 volts.

cases, ductwork is accessible from an unfinished attic.

Shortening a duct can often be done by trimming off excess sheet metal with sheet-metal shears. More extensive changes often require removing the section of duct involved. Open the wall or ceiling back to the first joint in the system. Measure and sketch the changes to be made before removing any sections of duct to be modified.

In some duct systems, sections are held together with sheet-metal screws. Some systems are assembled with *interlocking joints,* made by folding the edges of the metal duct back on themselves to form a "U". C-shaped metal slides drive onto the folded ends to lock them together.

To remove a duct section with interlocking joints, remove any duct tape sealing the joint and straighten out the end tabs on the metal slide. Then drive the metal slide off the duct ends with a hammer and a screwdriver. If the duct was assembled with sheet-metal screws, remove duct tape, then remove the screws. Disconnect any hangers attached to the duct section.

SHEET METAL JOINTS

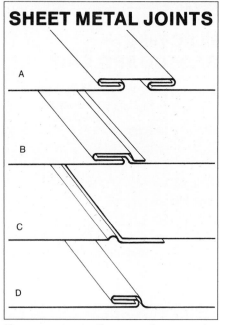

Here are connections most commonly used to assemble and connect ductwork: A. *Drive clip* is used to lock sections of rectangular duct together. B. *Snap lock* is used on long, side seam of round duct. C. *Crimp* allows one length of round duct to plug into the next. Secure with self-tapping screws. D. *Hammer lock* is earlier, simpler version of snap lock. It must be hammered closed to hold securely. For best sealing, all joints should be covered with duct tape.

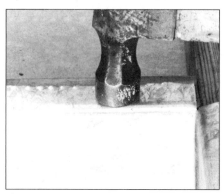

When terminating a duct at a register location, install framing members on all four sides—even 2x2s are enough. Flange end of duct outward on face of framing members before installing wall finish. Flanging can be fairly rough—it doesn't show after register is in place.

Given detailed measurements, a sheet-metal fabricator will either rework the existing piece to suit the new dimensions or fabricate a new piece that replaces or attaches to the old. Sheet-metal shops are listed in the Yellow Pages. They should also be able to supply you with new attaching parts or new registers. Before replacing duct sections, reshape any joints that may have been deformed when

VENTILATING FAN SIZING

Floor area for rooms with 8' ceiling or lower Maximum sq. ft.	Room volume with higher ceilings Maximum cu.ft.	Minimum required fan capacity (most code areas) Cubic feet per minute (CFM)
35	280	24
40	320	27
45	360	30
50	400	33
55	440	37
60	480	40
65	520	44
70	560	47
75	600	50
80	640	54
85	680	57
90	720	60
100	800	67
120	960	80
140	1,120	94
160	1,280	107
180	1,440	120
200	1,600	134
250	2,000	167
300	2,400	200

Sheet-metal fabricator can provide ready-made register flanges for duct ends. These are mandatory for flexible-duct installations like this one.

taking sections apart. Replace insulation and duct tape after sections are installed.

When installing a sheet-metal duct, frame in the duct end on all four sides. Bend the four sides of the duct down flat against the framing members to form flanges. After the wall-surface material is installed and painted or papered, install the register. Make sure the register-attaching screws extend through the wall-surface material, through the flanges at the end of the duct into the framing.

PATHS FOR VENT DUCTS

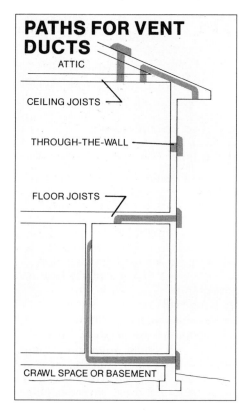

VENTILATION

Codes require that every bathroom have some method of exhausting heat, moisture, and odors. An operable window can meet the legal code requirements, but in practice every bathroom needs a fan. Fans come in so many shapes and sizes that you'll have to depend on the installation instructions packed with the fan for mounting details. Generally, installa-

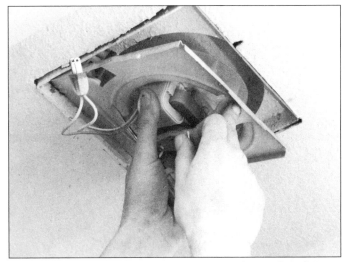

Ventilating fans rough in much like recessed light fixtures. Housing shown is ready for ceiling drywall. Operating parts of fan are stored for installation at trim stage.

Working parts of fan can be installed at same time as light fixtures and other finish electrical equipment.

tion and hookup is much like a recessed light fixture. All connections are made inside an integral junction box. Connection details will be covered in the installation instructions.

There are some ceiling-fan units that combine functions, usually fan/light units and fan/light/heatlamp units. Electrical wiring is similar to a simple fan, though the unit itself might be more complex. Check the installation instructions for any additional steps that might be required.

Planning a Duct Layout—A duct will be needed to carry exhaust air outside. Start by planning a path for the duct. The shortest path is the best, consistent with avoiding framing members. The best place to run a duct is through an attic, basement, or crawl space, if possible, to the outside. If not, find space between floor joists or ceiling joists for a run to an outside wall.

In a flat-roof house or on the top floor of any house, the easiest path for the duct may be through the roof, but roof flashing will be necessary. The duct outlet should never terminate in an attic, basement or other enclosed area. To cut down on moisture condensation within the duct, insulate sections of duct that run through unheated areas.

Vent duct is made in many sizes, in round and flat shapes, in both metal and plastic. Flat duct is made 3-1/2 inches wide to fit inside a standard stud wall. It's also useful in other places where space is limited.

Depending on the shape of the duct you're planning to install, *transition fittings* may be needed to connect the fan to the duct, or to connect one duct shape to another. The fan supplier or a sheet-metal fabricator should be able to supply these fittings.

You'll also need an outlet fitting such as a roof cap or wall cap, and appropriate flashing. Pick an outlet fitting that includes a gravity-operated damper to avoid heat loss and backdrafts when the fan is off. A transition fitting may also be needed to connect the duct to the outlet fitting.

The fan manufacturer's literature usually specifies limits on lengths of duct runs. Elbows and other fittings count as the equivalent of extra duct length. As a rule of thumb, add 4-5 feet to the total duct length for each 90° elbow in the system. On a long duct run, you may have to use a larger duct, a more powerful fan or a booster fan.

Installing the Duct—Vent ducts are best installed while doing rough electrical or plumbing work so all patching can be done at once. The details of vent-duct connections are similar to those of warm-air heating systems.

Remove finish material where necessary, to provide access. Then cut holes needed for passage of the duct. Avoid cutting vital framing members. Loosely assemble the duct in place. Use sheet-metal screws to fasten duct sections solidly together. Wrap all joints with duct tape. When the duct is assembled in its final location, make sure it's securely anchored. Perforated-metal strapping tape is most often used for anchoring.

Installing the Fan—Most ventilating fans are installed much like a recessed light fixture. A separate sheet-metal housing fastens between joists or wall studs with round-head screws. Slip the end of the duct over the outlet flange of the housing and fasten with sheet-metal screws and duct tape. Connect wiring according to fan instructions, within the junction box attached to the housing.

After the wall-finish material is in place, you can then insert the motor-and-fan assembly. Some motor-and-fan assemblies are held in with screws, others just snap in. Most are electrically connected by plugging them into an outlet on the face of the junction box inside the housing. Complete the installation by installing the grille or register, if it's separate.

It's sometimes difficult to reinstall registers, grilles and fan covers after they've been removed. Realigning the screw holes is usually the difficulty. In wood framing, tap a finish nail lightly into each of the old screw holes before installing the cover. Then pull out one nail at a time and replace it with the correct screw. If the screws aren't holding well, replace them with slightly longer or thicker ones.

If the fasteners involved are machine screws, use a large finish nail to align the holes, one at a time. Or find some longer machine screws with the same thread. Cut the heads off, and start the threaded part into the hole. Then line up the cover on the machine screws, remove them one at a time, and replace with the original screws.

11

Ceramic Tile

Hand-painted decorator tiles add unique touch to vanity top and surround. Note matching vanity bowl. Such tiles can also be used as random accents for solid-color background tiles. *Photo courtesy of Country Floors Inc.*

The old way of installing ceramic tile was to lay it on a thick mortar bed. The work was difficult and was done by a specialized group of craftsmen. Today, ceramic tile is installed with mastic adhesives on drywall, plaster or plywood. Relatively thin and regular ceramic tiles are usually laid in mastic adhesives. Thicker tiles such as Mexican tile and quarry tile are set with thinset-type cement adhesive. Application techniques for tile are much the same for both adhesive types. The traditional mortar-bed method can still be used, but isn't worth the bother.

Usually, the larger the individual tile, the faster the work goes. But most small mosaic tiles now come pre-mounted on either a backing mesh that stays on after installation, or a facing paper that is soaked off after installation. Therefore, mosaic tiles go on as fast as bigger tiles.

Some tiles are made with spacer lugs on the edges to automatically provide uniform grout joints. Plastic spacers are used to control grout-joint width on tile without lugs, or if you want wider grout joints than provided by the lugs on the tiles.

Fastest of all are flexible pregrouted tile sheets. These are sheets of full-size ceramic tiles bonded together with silicone grout. They're applied much like mosaic tile, but on a larger scale. After the panels are installed, remaining grout joints are finished with a matching silicone grout.

Many tiles have *spacer lugs* along their edges to provide for grout joints. Spacer lugs are protrusions molded into the tile edges to keep them evenly spaced. If your tiles don't have these, buy a sufficient quantity of *spacers*. These small plastic crosses are sold by the bag, and fit into the corners between tiles. They're available in several sizes at the tile dealer.

TOOLS

It's only necessary to assemble a small group of tools to install ceramic tile. General tools required include a hammer, level, framing square, tape measure and chalk line.

There are several tools used for cutting tiles. If you're working with glazed ceramic tiles, and only need to make a few cuts, you can use a glass cutter. If you need to make many straight cuts, you can rent a tile cutter, available from the tile supplier or a tool-rental company. Large tiles can be cut with a carbide-tip blade in a hacksaw, as described on page 149. To make irregular cuts, you'll need special *nibbling pliers*, available at the tile dealers or a hardware store. A utility knife is useful for separating small mosaic tiles from their backing.

You'll need a special notched trowel for spreading adhesive. After you've chosen the adhesive, check the label for the recommended trowel-notch size. Trowel notches control adhesive-film thickness, critical to good adhesion. If you'll be setting tile for more than a day, buy a second trowel for the second day. It's much easier and less expensive to discard the used trowel than it is to clean one properly. Trowels are available in reusable, and less-expensive throwaway versions.

Grouting will require a sponge-float or squeegee, along with buckets and

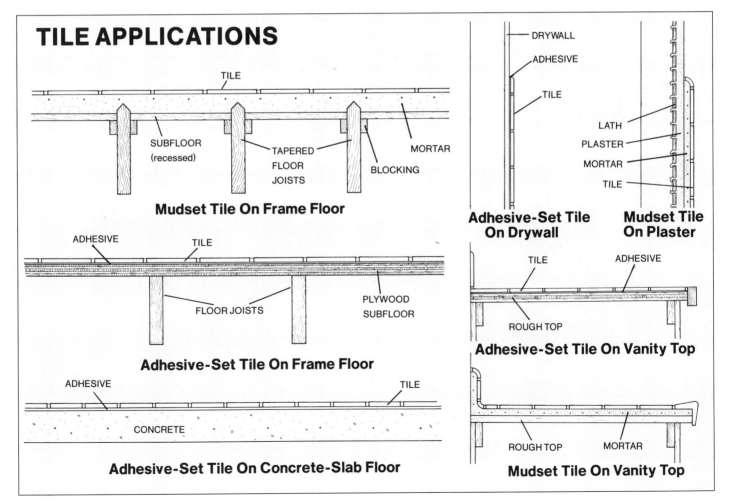

TILE APPLICATIONS

Mudset Tile On Frame Floor
TILE
SUBFLOOR (recessed)
TAPERED FLOOR JOISTS
BLOCKING
MORTAR

Adhesive-Set Tile On Frame Floor
ADHESIVE
TILE
FLOOR JOISTS
PLYWOOD SUBFLOOR

Adhesive-Set Tile On Concrete-Slab Floor
ADHESIVE
TILE
CONCRETE

Adhesive-Set Tile On Drywall
DRYWALL
ADHESIVE
TILE

Mudset Tile On Plaster
LATH
PLASTER
MORTAR
TILE

Adhesive-Set Tile On Vanity Top
TILE
ADHESIVE
ROUGH TOP

Mudset Tile On Vanity Top
ROUGH TOP
MORTAR

Shown are the few tools you'll need to apply ceramic tile. Tile cutter and notched trowel are the only specialized ones.

sponges or cloths for cleanup. Additional specialized tools and materials are listed where required in following instructions.

ADHESIVES

New adhesives have made tile work easy. Adhesive types are *organic water-base, organic solvent-base* and *epoxy*. Organic water-base adhesives will tolerate some water exposure, but not a lot. Organic solvent-base will withstand a lot of water exposure. Epoxy will stand up to anything the tile will, except a few industrial solvents.

Areas where tile comes in direct contact with water, such as showers and tub surrounds, will require a highly water-resistant adhesive. Have the tile dealer recommend the adhesive best suited to your circumstances.

If you're planning to use a solvent-base adhesive or an epoxy, be sure to allow adequate ventilation. Also, eliminate any possible source of ignition of the fumes. More safety information on solvents is on page 87. Also read safety precautions on the adhesive label.

Most tile adhesives come in *floor* and *wall* grades. Either grade can be used in either area. But there's a difference in setting times. Wall grades set up more slowly and take more time to set completely. Floor grades are completely set in 24 hours, but you have to work quickly. Pick the grade best suited to your working speed and the job circumstances.

Some adhesives used over bare wood may require a sealer or preliminary skim coat. If yours does, brush or trowel on the sealer or skim coat and let it dry. If you've removed existing finish materials, make sure the new adhesive will stick to the surface. For more on surface preparation, see page 81.

CUTTING TILE

How you cut ceramic tile depends on the kind of tile and the nature of the cut. To make a quantity of straight cuts on medium-to-large, glazed or semiglazed tile, use a device called a *tile cutter*. A tile cutter has a scoring wheel on the central handle. Score the tile on the cut line, and then push down on the handle to snap the tile at the score.

If only a few cuts are needed, you don't need a tile cutter. Score the cut line with a glass cutter. Position the score line over a pencil or piece of wire and press down sharply with both hands to snap the tile. Small or irregular cuts are best made with nibbling pliers, also available at the tile dealer.

It's usually best to make all cuts for a surface at one time, though some tilesetters like to cut and fit as they go along. Put cut pieces near their final location—or number the backs—so you don't mix them up. Then butter the back of each cut piece and ease it into position. The adhesive under the cut pieces should be the same thickness as the rest of the adhesive layer.

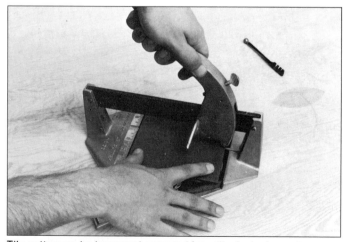

Tile cutter can be borrowed or rented from tile dealer in most cases. Pull up on handle to press cutting wheel against tile, pull handle along to score tile, then push down on handle to snap tile on scored line.

If only a few tiles must be cut, glass cutter and straightedge work well. This method provides extra control for cuts on small-size tile.

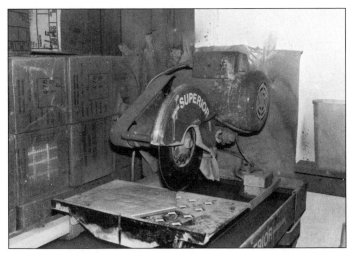

Commercial-type tile saw makes short work of cutting tile. These saws can be rented, and many tile dealers have one. They'll make cuts for a small fee.

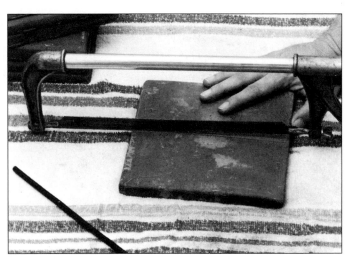

Soft unglazed tiles can't be scored and snapped. Groove face of tile—and back if tile is very thick—with saw. Then snap over a wire.

When cut tiles are in place, tap them with a padded wood block and hammer until they are level with surrounding tiles.

Cutting Large Tiles—Large, unglazed quarry tiles and large Mexican tiles are too thick to be cut by scoring and snapping. Some tile dealers have water-cooled *tile saws* and will make cuts to your marks for a small fee. If you have a large quantity of cuts to make, it might be worthwhile to rent a tile saw from a local tool-rental company.

You can also cut large tiles by hand. Most hardware stores carry hacksaw blades that have carbide grit bonded to the edge. Installed in a standard hacksaw frame, one of these blades will make hundreds of cuts in large tile. Don't use the blade to cut soft materials like wood—the cutting edge will get clogged. There is also a wire version of this blade for making tight, curved cuts in glazed and unglazed tiles. Wire-type blades are most useful in a coping saw.

When making straight cuts with a carbide-grit hacksaw blade, cut with the blade parallel to the surface of the tile to make a groove about 1/16-inch deep. In other words, cut the whole length of the groove at once. Extend the groove down the radii on curved-tile edges. Place the tile on a towel, over a length of insulated wire. Push down sharply on both sides to snap it. For extremely thick tile, you may have to groove both face and back to get a clean snap. Don't use a straightedge to guide a carbide-grit blade. It will ruin the straightedge in two or three strokes.

Curved Cuts—Use nibbling pliers to make curved or irregular cuts in tile. These are available at the tile dealer. Nibble away at the surplus part of the tile until you've gnawed it down to the desired shape. The tile need only have an even contour at the finished surface. If the cut edge is uneven down in the grout joint, it won't show.

Cutting Mosaic Tiles—Whole mosaic tiles are easy to separate from the sheet with a utility knife. Cutting individual tiles is more difficult. They can be cut with nibbling pliers, but the pliers may leave surface fractures on highly glazed mosaics. It's hard to get a straight clean cut.

The diamond cutter's method works well with some mosaics. Turn the tile face down on a piece of plywood and support each edge with lengths of wire. Then place the cutting edge of a chisel over the cut line. Make sure the cutting edge is squarely in contact with the back of the tile, and the front of the tile is squarely in contact with the wires. Then strike the chisel handle with a hammer. You may have to try this several times before you can get the tile to break where you want it to. Don't use your best wood chisel for this—the tile will chip or dull the cutting edge.

TILE LAYOUT

There are some basic rules that apply to laying out ceramic tile:
- Plan the layout so all cut pieces are more than half a tile in size.
- Never place a cut edge of a tile in an exposed location, such as an outside corner.
- Always lay out locations of trim pieces before laying out field tiles (whole tiles).
- Try to locate cut tiles in the least obtrusive location.

In almost every case, the easiest sequence of tile application is the same. Install any bathtubs and preformed shower pans first. Then lay out and install tile on all vertical surfaces, such as walls and tub surrounds. Finally, lay out and install tile on floors and other horizontal surfaces. The exception to this rule is vanity tops, discussed on page 152.

WALLS

The first step in laying out wall tile is to measure and mark layout lines on the wall. Start the wall layout by marking the locations of any trim pieces. Then lay out horizontal lines, and finally, vertical lines. The basic unit of tile layout is the width of a tile plus one grout joint.

In terms of design, most of the important lines in any bathroom are horizontal. It's important that the horizontal grout joints of the tile harmonize with them. The fixed spacing of tile makes it impossible to match all other horizontal lines in the bathroom, so you'll have to pick what seems to be the most obvious horizontal line and lay out the tile from that point. In most cases, this will be the floor line, but in some cases, the top edge of the tub will be a more obvious focal point.

Use a level and pencil to draw a level line a foot or so above the horizontal line you'll be laying out from. Then measure down at closely spaced

LAYING OUT WALL TILE

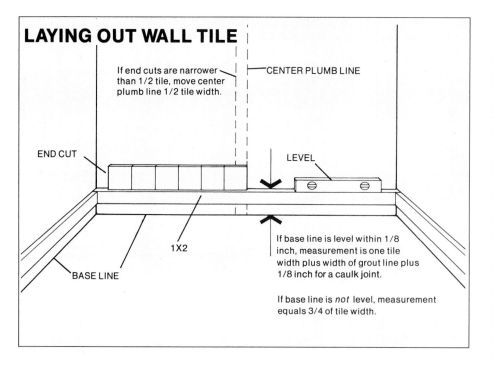

If end cuts are narrower than 1/2 tile, move center plumb line 1/2 tile width.

CENTER PLUMB LINE

END CUT

LEVEL

1X2

BASE LINE

If base line is level within 1/8 inch, measurement is one tile width plus width of grout line plus 1/8 inch for a caulk joint.

If base line is *not* level, measurement equals 3/4 of tile width.

TILE STICK

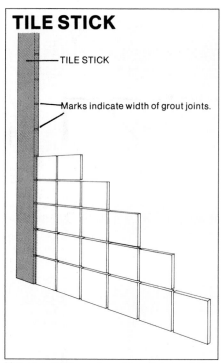

TILE STICK

Marks indicate width of grout joints.

You can easily make a tile stick to aid in layout work. Mark one edge with a felt-tip pen to match a row of the tile. Same stick will work for four different sizes of tile—but don't get mixed up when you're using one with multiple markings. The stick is most useful for laying out wall tile.

points to find the highest and lowest points on the horizontal line. Bear in mind that the horizontal line you're laying out from may extend along several walls.

If the line is within 1/8 inch of level, you can work from the highest point. If the line is more than 1/8 inch

out, move the tile layout down so you can cut the bottom row of tile to fit the irregularity.

Measure up the width of a tile and a grout joint, or about 3/4 of a tile if you've decided to cut the bottom row. Add about 1/8-inch for a caulk joint, and mark. Use your level to extend a horizontal line through the mark, as far as the tile goes.

Measure from the level line, or use a tile stick, described below, to see how the tile will work with any other horizontal surfaces in the room. Narrow cuts at the floor line often aren't objectionable, but they usually are objectionable at a vanity top or over a tub. Make any adjustments before starting on the tile.

Tile Stick—A useful device for determining tile layout on walls and other vertical surfaces is called a *tile stick*. This is any straight piece of wood that has one edge marked with the particular tile spacing you're using.

You can easily make a tile stick. Lay out a row of the wall tiles you're installing on any flat surface. Then place a straight length of 1x2 alongside the row and mark stick with a felt-tip pen at each grout joint.

If you're working with more than one size of tile, you can fit up to four sets of markings on the one stick. But make sure they're clearly identified so you don't mix them up.

When tiling to an out-of-level horizontal surface—often a problem with existing tubs—be cautious if the tile

has a pronounced radius or 'pillow' at the edges. Because you're laying out from the lowest point on the surface, you'll have to cut the tiles to fit all higher points to avoid ending up with an unsightly tapered caulk line between the bottom row of tiles and the tub or floor.

The pillow-shape edge will cut off everywhere *but* at the lowest point. This in itself will make the caulk line irregular. If you run into this problem, move the level line down by 1/4 to 1/2-inch so the pillow-shape edge is cut off all tiles in the bottom row. Also check for this problem on any other horizontal surfaces you're tiling.

You may have two or more areas of wall tile in a bathroom, with wall space between them. You usually can't get away with working with two different horizontal level lines, one in each area. It's only possible when the space between the areas is wide, the grout lines are all but invisible or the horizontal lines are aligned closely enough to fool the eye. Work both area layouts to the same level line. In fact, if the areas are close together, you'll probably get better results by eliminating the wall space between and running the tile straight through.

When you're satisfied with the horizontal level line, tack strips of 1x2 to all the walls. The top edge of the 1x2s should just meet the level line. These strips support the tile and keep it from slipping down while the adhesive sets. You can then remove the strips and set the bottom row.

To determine the vertical alignment of the wall tile, treat each wall surface individually. Strangely, the vertical tile joints don't have to be equally spaced from panel to panel. The job will look good as long as the partial tiles at the left and right edges of each panel are equal.

Use a tape measure to mark the midpoint of the wall on the top of the 1x2 strip. Stand tiles on top of the 1x2 strip, leaning against the wall and with correctly spaced grout joints. If you've made a tile stick, you need not set up the tiles in the middle of the run—just set up the last few tiles at each end and align them with the tile stick. If the remaining space at each end is less than half a tile, shift the whole row left or right half a tile. That way the cut tiles at each end are more than half a tile wide.

There are several special cases to

Continued on page 152

LAYOUT LINES

The method of establishing layout lines described here works for resilient and ceramic tiles and other block-flooring materials. It can be used to lay out tiles for larger bathrooms. Small bathrooms may not require establishing layout lines by this method. You can either use a tape measure and framing square to establish the lines or lay out the tiles directly on the floor to see how they fit.

Check room dimensions. Divide length and width of room by width of tiles. If the result is an odd number of tiles and a partial tile, center the layout line and run tiles in each direction from it. See top drawing at right. If the result is an even number and a partial tile, working from a centered layout line will cause cut pieces at walls to be less than half a tile. Move the layout line half a tile to either side of center to end up with tiles over half size at walls.

Layout lines should average out the variance in direction of each pair of walls, and should cross in the middle at an exact right angle.

Measure and mark centerpoints of long walls. In top drawing at right, distances A and B should be equal, as should distances C and D. Snap a chalk line between centerpoints of opposite walls. Mark centerpoints of short walls, E equal to G and G equal to H.

Use two nails to string a chalkline between centerpoints of short walls. Before you snap the line, use a rafter square to see if intersection in middle is an exact 90° angle. If it is, distances A to H are all equal—all walls are square and the same length. Snap chalkline and get on with the job. If intersection of layout lines is not 90°, adjust them.

To adjust, mark center intersection on floor. Then move end points of chalkline until intersection in middle is 90°, and mark two new end points. Don't move the intersection as you do this. Find the midpoint between old and new marks at each end of the chalkline. Connect the chalkline to midpoints at each end and snap.

Rub out the first center line that runs perpendicular to the one you just marked. Set the chalkline over the rubbed-out line, across the short dimension of the room. Adjust the chalkline until it's exactly at 90° to long chalk mark, through the original center intersection. Snap chalkline. Both center lines should now intersect at 90°.

To make layout lines for a diagonal floor, first set up layout lines as described above. Measure several feet out from the center intersection, in any three directions along lines—points A, B and C in bottom drawing at right. All measurements from the center should be equal.

Tack a nail into floor at points A, B and C. Hook the end of a tape measure on each nail in turn. Hold a pencil against the tape measure at a distance equal to that between nails and centerpoint.

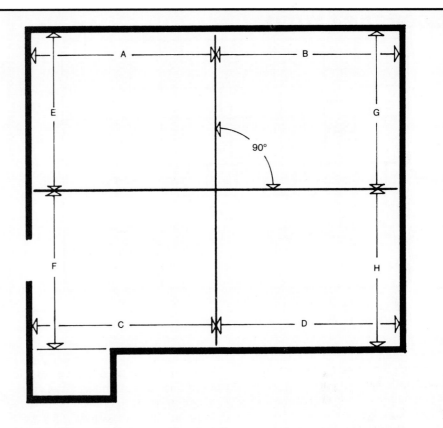

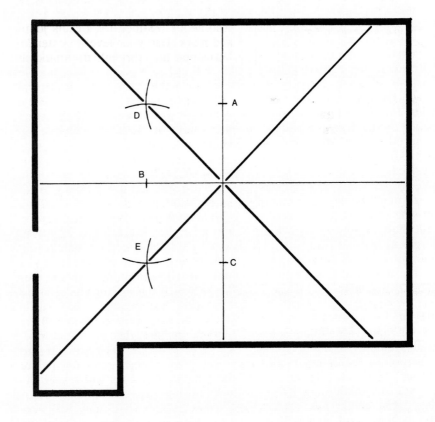

Draw four arcs on the floor, as shown in drawing. Arcs should intersect at points D and E. Snap chalklines between D and center intersection, and E and center intersection. Continue lines to the wall.

On a diagonal floor, you'll have small, partial tiles at walls. Lay out a row of diagonal tiles to see what size partial tiles are required at walls. Adjust layout lines for best pattern of cut pieces at walls.

FLOOR TILE LAYOUT

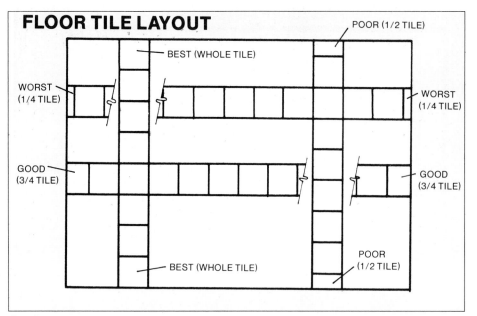

POOR (1/2 TILE)

BEST (WHOLE TILE)

WORST (1/4 TILE)

WORST (1/4 TILE)

GOOD (3/4 TILE)

GOOD (3/4 TILE)

BEST (WHOLE TILE)

POOR (1/2 TILE)

Cut tiles at walls should be 1/2 tile or wider.

Continued from page 150

watch for when laying out the vertical lines for wall tile. If you plan on applying cove tile at an inside corner, allow for it when doing the trial layout—and allow for the layer of mastic underneath the cover tile. Plan all corner overlaps carefully.

The neatest way to handle an inside corner is to run cut tiles into the corner and then cover up the cut edges with whole tiles on the adjoining wall. That way, the cut doesn't have to be exact. Outside corners are best arranged so the edge of a whole tile is just covered by the edge of a bullnose tile on the other wall. Allow for the correct thickness of tile, grout joints and adhesive layers.

Outside-corner trim pieces work best if they meet whole tiles on both sides of the corner. While you're laying out the vertical lines, check all the trim pieces and make sure they'll work out. Sometimes rearranging the layout is the only way to get by with the trim pieces available.

FLOORS

Layout for ceramic-tile floors is the same as for resilient-tile floors. To establish layout lines, follow instructions on page 151.

When you've established layout lines, lay out a single row of tiles along the longest layout line, in both directions from the centerpoint. Do not adhere tiles to floor at this time. Make sure you allow for grout joints. If the tiles have spacer lugs, the joints are predetermined. If they don't, use

the plastic spacers to determine joints.

Use a framing square to run single rows of tiles at right angles to the long rows. Or you can use the tile stick to determine tile locations. This will reveal any awkward-looking areas or small cuts.

Cuts less than a half tile in width should be avoided wherever possible. Small cuts can usually be eliminated by shifting the whole layout half a tile one way or the other. Rework the trial layout until it suits you. Then make a sketch, or use a pencil to make reference marks on the floor. Remove the single rows of tile.

VANITY TOPS

Layout lines are not necessary to do a trial layout for vanity tops. Starting with an outside corner, lay single rows of tile in both directions. If you're using an outside-corner tile at the corner, position this tile first, mark its location on the top and run whole tiles from there.

Because vanity tops are usually small, you may want to lay out all the tiles to see how they fit. Otherwise, use a carpenter's square to lay out single rows of tiles perpendicular to the longest row. This will reveal any awkward-looking areas or small cuts.

Cuts less than a half tile in width are less obtrusive at the back edge of the vanity top. Small cuts at either side of the top can usually be eliminated by shifting the whole layout half a tile left or right. Also, try to work the layout so you have as few small cuts as possi-

ble around the lavatory cutout, and tiles on both sides of the cutout are equal in size.

Rework the trial layout until it suits you. Then make a sketch or draw reference marks on the rough top. Remove single rows of tile.

TILE APPLICATION

Before you start, refer to pages 147-149, for information on required tools, adhesives and tile-cutting techniques. Basic instructions are given here for floors, walls and vanity tops. If you're installing tile in a shower, do the walls first, then the floor.

FLOOR TILE APPLICATION

After you've set up your layout lines, apply as much mastic to the floor as you can cover with tile before the mastic sets. Start setting whole tiles diagonally out from the intersection of the layout lines.

Don't bed tiles solidly into the mastic until you have a number of them down and you're satisfied with the alignment and spacing. Then use a short length of 2x4 wrapped in an old towel and beat the tiles into solid contact with the adhesive. Be careful not to push any of the tiles too far into the mastic at the edges of the field.

If the tiles you're laying don't have spacer lugs at the edges, use tile spacers, available at the tile dealer.

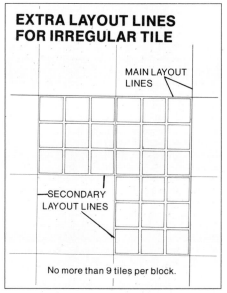

EXTRA LAYOUT LINES FOR IRREGULAR TILE

MAIN LAYOUT LINES

SECONDARY LAYOUT LINES

No more than 9 tiles per block.

Large, irregular floor tiles with wide grout joints may require two sets of layout lines. Starting from main layout lines, establish secondary layout lines to form a grid block. Evenly space tiles within each block.

For larger grout joints, space tiles with small strips of wood or hardboard.

Large, heavy tiles, such as quarry tiles, require additional layout lines to end up with even grout joints. Overall size, shape, and thickness of individual tiles can vary greatly, and the tiles don't have spacer lugs. So you can't use a spacer system to make uniform grout joints. As you work, add extra chalk lines to form a *grid block* that's two tiles on a side, two by three tiles, or three by three tiles, depending on tile size. Run the chalk lines down the centers of the grout joints. It's easiest to do this with the completed trial layout still in place as a guide.

Apply adhesive to one grid block at a time. Place and level the tiles in that grid block. Then ease the tiles around until all grout joints are evenly spaced. Remember that the edges of most quarry tiles are curved. The spacing at the shoulder of the tile, not the actual gap between the tiles, controls the width of the grout joint. Recheck level and give each tile a firm push with the flat of your hand to ensure solid bedding. Then start with the next grid block.

Lay out whole tiles in a room before you start fitting and laying cut tiles. Avoid standing or kneeling on newly laid tiles because you can easily sink tiles into the adhesive or slide them out of position. If you must stand or kneel on newly laid tiles, place large pieces of plywood or hardboard on the tiles to distribute your weight. Move carefully so you don't slide the plywood. To avoid this, you can set cut tiles around room edges the following day.

WALL TILE APPLICATION

Applying ceramic tile to walls is a more intricate process than on floors. Careful planning and laying out before starting can eliminate much of the intricacy.

Porous subsurface materials will often require a prime coat of adhesive to seal them before applying the coat that holds the tile. Check the label on the adhesive for recommendations. If a prime coat is called for, trowel on a smooth film with the straight edge of your adhesive trowel, and let it dry completely.

Apply a smooth coat of adhesive under the layer that holds the tile anywhere the tile will be subjected to severe water exposure, such as in a

Large tiles go down fast, quickly cover large areas like this floor. Keep adhesive from piling up in grout joints as you work. Make sure tiles are evenly bedded in adhesive to avoid cracking, due to lack of support.

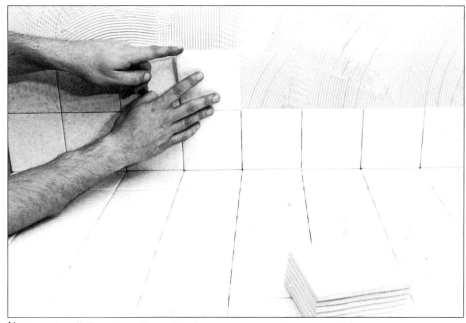

Always set wall tile across the wall, not up the wall. That way the adhesive holding the lower courses has a chance to set up some before too much weight is stacked on it.

shower. The adhesive provides an additional barrier to water penetration.

Apply adhesive over the surface of one wall with the notched side of an adhesive trowel. Do not let adhesive obscure the layout lines. Don't apply any more adhesive than you can cover during its open time. Also, make sure you're doing the sections in the right sequence, so any planned overlaps at corners work out correctly.

Working outward from the center of your horizontal layout line, set all the whole tiles that rest on the 1x2 strip, page 150. Then add tiles stair-step fashion, working out in both di-

rections from the center vertical line. This method allows adhesive the maximum time to develop bond before tiles above are added. In other words, don't put the tiles on in vertical rows.

Be sure to push each tile firmly into the adhesive as you go along. Each tile rests on the one below, and a loose tile can cause several below it to fall off the wall.

If you're installing tiles with spacer lugs, setting the whole tiles is relatively easy. If the tiles don't have spacer lugs, some other means of spacing will be necessary so all the grout joints don't creep closed as the adhesive is setting.

If the desired grout-joint width matches a size of available tile spacers, use them. If the desired width doesn't match a standard spacer, use anything that works. Narrow strips cut from scrap plywood, hardboard or plastic laminate work well. Other possibilities are slips of cardboard or finish nails.

A traditional spacing method uses hard-woven cord of an appropriate size. The cords are inserted into the horizontal grout joints as the tile goes on, then removed after the adhesive sets. This method still works if you can find the right-size cordage. Try woven clothesline for wide joints, venetian-blind cord for medium joints, or masons' twine for narrow joints.

Whatever you use for spacers, don't let the spacers bond to the adhesive so strongly that you have trouble removing them. Dampening the spacers helps, but do not oil them as you would concrete forms. The oil will penetrate the body of the tile and permanently stain it.

After all the whole tiles are in place on one wall, mark, cut and install any cut tiles. Tile-cutting techniques are shown on pages 148-149. Clean excess adhesive from tile faces. Then wrap an old towel around a short piece of 2x4 and beat the tiles firmly into the adhesive. As you beat in the tile, check for and correct any tiles that might be slightly out of position. Remove any adhesive from grout joints where it might interfere with grout application.

After the adhesive has set com-pletely—24 to 48 hours—remove the 1x2 strips at the bottom. Cut, if necessary, and install all of the bottom tiles. Be sure to beat the bottom tiles down level with the rest of the tile. You'll need to use shims under the bottom tiles so they don't drift downward before the adhesive sets. Cardboard or Bristol board works well for this purpose.

VANITY-TOP TILE APPLICATION

Before you can put ceramic tile on a vanity, it's necessary to build a rough top. This process is described on pages 162-163. When making and installing the rough top, keep the dimensions of the tile in mind. It's often possible to adjust rough-top measurements to eliminate much of the later cutting and fitting of tile.

TILE TRIM PIECES

Before selecting and buying tile, make a list of required trim pieces. Not all of the trim pieces shown here are available for all tile that's on the market. While certain substitutions are possible, sometimes the absence of a matching trim piece is critical.

An excellent solution for the problem of unobtainable trim pieces is the use of contrasting trim. You can trim either in an accent color, or with a plain color that matches the background of a patterned tile. If you trim with an accent color, note that the louder the color, the better the installation workmanship has to be.

Also, make sure you can get a grout color that works with both the main tile selection and the trim tile. It's not feasible to apply two different grouts to a tile area.

Two Kinds of Trim—Field tiles are much the same no matter how you plan to install them. But trim pieces can be different, depending on whether the tile is being set with adhesive or in mortar. Trim pieces for adhesive-set tile are flat, but have finished edges in the right places.

Outside corners are fairly sharp. Trim pieces for installation over mortar must curve back to the wall to hide the edge of the mortar bed. Outside corners for installation over mortar have the same wide curve as the edge pieces. Inside-corner trim for both applications are much the same.

The three basic situations where trim pieces are used are inside corners, outside corners, and edges. Inside corners are covered with cove trim. Locations where three inside corners come together utilize an inside-cove corner.

Usually, edges and outside corners are finished with the same trim pieces. The basic outside-corner and edge-trim piece is the bullnose, radiused on one edge. A double bullnose is radiused on two opposite edges, used for shower door jambs and curbs. If a trim piece is radiused on two adjacent edges, it's called a down-corner. An up-corner is square on all four edges, but turned down on one corner. It fits on a projecting corner against a down-corner and a bullnose. There are many more specialized trim pieces for special situations.

Visualizing how all these trim pieces go together can be nearly impossible. If you have a fairly complicated tile job to do, there's a simple way to work out what trim pieces to use. Take a trip to the tile dealer and buy one or two of each trim piece, along with a couple of field tiles, of the tile you're going to use. Write the name of each trim piece on the back with a pencil.

Use the pieces to experiment with different tile layouts on the surface you'll be covering. When you figure out a particular trim situation, trace around the trim pieces, and pencil in the name of the pieces right on the surface. You can work your way through the most complicated trim problems this way. Make sure your solutions are consistent. For instance, don't trim out opposite ends of a window sill in two different ways.

Shown here are common tile trim pieces. Not all of them are available to match all tile lines. Some manufacturer's trim pieces may vary slightly from patterns shown here.

If you're using outside-corner tiles on the edges, apply them first. Butter the backs of the outside-corner tiles with adhesive and apply them according to your layout marks.

Spread adhesive with a notched trowel over a portion of the rough top. Spread only as much adhesive as you're sure you can cover before the adhesive sets up. If you're using a wood edge strip, the first row of tiles should be a grout joint's width back from the strip.

Install all whole tiles first. Set down whole tiles slightly out of position. Then twist or slide them into final position. The movement should be slight, so you don't pile up adhesive in the grout spaces. It is easier to cut and fit all partial tiles at the same time, after you've done the whole tiles.

After all tiles on a surface are in place, lightly tap them into the mastic with a padded wood block and hammer. This levels the tiles and ensures good contact with the mastic. A towel wrapped around a piece of 2x4 or 2x6 will do.

Lavatory Cutouts—How you tile a lavatory cutout depends on the kind of lavatory installation. For a drop-in lavatory, the lavatory should be installed after the tile, but before the grout. Run the field tile to the edge of the cutout in the top, making all necessary cuts.

A few lavatories are meant to be installed directly in the tile field. These should be installed before the tile so you can tile to them. Pay particular attention to the relative thicknesses of such lavatories and the tile. You may have to shave down the rough top at the edge of the cutout, or build it up, to get the finished surfaces to come out even.

Undercounter lavatories should be in place before the tile goes on, so you can complete the tile trim. Quarter-round trim pieces are the easiest way to finish off top edges. As with the tile-in lavatories, some adjustment of lavatory position may be needed to fit the dimensions of the trim.

GROUTING AND FINISHING JOINTS

After all tiles are in place and the mastic has set, grout the joints. If you're using wood edge strips, install and finish them before grouting.

Drop-in lavatories are installed after setting tile but before applying grout. Grout can be used to fill gap around lavatory rim. *Photo courtesy of American Olean Tile Co.*

Grouting is a messy job. Protect or mask off nearby surfaces. Wear rubber gloves—most grouts are slightly caustic. Mix powdered grout according to the package directions, usually to a consistency a little thicker than pancake batter. Pigment particles in powdered grout should be broken up and evenly distributed throughout the mixture. Even some white grouts contain pigment for a uniform color.

Spread grout over the entire surface with a squeegee or sponge float. Working on the diagonal, force grout into all joints. Use the squeegee to remove as much surplus grout as you can. Then remove some more with an almost-dry sponge. Do this until the grout is level with the tile surface or slightly below it.

In an hour or so, the grout will be ready for another cleanup. Package instructions will often tell you to let the grout set overnight. If you do, the tile won't clean up as easily. Wait until grout is starting to show dry patches. Use a cloth wrapped around a wood block to remove surplus grout from tiles and polish off the grout haze. Don't use terrycloth or other fabric with a nap. It will dig the soft grout out of the joints. Burlap is the best material for this. Work the grout in the joints down to its final level and contour. Don't try to remove every last trace of grout haze at this time.

Touch up low spots or air bubbles with more grout. You can use any smooth object to shape the grout as needed. The handle of an old toothbrush works well. Use an old spoon for wider grout joints.

When the grout is completely dry, buff off haze or surplus grout with a coarse cloth. High spots in grout joints can be leveled by wrapping the coarse cloth around your joint-striking tool and buffing vigorously.

MORTAR GROUT

Large tiles with large joints are generally grouted with mortar—a mixture of Portland cement and sand. Ordinary sand is unsuitable for mortar grout because the color and grain size is variable. Use uniformly graded No. 30 white silica sand, sold in sacks at a masonry supplier.

One part Portland cement to 3 parts sand is a good starting point for the mix. To improve plasticity, you can add a small amount of *hydrated lime.* Lime content is not critical, but should not exceed 10%, or the grout will be too stringy.

Use the basic 1 to 3 mix for grout joints 1/2 inch or wider. For narrower grout joints, the mix should be proportionally richer, up to 1 part cement to 1 part sand for the narrowest grout joints. Joints narrower than 1/4 inch or so should be grouted with prepared grout.

Mortar grout won't stick to the surface of glazed tile. You can shovel grout into place with a trowel and strike it off with a flat piece of wood or squeegee. Mortar grout will cause permanent stains on the faces of unglazed tiles. For these tiles, mix mortar with more water—almost a slurry—and carefully pour into place. Use a plastic watering can with a long, thin spout or a sturdy canvas bag with a hole in it, similar in use to a cake decorator's pastry bag.

Tooling—The mortar will take an initial set a few minutes after application. This stage is easy to determine because the mortar becomes dull in appearance and starts to stiffen up. Tool the mortar to final shape and surface compactness before it sets completely.

Masons' joint tools work well on glazed tile, but they're difficult to use on unglazed tile. For unglazed tile, put in only as much mortar as needed. Tool it with something that can be handled more carefully, such as an old stainless-steel tablespoon.

Immediately after tooling grout joints on unglazed tiles, clean tile faces with a damp sponge or cloth wrapped around your index finger. This removes minor mortar stains on the tiles. It also evens and compacts the edges of the mortar grout. If you

Spread grout with a squeegee or a sponge float. Work diagonally so you don't scrape grout back out of joints.

Keep grout off faces of porous tile by using watering can or canvas bag to apply. In problem situations, it helps to coat faces of tiles with silicone sealer before applying grout. Use a sponge or paintbrush so you avoid getting sealer into the grout joints, where it will interfere with grout bonding.

find the mortar grout is drying out too quickly during or after application, the tile itself is probably too dry. If so, use water in a spray bottle to moisten the grout joints before you apply the mortar grout.

SEALING GROUT
AND UNGLAZED TILES

While glazed tile is impervious to most dirt and stains, grout is not. Especially in a bathroom, grout joints should be sealed. The surface of unglazed tile is susceptible to dirt and stains. Unglazed tile should be sealed with the same sealer used for grout, if it's given no other finish.

Several materials are available to seal tile and grout. If you don't want the sealer to show, use *silicone sealer*. Silicone sealer is swabbed on with a brush, sponge or cloth, and the surplus wiped up a few minutes later. After drying, it's invisible. Test by pouring on some water and wiping it up after a while. If the surface shows a damp spot after wiping, apply another coat of sealer.

If you want a semigloss surface, use an *acrylic emulsion*. For a small area, use one of the self-polishing floor waxes, such as Johnson's Futura. For big areas, use commercial concrete sealer, available from a janitorial supplier.

The easiest way to apply acrylic emulsion is with a 4- or 5-inch paintbrush or a thick lambs-wool paint roller. Don't apply too vigorously or you'll create bubbles that will show after the acrylic emulsion dries. On porous tiles and grout joints, several coats may be necessary. To get a uniform satin gloss, use an electric floor buffer after the acrylic emulsion is dry.

Floors sealed with acrylic emulsion should be damp-mopped periodically, and need a light reapplication of sealer every 6 to 12 months. Some commercial maintenance services add a small amount of acrylic emulsion to the water when damp-mopping and follow up with a light buffing. Unglazed-tile floors treated this way never need full reapplication, yet don't build up an excess of acrylic.

CAULKING

The final step in preparing the tile job to withstand water is to caulk any joints where tile meets any other surface. Use silicone tub-and-tile caulk if white is acceptable. To match colors, use exterior acrylic caulking in a cartridge, available in many colors.

Force the caulk well into the joints, running along the joint a few feet at a time. Go back immediately and smooth out the caulk with a wet finger. Finish with a damp cloth, removing any excess from the tile as you go.

There's a way to avoid problems with that perennially troublesome caulked joint between the tub and the wall. First, fill the tub all the way up with water. Then take off your shoes and socks, roll up your pantlegs, and step into the tub. The weight of you and all that water ensures that the tub and the floor beneath it are flexed downward as far as they'll ever go. Caulk the joint and leave the water in the tub until the caulk sets completely.

Because wall and floor tiles in this bathroom are same color, a dark colored grout was used on floor tile to visually separate it from the wall. *Photo courtesy of United States Ceramic Tile Co.*

Vanities & Tops

Suspended vanity is major element in modern bathroom design based on rectangles. Under-counter lighting adds impact to design. Owners sacrificed vanity-storage space to achieve desired effect. *Photo courtesy of American Olean Tile Co.*

Vanities and storage cabinets are common features in today's bathroom. If they're to look good and function well, cabinets and vanity tops must be installed as carefully as any other bathroom fixture. Because bathrooms are relatively small spaces, errors in cabinet and top installation are more likely to be noticeable. This chapter covers correct installation techniques.

Vanity tops deserve particular attention because of water and other substances they're exposed to. Top materials must be waterproof. They should be resistant to all the oils, stains and chemicals found in makeup, cleansers, and other personal grooming substances kept in a bathroom. All cracks and seams must be well sealed. Porous or rough surfaces should be waterproofed.

Common materials for vanity tops include plastic laminate, synthetic marble, DuPont Corian, and ceramic tile.

Because the installation methods for ceramic tile are similar for floors, walls, around fixtures or on vanity tops, the methods are covered separately in the previous chapter, starting on page 146. To apply tile, you'll first have to install a rough top, as described on pages 162-163 in this chapter. Installation of the other top materials mentioned are covered in this chapter.

PREPARATION WORK

Vanities and storage cabinets must be installed level and square, whether the surface to which they're attached is level and square or not. Use a level and a straight, 6- to 8-foot length of lumber to locate and mark the high spots on the floor and walls where the vanity or cabinet will contact. If high spots can't be sanded or chipped down, shim out the cabinets to clear high spots as you install.

When the high spots on floor and wall have been located and marked, draw a full-size layout of the vanity on the walls and floor. The layout should be drawn to fit the high spots. Use the level to transfer the height of the highest spot on the floor to the walls. See drawing at right. Draw a level line on the wall at that height. Then lay out the vanity cabinet up from the level line rather than from the floor.

Review the layout on the wall to make sure any gaps can be covered by moldings and fillers. Don't be tempted to adjust the vanity cabinet to close the gap, or the vanity will not remain plumb and level.

Raising the vanity to clear a high spot usually creates a gap where the vanity *toe board* meets the floor. The toe board is a wide strip of molding between the bottom front of the vanity and the floor. If the toe board doesn't completely cover the gap, scribe and cut a wider toe board to fit, or attach a piece of base-shoe or quarter-round molding to cover the gap.

Tap with a hammer to find the studs in walls where the vanity cabinet will be attached. Then use a nail to verify exact locations of stud centers and mark them on the walls a few inches above the cabinet layout lines. If you make the marks small, you can later cover them with the backsplash on the vanity top.

INSTALLING VANITY CABINETS

You may be installing many cabinets in a large and elaborate vanity, or only one or two in a modest one. When many cabinets are involved, it's generally best to install them one at a time. If a few cabinets are to be installed, it's sometimes better to line up the cabinets in the middle of the room. You can then align them and screw them together at the front frames. The whole assembly can then be slipped into place.

The following text details the process of installing one cabinet at at time. If you're installing one cabinet

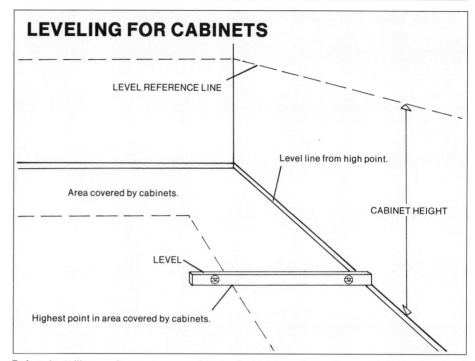

LEVELING FOR CABINETS

LEVEL REFERENCE LINE

Level line from high point.

CABINET HEIGHT

Area covered by cabinets.

LEVEL

Highest point in area covered by cabinets.

Before installing vanity or storage cabinets, find high spots on floor or wall. Use level and long, straight 1x2. Set up reference marks on wall and floor, level and plumb with high spots. Extremely high spots may need fixing before vanity goes in. At same time, check any wall-mounted mirror locations for same problem.

only, follow instructions for the first cabinet only.

First Cabinet—If the cabinet run starts at a corner, install the corner cabinet first. Shim the cabinet and level it to the wall reference line. Then drill a 3/32-inch hole through the mounting rail at the back of the cabinet at each stud mark. The hole should be about 1 inch down from the cabinet top. Drive a No. 7x2-1/2-inch pan-head screw through each hole and into the stud.

Draw the screws down lightly and check cabinet for warpage. It's easy to see warping or twisting taking place as you tighten the screws. Doors should remain in alignment with the face frame and each other. They should not look warped. Shim as necessary to eliminate any warpage.

The Next Cabinet—Place the second cabinet next to the first, and shim it to the reference line on the wall. Then clamp the front faces of the two cabinets tightly together with two padded C-clamps. Drill and countersink two 3/32-inch holes edgeways through

Continued on page 161

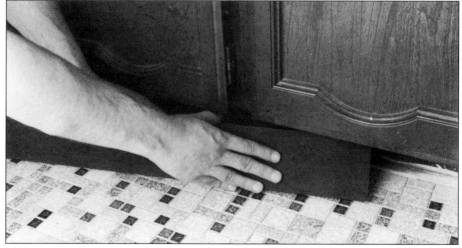

If floor is sloped or uneven, use extra length of prefinished toeboard to cover gap and shims.

INSTALLING FACE FRAMES

A *face frame* is the front part of a cabinet, without the box and internal parts. Face frames are useful for closing off spaces where there isn't room for a conventional door of any kind. Face frames can be installed in a recess or alcove, between two walls. A face frame can also be applied to the surface of a wall. The five basic installation situations you're likely to meet are shown here. The degree of care you'll have to use in fitting depends on whether you can use molding to close gaps, and how straight the walls are.

First, check the bathroom to see if the face frame needs to be positioned to match the height of anything else. If so, use a level to transfer and mark a reference point to work from.

Plant-on—The application shown at (A) is the simplest. Hold the face frame in position and level it. Check to be sure there are no unsightly gaps between the frame and the wall. If you're not applying moldings around the perimeter, you may have to scribe the frame to fit the wall. Scribing techniques are given on page 177.

Caution: If you drive in screws to pull the frame down to the wall, you'll just transfer the frame-to-wall gap to frame-and-door. Scribe to fit, shave down the wall to fit, or use a perimeter molding.

The best way to attach a plant-on face frame is to drive flat-head wood screws through the frame into the wall structure where the heads will be concealed by the door. If this isn't possible, mark the outline of the wall opening on the back of the frame and remove it from its position. Install 1/2x1/2" wood strips just inside the outline on the back of the frame. Use short screws to attach the strips. Replace the face frame in position. Drill, countersink, and drive flat-head screws through the strips into the wall framing. Two or three screws on each side are usually enough, unless the face frame is extremely large or heavy.

Recessed—The recess application at (B) will always require scribing or perimeter moldings. Place the face frame against the opening, in line with any reference marks, and level it. With the door open, mark the outline of the wall opening on the back of the frame. Trim the frame to the mark. Insert the trimmed face frame in the opening and adjust it. No wall is ever completely flat, so final adjustment may take some compromising.

Then drill, countersink, and drive flat-head wood screws edgewise through the sides of the frame into the wall structure. If you can't get a solid mounting this way, try setting the face frame deeper, or using the interior mounting strips discussed above, for (A).

Half Alcove—The half-alcove applications at (C) and (D) are similar. Hold the face frame in place and plumb up the side of the frame that's perpendicular to the wall. Scribe and trim to fit the wall. Then fit the other sides of the frame, either similar to (A) above, or (B) above. Best anchorage is by driving screws through the inside edge of the frame into the wall framing.

Alcove—The full-alcove application shown at (E) is the trickiest, but not very common. It's usually necessary to make a cardboard pattern. When the cardboard pattern fits perfectly, hold it in place and use a level and a felt-tip pen to draw a plumb line or level line on the pattern. Then position the cardboard pattern on the frame for trimming.

Use the plumb or level line to make sure the door and opening will come out level and plumb after installation.

Caution: It's possible to reverse the pattern and end up with a backwards fit. Once the face frame is fitted into the alcove, anchor by driving flat-head wood screws through the edges of the frame into the wall structure.

Problems—A chronic problem with alcove and half-alcove installations is the absence of a handy framing member in the wall for good anchorage. In such cases, use molly bolts for mounting. Use one bolt for each foot of frame. Add wood screws where the frame contacts a crossmember, such as bracing or a plate in the wall.

In difficult anchoring situations, you may have to install metal angle brackets on the back of the face frame. You can then run fasteners into the wall through the angle brackets. This works well if there's a framing member only an inch or two behind the face-frame location.

Especially in remodeling situations, there are times when new work installed plumb, level and square looks out of place. This happens when adjacent materials are not plumb, level, or square. There are no general rules for dealing with such situations, because each is often unique. In some cases, you may have to install a face frame slightly "off" to have it come out looking right.

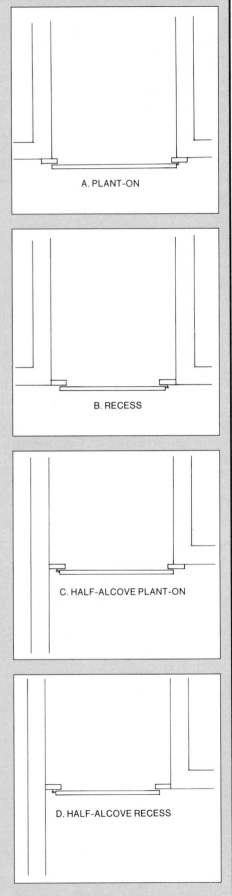

A. PLANT-ON

B. RECESS

C. HALF-ALCOVE PLANT-ON

D. HALF-ALCOVE RECESS

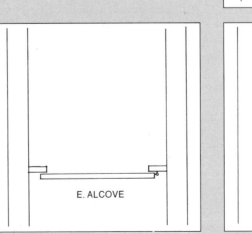

E. ALCOVE

Align front frames of separate cabinets using padded C-clamps. Drill and countersink for two flathead wood screws to tie cabinets together, as shown here.

Continued from page 159
one of the front frames and partway into the other. Countersink the holes and drive in two No. 7 flat-head screws. Shim the back edge of the cabinet as required. Screw the cabinet to the studs as you did with the first one. Repeat this process for successive cabinets.

To bridge the gap, such as kneespace, use two straight 6- or 8-foot lengths of 1x3 or 1x4. Clamp these to the top front and top rear of the cabinets you've already installed, so they extend across the gap. Strips should be level with cabinet tops. Measure and mark on the wood strips the width of the gap. Use the wood strips as guides for setting the next cabinet.

VANITY TOPS AND BACKSPLASHES

After the vanity cabinets are installed, install the top or tops. The easiest type to install is the *post-form top*, though its use has limits. Synthetic marble and DuPont Corian complete the list of materials that can be applied directly over the base cabinets. Plastic laminate and ceramic tile require the construction of a rough top on the cabinets. Installation of synthetic marble and Corian start on page 162, plastic laminate on page 163. Tile installation is discussed on pages 154-155.

POST-FORM TOPS

When buying post-form tops, make sure you allow an extra 3 inches for each overhanging end and an extra inch for each flush end. Mitered ends for corners are precut left-hand and right-hand. Make sure you get the correct ones. If you're replacing an existing top, instructions for removing the old top are on page 74. If walls and corners aren't relatively square and level, avoid using a post-form top.

Rough Cutting—Before you make any cuts, use a framing square to check all factory cuts, especially miters, to make sure they're true. Square cuts should be exactly 90°, miters excatly 45°. If cuts are off, you can either recut the top or return it to the dealer. If a miter cut is off, return the top—don't try to recut it.

If necessary, cut the material into the correct number of pieces. To allow for trimming, add 3 inches to each overhang and at least 1 inch to each flush end. Use a framing square to mark for cutting.

If you're cutting with a circular saw or saber saw, mark and cut the top from the underside. That way the saw teeth cut into the finish surface instead of out of it. If you're cutting with a handsaw, keyhole saw or table saw, mark and cut from the top side. For a clean cut, use a plywood blade or finish blade. Make cuts to the outside of your marks, especially on the finish cuts. Don't cut down the middle of the line.

Fitting—Trial fit each piece. Mark each end on the underside where it clears the cabinet below. If any pieces are similar, number them to avoid confusion.

Remove the top sections and mark for final cutting. Any overhanging ends should equal the front overhang. Cross out any earlier marks so you don't cut off the overhang by mistake.

Cutout for Lavatory—Position the lavatory upside-down on the vanity top. Use a tape measure to make sure the lavatory is square to the top and correctly positioned. Trace the outline of the lavatory on the vanity top. Measure in from your marks the width of the lavatory rim and lay out the cut lines.

If you have any trouble working out the exact location for the lavatory cutout, put the vanity top in place. Measure inside the cabinet on the underside of the top to find the center-

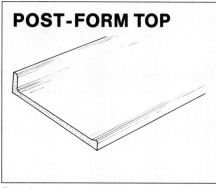

POST-FORM TOP

Post-form top material is sold by running foot, usually in 2-foot increments.

point of the cutout. Drive a nail through from underneath and measure out from the nail. While under the cabinet, make sure that the lavatory bowl will clear the cabinet structure below the cutout. If it doesn't, reposition the cutout.

If the lavatory is square or rectangular in shape, avoid square corners on cutouts. Make cutouts after you've made the final end cuts. Match the corner radius of the fixture that goes in the cutout. Bore a hole at each corner, then use a saw to connect the holes.

End Caps—When all cutting is completed, sand any exposed ends to prepare them for the precut end caps. Use a sanding block to avoid curving the cut surface. Sand away from the finished surface to prevent it from chipping. Trial-fit end caps frequently as you sand. When you're satisfied with the fit, attach the end caps with contact cement, following label directions.

Mounting—Remove the top and drill vertical 3/16-inch holes in the front

Even if lavatory cutout is rectangular, drill corners to provide radius. Square corners can start cracks, especially in plastic laminate.

and back corner-blocks of the cabinets. Holes should clear the threads of the screws you're using to anchor the top—No. 7 drive screws are recommended. Screws should be only long enough to extend about two-thirds the way into the vanity top.

If the top has any miter joints, bolt miters solidly together before driving in screws. Use special *miter bolts*, usually available from the top supplier.

Drop the assembled top into position. If you don't have help for a large assembly, position pieces on the cabinets before you assemble miters. Insert screws up through the pre-drilled holes in the cabinet and drive them into the top. You may need to drill pilot holes in the top to get the screws started.

Caulking—When the top is fastened in place, apply tub-and-tile caulk along the joint between the wall and the backsplash. Pump some of the caulk down behind the backsplash as you go. As soon as you're finished caulking, squeegee off the excess with a wet finger.

SYNTHETIC-MARBLE AND CORIAN TOPS

Synthetic marble and Du Pont *Corian* are mineral-filled acrylics. Synthetic marble gets its gloss from a surface coating, so it isn't feasible to cut and fit pieces on the job unless the cut edges will be concealed when you're done. For this reason, you'll have to either buy a factory-made, stock-size top, or have the top made to exact measurements.

Du Pont Corian can be polished to a gloss after cutting, so it can be cut and fitted on the job. Corian can also be routed, sanded or planed to complex shapes. Corian is also available in prefabricated tops. Smaller, prefabricated tops with integral lavatories are available in both Corian and synthetic marble.

Both materials should be worked with carbide-tip tools. Standard tools and saw blades will dull quickly, due to the mineral dust in the material. It is also a good idea to wear a respirator while cutting, to avoid inhaling the dust. Use a circular saw to make straight cuts, a saber saw to make curved cuts and cutout for lavatory bowl. Cut both materials from the underside avoid chipping the surface. Use padded sawhorses or wood blocks to protect the finished surface while you're working.

Once synthetic marble or Corian tops are fabricated, installation is fairly easy. The materials are dense and fairly brittle, so have enough help on hand to handle the biggest piece.

Apply 1-inch strips of adhesive to the tops of the cabinets, every 6 or 8 inches. There's a special adhesive for these tops, but if stresses are low, you can get by with silicone sealer. Lower the slab onto the cabinets and let its weight bed it in the adhesive.

The adhesive strips form a uniform supporting cushion. Don't disturb the slab until the adhesive cures completely. If you ever have to remove such a top, saw through the adhesive strips with a wavy-edge bread knife.

Apply backsplash pieces the same way as the main piece. Adhere the pieces with adhesive or silicone sealer, applied in 1-inch strips every 6 or 8 inches. After all pieces are in place and the adhesive has cured, caulk all seams and joints with tub-and-tile caulk or silicone sealer. Apply caulk or sealer and immediately smooth off the joint with a wet finger. Clean off surplus caulk before it sets.

ROUGH TOP FOR LAMINATE OR TILE

If you're applying plastic laminate or ceramic tile, you'll need to build a rough top to put them on. Particle board works well under plastic laminates but can disintegrate when repeatedly exposed to water. On installations where structural strength is a factor, or where there's potential for water exposure, use plywood. This especially applies to ceramic-tile tops because grout joints are susceptible to water leaks.

Whichever material you use, the thickness should be 3/4 inch. Plywood should be grade-marked PTS (plugged, touched, sanded) on at least one side. Exterior-grade plywood is recommended.

Layout and Cutting—If you're using laminate, work out the locations of laminate seams *before* cutting pieces for the rough top. Seams in the laminate should not coincide with seams in the rough top.

Measure, cut, and fit to provide a 1-1/2-inch overhang on all open edges. If the top will have a wood edge strip, make the overhang 1-1/2 inches minus the width of the wood edge strip, usually 3/4 inch. On difficult or

odd-shaped pieces, rough out a piece, put it in place, and mark for finish cutting.

If the bathroom has wavy walls, the rough top should be fitted to them. Cut to the finish-top width plus a little more than the maximum depth of the wall irregularities. Then scribe the top pieces to fit. Scribing techniques are shown on page 177.

Assembly—After the pieces for the rough top are made up, lay them out, upside-down, on a reasonably flat and level floor. Before assembling the rough top, make sure you can maneuver it into the bathroom after assembly.

Tie any seams together with corrugated fasteners and glue. Cut 3-inch-wide trim strips of the same 3/4-inch material. Glue and nail strips to the perimeter of the top, as shown in the drawing below. Use 1-1/4- inch annular-ring nails. Carefully line up outer edges. Stagger splices in strips so they stiffen any seams in the rough top.

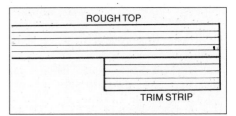

Cut and attach 3-inch-wide trim strip to bottom edges of rough top. Strips are cut from same material used for top.

Final Fitting and Cutouts—Replace the assembled rough top on the cabinets. If you've misaligned any of the pieces during assembly, small corrections may be required. Trim or fill to correct the fit. The fit doesn't have to be perfect: within 1/16 inch or so is OK.

Mark exact locations of cutouts. Lavatories can be turned over, positioned on the rough top, and traced in. Offset the cut lines inside the mark by the width of the lavatory rim. Make sure there is clearance underneath the counter for the lavatory. If you have difficulty centering a cutout, find its center underneath the top by measuring. Drive a nail up through the top and take measurements from the nail.

Once the cutouts are marked—and checked—drill a hole that matches

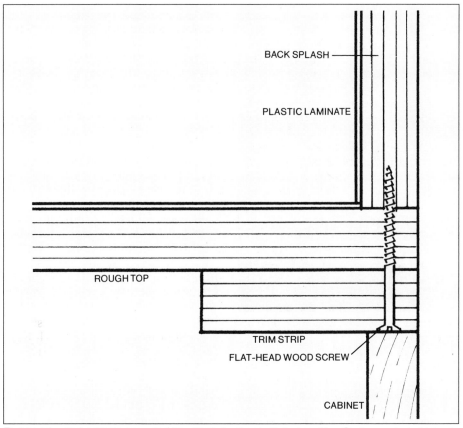

Flat-head wood screws are used to attach backsplash to top. Use C-clamps to hold back-splash in position while drilling pilot holes and attaching screws.

the radius at each corner of each cutout. Make straight cuts with a circular saw, curved cuts with a saber saw. Make cuts carefully, because you'll be trimming the finish material to the cutouts. Excess cutout could be visible in the finished job.

Backsplashes—While the rough top is sitting in place, cut and fit back-splashes, if any. The standard height for vanity backsplashes is 4 inches.

Remove the top from the cabinets to mount backsplashes. Drill a row of 3/16-inch holes in the top about 1 foot apart. Center holes on a straight line, 3/8 inch in from the back edge of the top. Countersink holes on the underside of the top to accept flat-head wood screws.

Line up backsplash sections and clamp them in place with C-clamps. Drive in flat-head screws from the bottom. Also use wood screws to tie the backsplash pieces together at any corners.

Mounting—Do any sanding and squaring up before mounting the rough top. If you're going to apply plastic laminate to the top, all surfaces should be flat and all edges square.

Use a hard sanding block and a small plane to smooth any rough edges.

Drill vertical 3/16-inch holes in the corner blocks of the cabinets. Then move the top into final position and drive in screws from underneath. Use No. 10x1-1/4'' hex-head drive screws. A magnetic screw bit in a variable speed drill is the quickest way to drive the screws. Do not use glue to attach the top—you might need to remove it in the future.

APPLYING PLASTIC LAMINATE

Plastic laminates are most often applied with solvent-base contact cement. If you're using a solvent-base cement, carefully read label directions, and follow them. Solvent fumes are both toxic and explosive. Provide adequate ventilation to prevent buildup of fumes. Extinguish all open flames, including pilot lights. If possible, do all cementing outside. See page 83 for more on safety procedures.

Preparation—Remove all grease, oil, wax and sawdust from the plastic laminate and the surface you're applying it

to. New laminate can be applied over existing laminate. Thoroughly roughen the existing surface with coarse sandpaper and clean with mineral spirits or alcohol.

If the old surface is loose, remove all loose material. In this case, check the compatibility of the new adhesive with the old. If the old surface is in poor condition, you may prefer to rip it out and build a new rough top. Small surface imperfections can be filled with floor-patching compound.

Layout and Cutting—Mark all cuts on plastic laminate with a grease pencil or washable felt-tip marker. Leave 1 inch excess material on all open sides to allow for trimming. Use the straight, factory edges for seams. You may have to make paper patterns if the job is complicated, or if you don't have enough extra material.

Most straight cuts in plastic laminate can also be made with a special carbide-tip scriber and a steel straightedge. Deeply score the face of the plastic laminate with the scriber. Then insert a strip of wood under the score line and push down to snap off the piece. Or you can use a circular saw or saber saw with a fine-tooth blade.

Cementing—Contact cements have open times from 20 minutes to 2 hours. Check label specifics. Coat both surfaces with cement. After application, the contact cement is ready when it's tacky, but no longer tends to lift when you touch it with your finger. If dull spots appear anywhere on the cement coatings, it means the cement has been absorbed and will not bond. If this happens, let the surface dry, then recoat. The first coat will serve as a sealer.

The standard sequence of applying laminate pieces is do all vertical surfaces, then do horizontal ones. Start with the side edges of the top, then the front edge, then the backsplash, if any. Trim all edge strips as described on page 164, then apply the top pieces.

Edge Strips—Edge strips over 3 feet in length require a helper when you attach them to the top. On long pieces, alignment is difficult. A small misalignment at one end can turn into several inches misalignment at the other. Once the two coated surfaces come into contact, they're permanently stuck in that position. You can't adjust them. Clean any contact

Apply plastic laminate to ends of vanity top and backsplashes, then on long ends, then on main surfaces. Make exposed edges as unobtrusive as possible.

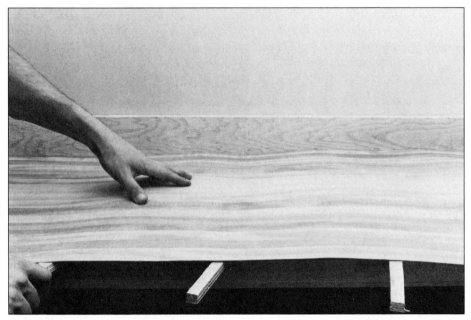

Use spacers when applying laminate to long, horizontal surfaces. A small misalignment at one end can grow to a large misalignment at the other. Brown wrapping paper keeps laminate between strips from contacting adhesive on rough top. Carefully remove strips and paper as you press laminate into place.

cement off your hands before touching coated surfaces. After you've applied laminate to the edges, tap it into contact with a padded wood block and hammer.

Trimming—The overhanging edges of each laminate piece must be trimmed flush with the rough top before adjoining pieces can be applied. Trimming can be done with a saw, plane, file and sandpaper. But it's tedious that way. The best way to trim laminate is with a router.

Special router bits are used to trim plastic laminate. These bits have small ball bearings to guide the bit. For small jobs, trimming bits are made to be chucked in an electric drill.

Horizontal Surfaces—After the plastic-laminate edge strips are trimmed flush with the surface of the rough top, apply contact cement to the top and to the laminate. On large, horizontal surfaces, use spacers between the top and the laminate to keep the two separated while you posi-

tion the laminate over the rough top. You can use wood strips, metal rods, thin strips of cardboard or even grocery bags for spacers. Position spacers so you can withdraw them as you lower the laminate to the top. Make sure spacers won't leave any debris, such as splinters or sawdust, in the cement.

When the laminate is positioned, start sticking it down at the most difficult location, such as in a corner. Ease out the spacers and let the laminate down until all the spacers are out.

Beat the laminate firmly into place with a padded block and a hammer, especially along the edges. Trim it with a router. The final edge can be trimmed square, or with a bevel. Use fine sandpaper and a block to remove any sharp edges. Make any cutouts, then trim off the surplus material with a router.

WOOD EDGE STRIPS

Wood edge strips are one of the handsomest edge treatments for vanity tops. Wood edge strips can either match or contrast with the vanity cabinets.

You may be able to buy wood edge strips from some cabinet suppliers, or you can make them from available molding stock. If you're working with a custom cabinetmaker, he can easily make matching edge strips. You can even have them milled to match the vanity cabinets or other trim in the bathroom.

Wood edge strips are usually 1-1/2 to 2 inches wide and 1/2 to 3/4 inch thick. They can be applied to almost any vanity top. Use a close-grain hardwood with no splinters and good wear characteristics. Birch, ash, oak, walnut and cherry are popular trim materials.

Check for adequate clearance between the bottom of the wood edge strip and doors or drawer tops. If clearance is too tight, or appearance isn't good, remove the top, add plywood spacer strips and reinstall top.

On ceramic-tile counters, strips are best applied after the tile but before the grout. On plastic laminate, synthetic marble or Corian tops, wood edge strips are best installed last.

If you've ordered from a fabricator, it may be possible to have edge strips installed at the shop. At least tell the fabricator where you'll apply wood edge strips so he can prepare the edges for you.

Installation—All wood edge strips should be sanded and finished before final installation. Sanding and finishing after installation may damage adjoining finished surfaces. Keep oil- and wax-base finishes off areas where adhesives will be applied.

Grout will hide small irregularites on ceramic-tile tops, so alignment of the wood strip is not critical. The top edge of the strip should be even with the tile surface.

On plastic-laminate tops, all irregularities must be taken care of during edging installation. It's difficult to remove high spots and refinish the strip without marring adjoining laminate.

You can mount edge strips without visible attachments by using contact cement—but this can be tricky and there's no room for error. Otherwise, use countersunk screws with matching or contrasting plugs made from wood dowel, brass rod or aluminum rod.

Screws and Plugs—Roughly fit the wood edge strips and lay out the fastener locations in a neat and evenly spaced pattern. Use finish nails to tack the strips in place. Place one nail at each fastener location, and drive it through the strip and partway into the top. Nails and holes will relocate the pieces as you remove and replace them.

To fit strips perfectly, mark any high spots by scribing a line on the back of the strip with the point of a utility knife. Remove the strip with the nails still in it, sand it down, and replace it. Repeat the process until each strip fits perfectly.

When all strips are fitted and replaced, remove one nail. Use the nail hole as a guide to drill a plug pocket and a pilot hole for the screw. Drive the screw in the hole. Repeat with succeeding nails.

When all screws are in place, remove screws and strips. Stain and seal strips. Apply woodworking glue to the back of each strip and to end joints. Reinstall the strips and tighten screws. Remove excess glue with a damp cloth.

To plug the holes, start with a dowel or metal rod of appropriate diameter. Sand dowel end to a smooth, square finish surface. Sand sides of dowel as needed to get a light press-fit. To mark the dowel, insert and pull end slightly clear of the hole bottom. Mark the dowel at the surface and cut the plug off. Slightly taper the

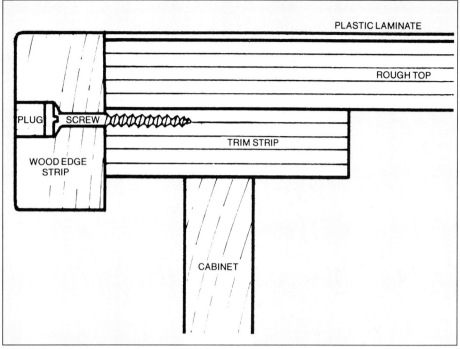

Wood edge strip is attached to plastic-laminate top with countersunk wood screws. Glue dowel plugs into screw holes, pushing them flush with surface. Align top of edge strip with laminate surface.

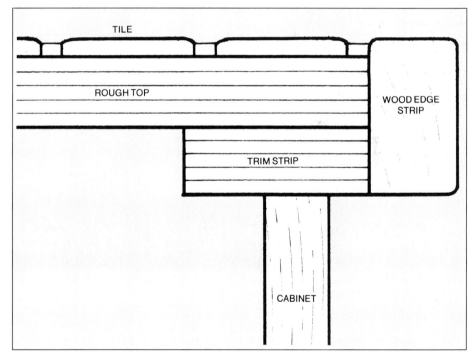

Edge strip for tile top is attached the same as for plastic-laminate top above. Leave room for grout joint between edge strip and tile. Use masking tape to protect edge strip while grouting.

cut end with sandpaper.

Put a small amount of glue into the hole and line up the plug grain with the wood-strip grain. The smooth-finish end of the plug should face out. Carefully push the plug into the hole with a smooth, flat metal object.

Air pressure sometimes builds up when the plug is pushed in and will force the plug out again before the glue dries. Check plugs every few minutes while the glue is drying and push in any that move out. The air pressure will eventually dissipate, and plugs usually stay put the second time.

Finish Work

The trim in a bathroom encompasses doors, window trim and all the little items that aren't structural and aren't part of the plumbing and electrical systems. Trim can help unify bathroom design by tying all other elements together.

An amazing number of finish pieces must be installed before a new bathroom can be called complete. Finish work includes installation of doors, windows, trims and moldings, and bathroom accessories, such as towel bars, soap dishes and medicine cabinets. All of these are in plain sight, so they must be installed with attention to detail. The finish pieces not already covered in other chapters are covered here.

While doors and windows might be thought of as part of the structure, they must be installed as carefully as any other trim. Detailed installation and finishing techniques for doors, windows, skylights and luminous ceilings are covered here, as well as installation of trim, moldings and bathroom accessories.

WINDOW INSTALLATION

If you've done work on outside walls, you'll probably have one or more windows to install. No matter what type of window it is, installation basics are similar.

Use a framing square to check the window assembly to make sure it's square. If the window assembly is wood, attach a 6- to 8-inch-wide strip of 6-mil polyethylene around the outside edges of the window frame. Staple it onto the sides so you can lap it over wall framing for an air seal. Then trial-fit the window in the opening. If opening is too small, rework it. For information on making window openings, see pages 92-93.

Aluminum-frame windows have a flange that seats against the outside edges of the framed window opening. The windows can be installed before the finish siding, with siding covering the flange, or after the finish siding. See drawing at right. If your house has lap siding, it's best to install the window first, then fit the siding to it. If the window is installed over the siding, the flange can be covered with 1x3 or 1x4 trim.

Installing a window in a frame wall covered with stucco is similar to working with a plaster wall. The stucco and reinforcing can be cut with a circular saw, using a carbide-tip blade or a masonry blade.

Set the saw to cut only through the stucco, not into the framing. An aluminum window requires an opening large enough to allow you to attach the mounting flange to the framing.

Once the aluminum window is installed, you can either use stucco patch to patch the opening around the window, or cover the opening with 1x3 or 1x4 wood trim. Another alternative is to use a wood or vinyl-clad window. The stucco can be cut for an exact fit, so trim strips that come with the window will cover the opening. No patching will be required.

After the hole is cut in the stucco, the interior wall-finish material is also removed and the framing reworked to fit the new window. Remember that all exterior walls should be considered bearing, so shoring will be required while modifications are being made to the framing. See pages 92-93 for details on framing window openings. Shoring for bearing walls is discussed on page 86.

Wood and vinyl-clad wood windows have molding that attaches to the outside of the frame. They can be installed before or after the finish siding, depending on the type of siding involved. Lap siding is usually fitted to the sides of the window frame after installation. See drawing at right.

HOW TO INSTALL

To install the window, place it in the opening and level it. The window should be level, even if the framed opening isn't. Leave a gap of 1/4 to 1/2 inch at both top and bottom be-

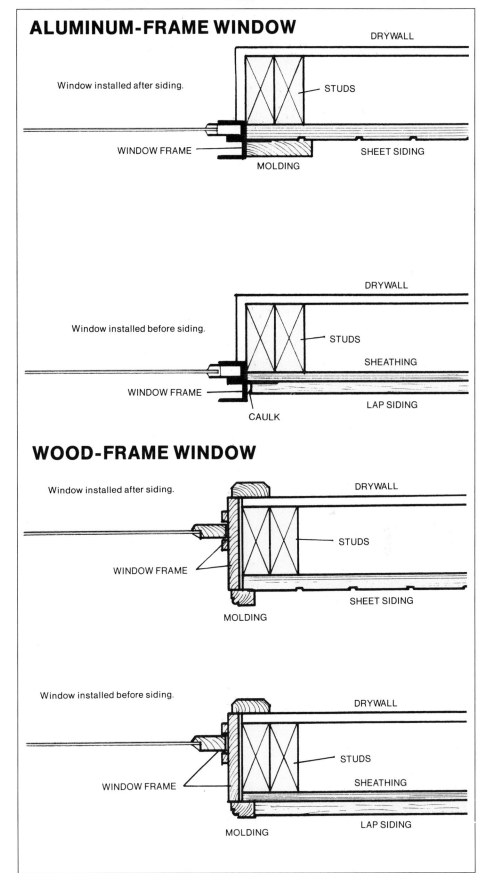

Wood-frame and aluminum-frame windows can be installed before or after exterior siding, depending on type of siding used. Wood-frame windows are easier to install in existing stucco walls because no patching is required.

NAILING WOOD WINDOWS

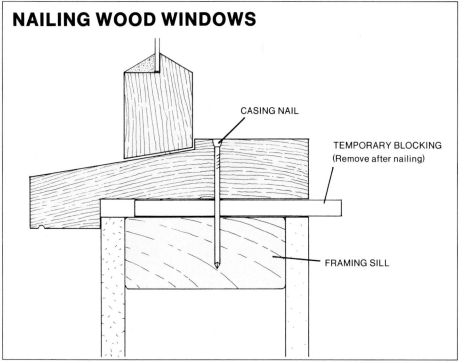

CASING NAIL

TEMPORARY BLOCKING
(Remove after nailing)

FRAMING SILL

Use casing nails to attach wood windows to window frame. Removable blocking provides space around window for expansion and contraction.

tween the window frame and the header and sill. This prevents the window from jamming if the header or floor ever sags in the future.

On horizontal-sliding windows, the gap at the top should be slightly larger

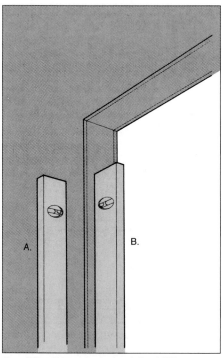

If wall itself is out-of-plumb by 1/8" or more (A), you'll probably have problems installing the jamb and door trim. If door opening is out of plumb up to 1/4" in line of wall (B), it can be corrected when shimming door jamb.

than the one at the bottom. The rough opening should not be so large that you can't nail the flange or outer molding on all four sides.

After the window is positioned and leveled, drive two or three nails through the flange or outer molding on each side. Don't drive nails through the top or bottom flange or molding.

If you're installing a wood-frame window, go inside the house and fit temporary shims or wood blocks every foot or so between the bottom of the window and the sill. Also fit shims or wood blocks between the top of the window and the header.

Drive *casing nails* through the window frame next to each of the temporary shims. Casing nails look much like finish nails. Remove the temporary shims. This locks the window into the opening, but allows it to move independent of the header and sill. Complete the fastening of a wood-frame window by nailing through the exterior moldings at the sides of the window.

On aluminum-frame windows, use a screwdriver to punch vertical slots every foot or so in the top and bottom flanges. Some aluminum-frame windows come with prepunched slots or stamped indentations where slots can be punched. Install nails at the centers of the slots. Leave a small gap between

the nailhead and the slot, so nails can move in the slots if the header sags.

In severe-climate areas, consider installing a metal drip cap at the top of the window to protect the top joint from water penetration. In all cases, caulk joints where the window assembly meets siding or trim.

DOORS

Doors provide a different set of installation problems from windows. Doors can become misaligned due to constant stress placed on the jamb from opening and closing the door, and from the weight of the door itself. Doors must be installed in correct alignment and fastened solidly enough to keep them that way.

PREHUNG DOORS

Prehung doors are factory-assembled units that consist of the door, the *jamb*, or door frame, the *door stop* and *hinges*. The door usually has predrilled holes for a *lockset* and the jamb is mortised for the *striker plate*. *Case trim pieces* are usually precut by the factory, and often installed on one side of the door.

Prehung doors cost little more than if you buy the pieces separately. They save hours of work in installation. Doors come in left- and right-hand swing. Make sure you order the correct ones.

Installing a Prehung Door—Use your level to determine if the floor is level across the door opening. If it isn't, measure and note the amount of offset. Then measure down the side jambs and mark and trim the jamb bottoms to fit.

Hold the level against the wall to make sure it doesn't lean in or out. The rough opening in the wall doesn't have to be perfectly plumb. Small misalignments can be corrected by shimming when the door jamb is nailed into the rough opening. See drawing at left.

On prehung exterior doors, side jambs should be pretrimmed to suit the height of the *threshold*. Check threshold height and trim the jamb for it, if necessary.

On interior doors, check the offset between the door bottom and the bottoms of the jamb. If the finish flooring is already in place, trim the jamb so the door bottom clears the floor sur-

PREHUNG DOOR INSTALLATION

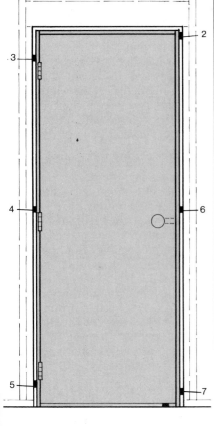

To fit prehung door into rough opening, follow this sequence: Loosely fit door and jamb into rough opening. Shim frame at position 1 to raise door to correct position in jamb. Shim at position 2 to hold jamb in position. Shim at positions 3 and 4; check upper half of hinge side of jamb for plumb. Shim at position 5 without loosening position 4. Shim at positions 6 and 7. Recheck plumb on hinge side of jamb. Check fit and alignment of door in jamb, and jamb in wall. Adjust if needed. Drive two casing nails through jamb just below each shim location. Open door to make sure it doesn't fall open or closed. Remove cardboard shims on door and check for free operation. Install one long screw in center hole of each hinge. Screw should extend into jackstud of rough opening. Break off projecting shims, install case trim, lockset and threshold.

face in both open and closed positions. If you've not yet installed the finish flooring, adjust jamb length to provide clearance under the door for it. If asked, the door supplier may be able to provide a door and jamb assembly precut to suit the flooring you're installing.

Pull any nails or staples holding the door and jamb together. Holding the assembly by the door so the jamb hangs on it, stand it in the opening. *Don't pick up the assembly by the jamb.*

Drive shims under the door on the lockset side until the door just contacts the jamb at the top. Most prehung doors are shipped with a series of cardboard spacers tacked between the door and jamb. Don't remove them until the door is completely installed—the spacers allow for correct operating clearance.

Wedge two or three shim shingles between the top of the jamb and the side of the opening on the lockset side. Fit a similar group of shim shingles behind each hinge. Shimming should be done without disturbing the position of the door and jamb assembly. Both sides of the jamb should be sitting squarely on the floor. The top of the jamb should be aligned with the top of the door. Check shimming with your level. The hinge side of the jamb must be plumb in both directions.

Double-check shimming by pushing the lower end of the jamb on the lockset side away from the door, then opening the door. It should stay still in any position. If it falls open or closed, the hinge side of the jamb is out of plumb. Use your level to find

the problem. Realign the hinge side of the jamb by adjusting shims. *Note:* This test won't work if the hinges are tight or binding. If hinges are binding, use a level to check the hinge side of the jamb at several locations and reshim. This should relieve the stress on the hinges. Lubricate tight hinges with light oil or WD-40.

When the hinge side of the jamb is plumb, drive pairs of casing nails on either side of each hinge, just below the shims. That way, if the jamb loosens and the shims slip, they will be stopped by the nails. Try the door again to make sure you haven't misaligned the jamb while nailing.

Close the door and move the lockset side of the jamb into alignment with it. Insert shims behind the striker-plate location and near the bottom of the jamb. When shims are aligned, drive pairs of casing nails just below each shim. Line up the jamb to the door, not to the wall.

If the jamb doesn't line up to the wall, either the door or wall is warped. Find out which has the problem and fix it. Small warpage of the door can be corrected by removing the *stop strips* on the jamb and relocating them. Minor warpage of the wall opening can be hidden with the case trim.

Remove spacers on the edges of the door itself. Check the door for

TYPICAL DOOR OPENING

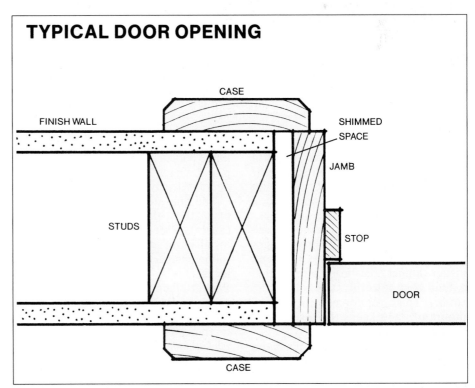

Whether you buy a prehung-door assembly or individual components, the opening will include parts shown here.

Pocket door separates powder room from makeup area in this compartmented bathroom. Frame for door is installed when the walls are framed.

smooth operation and make any needed adjustments. Break off shim shingles level with the wall surface. If shingles are not easily broken, cut them with a hammer and a wood chisel. Then attach wood casing strips.

For heavy doors, remove the middle screws from all three hinges on the jamb side. Drill pilot holes and install longer flat-head screws that extend back into the stud behind the jamb. This reinforces the hinge mountings and keeps the casing nails from withdrawing.

On a three-hinge door, attach the top and bottom hinges first. Pull the hinge pin on the middle hinge and put in the long screw for the middle hinge. Adjust the long screw in the middle hinge in and out until the hinge halves are lined up for the hinge pin. Recheck the door to make sure it operates freely.

The final step in door assembly is to install the lockset and striker plate. Because locksets differ in assembly and installation, the best advice is to follow instructions that come with the lockset.

Pocket Doors—Whenever there isn't swing space for a standard door, but there is a stretch of blank wall adjacent to the opening, consider installing a *pocket door.* A pocket door is hung on a top track so it can slide into a pocket built into the wall alongside.

Pocket doors are simpler to install than you might think. The prehung

door companies can supply preassembled door, pocket and frame with track.

You must prepare for a pocket door and install the frame before the wall-finish material goes on. The opening is rough framed the same as for a swing door. But the opening must be sized to accept the whole frame, roughly twice the width of the door itself. Because pocket construction varies, check with the supplier for exact measurements of the rough opening.

Install the frame itself in the rough opening, using the same shimming and nailing technique as shown on page 69 for a prehung swing door. It helps to have the door available to assist in squaring the open edge of the frame before nailing. It's sometimes necessary to drill, countersink, and drive in a flat-head wood screw every foot or so, up through the top of the frame into the header. Countersunk holes are then filled with wood filler or short lengths of dowel. This procedure is especially important if the door is large and heavy.

After the frame is in place, remove the door from the track and store it out of the way until you're ready for final installation. Usually, you must gently pry off a stop strip or two to free the door from the frame.

When installing wall-finish material and moldings on the pocket area of the pocket-door frame, be careful not to use nails that protrude into the pocket. These can block or scratch the door. To avoid loosening joints while nailing, support the pocket framing with your hand or with wood blocks.

BYPASS AND BIFOLD DOORS

Unlike swing doors, bypass and bifold doors can be installed without a separate jamb and case trim, directly in an opening. The rough opening is then finished with with drywall or plaster. Often, the only trim used is a strip, called a *valance,* to hide the top track.

Installing these doors without a jamb requires that the rough opening be square, plumb and level, and sized to finish-door dimensions, plus the width of the drywall or plaster layer. Frame such openings carefully. If you're installing bypass or bifold doors in an existing opening that's out of square, plumb or level, consider installing a jamb and case trim, and using a smaller door size.

Install Jamb—The procedure is the same as detailed on page 169 for prehung doors, except the jamb parts won't be preassembled. Also, you won't have the door in place to help keep the jamb square.

Check instructions packed with the door hardware for overall clearances needed at top and bottom of the doors. These measurements vary. Be sure to allow clearance for any floor coverings not already in place, to save door trimming later. Add required clearances to the door height to get an overall minimum jamb height. Use a 4-foot level to determine which side of the opening is high at the floor. Mark the low side at a point level with the high side.

Check the floor with a level on either side of the opening to make sure the floor doesn't slope perpendicular to the opening. If either side of the opening slopes by more than the floor covering will conceal, allow for it when you cut the jamb sides. If the finish floor is already in place, you may have to scribe and trim the bottoms of the jamb legs to get a good fit.

Measure down each jamb leg from the bottom of the rabbet where the jamb top fits. The measurement will be the actual height of the finished opening. Then mark the bottoms of the jamb legs, and cut to fit. Lay the jamb parts on the floor and assemble.

Use nails or screws to attach jamb legs to jamb top from the outside. Use a rafter square to square up the top corners of the jamb. Tack scrap strips of plywood or 1x2 diagonally across each top corner of the jamb to keep it square. Stand the jamb in the opening and attach it, following the same instructions as for prehung doors, page 169.

Install Top Track—Position the track at the top of the opening and adjust in or out according to the instructions with the hardware. Make sure the front of the track faces out. Then drive the screws—usually provided—through the holes in the track into the top of the opening. Make sure the screws are long enough to get a good bite into the header behind the top jamb, especially in the case of bypass doors. All the weight of a set of bypass doors hangs on the track. Substitute similar but longer screws if you have to.

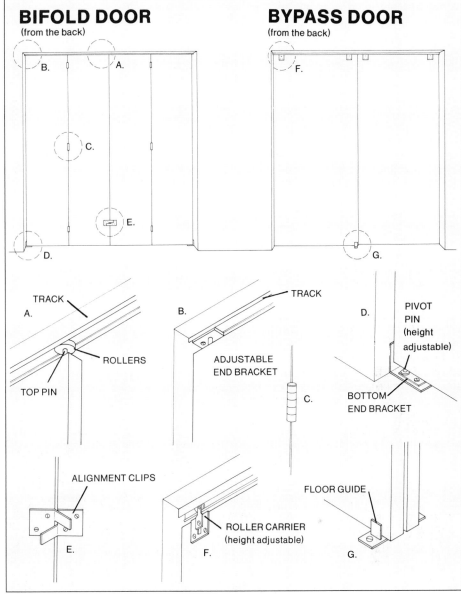

Letters on doors above indicate positions of hardware shown beneath them.

Bifold Doors—Use a plumb line or a 4-foot level to position the bottom brackets directly below the track. Screw the bottom brackets to wall or floor—see hardware instructions. If the finish floor covering isn't down yet, insert a spacer—a scrap of cardboard, floor covering or thin plywood—under the bottom bracket to make sure the door bottoms will clear the floor covering.

If the doors aren't preassembled, hinge them together. Install the end pins in each pair of doors. The end bracket goes on the top corner near the wall, the pivot pin on the bottom near the wall, and the roller on the top near the free edge of the door pair. See drawing above.

Loosen the screw on the top bracket

in the track and slide it out from the corner. Fold up the pair of doors, engage the bottom pin in the bottom bracket, then engage the top pin in the top bracket. Lining up the roller with the track, tip the door pair upright by sliding the top bracket to the corner. Retighten the top bracket screw. Install the other door pair the same way.

Adjusting Bifold Doors—Adjust the bolts or screws in top and bottom brackets so doors clear the wall or jamb as they close. When both door pairs are adjusted to clear the wall, close both to see if they meet correctly at the center.

Adjust the top and bottom brackets on both sides until the door pairs just clear in the middle. Doors should be evenly spaced at the edges of the opening, along the top and where they meet in the middle. If the opening isn't perfect, adjust doors until the gaps at top and sides are as straight as possible.

Set the height of the door pairs last. To do this, adjust the bottom pin with a wrench so the door tops just clear the top track. Both doors should be aligned vertically. Double-check doors for operation and retighten all adjusters so they don't shift later. The final step is to install the aligning clips on the backs of the free edges of the doors so they mesh when the doors close. See drawing on page 171.

Bypass Doors—Install the *roller carriers* on the backs of the doors, spaced according to the instructions with the hardware. See drawing on page 171. Tilt the innermost door at an angle and hook the rollers onto the rear track channel. Then hook the other door on the front track.

Adjusting Bypass Doors—Use the adjuster screws on the roller carriers to adjust each door so it meets the wall or jamb evenly. The gap at the top should be uniform. Doors should be set high enough to clear floor coverings, and also high enough to fit

correctly into the *floor guide*. The floor guide keeps bypass doors in alignment at the bottom and prevents doors from swinging in and out. Do not install the guide until the finish floor covering is down. If you haven't yet installed the floor covering, make sure door bottoms will clear it *and* fit into the floor guide once the floor covering is down.

Centering Floor Guide—After all final adjustments are made to the doors, move both doors into their closed positions. With a pencil or piece of tape, mark the floor directly below the end of the front door. Then open the front door all the way and make another mark directly below the end of the rear door. The guide should be positioned midway between these two marks.

Installing Floor Guide—Slip the guide into position on the door bottoms. Use a level to make sure the doors are hanging plumb. Mark the final in-and-out position for the floor guide. Anchor the floor guide as shown in manufacturer's instructions, usually with wood screws. The outer ears on the floor guide should be adjusted so the doors can operate freely without binding.

GLASS ENCLOSURES FOR TUBS AND SHOWERS

Though glass panel doors for tubs and showers are adjustable to some extent, it's best if the surfaces they're attached to are relatively plumb and level. Before you start the installation, check tub or shower surfaces with a level to make sure they're within the adjustment range of the enclosure you're installing.

Check all dimensions against the installation sheet packed with the enclosure. If you anticipate any problems fitting the enclosure to the opening, consult the dealer before trying to install the enclosure.

Some panels are glazed with plastic, but most are glazed with *tempered glass*. Check the corners of each glass panel for an etched emblem to make sure all panels *are* tempered. If the emblem is missing on a piece of glass, check with the dealer. Ordinary glass in a tub or shower is dangerous and is usually prohibited by the codes.

Note: Do not attempt to cut tempered glass. It cannot be cut or scratched by any means without shattering. If the glass panel is the wrong size, take it back to the glass shop for a replacement.

Bottom track of shower enclosure is usually just trapped in place by the vertical end tracks. Gasket provides a watertight seal around edges of tracks. On irregular surfaces such as tile, supplement gasket with tub and tile caulk. Plastic screw anchors work well in synthetic marble.

Sliding door panels hang from nylon rollers in top track. Plastic guides center panel in bottom track.

Tempered-glass panels can be made that are slightly smaller, larger, or oddly shaped to fit a peculiar situation. Take detailed measurements, make drawings, and consult your dealer. The dealer in this case should be a glass company. Special size and shape tempered-glass panels may take a week or two to fabricate, and will cost extra. Be sure you get the right-size aluminum-frame pieces to go with the panel.

Check all pieces of the glass enclosure before installing it. Stand each glass panel upright. Use a level or a straightedge to find any warpage in the panel. When glass is heat-treated during manufacturing, it sometimes develops a slight residual bow. If there are any bowed panels, adapt to fit them as you install.

If two or more panels of an enclosure are bowed, assemble and install them so they bow in the same direction, not opposite each other. Then warp the aluminum tracks slightly so they match the bow. That way, the installation will come out looking straight. The bow is rarely more than 1/8-inch in 4 or 5 feet, but when the track is straight and the panels bow by 1/8-inch, it shows.

Enclosure Installation—Use a level to lay out the position of the enclosure frame. Depending on the finish material around the opening, you can mark with a crayon, a grease pencil, a sliver of soap or chalk. Make sure marks can be erased after installation. Mark the base track and cut it to length with a hacksaw and a miter box. You may need to insert a block of wood inside the aluminum channel to keep its thin flanges from bending or buckling while you cut. Remove burrs with a fine file or emery cloth.

If the enclosure has a flexible gasket or sealing strip, install it on the base track. Slightly compress the gasket or strip lengthwise before cutting it to length. If you don't, the strip can shrink after installation, leaving gaps at the ends.

When the sealing strip is down, position the base track over it. Consult installation instructions to see if adhesive or fasteners are needed to attach the base track to the floor, sill or tub. On most enclosures, the base track is held in place by the end tracks. Make sure drain openings in the base track face toward the tub or shower enclosure.

Custom shower doors fold back against back wall of enclosure to allow easy access. Installation is basically the same as for other enclosures.

Trial-fit the end tracks. Trim if necessary, and mark the fastener locations. The method used to anchor fasteners depends on what material you're anchoring to. To anchor to wood framing, drill a small pilot hole and drive in the screws. Put a small blob of silicone sealer over each pilot hole to seal the wood against water penetration. To anchor to synthetic marble, drill an oversize hole and insert a plastic screw anchor. Then drive the screws into the anchors.

To attach strips to ceramic tile, use a variable-speed drill with a special carbide-tip bit to drill screw holes. These bits are made for drilling holes in ceramic tile. Insert plastic or fiber screw-anchors into the holes. Drill holes carefully—ceramic tile cracks easily. Use a slow drill speed and light pressure while drilling. As you drill, frequently immerse the bit in water to keep it cool and lubricated.

Some end tracks come in two pieces to allow adjustment for slightly over-size openings. Measure the remaining space and the panels to fit into it. Anchor one part of the end track to the wall and attach the other part to it to fit the measurements. Fit and install the top track, if there is one.

Fixed panels and swing doors attach to the tracks with sheet-metal screws, often through attaching tabs. Sliding panels are usually installed by hooking rollers into the top track and setting the panel bottom into the appropriate channel in the base track.

Once all the parts are in place, install pulls or handles. Adjust the moving parts of the door for free operation and correct alignment. Clean the entire enclosure with glass cleaner to remove fingerprints and any traces of leftover sealant.

SKYLIGHTS AND LUMINOUS CEILINGS

From the inside of a bathroom, skylights and luminous ceilings are much alike. Trim involves diffuser panels and moldings to support them. Above the diffuser panels, luminous ceilings and skylights are quite different.

All the structure required for a luminous ceiling is a drywall box, either between joists, or framed into a furred-down space. The fluorescent fixtures are wired the same as any other switched fixtures—see page 140.

A skylight requires a framed-in light shaft extending from the ceiling to the underside of the roof, preferably lined with drywall painted white. The sides of the light shaft don't have to be straight. You can angle them to match up different-size skylights and diffusers, or to adapt to misaligned ceiling and roof framing.

SKYLIGHTS

Before planning or buying a skylight, check the roof and ceiling framing. The easiest skylight to install is one that fits multiples of the rafter and ceiling-joist spacing. If the installation requires cutting any framing members, plan on doubling adjacent members and installing headers across the opening at top and bottom. You may then have to box in the sides of the opening to fit the skylight size. It's also possible to leave an interfering rafter or ceiling joist in place, wrapping it either with wood trim or drywall to make it less unsightly.

If a translucent diffuser panel is to be installed at the ceiling line, the rafter or ceiling joist can be painted white and left in place. If you decide to leave a rafter or joist in place, consider the effect it will have on the appearance of the finished skylight or luminous ceiling.

Do not cut trusses under any circumstances. A truss is a one-piece framing unit that takes the place of rafters and joists. Modifying one requires re-engineering the entire roof system. If there's a truss in the way, move the opening to avoid it, or wrap the truss with drywall and leave it in place.

Before starting installation, make sure there are no pipes, wires or ducts in the way. Rework them beforehand, or relocate the skylight. Gather all

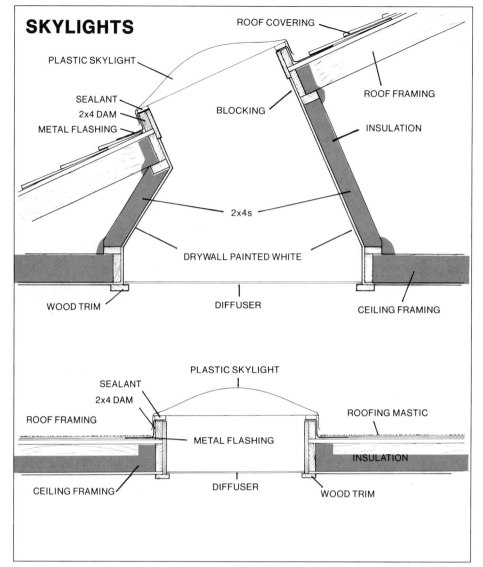

SKYLIGHTS

Skylights must be correctly flashed and sealed to prevent leaks. A 2x4 dam is required for all roofs less than 12/12 pitch. See text below.

necessary materials before you start.

Skylight Installation—Mark the skylight opening on the ceiling and cut a small hole in the ceiling at the center of the proposed opening. Use a tape measure to probe sideways through the hole to find locations of framing members on all sides. Transfer measurements and mark framing locations on the ceiling. Mark skylight-opening dimensions on the ceiling, making any adjustments to fit framing. Then cut the ceiling opening.

Working from the ceiling opening, use a level to locate the skylight opening on the underside of the roof. Remember, the two don't necessarily have to coincide. You can slope the sides of the light shaft if you want, as shown in the drawing above. Drive a nail up through the roof at each corner of the skylight opening.

Carefully remove roofing materials within the opening location, and in a strip about 6 inches wide around it. The strip will allow you to install the *dam* and *flashing*, as described below. Asphalt shingles can often be laid back out of the way at the sides of the opening.

Drive the locating nails out of the roof sheathing and mark and cut out the opening. Use a circular saw with a carbide-tip blade. Nails and roofing debris can ruin an ordinary blade. Wear eye protection while cutting. Take care not to damage and weaken rafters as you cut.

Most building codes require a 4-inch-high *dam* under a skylight on a roof less than *12/12 pitch*. A dam is a frame of 2x4s or 2x6s on edge, that elevates the skylight above the roof surface. A roof with a 12/12 pitch is one with a slope that rises 12 inches for every 12 inches of horizontal run, or one that forms a 45° angle to the ceiling joists.

The dam should have the same interior dimensions as the skylight opening in the roof. To attach the dam, toenail into the roof from the outside of the frame. See drawing on page 174.

Cut four pieces of 12- or 14-inch-wide metal flashing, one for each side of the dam. Aluminum flashing is easiest to work with. Each strip should be 16 or 18 inches longer than the side to which it will be attached.

Starting at the lower end of the dam, nail the edge of the first piece of flashing onto the top edge of the dam. Center flashing so overlap is equal at each end of the dam. Fold the flashing down, form a curve where it meets the roof and bed the free edge of the flashing in roofing mastic. Pleat and fold the corners around and up at the sides.

Attach the two side flashing strips the same way, but fold only the upper corners. Trim the lower corners to fit, and adhere them with roofing mastic. You can nail the sections of the side flashings that lie flat on the roof, if necessary.

Cover nailheads with a dab of roofing mastic. Attach the top flashing strip, fit it, and fold both corners. Cover top and side flashing strips with roofing. At the bottom end of the dam, slip the roofing material *underneath* the flashing so the flashing rests on top of it. Use roofing mastic to attach the roofing material to the flashing and surrounding roof sheathing. This avoids putting excessive nail holes in the flashing. The flashing and the replaced roofing must be absolutely weathertight.

Apply a band of silicone sealer-adhesive or self-stick foam weatherstripping all the way around the top edge of the dam. Drop the skylight into place over the top of the dam and press down to get a good seal. Fasten with screws through the side flanges, if required by the manufacturer's instructions.

Finishing the Installation—The inside of a skylight installation involves framing, drywall installation, insulation replacement, and trim or diffuser installation.

LUMINOUS CEILINGS

Rather than installing a surface-

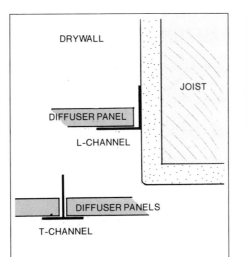

Metal L-channels, top, and T-channels, bottom, are most often used for luminous ceilings. Use T-channels to make panels flush with ceiling, L-channels for recessed panels.

mounted ceiling light, you can often install a flush or nearly-flush luminous ceiling. If ceiling height permits, a whole-bathroom luminous ceiling is just a matter of installing fluorescent light fixtures flush on the existing ceiling and suspending diffuser panels about 6 inches below the tubes.

You can install a smaller luminous area between the ceiling joists, if there's enough vertical clearance. You should provide for about 6 inches clearance between the fluorescent light tube and the diffuser panel—about 8 to 9 inches total vertical clearance. If there's a layer of insulation directly above, you also need enough additional space above the box to preserve the insulation layer without compressing it.

Use a hammer and nail to locate the ceiling joists from beneath. Mark the opening to be cut, using a framing square to square up the cutout. Cuts along joists should be at the inner edge of the joists. Before cutting into the ceiling, make a small hole in the middle of the cutout area—or check in the attic—to make sure there are no pipes, wires or ducts in the way. Sometimes it's easier to reposition the luminous panel than to relocate pipes or ductwork.

If you're working with drywall, use a utility knife to cut out the opening. If you're sure nothing's in the way, you can use a keyhole saw. To cut out an opening in a plaster ceiling, see page 79.

Wood moldings can be used to hold diffuser panels. Moldings should be firmly attached to framing with screws or annular-ring nails to support weight of panels.

Nail in 2x2 or 2x4 cleats and cross-blocking to provide nailing for the drywall box. You'll have to size up your own framing here, because framing methods vary greatly. As mentioned, the resulting box must provide about 6 inches vertical clearance between the fluorescent tubes and the diffusers.

Line the box with drywall after running and pigtailing fixture wires. Make sure enough wire extends through the finished box so you can hook up the fixture. Then tape and finish the drywall. Drywall installation and finishing is covered on pages 94-99.

After taping and finishing, paint the inside of the box flat white to provide maximum reflectivity and even light distribution. Install the light fixtures and you're ready to install the trim.

TRIM FOR LUMINOUS CEILINGS AND SKYLIGHTS

Diffuser panels are used to cover a luminous ceiling, and sometimes a skylight. These translucent panels are usually made of acrylic plastic and come in a number of surface textures. For safety reasons, glass panels are not recommended. A metal or wood molding is used to hold the diffuser panels in place, as shown in the drawings above.

The simplest means of holding diffuser panels in place are metal L-channels and T-channels made for suspended ceilings. The opening should be framed to fit standard 2x2' or 2x4' diffuser panels. If it isn't, measure and mark the opening so that cut diffuser panels on the opening sides or ends are equal in size.

Install channel all the way around the opening. If the diffuser panels will be flush with the ceiling, use T-channel. If the diffuser panels are to be recessed into the opening, use L-channel. See drawing on page 175.

Recessed diffusers should not be leveled when installed. They should follow the slope of the ceiling, if any. If the ceiling isn't level, make the recess measurement equal all the way around the opening. Twist diffuser panels slightly to fit.

Install T-channel across the shortest dimension of the opening, spaced to accept the diffuser panels. You may need to add screw-eyes and suspension wires to support the channel if spans are long. Consult manufacturer's instructions. Then snap in *cross-Ts* in the opposite direction and drop in the diffuser panels.

Luminous ceilings and skylight openings can also be trimmed with wood, either to match other openings in the ceiling, or to match cabinets or other wood trim. Installation techniques are the same as detailed under moldings below, but you should use annular-ring nails or screws to attach moldings. Smooth-shank finish nails tend to pull out, due to gravity.

Sagging can be a problem with wood-trimmed luminous ceilings. If moldings don't have sufficient thickness to keep from sagging, install vertical 1x2 or 1x3 stringers and attach the crossbars to the stringers. On long spans, use screw-eyes and suspension wires if you have to.

WOOD MOLDINGS

Fitting together various materials leaves gaps and expansion-contraction spaces. If you've installed vanity cabinets, gaps should be covered by the moldings and fillers of the cabinet system. Gaps around doors and other openings, and along the bottoms of walls, will be covered by moldings, to be discussed here.

You can use a number of materials for door, window and base moldings. Strictly speaking, the term *molding* applies to wood that has been milled to a decorative surface. But unmilled materials such as rough-sawn cedar or

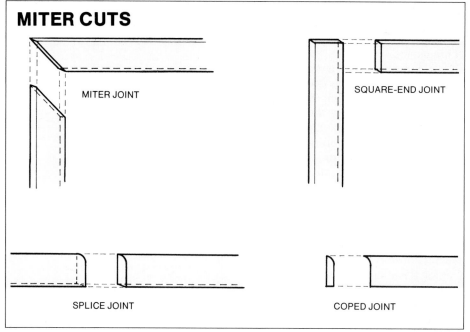

MITER CUTS

MITER JOINT

SQUARE-END JOINT

SPLICE JOINT

COPED JOINT

Accurate miter cuts can be made with a saw and miter box, radial-arm saw or *chop saw* (power miter box).

The most dependable of the hand-operated miter boxes has adjustable guide towers to hold saw. It is bulky but accurate and easy to use.

redwood can be used as moldings, so the strict definition won't apply in this chapter. You can use anything that works and looks good. Molding can match walls, floors, cabinets or doors, or you can choose a contrasting molding. Installation techniques are similar for all types.

All moldings should be painted or otherwise finished before installation. This saves work cutting in paint or finish next to other surfaces. The trim can then be touched up after mounting.

Joints—Basic joints in moldings are the *square end,* the *splice,* the *coped joint,* and the *miter joint.* Except for the coped joint, all should be made with a good-quality miter box. Simple wooden miter boxes work for a few cuts, but the guide slots soon become frayed and inaccurate. If you have many miter cuts to make, buy a good metal miter box, either the U-channel type or the blade-guide type.

If you have a lot of miter cuts, rent or buy a power tool called a *chop saw*. This is basically a power miter box. The saw portion is similar to a circular saw, mounted on an adjustable pivot. If you have a good table saw or radial-arm saw, you don't need a miter box or a chop saw.

Check the accuracy of the angle settings of your mitering tools before you start. When working with moldings, consider not only the angle of a cut in one plane, but in two.

The square-end joint is the simplest cut to make—the name is self-explanatory. To make this cut, position the angle setting on your miter box or saw at exactly 90°.

A splice is used to connect two short pieces of molding to make a long piece. Cutting is straightforward, but the installation of a splice joint can be tricky. Splices tend to gap after the pieces are firmly attached. Crowd the joint slightly as you're attaching the

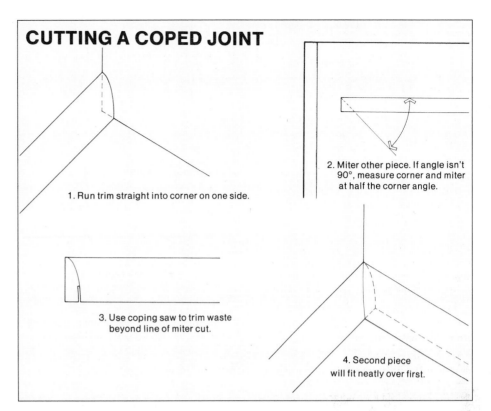

CUTTING A COPED JOINT

1. Run trim straight into corner on one side.

2. Miter other piece. If angle isn't 90°, measure corner and miter at half the corner angle.

3. Use coping saw to trim waste beyond line of miter cut.

4. Second piece will fit neatly over first.

SCRIBING

Not all surfaces you want to fit a molding against are straight. You may have to recut the edge or end of a molding to fit an irregular contour. Start by placing the length of molding as close as possible to its final position. Use a compass to measure the width of the widest space between the molding and the irregular surface. An inexpensive pencil compass will work.

Draw the compass along the length of the molding. The point should follow the line on the surface where you want the molding to fit, while the pencil makes a parallel mark on the molding.

To cut to the line you've marked, use any tools that seem suitable. On small moldings, scribe along the pencil line with the point of a utility knife. Then shave off surplus material, using the utility knife or a wood rasp. Smooth the shaved surface with sandpaper. On larger moldings and hardwoods, a coping saw or saber saw may be needed to remove surplus material.

When you've cut the molding back to the marked line, remove some extra material behind the visible surface. This enables the molding to clear any projections on the irregular surface behind it.

Trial-fit the molding as you work, to detect any problems. If you must have a perfect fit, apply chalk to the irregular surface. Trial-fit the molding and tap it a few times. Shave or sand off the places where the chalk transfers, until the chalk transfers along the whole length of the molding.

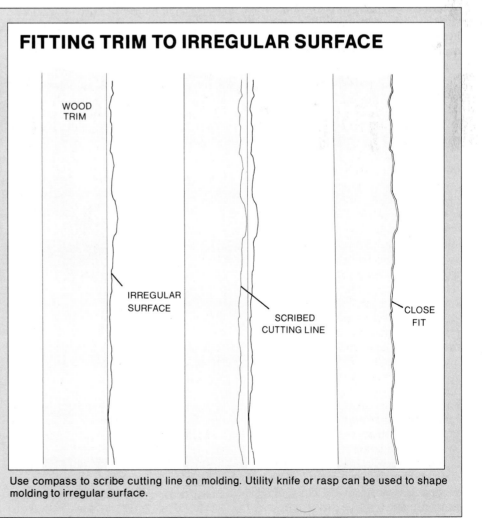

FITTING TRIM TO IRREGULAR SURFACE

WOOD TRIM

IRREGULAR SURFACE

SCRIBED CUTTING LINE

CLOSE FIT

Use compass to scribe cutting line on molding. Utility knife or rasp can be used to shape molding to irregular surface.

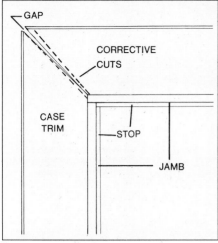

Door and window case corners may need adjusted miter cuts for good fit. Even if corner is square, jamb may be in or out from wall.

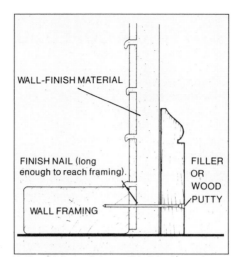

Nail moldings into solid framing when possible. Here, base shoe is nailed to bottom plate of wall framing. Nail must be long enough to go through molding, wall-finish material and well into the framing. For moldings at mid-wall height, locate all studs and nail molding at stud locations.

pieces, but not enough to cause an overlap.

The miter joint comes in inside and outside forms, and consists of two 45° cuts. Miters can be cut from the narrow or wide face of the molding.

The coped joint makes a much smoother inside corner than an inside miter does. Make a miter cut on the end of the piece at one side of the inside corner. Let the piece on the other side of the corner run straight through. Then use a coping saw to cut out the section of wood on the second piece beyond the miter line of the first. If you saw carefully, the cutout section will fit neatly over the molding on the other side of the corner. See drawings on page 177.

Especially in remodeling work, true cuts on moldings are as rare as straight walls. To make a good fit, some variation from the expected cut will often be required. Unfortunately there's no good way to measure these small variations in advance. The expert trimmer sees the needed adjustment and makes it. For the novice, it's usually a process of trial and error.

Moldings that are small in width and thickness can usually be cut true and installed without making adjustments. But moldings over 1 inch or so, in either width or thickness, may need adjustment as you cut.

For the novice, the best substitute for experience is to use precut guides to test the accuracy of cuts. Guides can be cut from two short lengths of

the molding you're using. Cut one end of each piece exactly square and the other end at a 45° angle. These pieces can be pushed into the position of most joints, and will make the needed adjustments obvious. Then adjust cuts on the molding you're installing to fit the space.

Always cut molding an inch or two longer than the final, installed length. This allows you to make adjustments to the cut without ending up with a too-short piece. Surplus molding at the opposite end can then be trimmed off or cut to fit.

All screw-mounted accessories install much the same. Some are provided with separate mounting plates so screws don't show—accessory is held on with concealed fasteners. Make sure anchorage is suitable for load on accessory.

The only time guide pieces won't work is when you're fitting moldings around doorways. Door jambs are rarely flush with the surrounding wall surface. If you put your guide piece in place, you'll find the jamb is either in or out from the wall. If it's out, the miters at the top corners will gap at the inside. If the jamb is in from the wall, the miters at the top corners will gap at the outside. The angle of the cut must be adjusted to fit, in both planes, and the adjustment should be the same for both halves of each cut.

Moldings—Finish nails are most often used to attach moldings. The nail size should be suited to the molding thickness, not width. Use the smallest nail that will reach through the molding and 1/2 inch or so into solid wood behind any intervening softer material, such as drywall. If wood tends to split near the molding ends, chuck a finish nail of the same size in an electric drill and use it to drill pilot holes. Construction adhesive can also be used where necessary, to minimize nail holes or to cope with difficult situations.

Finish materials such as wood flooring are subject to expansion and contraction. Make sure adjoining moldings don't bind against these materials. Don't nail the moldings to them, but to the adjacent surface. For instance, if the floor is subject to expansion and contraction, nail the molding to the wall. Insert a piece of thick paper or thin cardboard between the molding and the finish-flooring material to maintain clearance while you're nailing.

ACCESSORIES

While at first glance a soap dish doesn't much resemble a medicine cabinet, the installation technique might well be identical. So installation techniques for all such accessories is covered in two basic groups; screw-mounted and adhesive-mounted. There's some variation in each basic group for surface-mounted and recessed accessories, noted where applicable. When installing these accessories, frequently use a level to make sure they're installed level.

Screw-Mounted Accessories—These accessories must be attached firmly to the wall. Common screws—even ones with plastic plugs—will not hold in drywall or thin paneling. You must either provide solid backing in the framed wall, or use a different fastener to mount these accessories.

When framing, run blocking between studs at locations where you'll install towel bars, soap dishes, surface-mounted medicine cabinets and other accessories. If you can't provide backing, substitute molly bolts or toggle bolts for screws.

Molly bolts have the advantage that you can unscrew the bolt from the body if you need to remove the accessory for painting walls or other reasons. Once a toggle-bolt is in place, you can't remove the bolt or screw without losing the toggle inside the wall. Some accessories attach directly to the wall, using exposed screws. Others come with attaching plates, and the accessory attaches to the plates with concealed fasteners.

Another category of screw-mounted accessories is recessed or semi-recessed. Paper-holders and some soap dishes fall in this category. They come with a bracket inside the opening as an attaching point for one or two screws. Check the installation instructions for details—mounting systems vary.

Recessed Medicine Cabinets—Most factory-made recessed medicine cabinets are sized to fit between wall studs on 16-inch centers. They are usually attached by two or three wood screws through each side of the cabinet into the adjacent wall studs. Use a short level inside the wall opening to determine if the studs are plumb. If necessary, tack shims to the studs at fastener locations to plumb the cabinet before mounting it.

Grab Bars—Safety rails and grab bars are most often installed in bathrooms for the handicapped and elderly. Locating safety rails and grab bars for these purposes is discussed on pages 64-65. Attachment methods are discussed here.

Most safety rails and grab bars are screw- or bolt-mounted. They should always be attached to solid framing. Don't use molly bolts or toggles that could fail under extreme loads. Nothing short of near-indestructible is good enough. If safety rails or grab bars are to be installed to the floor, they should be solidly attached with lag screws or bolts to the floor framing or concrete slab.

The *Federal Standards for Housing for the Elderly* require that grab bars

sustain 250 pounds for 5 minutes at any point without failure. If you can hang on a grab bar with your feet off the floor for a minute or so without hearing any creaking, it will probably meet these standards.

Because of the forces placed on the attachments, safety rails and grab bars should not be installed directly over brittle materials like ceramic tile. If the finish material is thin enough not to interfere with the flange of the bar or rail, cut out the finish material and and attach the bar directly to the wall or floor framing.

If the finish material is too thick for this approach, install a spacer. The spacer should be made of exterior plywood. Cut it the same shape as the end of the bar or rail, 1/16 inch smaller so it doesn't show when the bar is installed. The spacer should also be 1/16 inch thicker than the finish material.

After the finish material is in place, install the bar or rail. Use tub-and-tile caulk to close the gap between the bar or rail and the finish material. Do not use tile grout because it will eventually break out.

Adhesive-Mounted Accessories—Use higher-strength floor adhesives, rather than wall adhesives to install these accessories. Install surface-mounted accessories by buttering the back with adhesive and pressing into place. You may have to prop accessories in place until the adhesive sets, to prevent slipping or falling out. For recess-type accessories, cut a hole in the wall surface just big enough for the body of the accessory. Apply the adhesive to the face of the wall around

To save space that otherwise would be needed for door swings, these tambour doors roll up for access to medicine cabinet behind.

the hole, or on the back of the wall flange of the accessory. Press firmly into place. Clean off any adhesive that squeezes out.

Some of the less-expensive accessories, such as plastic towel bars or paper holders, use self-adhesive pads for mounting. As a rule, they're not as sturdy as screw-mounted or adhesive-mounted accessories. They must be mounted to a smooth, dry, clean and solid surface. They won't stick to surfaces with peeling or chalking paint.

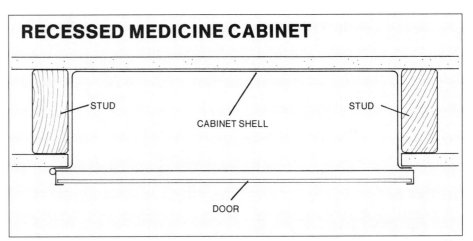

RECESSED MEDICINE CABINET

STUD

CABINET SHELL

STUD

DOOR

Most recessed medicine cabinets are designed to fit between studs on 16-inch centers. Use round-head wood screws to attach cabinet to studs.

Special Areas

Fanciful decorating adds interest to this powder room, primarily for use by guests. Full-wall mirrors visually expand space.

Not every bathroom-design question revolves around the conventional toilet-lavatory-tub/shower concept. There are other areas you'll sometimes need to think about. The four most useful of these special areas to look at separately are the *powder room,* the *mudroom,* the *makeup area,* and *bathroom storage.*

POWDER ROOMS

A powder room is much like any other bathroom, except it doesn't have a shower or tub. But a powder room is less oriented toward basic grooming, and more toward convenience. So the approach to a powder room is different. Much less storage is needed, and much less space.

Basically, a powder room reduces the traffic to other bathrooms. It keeps guests and other visitors who might be complete strangers out of more private areas of the home. It also keeps muddy-footed children close to an outside door. The key to getting good performance from a powder room is to determine what it's to accomplish, and for whom. The three basic location categories can be described as *formal, family* and *special-purpose.*

The *formal* powder room primarily serves guests and visitors. The location must be convenient to the formal areas of the home—the living room, dining room or main entry. The entrance to the powder room should offer some privacy, and perhaps a place to deposit coats and bags. Decorating can be quite ornate if you like. A medicine cabinet is unnecessary, but a mirror and good lighting for makeup repair are essential.

The *family* powder room also reduces the traffic to other bathrooms, but the emphasis is on family convenience. Anywhere you have a part of the home that's used by the family, but is remote from other bathrooms, consider slipping in a powder room. This might include a family room or recreation room in a basement, an indoor play area for children away from their normal bathroom, or a den or home office that's separated from the main living area. Such family-use powder rooms are essentially private rather than public, so they can be more utilitarian.

The *special-purpose* powder room usually serves a limited area. One major application is the powder room that serves a master bedroom when there isn't room for a full bath. A powder room convenient to a workshop, the garage or a greenhouse can be used for cleanup before entering the house.

Children's outdoor play presents problems when they have to travel through the house every time they want to go to the bathroom or get a drink of water. A powder room that's convenient to an outside entry can reduce traffic and mess.

A powder room related to a pool, spa or hot-tub area, close to the outside door or even in an outbuilding, can be handy for guests and family members. For guest use, some provision should be included for changing, and for hanging up street clothes and wet bathing suits.

Combined Bathrooms—Not every powder room is a separate room by itself, so don't despair if you're short of space. Almost any complete bathroom can be designed for use as a full bathroom part of the time, and as a powder room when necessary. This can be accomplished by careful fixture placement and dividing the bathroom into separate compartments.

In most cases, a combined-function bathroom has two separate entrances and a door or other movable divider between compartments. One example is a master bath that opens to a hall on one side, and to the master bedroom on the other. If it's planned so the toilet and a vanity are on the hall side, and the tub or shower and any dressing areas on the bedroom side, a pocket door or accordion door between the two areas can let you switch

Even in a fairly small space, a stylish powder room is possible. Accents must be carefully chosen to avoid a closed-in feeling.

the function back and forth. There are many such layouts possible. So if you're short of space and need a powder room, see if you can't get one by combining functions.

MUDROOMS

A powder room or bathroom can be combined with a laundry or utility room. This arrangement can serve all sorts of cleanup needs after gardening or some other messy activity. As the term *mudroom* suggests, surfaces, es-

pecially floors, should be able to withstand mud and grit.

A place to hang clean clothes and space to change into them make it easy to remove dirty clothes and deposit them in a hamper convenient to the washer or in the washer itself. If space permits, a laundry sink or large kitchen sink is often more practical in a mudroom than is a standard bathroom lavatory. Add a shower and the cleanup facilities will be complete.

If a shower or toilet is provided,

think carefully about privacy. The shower and dressing area can be combined in a separate compartment, as can the toilet. Or, you can install accordion doors to close off privacy areas when needed.

MAKEUP AREAS

Dry activities such as makeup application and hair care don't combine very well with wet activities such as hand and face-washing, tooth brushing and shaving. Often complaints of lack of bathroom space come from conflicts between wet and dry activities.

Even if there's not much space, try to separate the two activities. All that's really needed for makeup and hair care is a simple counter with a knee space below, a large mirror and a chair or stool. Some drawer space is helpful. An electrical outlet is a must. Careful attention should be paid to lighting, as discussed on page 56.

A makeup area doesn't have to be in the bathroom, though it's usually related to a bathroom. For a master bedroom, the makeup area might be in the master bath, in an adjoining dressing area or in the bedroom. In fact, the term *vanity* comes from a piece of bedroom furniture used for applying makeup. This type of vanity has drawers, a knee space and an attached mirror. The idea of a makeup area separate from the bathroom stems from the traditional bedroom vanity.

If there are any daughters in the family, they can spend several hours a day on makeup and hair care during their teenage years. If the only place available is the family bathroom, they can tie it up for hours. A makeup area in their own bedroom could be a worthwhile addition.

Whether such a makeup area is built-in or free-standing, not much space is required. If there's room for a counter that's a foot or more deep and 2 to 3 feet wide, one or two drawers and a stool or small chair, you can create a makeup area.

The materials used to build a makeup area should be durable. They should not be subject to staining or heat damage from hair dryers and curling irons. Otherwise, there aren't any restrictions. You can harmonize a makeup area with the room it's in, with the associated bathroom, or with the overall scheme of the home.

A makeup vanity need not be full depth, as long as the rest of the necessary elements are there.

Tambour doors conceal narrow storage area between vanity top and mirror. Counter space between twin vanities is used for makeup application.

STORAGE

A bathroom needs storage space. There are many kinds of things stored in a bathroom, but all must be readily accessible. The basic groups are linens (towels, washcloths and bath mats), soiled clothes headed for the laundry, appliances such as hair dryers, electric shavers and heating pads, and toiletries. A minor group is cleaning supplies. Storage needs are different for each group.

Towels and other linens can be stored in a vanity, but an actual linen closet in the bathroom is much more convenient. The size of a folded bath towel is the basic unit of space for linen planning in a bathroom. It is not a standard unit—bath towels vary, and methods of folding vary. Work from your own towels and folding methods, allowing enough space to avoid crowding. The principle here is that a bathroom linen shelf that's two and a half towels wide might as well be only two towels wide. The leftover space must either be filled with odd-size items, leading to jumbles, or left

Makeup area between vanities includes knee space, shallow drawer for makeup and toiletry items. *Photo courtesy of Armstrong World Industries Inc.*

Roll-out baskets provide plenty of room and ample ventilation for dirty laundry. Baskets are concealed behind solid-oak doors.

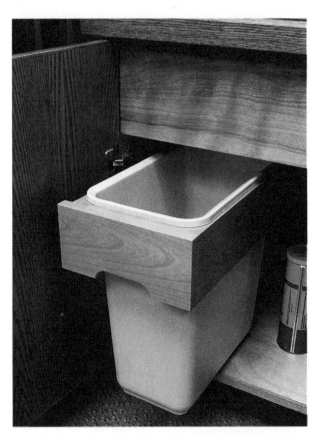

Storage also includes finding space to put the waste basket. Pull-out wastebasket holder can be installed in vanity cabinets or in a linen closet.

empty, wasting space. A linen shelf that's shallower than a folded bath towel is a real problem. Any space you can find that's one towel or more wide and deep is a candidate for linen storage.

In many house designs, more than one bathroom, or sometimes a laundry room or hall linen closet are clustered together. It's sometimes possible to arrange a storage space with two or more doors opening from different rooms. In this way, the storage area can be shared by two bathrooms, or fresh towels inserted from the laundry room and taken out from the bathroom on the other side. If you use this technique, watch that you don't introduce sound-transmission problems. Weatherstripping both doors can help.

Privacy problems can develop from some double-door storage arrangements—you can find yourself face to face with the occupant of the other room. For this reason, you should arrange doors carefully. Offset doors or ones at right angles to each other generally create fewer privacy problems than doors directly opposite each other. Of course, if one of the doors opens into a utility room and is opened only once or twice a week to deposit clean towels, there's little risk of intrusion.

Adjustable shelves are the most useful, no matter what you're storing. You can either use slotted-metal standards, or install a cabinet with multiple holes and movable shelf supports. Solid 1-by lumber or 3/4-inch plywood make the best shelving.

Appliances, including medical equipment, divide into two groups depending on size and frequency of use. Things that are bulky or rarely used can be stored on a closet shelf. Anything that's used nearly every day, like a hair dryer, should be stored as near as possible to the point of use. Multiple drawers in a vanity are handy for these items. Again, when planning storage space, work with the actual sizes of the items to be stored.

Toiletries and medicines are best stored at point of use, and that generally means a medicine cabinet. In some cases, a vanity drawer may be more useful for storing these items, especially if more than one person uses the bathroom.

Both cleaning supplies and medicines can present a similar problem,

This bathroom has storage to spare. Drawers usually make better use of space than shelves. Corner medicine cabinet and drawers beneath make use of otherwise wasted space. Bathroom still awaits a few finishing touches, such as its window trim.

Open shelves can be used to store and display more attractive bathroom items. Alcove in this bathroom provides perfect place for storage cabinets. Doors on lower storage cabinet open individually, are sized to clear toilet when open.

particularly if there are ever small children around the home. Many of either are poisonous, corrosive, or both. Even though it may be a little more trouble, arrange separate secure storage for any hazardous substances. An unobtrusive cabinet lock can be fitted to almost any cabinet door, or a keyed lockset to any swing door. This simple precaution can be life-saving.

When planning bathroom storage, provide individual storage space for each family member who uses that bathroom. An easy way to do this is to replace open shelf space with individual pull-out drawers.

Not all storage cabinets need to be built in. Wall-hung unit makes attractive addition to this bathroom.

15

Quick Projects

Ordinary fixture over vanity mirror can be replaced with an attractive multiple-bulb fixture like this one.

Bathroom fixtures and fittings are the basic framework of the bathroom. They're designed to last a long time. Those long-lasting qualities often make it necessary to find other ways to keep a bathroom looking up-to-date instead of outdated. This is accomplished through periodic redecorating. When accessories get a little shabby, or when you're tired of looking at the same old bathroom, there are a number of small improvements

you can make to beautify the room.

In addition to new paint or wall coverings, you can change shower curtains, towels, window coverings and rugs. In addition to these superficial redecorating projects, there are also other ways of updating your bathroom. The projects covered here can be done at relatively little cost and time, either in connection with a complete redecorating effort, or by themselves.

Along with periodic updating, a bathroom needs a certain amount of continuing service and repair. A section on basic repair and troubleshooting starts on page 188.

New Lighting

A chronic problem with older bathrooms is poor lighting. Often there's only one small light fixture over the lavatory. You can get a fresh look with one or more new light fixtures.

One good approach is to replace the existing fixture with a larger, wider one that has multiple bulbs. An example of this type is shown on page 186. Such fixtures will usually mount on the same electrical box as the old fixture.

If you need the light in a different place, think about using a swag lamp, as shown on pages 9 and 21. Make sure the light and its wiring are sized and positioned so accidental contact with plumbing fixtures and fittings is impossible.

The best type of swag fixture for a bathroom is one that comes with a cover plate that replaces the original light fixture. This type is connected directly into the circuit, rather than plugged into an outlet.

If the fixture you choose is a plug-in type, the fixture supplier can usually furnish you with a suitable cover plate. The plate should have a chain hook to support the weight of the lamp. In any case, the weight of the lamp should not be supported by the cord. To install the lamp, cut off the plug and wire the cord directly into the circuit, using wire nuts.

A third and somewhat more complicated approach is to add a light fixture where there is none, tied into the present bathroom light.

Replacing a Fixture—All permanent incandescent fixtures are installed in a similar manner. Turn off the power to the bathroom, dismantle the present fixture, and disconnect the wires from it. Hook up the wires to the new fixture the same way they were connected to the old one. Then assemble and mount the new fixture in place of the old, according to the instruction sheet that came with it. There's no need to concern yourself with any other wiring in the electrical box—just disconnect and reconnect. If there was no green or bare safety-ground wire in the circuit to the old fixture, connect the new fixture's safety-ground wire to one of the electrical-box screws.

Adding a Fixture—Installing an extra light fixture where light is needed is somewhat more complicated, but not much, especially if there's an attic up above. A tub or shower area is a prime candidate for an overhead fixture. Pages 138-140 give details on installing an electrical box at the new location, and running wire to it.

No matter what type of lavatory you have, you can usually find a variety of fitting styles for it. Most lavatories are drilled to accept standard fittings.

No circuit design is necessary. Turn off the circuit to the light at the main-entrance panel. Remove the cover plate on the existing fixture. Note the sizes, colors and number of wires in the cable serving the existing fixture. The cable used to tie in the second fixture should be identical, except it should include a safety ground wire, whether or not the existing cable has one.

If the circuit for the old fixture already has a green or bare safety connection, you can ground the new one through the old one. If it doesn't have a safety-ground connection, tie the one in the new cable to both the old electrical box and the new one. Then run an extra length of wire to the nearest metal pipe from new box or old and clamp it on. This will make both the old fixture and the new one much safer.

Run cable from the existing box to the new box. Remove the wire nuts connecting the existing fixture to the circuit. Connect the wires of the new cable to the existing circuit *and* to the existing fixture, matching the wire colors. *Do not* tie two different-colored wires together. You may need to replace the old wire nuts with slightly larger ones.

Once the wiring is done, assemble and connect the new fixture to the new box, according to the installation instructions that came with the fixture. Wiring hookup at the new fixture should be exactly the same as the hookup at the old one—just copy it. You now have two light fixtures in the bathroom that are operated by the same switch.

Big New Medicine Cabinet and Mirror

Many older bathrooms came equipped with a small medicine cabinet with a mirror door, recessed into the wall over the lavatory. If you have one and you're sick of it, replace it with a new surface-mounted unit. This is especially easy if the lavatory is near a corner. You can install a new unit with a large mirror on the back wall and a cabinet with a diagonal-mirror door in the corner.

Start by removing the old medicine cabinet. You'll usually find mounting screws inside. If it's completely recessed, you may be able to remove the door and leave the rest in the wall behind the new unit.

Fasten the new unit in place according to the mounting instructions that came with it—mounting procedures vary. Usually this involves establishing a level line, positioning the unit, and installing some anchoring screws. If studs aren't in the right places, you may have to put in some plastic screw anchors or molly bolts.

New Lavatory Fitting

Lavatory designs change slowly. Some that were first made 40 years ago are still being produced. However, lavatory fittings have changed radically in the last decade or two. They're easy to replace, and you can update the appearance of your lavatory by installing a modern single-handle faucet, or an up-to-date two-handle one.

Except for a few older models, lavatories are made with fitting holes on 4- and 8-inch centers. If yours has holes on 8-inch centers, there aren't any single-handle faucets to fit it—you'll have to use a two-handle one. If the holes are on 4-inch centers, both single-handle and two-handle models are available.

Before you buy the new fitting, measure the spread on the fitting holes, and make note of the overall length of the spout. The new fitting's spout doesn't have to be exactly the same length, but some lavatories re-

TROUBLESHOOTING BATHROOM FIXTURES

A bathroom contains a complex collection of plumbing fixtures. Modern engineering and manufacturing have made these fixtures almost, but not quite, trouble-free. Even the best bathroom equipment needs some service once in a while. Any older bathroom will need a fair amount of maintenance and repair. Most problems with bathroom fixtures and fittings are minor. It's often difficult to determine what the problem is from the symptoms. This chart will help you identify the problem and repair it.

SYMPTOM	POSSIBLE CAUSE	CURE
Toilet		
1. Runs, won't shut off.	Flush valve, ball cock.	Remove tank lid. Flush toilet, allow tank to fill to correct level. Lift up on ball-cock float and hold. If water level continues to rise, service or replace ball cock. If water level goes down, service and replace flush valve. If water level stays where it is, adjust float to produce correct water level.
2. Squirts water at tank lid.	Ball cock.	Remove tank lid, flush toilet, observe source of water. Source will be either refill tube or ball-cock upper seal. Service or replace.
3. Won't flush unless handle is held down.	Flush valve—linkage.	Remove tank lid. Clean and adjust flush-valve linkage so slip joint works freely. Flush and let go of handle. If flush valve does not stay up by itself for duration of flush, replace it.
4. Flushes sluggishly.	Ball cock, partial blockage.	Remove tank lid and adjust water level, if necessary. Add 1/2-cup of liquid detergent to bowl and mix. Add a bucket of water to bowl slowly. Wait 30 minutes, then flush repeatedly. If no improvement, remove toilet, clear drain line and trapway.
5. Stops up often.	Partial blockage.	Monitor for user-caused problems, such as deposit of unsuitable items. Remove toilet and clear trapway and drain line. Inspect drain line for inadequate slope or other construction problems, pages 122-123. Rework drain line, if needed.
6. Refills slowly, noisily.	Ball cock, supply.	Check that supply valve is fully open and supply riser isn't kinked or pinched. Dismantle ball cock, if possible, then clean, lube and reassemble. If problem persists, disconnect supply riser, slip on a rubber hose, put other end of hose in bowl, turn on water. If flow is full and quiet, replace ball cock. If flow from supply is slow or noisy, clear restriction in supply fitting or pipe.
7. Leaks at floor line.	Wax ring.	Remove toilet, make sure floor flange is still serviceable. Reinstall toilet with new wax ring and new flange bolts.
8. Low water level in bowl.	Ball cock.	Remove tank lid, check refill tube for kinking or wrong position. Refill tube should be squirting small stream down overflow tube during refill. Reposition or replace.
Lavatory		
1. Faucet drips.	Washer, seat.	Shut off water and remove stem or cartridge. Replace washer, check seat inside fitting body for rough surface. Replace or resurface seat, if needed. On cartridge type, remove debris or mineral deposits, reassemble and check. If leak is still present, replace cartridge.

quire a special long-spout fitting.

Use a mirror and a flashlight to check the supply-pipe arrangement on the present fitting. Some adapters or new supply risers may be needed to connect the new fitting to the supply pipe.

If the lavatory is an old wall-hung model with the fitting coming through the back, give up and replace the whole lavatory. New fittings of that type are nearly impossible to find, and new ones will look just as old-fashioned as the ones already on it.

Installation—To install the new fitting, first shut off the supply valves. Use adjustable wrenches to disconnect the supply risers, and to remove the large nuts and washers underneath that hold the fitting in place. If the space is tight, you may need a basin wrench to do this. Remove the fitting and clean the lavatory surface thoroughly. Stubborn deposits can usually be removed with paint thinner and steel wool, or a putty knife.

If the new fitting came with a base gasket, place it on the lavatory and position the new fitting. If there's no base gasket, put down a thin bead of plumbers' putty or tub-and-tile caulk to seal the fitting to the lavatory. Then position the fitting.

Assemble the anchoring washers and nuts from underneath and tighten securely. Clean up any extruded caulk, if you used it, with a wet paper towel.

Make any necessary modifications to the supply risers, and attach them to the new fitting. Tighten the water connections. Before turning the water back on, unscrew the aerator from the fitting. Turn on the water, flush thoroughly, check for leaks, and replace the aerator.

If the pop-up assembly is in prime condition and is compatible with the new fitting, you don't have to replace it. If it's necessary to replace the pop-up assembly, first dismantle the trap. Remove any pop-up operating linkage still on the drain body. Unscrew the large nut underneath that holds the drain body on, rap sharply upward on the bottom of the drain body, and remove it. Clean the inside of the lavatory around the drain fitting.

2. Slow water flow.	Aerator, supply.	Check water-supply lines—valves should be fully open and risers not kinked or pinched. Remove aerator, clean and replace. If problem persists, remove stems and check for flow with stems out. If full flow, clean passageways with wire, flush before replacing aerator. If flow is restricted with stems out, remove restriction in supply fittings or pipes.
3. Slow water drain.	Trap, drain line.	Lift out pop-up plug and check drain body for hair or other debris, remove. Readjust pop-up linkage for higher lift on opening. Dismantle trap, clear partial blockage in trap body or drain line.
4. Pop-up won't hold water.	Pop-up, linkage.	Lift out pop-up plug and check seal, replace if needed. Replace plug, readjust pop-up linkage to close correctly. If plug won't seat, remove and clean soap scum or mineral deposits in drain body at sealing surface.
5. Repeated hammering noise only when opening and closing valve.	Faucet washer, seat.	Remove faucet stems, tighten or replace loose parts.
6. Single hammering noise on opening or closing.	Loose pipes.	Water hammer—install air chambers or tie down loose pipes—see page 122.
7. Water leaks at handles.	Seal washers	Remove retaining nuts on stems, leaving stems in place. Check seal washers. If serviceable, reinstall retaining nuts and tighten until leak stops. If seal washers are not serviceable, replace and reassemble.

Tub or Shower

1. Leaks at sidewall seam.	Inadequate caulking.	Clean and recaulk.
2. Faucet drips.	Washer, seat.	Shut off water, remove handles, escutcheons, retaining nuts and stems. Install new washers. Inspect seats inside valve body for rough surface, replace or resurface if needed. Reinstall all parts.
3. Diverter won't stay in shower position.	Spout.	Unscrew spout, disassemble and clean out mineral deposits. Reassemble and reinstall. If problem persists or diverter parts are badly worn, replace spout assembly.
4. Leaks at handles.	Seal washers.	Remove handles, escutcheons, retaining nuts. Check seal washers. If still serviceable, reinstall and tighten until leak stops. If unserviceable, replace seal washers and reinstall parts.
5. Tub drain won't hold water.	Drain, overflow.	Disassemble overflow plate, withdraw plug and linkage. Readjust linkage to get good seal. If plug hangs up before dropping to closed position, dismantle drain pipe from behind and remove mineral buildup or soap scum. Reassemble and readjust plug linkage.
6. Drains slow.	Drain, drum trap.	Dismantle drain pipe and trap, clear hair or other debris. Reassemble.
7. Showerhead spray pattern poor.	Showerhead.	Unscrew showerhead, dismantle and clean. In hard-water areas, soak in strong vinegar-water solution overnight to loosen deposits. Reassemble and reinstall. If problem persists, replace showerhead.

Place a ring of plumbers' putty around the drain opening, inside the lavatory. Drop the new drain body into place and press down firmly. From underneath, assemble and tighten the attaching nut and washers. Assemble the new pop-up operating rod and linkage according to the instructions with the fitting, and adjust. Thread up and tighten the tailpiece in the bottom of the drain body. Reassemble the trap and tighten nuts. Test for leaks.

New Toilet Seat

Unless your bathroom is recent or quite fancy, chances are the toilet seat is poor quality, worn, or both. Most standard seats are molded wood covered with enamel paint. On such seats, the durability of the paint is fairly low.

You can quickly improve the appearance of the bathroom with a new seat. There are many options in toilet seats, discussed on page 46. Before buying a new seat, determine whether the toilet bowl is *round-front* or *elongated*. If you can't tell, take an overall measurement from the seat bolts to the front edge of the bowl. Also measure the distance between the seat bolts—most bowls are standardized, but a few aren't.

After you have the new seat and you've checked that it will fit, remove the old seat by unthreading the nuts from the two seat bolts. If the nuts are corroded fast, use an automotive-type nut splitter or a hacksaw to remove them. *Don't* use a hammer and chisel—one slip can crack or break the bowl.

After the old seat is off, thoroughly clean the areas around the seat-bolt holes. Drop on the new seat, and thread on and tighten the new nuts, along with any washers provided. The nuts should be snug, but not tight enough to crack the bowl. ▫

Where to Find Out More

The following list includes many manufacturers of equipment and supplies used in bathrooms. You can write to manufacturers for product information and brochures, or for the names and addresses of local suppliers of their products.

CABINETS

Aristokraft Cabinets
P.O. Box 420
Jasper, IN 47546

Belwood Division of U.S. Industries Inc.
P.O. Drawer A
Ackerman, MS 39735

Coppes Inc.
401 E. Market St.
Napannee, IN 46550

Diamond Cabinets, Division of Medford Corp.
P.O. Box 547
Hillsboro, OR 97123

H.J. Scheirich Co.
P.O. Box 37120
Louisville, KY 40133

Haas Cabinet Co.
625 W. Utica St.
Sellersburg, IN 47172

Kemper Division of Tappan Co.
701 S. N St.
Richmond, IN 47374

Long-Bell Cabinets Inc.
KK Plaza
Jeffersonville, IN 47130

Mastercraft Industries Corp.
6715 E. 39th Ave.
Denver, CO 80207

Merillat Industries Inc.
2075 W. Beecher Road
Adrian, MI 49221

Poggenpohl U.S.A. Corp.
222 Cedar Lane
Teaneck, NJ 07666

Quaker Maid Division of Tappan Corp.
Route 61
Leesport, PA 19533

Triangle Pacific Corp.
P.O. Box 220100
Dallas, TX 75222

Westinghouse Corp. Micarta Division
P.O. Box 248
Hampton, SC 29924

CERAMIC TILE

American Olean Tile Co.
P.O. Box 271, 1000 Cannon Ave.
Lansdale, PA 19446

Cambridge Tile Mfg. Co.
P.O. Box 15307
Cincinnati, OH

Country Floors
300 E. 61st St.
New York, NY 10021

Florida Tile Division of Sikes Corp.
P.O. Box 447
Lakeland, FL 33802

Marazzi U.S.A. Inc.
P.O. Box 58163, Suite 9063
World Trade Center
Dallas, TX 75258

Monarch Tile Mfg. Inc.
P.O. Box 2041
San Angelo, TX 76901

U.S. Ceramic Tile Co., Division of Soartek Inc.,
1375 Raff Road S.W.
Canton, OH 44710

Wenczel Tile Co.
P.O. Box 5308, Klagg Avenue
Trenton, NJ 08638

EXHAUST FANS & VENTILATORS

Aubrey Mfg. Co.
S. Main Street
Union, IL 60180

Broan Mfg. Co. Inc.
926 W. State St.
Hartford, WI 53027

Dayton Electric Mfg. Co.
5959 W. Howard St.
Chicago, IL 60648

Miami-Carey
203 Garver Road
Monroe, OH 45050

Nutone Division of Scovill Inc.
Madison & Red Bank Roads
Cincinnati, OH 45227

Rittenhouse Division of Emerson Electric
475 Quaker Meeting House Road
Honeoye Falls, NY 14472

Thermador/Waste King
5119 District Blvd.
Los Angeles, CA 90040

LIGHTING

Day-Brite Lighting Division of Emerson Electric Co.
1015 S. Green St.
Tupelo, MS 38801

Dayton Electric Mfg. Co.
5959 W. Howard St.
Chicago, IL 60648

Duray Fluorescent Mfg. Co.
2050 W. Balmoral Ave.
Chicago, IL 60625

Eagle Electric Mfg. Co.
45-31 Court Square
Long Island City, NY 11101

General Electric Co., Lighting Systems Dept.
Hendersonville
NC 28739

GTE Products Corp., Lighting Products Group
100 Endicott St.
Danvers, MA 01923

KEENE Corp. Lighting Division
2345 Vauxhall Road
Union, NJ 07083

Lightolier Inc.
346 Claremont Ave.
Jersey City, NJ 97305

McGraw Edison Co., Lighting Products Division
P.O. Box 1205
Racine, WI 53405

Nutone Division of Scovill Inc.
Madison & Red Bank Roads
Cincinnati, OH 45227

Omega Lighting Co., Division of Emerson Electric
270 Long Island Expressway
Melville, NY 11747

Panasonic Co.
1 Panasonic Way
Secaucus, NJ 07094

PLUMBING FIXTURES & FITTINGS

American Brass Mfg. Co.
5000 Superior Ave.
Cleveland, OH 44103

American-Standard
P.O. Box 2003
New Brunswick, NJ 08903

Brass-Craft Mfg. Co. Inc.
700 Fisher Building
Detroit, MI 48202

Briggs
P.O. Box 22622
Tampa, FL 33622

Central Brass Mfg. Co.
2950 E. 55th St.
Cleveland, OH 44127

Chicago Faucet Co.
2100 S. Nuclear Drive
Des Plaines, IL 60018

Crane Co., Plumbing Division
300 Park Ave.
New York, NY 10022

Delta Faucet Co.
P.O. Box 40980, 55 E. 111th St.
Indianapolis, IN 46280

DuPont Co.
1007 Market St.
Wilmington, DE 19898

Eljer Plumbingware—Wallace Murray Corp.
3 Gateway Center
Pittsburgh, PA 15222

Elkay Mfg. Co.
2222 Camden Court
Oak Brook, IL 60521

Fiat Products Inc., Division of Mark Control
3400 Oakton
Skokie, IL 60076

Gerber Plumbing Fixtures
4656 Touhy
Chicago, IL 60646

Grohe
2677 Coyle Ave.
Elk Grove Village, IL 60007

Indiana Brass Inc.
P.O. Box 369
Frankfort, IN 46041

Jacuzzi Whirlpool Bath Inc.
298 N. Wiget Lane
Walnut Creek, CA 94596

Just Mfg. Co.
9233 King St.
Franklin Park, IL 60131

Kohler Co.
High Street
Kohler, WI 53004

Manville Mfg. Co.
342 Rockwell Ave.
Pontiac, MI 48053

Masonite Corp., Fiberglass Division
P.O. Box 830
Rock Falls, IL 61071

Milwaukee Faucets Inc.
4250 N. 124th St.
Milwaukee, WI 53222

Thomas Industries Inc.
P.O. Box 35120, 207 E. Broadway
Louisville, KY 40232

Westinghouse Electric Corp., Lighting Division
P.O. Box 824
Vicksburg, MS 39180

Moen Division of Stanadyne
377 Woodland Ave.
Elyria, OH 44036

Norris Plumbing Fixtures
P.O. Box 370
Walnut, CA 91789

Owens-Corning Fiberglas
Fiberglas Tower
Toledo, OH 43659

Peerless Pottery Inc.
P.O. Box 5581
Evansville, IN 47715

Piazza Faucet Inc.
11602 Knott Ave., Suite 13
Garden Grove, CA 92641

Price Pfister Division of Norris Industries
13500 Paxton St.
Pacoima, CA 91331

Sherle Wagner International
60 E. 57th St.
New York, NY

Speakman Co.
301 E. 30th St.
Wilmington, DE 19899

Sterling Faucet Co.
1375 Remmington Road
Schaumburg, IL 60195

Symmons Industries Inc.
31 Brooks Drive
Braintree, MA 02184

U. S. Brass Division of Wallace Murray Corp.
901 10th St.
Plano, TX 75074

Universal-Rundle Corp.
P.O. Box 29
New Castle, PA 16103

Vance Industries Inc.
7401 W. Wilson Ave.
Chicago, IL 60656

RESILIENT FLOORING

Amtico Flooring Division of American Biltrite Inc.
3131 Princeton Pike
Lawrenceville, NJ 08648

Armstrong World Industries Inc.
P.O. Box 3001
Lancaster, PA 17604

Azrock Floor Products
P.O. Box 34030
San Antonio, TX 78233

Congoleum Corp.
195 Belgrove Drive
Kearny, NJ 07032

Kentile Floors Inc.
58 Second St.
Brooklyn, NY 11215

Mannington Mills Inc.
P.O. Box 30
Salem, NJ 08079

Masonite Corp.
29 N. Wacker Drive
Chicago, IL 60606

VANITY TOPS

Also see Ceramic Tile

DuPont Co.
1007 Market St.
Wilmington, DE 19898

Formica Corp., Subsidiary of American Cyanamid
859 Berdan Ave.
Wayne, NJ 07470

Nevamar Corp.
8339 Telegraph Road
Odenton, MD 21113

Westinghouse Corp. Micarta Division
P.O. Box 248
Hampton, SC 29924

Wilsonart Division of Ralph Wilson Plastics Co.
600 General Bruce Drive
Temple, TX 76501

WINDOWS AND SKYLIGHTS

Alcan Building Products
P.O. Box 511
Warren, OH 44482

Caradco
P.O. Box 920
Rantoul, IL 61866

Crestline
910 Cleveland Ave.
Wausau, WI 54401

Filon Division of Vistron Corp.
12333 S. Van Ness Ave.
Hawthorne, CA 90250

Howmet Aluminum Corp., Building Products Division
P.O. Box 4515
Lancaster, PA 17604

Hurd Millwork Co.
520 S. Whelen
Medford, WI 54451

Kalwall Corp.
P.O. Box 237, 1111 Candia Road
Manchester, NH 03102

Louisiana-Pacific Corp.
1300 S.W. Fifth Ave.
Portland, OR 97201

Peachtree Doors
P.O. Box 700
Norcross, GA 30091

Pella/Rolscreen Co.
100 Main St.
Pella, IA 50219

Velux America Inc.
P.O. Box 3208
Greenwood, SC 29646

WOOD FLOORING

Bruce Hardwood Floors, a Triangle Pacific Co.
16803 Dallas Parkway
Dallas, TX 75248

Comtex Industries Inc.
1666 Kennedy Causeway, Suite 503
Miami Beach, FL 33141

Connor Forest Industries
P.O. Box 847
Wausau, WI 54401

Crown Mosaic Parquet Flooring Inc.
P.O. Box 272
Sevierville, TN 37862

Masonite Corp.
29 N. Wacker Drive
Chicago, IL 60606

Weyerhaeuser Co.
Tacoma, WA 98401

Wood Mosaic, Olinkraft Division
P.O. Box 21159
Louisville, KY 40221